CW00670889

DUMBARTON OAKS
MEDIEVAL LIBRARY

Jan M. Ziolkowski, General Editor

OLD ENGLISH PSALMS

DOML 42

DUMBARTON OAKS MEDIEVAL LIBRARY

Jan M. Ziolkowski, General Editor
Daniel Donoghue, Old English Editor

Old English Editorial Board
Peter S. Baker
R. D. Fulk
Antonette diPaolo Healey
Susan Irvine
Christopher A. Jones
Katherine O'Brien O'Keeffe
Andy Orchard
Elizabeth Tyler

Old English Advisory Board
Rolf Bremmer
Roberta Frank
Simon Keynes
Patrizia Lendinara
Donald Scragg

Old English Psalms

Edited and Translated by

PATRICK P. O'NEILL

DUMBARTON OAKS
MEDIEVAL LIBRARY

HARVARD UNIVERSITY PRESS
CAMBRIDGE, MASSACHUSETTS
LONDON, ENGLAND
2016

Copyright © 2016 by the President and Fellows of Harvard College

ALL RIGHTS RESERVED

Printed in the United States of America

Library of Congress Cataloging-in-Publication Data

Names: O'Neill, Patrick P., editor, translator.

Title: Old English psalms / edited and translated by Patrick P. O'Neill.

Other titles: Dumbarton Oaks medieval library ; 42.

Description: Cambridge, Massachusetts : Harvard University Press, 2016. |
    Series: Dumbarton Oaks medieval library ; 42 | English translation on
the rectos, and Old English on the versos; introductory matter in English. |
    Includes bibliographical references and index.

Identifiers: LCCN 2015037316 | ISBN 9780674504752 (alk. paper)

Classification: LCC BS1421 .O43 2016 | DDC 223/.20529 — dc23 LC record
available at http://lccn.loc.gov/2015037316

Contents

Introduction

The Psalter, with its 150 psalms, is the longest book of the Bible. For the Anglo-Saxons it was also the preeminent work of the Old Testament, the one they knew best and recited most frequently.[1] It had several claims on them: as a wisdom book composed in poetry, a genre that their learned classes cultivated and cherished; as the basic classroom text used to teach clerical students how to read and write Latin, a process that entailed memorizing large portions of the psalms; and, most important, as the central text of the Divine Office. In this last function the psalms were recited at seven mandated times of the day (the Hours), in what was the most important ritual of Christian liturgy after the Mass. This practice was obligatory for ecclesiastics, but it also found its way into the lives of the secular elite as a private devotion; we find it used in France by the late eighth century and in England by the ninth, as attested by Bishop Asser in his Life of King Alfred of Wessex.[2]

But what sets the Anglo-Saxons apart from other western European cultures was their engagement with the psalms in the vernacular. They knew that the Latin Psalter, which they inherited from Roman and Irish missionaries, had undergone several stages of translation, from its original Hebrew into Greek, and from Greek into Latin. This awareness may well have encouraged them to embark on the hazardous undertaking of translating it yet again from Latin into Old English. Even more remarkable was that Anglo-Saxon vernacularization of the psalms took three different forms. The most elementary was the word-for-word translation (often called a "gloss"), with the Old English rendering in each case written in smaller script above the corresponding Latin word of the main text. As many as twenty such glossed Psalters have survived. The second mode of translation was prose paraphrase, an advance on the gloss, since the emphasis shifted from focus on the individual word to conveying the meaning of psalm verses in idiomatic sentences. The Old English paraphrase of Psalms 1 to 50 (hereafter referred to as the Prose Psalms), generally attributed to King Alfred, exemplifies this development. The third mode of translation, adopted in the Metrical Psalms, maintained the focus on a literal rendering, while recasting the psalms in the medium of Anglo-Saxon poetry.

By a happy coincidence the Prose Psalms and the Metrical Psalms have survived in a single manuscript, Paris, Bibliothèque nationale de France, fonds latin MS 8824, which was copied about the middle of the eleventh century, more than a century after their likely date of composition.[3] In this manuscript the two Old English versions and the corresponding Latin text of the Roman Psalter are copied in long parallel columns, the Latin on the left, the Old English on the right; the remaining contents comprise twelve Canticles, a litany, and a collection of eight prayers, all in Latin. The combination of texts resembles that found in other Psalters known to have been intended for private devotions (rather than monastic observance), while the prominent position of the vernacular translations, which enjoy equal visual status with the Latin, suggests a lay audience of pious readers and reciters of the psalms.

On the final page of the manuscript, at the very end, the scribe adds a colophon, in which he identifies himself as Wulfwinus, "the one dedicated to God" *(sacer Dei),* "with the surname Cada" *(cognomento Cada).* Although the name has not been identified, he may be "Wulfwinus the scribe" *(Wulfwinus scriptor),* who was a member of the community of Saint Augustine's, Canterbury, around the time when the Paris Psalter was copied.[4] Whatever his identity, he does not seem to display any special interest or expertise in Psalter matters, judging by the significant number of copying errors, some of them involving whole sentences, in both the Latin and the Old English parts. Indeed, the indifferent quality of the copied texts, and the use of the Roman Psalter at this late date rather than the widely used Gallican version, fits well with the proposed lay audience.

Within the Paris manuscript, the Prose Psalms provide the text of Psalms 1 to 50, and the Metrical Psalms the remaining Psalms 51 to 150. The most likely explanation for this arrangement is that only the first fifty psalms of the prose were available, and so for the remaining psalms the metrical version (which evidently covered the full Psalter)[5] was supplied for want of a better alternative. The present edition combines the Prose and Metrical Psalms in the same complementary sequence, to provide a full vernacular rendering of the 150 psalms.

The Prose Psalms, on linguistic grounds, are generally accepted as having been composed in the early West-Saxon dialect of Old English, probably in the late ninth century, a combination of circumstances that would locate it in the kingdom of Wessex during the reign of King Alfred (871–899). Indeed, many scholars believe that they are a product of his ambitious plan to translate from Latin into English "certain books, those which are the most necessary for all people to know" *(sumæ bec, ða ðe niedbeðearfosta sien eallum monnum to wiotonne).*[6] In support they point to Alfred's daily recitation of the psalms as a personal devotion, attested by Asser,[7] and the statement of William of Malmesbury (ca. 1125) that at the time of his death the king had just finished translating the first fifty psalms.[8] William's statement would accord neatly with the fact that the prose version in its extant form contains precisely that number of psalms. But the most compelling evidence for Alfredian authorship is internal; the vocabulary and word usage of the Prose Psalms, which, as demonstrated by Bately, show a remarkable degree of agreement with that of other works attributed to Alfred, notably, his translations of Pope Gregory the Great's *Pastoral Care,* Boethius's *Consolation of Philosophy,* and Saint Augustine's *Soliloquies.*[9] There seems to be a general, if not unanimous, consensus that the work is a product of Alfred's circle of scholars and that the king played an active role in the process.

By almost any standard, the Prose Psalms are a remarkable piece of work; indeed, there is nothing quite like them among the other early medieval vernaculars of the West. For one thing, the work represents a bold foray into the perilous field of scriptural translation, which, while not expressly forbidden by the Roman Church, was hardly encouraged. And in the same venturesome spirit, it offers not so much a "safe" literal translation as a genuine paraphrase, one focused on conveying the meaning of the psalms in expository prose. The base text for this translation was the Roman Psalter (Ro), the version of the psalms current (and dominant) in England from the early eighth to the late tenth centuries. However, as part of his effort to convey the literal meaning as accurately and intelligibly as possible, the author had recourse to two other versions of the Latin Psalter then available in the medieval West, the Gallican (Ga) and the Hebrew (He) versions. Quite frequently, he drew from them readings to parallel or even replace the corresponding reading of the Roman Psalter. For example, Psalm 11.3, *þa ofer-spræcan and þa yfel-spræcan tungan* (those boastful and those malicious tongues) combines Ga *magniloquam* and Ro *maliloquam;* Psalm 34.15, *hi blissedon . . . on minum ungelimpe* (they rejoiced . . . in my misfortune) reflects He *in infirmitate mea laetabantur* (Ro and Ga *aduersum me laetati sunt*).[10]

The defining feature of the Prose Psalms is their combining of literal translation with historically oriented interpretation. In practice this meant accounting as far as possible for the full Latin text, even to the level of the individual word, while at the same time ordering the text of the psalms as a record of King David and other major figures (and events) of Jewish history after his time, such as the Babylonian Captivity, King Hezekiah, and the Maccabees. While this approach to reading the Old Testament might seem obvious to modern readers, it was exceptional for its time and place, running counter to the type of scriptural exegesis generally practiced in the medieval West, which was based on the allegorical approach developed at the school of Alexandria. The mode of interpretation adopted in the Prose Psalms might loosely be described as Antiochene, a type of

exegesis practiced in the school of Antioch, which empha-
sized the literal meaning of the psalms. Its most influential
exponent was Theodore of Mopsuestia (ca. 350–428), whose
commentary on the psalms heavily influenced the Prose
Psalms, though indirectly through Latin translations and
abridgments.[11]

Although foregrounded in a literal and historical approach, the Prose Psalms quite frequently advert to allegorical interpretation, especially of the type that treated the
psalms as signifying events in the life of Christ and the contemporary Christian community; for example, the psalmist
suffering at the hands of his enemies could be read allegorically as Christ, or the Church, or the individual Christian
enduring similar difficulties at the hands of the Jews or the
devil. The Prose Psalms acknowledges this approach by frequently supplying allegorical renderings in juxtaposition to
their literal counterparts, though normally confining them
to individual words or phrases. Noteworthy is its translation
of Psalm 44, where more than half of the verses pair a literal with a corresponding allegorical interpretation, the latter introduced by the formula *þæt is/þæt synt.*

In a remarkable innovation, the Prose Psalms incorpo-
rated allegorical interpretation more formally by means of
an introductory paragraph entered at the head of each psalm.
The "Introduction" lays out in formulaic style a set of possible interpretations (normally four) for its particular psalm.
Thus, the typical Introduction provides: (1) a first historical
interpretation, referring to King David and his time; (2) a
second historical interpretation, referring to post-Davidic
figures (and events) of the Old Testament, for example, King
Hezekiah or the Maccabees; (3) a moral clause, designed, for

"every just person who sings this psalm either on his own behalf or on behalf of another person"; and (4) a Christological clause, referring to Christ's time on earth.[12] Other fourfold systems for interpreting Scripture were common in the
West, notably that of Saint Augustine of Hippo (historical,
allegorical, anagogical, and moral), but the Old English Introductions differ significantly in assigning a dominant role
to David in the psalms, both as king and prophet, and in
having two historical interpretations. For both its distinc-
tive fourfold scheme and its historical, Davidic emphasis,
the Prose Psalms drew heavily on a putative Irish (Hiberno-
Latin) Psalter commentary.[13]

Among Old English translations of the Latin Bible, the
Prose Psalms stand apart as a stylistic tour de force, in which
translation becomes "transformation" of the original (to use
Bately's term).[14] Thus, the characteristic style of the Latin
psalms, where clauses within a verse are sometimes left un-
connected or, more often, simply linked by *et* (and), is transformed mainly by adding relative clauses, conjunctions, or
adverbs.[15] Take, for example, Psalm 10:5, *Dominus in templo
sancto suo Dominus in caelo sedis eius,* which translates literally,
"The Lord in his holy temple, the Lord in heaven his seat."
Compare the rendering of the Prose Psalms 10.4, *Drihten ys
on his halgan temple, se Drihten se þæs setl ys on heofenum* (The
Lord resides in his holy temple, that Lord whose seat is in
the heavens), where two phrases are made into two clauses
by supplying a verb for each, with the second clause connected to the first by means of a relative construction *se þæs*
(whose). Likewise, Psalm 36:35–36, *vidi impium superexalta-
tum et elevatum super cedros Libani* (36) *transivi et ecce non erat
quaesivi eum et non est inventus locus eius* (I saw the wicked one

highly exalted and lifted up above the cedars of Lebanon. I passed by and behold he was not; I sought him and his place was not found). In the Prose Psalms (vv. 34–35) this becomes *Ic geseah þone unrihtwisan swiðe up ahafenne, swa swa sum ceder-treow on Libanus munte,* (35) *and ic þa þanon for and eft ðyder com, þonne næs he; and ic acsode æfter him and hine sohte, and hine ne funde, ne furþum þa stowe, þe ic hine ær on geseah, gecnawan ne mihte* (I saw the wicked one greatly exalted, just like some cedar tree on Mount Lebanon, and I then journeyed from that place and afterward came back there, and by then he had vanished; and I asked after him and looked for him, and did not find him, nor could I even recognize the place where I previously saw him.) In this rendering the two verses are connected not only by "and" but also the adverb *þanon* (from that place) in verse 35, which refers back to verse 34; at the same time adverbs of time (*þa, eft, þonne, ær*) have been added to enhance the clarity of the narrative sequence, while additional adverbs of place (*þanon, ðyder*) and the clause *þe ic hine ær on geseah,* strengthen the sense of physical location.

Moreover, knowing that the original psalms were poetic compositions, the author of the Prose Psalms attempted to convey something of their literary character in his work. Although restricted both by medium (prose) and strategy of translation (exposition), his efforts to embellish the style are evident throughout. One such is deliberate lexical deviation from his normal word choice for translating a particular Latin word, either to avoid the stylistic awkwardness of repeating a word used just before, or to achieve the euphonic advantages of alliteration or assonance. For example, Psalm 15.11, *Þu . . . gefylst me mid gefean* (You . . . will fill me with joy), where *bliss,* the regular translation of Ro *laetitia,* is replaced by *gefea,* which normally translates Ro *gaudium,* for the sake of its alliteration with *gefylst.* Another technique is the use of rhythm to enhance meaning, for example at Psalm 2.6, *And ic eam, þeah, cincg geset fram Gode ofer his ðone halgan munt Syon, to þam þæt ic lære his willan and his æ* (But I, however, am appointed by God king over Zion, that holy mountain of his, to teach his will and his law), where the solemn, measured pace, and the expansive purpose clause (Ro has only *praedicans*) convey an appropriate sense of David's divinely inspired mission.

The Metrical Psalms, represented by Psalms 51 to 150 in the present edition, are a bold, if not entirely successful, attempt at translating the Latin psalms in the medium of traditional Old English poetry.[16] They are generally thought to have been composed some time in the tenth century. One piece of evidence in support of that date is another Old English poem known as the *Menologium,* a type of vernacular martyrology, which contains a direct quotation from the Metrical Psalms.[17] Even though the *Menologium* itself cannot be precisely dated, it appears to have been composed sometime between the early and the late tenth century, thus providing a broad *terminus ante quem* for the Metrical Psalms. The author's close adherence to the Roman Psalter, which was becoming obsolete in monastic circles by the end of the tenth century, points to a date before that time.[18] Also consonant with the same conclusion are the textual affiliations of his putative Latin original (insofar as it can be reconstructed from his translation), which seem to reflect a type of Ro current in the ninth rather than the late tenth century, when it had become markedly contaminated by readings from the Gallican.

As with most other extant Old English poems, the Metrical Psalms are anonymous, and so what little can be gleaned about its author must come from internal evidence. The mere fact of translating the psalms indicates someone who knew Latin, and that consideration, coupled with the scriptural nature of the work and the occasional recourse to patristic commentaries, strongly suggests an ecclesiastic. The author was evidently familiar with other parts of the Bible, as indicated by sporadic additions supplied in the translation. Significantly, almost all the additions lend themselves to a Christian reading of the Old Testament as Salvation History, an activity most likely to have been conducted by an educated ecclesiastic. Some may have been added for the purpose of drawing a suitable Christian moral, as with the reference to the miraculous crossing of the Jordan (Psalm 104.36), the zeal of Phinehas (Psalm 105.24), and the testing of Job (70.19). Others (Psalms 67.25 and 113.2) serve to emphasize the dominance of the kingdom of Judah over that of Israel, a concern that might at first blush seem arcane until one realizes that Christ was believed to have been descended from the house of Judah through David.[19] A hint that the translator was also a monk lies in his treatment of certain passages in the original Latin referring to formal prayer, which in his translation are expanded in such a way as to make them consonant with the monastic observance of the Divine Office. Thus, at Ro 140:2, *sacrificium vespertinum* (an evening offering) is rendered by "whenever I devoutly recite to you the evening service" *(þonne ic þe æfenlac estum secge),*[20] where the addition of the verb *secge,* "I will recite," transforms a Hebrew sacrifice into a recitation reminiscent of the Hour of Vespers. Likewise, his enthusiastic rendition of Ro 84:5, with an anachronistic appeal to "Christ almighty" (Ro has *Deus,* "God"), probably reflects its frequent use as a versicle in the Divine Office and other liturgical settings. At Ro 90:6, *a (ruina et) daemonio meridiano* (from . . . the noonday devil) is translated at Psalm 90.6 by *on midne dæg mære deoful* (the notorious noonday devil), where the notoriety would likely be recognized only by those in monastic circles familiar with this personification of *acedia,* the vice of spiritual sloth.

Like the Prose Psalms, the Metrical Psalms seem to have been intended as a literal rendering, but in that respect they are no match for their West-Saxon predecessor. A comparison with the Latin original uncovers in the Metrical Psalms not only egregious errors of translation[21] but a significant body of omissions and additions.[22] Of course, similar changes are evident in the Prose Psalms but, with the notable exception of interpretative additions, they occur infrequently. The omissions in the Metrical Psalms often have to do with matter evidently deemed superfluous to the main idea. For example, the final clause, *ibi laetabimur in idipsum* (Ro 65:6), was not translated, presumably because it would have distracted attention from the enumeration of God's mighty deeds, preceding and following it; likewise, the final clause of Ro 99:5, *et usque in saeculum veritas eius,* a translation of which would have switched the main focus from divine benevolence to the less relevant theme of divine verity. Overall, the Latin text is subjected to numerous modifications, notably changing of tense, person, or mood in verbs; of subject to object, and vice versa; of independent to dependent clause, and vice versa; or direct to indirect statement. Indeed, it is fair to say that one rarely finds a verse of the translation without some modification, however minor, of the Latin.

Many of these changes have been documented by Bartlett, who concluded that "while reproducing without essential omissions or additions the matter of the Latin text, the translator has, nevertheless, permitted himself considerable freedom in his manner of expressing what he conceives to be the sense of the original."[23] Her assessment is surely accurate, but it leaves unanswered the larger question of how the translator conceived of the psalms and their meaning. One can begin by suggesting that he did not follow the conventional interpretations of the psalms found in the Latin commentaries that were then in vogue. He was evidently familiar with such commentaries—for example, Cassiodorus's *Exposition of the Psalms*—which he occasionally used. But the dependence is usually confined to single words or phrases and never embraces the holistic interpretation of a full psalm, as Cassiodorus had advocated. This reluctance—for so it seems to be—might be partly explained by his choice of the Old English poetic medium, with its structural basis in the half-line, a unit whose brevity did not lend itself to the kind of expository expansion evident in the Prose Psalms.

But more likely he deliberately eschewed commentary in order to focus on what might simplistically be called the "immediacy" of the psalms, the meaning they would have for contemporary Anglo-Saxon Christians who read and sang them as prayers, outside the formal setting of the Divine Office. Interpreted this way, their thematic alternation between appeals for divine help and expressions of gratitude on its reception could serve as models for Christians to fashion their own prayers to God, while the substance of the psalms could provide moral guidance for proper Christian conduct. Arguably, this was the sense of the psalms that the metrical translator wished to convey.

Evidence of his agenda is found throughout the work. One obvious clue are the occasional references to Christ that have no basis in the Latin text; for example, Psalm 84.5, *gecyr us georne to ðe, Crist ælmihtig,* in which *Deus* of the corresponding Ro 84:7, *Deus tu convertens vivificabis nos,* has been changed to Christ, the present participle *convertens* turned into an urgent command, and the words *vivificabis nos* omitted, all with a view to emphasizing the personal appeal to Christ's salvific power.[24] Other references to the Godhead in the psalms are embellished in such a way as to fortify the bond between suppliant and God; for example Ro *Dominus* is rendered *Drihten user,* "our Lord" (54.8, 64.1, 67.19); Ro *rex meus* becomes *deore cynincg,* "beloved king" (83.3); Ro *dilexi* is expanded to *Ic lufie þe, leofa Drihten,* "I love you, dear Lord" (114.1), with a vocative of endearment and the change of preterite to present tense to convey immediacy. At the beginning of Psalm 79, the translator adds *nu we biddað þe,* "we beg you now" (79.2), a direct supplication of God, which, coming at the beginning of the psalm, imparts to what follows the tone of a Christian prayer.

To the same end the grammatical number and person of Latin verbs are altered by recasting them in either first or second person singular. A striking example is the treatment of Ro *Confitemini* (acknowledge), the opening word of Psalms 105, 106, and 135, a command from the psalmist to his people to acknowledge God's favors. In the hands of the metrical translator, it becomes a single person acting of his own volition, *Ic andette* (I will acknowledge), thereby recasting the psalm as a personal prayer to God. A more explicit example is Ro Psalm 117:29, *confitemini Domino . . . quoniam in saeculum misericordia eius,* which is rendered at Psalm 117.28 *Eac ic andette eceum Dryhtne, . . . and ic ful geare wat þæt þin mild-heortnyss ys mycel to worulde* (I will also acknowledge the eternal Lord . . . and I truly know that your mercy is great, forever), where besides the change from a plural to a single speaker we have the addition of an asseverative, *ic ful geare wat,* and the altering of *eius* (his) to the more personal *þin* (your), all reminders that the translation is a personal prayer to God. Even more ambitious is the treatment of Ro Psalm 103:14–16, where a series of third person verbs and a present participle are translated by *you*-forms, thus *þu . . . lætest alædan . . . þu geworhtest* (Ro *producens*), *þu . . . ut-alæddest* (Ro *educat*); *þu gefyllest* (Ro *satiabuntur*), "you cause to grow, you provided, you produced, you will furnish." The effect of the changes is to emphasize God's personal intervention in providing for mankind, and thus provoke feelings of gratitude among contemporary Christians. That this latter community was the translator's focus is indicated by his treatment of Ro *ecclesia.* In a Hebrew context, and in the literal Old English translations of the glossed Psalters, it simply means "an assembly,"[25] but in the Metrical Psalms it becomes explicitly Christian, as in Psalm 106.31, *on cyrcean cristenes folces hean,* "in the exalted assembly of the Christian community" (Ro Psalm 106:32, *in ecclesia plebis*).[26]

How far the Metrical Psalms differ from the Prose Psalms as a result of this Christian coloring is well illustrated in their respective treatments of Psalm 50.[27] Predictably, Alfred's prose treats the psalm historically as David's prayer of contrition after his adultery with Bathsheba and provides a translation close to the original in its literalness. By contrast, the metrical translator employs many of the modifications identified above, such as embellished invocations of the deity (*mihtig/halig Drihten,* "mighty/holy Lord"), additions of personal pronouns (*min Drihten,* "my Lord," and *on ðinne willan,* "in your will") and of adverbs that convey the timeless applicability of the psalm (*a,* "always," *æfre to feore,* "ever at any time"), and the interpretation of Ro 50:14, *spiritu principali* (a perfect spirit) as *þone halgan gast* (the Holy Spirit). The overall effect is to change Psalm 50 into a prayer of Christian repentance with universal applicability, consonant with its widespread use as a "Penitential Psalm" among contemporary Anglo-Saxons.[28]

The precatory character of the Metrical Psalms may help to explain their popularity in late Anglo-Saxon England. As already noted, they are quoted in the *Menologium* and passages were inserted verbatim into the so-called Old English Benedictine Office.[29] Two more passages, one of them substantial, served to fill a lacuna in the Old English interlinear gloss of the Eadwine Psalter, which was compiled around 1165 at Canterbury; and while this latter use of the text may reflect necessity rather than predilection, it does show that a copy of the work was still being used at Christ Church Canterbury a century after the Norman Conquest.

Given the complexities of both the Latin Psalter and the vernacular versions, an explanation of the editorial procedures and conventions adopted in this edition is called for. For the Old English text of the Prose Psalms, the edition by O'Neill, *King Alfred's Old English Prose Translation of the First Fifty Psalms,* is used; for the Metrical Psalms, that of Krapp (in Anglo-Saxon Poetic Records 5), with some modifications (see the Note on the Texts). On the whole, both of these editions eschew normalization, and that policy has been maintained for the present edition, though modern punctuation, in line as far as possible with that of the facing modern English translation, has been supplied. Emendation is kept to a minimum and attempted only where the proposed reading seems plausible by virtue of grammatical, semantic, or paleographical considerations. Both prose and metrical versions follow the conventional numbering system used by scholars of Old English, which reflects the sequence of verses in the Paris Psalter and which differs from what is used in the Latin Vulgate psalms.

The facing modern English translations of both the Prose and the Metrical Psalms are entirely new; no previous translations of either work exist, as far as I know. Translating two works that are themselves translations of a Latin original poses a challenge, especially when, as is often the case, the Old English does not seem to render that original with a predictable translation. The problem is aggravated by the fact that many of the stylistic and syntactical difficulties of the Latin psalms, a reflection of their Hebrew origins, were transferred to both Old English versions. The present translation, while not pretending to literal fidelity, attempts to preserve the stylistic peculiarities of each work. For example, a feature common to both is the syntactical construction *apo koinou,* in which "a word or closely related group of words, occurring between two portions of discourse, contains an idea which completes the thought of the first part . . . [and] at once supplies the thought essential to the following part. . . ."[30] In the present edition (text and translation) the *koinon* (common element) is set off by bounding commas.[31] A special difficulty in the Metrical Psalms is how to deal with the numerous adverbs that seem to function mainly as alliterative fillers with little semantic force, such as *neode* (diligently, zealously), *swylce* (likewise, also), and the like. I have tried to retain them in the translation, except in cases where there are more of them than a modern English clause could reasonably carry.

In the translation the division of verses and their numbering follow that of the facing Old English. In addition the translation incorporates the numbering of the Latin Vulgate (Gallican), by means of a superscript number at the head of each new verse. The dual system of numbering verses is explained more fully in the Note on the Texts. In the edition and translation, an ellipsis (. . .) indicates any gap in the text, from single words to missing folios. Capitalization of epithets identified with the deity is confined to *God* (*God*) and *Lord* (*Drihten, Ealdor*). Onomastica in the translation, in the form of proper names and place-names, are spelled as found in the New Revised Standard Version.[32]

Those interested in the Latin and vernacular sources that may have influenced the Prose Psalms should consult O'Neill, *Prose Translation,* as discussion of this aspect has been omitted from the Notes to the Translations. Since no obvious major external influences on the Metrical Psalms are evident to the present editor, selective parallels from Latin Psalter commentaries (mainly Cassiodorus) have been given in the Notes to the Translations, but only when they shed light on the meaning of particular passages of difficulty.

Notes

1 For an excellent study of how the psalms influenced multiple facets of Anglo-Saxon life, see M. J. Toswell, *The Anglo-Saxon Psalter,* Medieval Church Studies 10 (Turnhout, 2014).

2 W. H. Stevenson, ed., *Asser's Life of King Alfred* (Oxford, 1959), 59; trans. by Keynes and Lapidge, *Alfred the Great: Asser's Life of King Alfred and Other Contemporary Sources* (Suffolk, 1983), 91.

3 B. Colgrave, *The Paris Psalter;* on the dating of the manuscript, see page 13. An online facsimile of the manuscript is available at http://gallica.bnf.fr/ark:/12148/btv1b8451636f.

4 See R. Emms, "The Scribe of the Paris Psalter," *Anglo-Saxon England* 27 (1999): 179–83.

5 Fragments of the Metrical Psalms for Psalms 1–50 have survived; for text and translation, see C. Jones, *Old English Shorter Poems, Volume 1: Religious and Didactic,* Dumbarton Oaks Medieval Library 15 (Cambridge, Mass., 2012), Appendix B, 284–343.

6 Translation from Keynes and Lapidge, *Alfred the Great,* 126.

7 "He was also in the invariable habit . . . of participating in certain psalms and prayers in the day-time and night-time offices"; Keynes and Lapidge, *Alfred the Great,* 91.

8 "He undertook a translation of the Psalter, the first division [Psalms 1–50] having scarcely been completed, he passed away"; W. Stubbs, ed., *Willemi Malmesbiriensis Monachi De Gestis Regum Anglorum Libri Quinque* (London, 1887–1889), Vol. 1, 132.

9 J. M. Bately, "Lexical Evidence for the Authorship of the Prose Psalms in the Paris Psalter," *Anglo-Saxon England* 10 (1982): 69–95; and "Alfred as Author and Translator," in *A Companion to Alfred the Great,* ed. N. G. Discenza and P. E. Szarmach, (Leiden, 2014), 113–42. On Alfred's personal involvement with the psalms, see Toswell, *The Anglo-Saxon Psalter,* 67–82.

10 The Roman Psalter was edited by R. Weber, *Le Psautier romain et les autres anciens psautiers latins* (Vatican City, 1953); the Gallican and Hebrew Psalters by R. Weber, *Biblia Sacra iuxta Vulgatum Versionem* (Stuttgart, 1969; 2nd improved ed., 1975).

11 P. P. O'Neill, *King Alfred's Old English Prose Translation of the First Fifty Psalms* (Cambridge, Mass., 2001), 37–39.

12 See P. P. O'Neill, "The Old English Introductions to the Prose Psalms

of the Paris Psalter: Sources, Structure, and Composition," *Studies in Philology* 78.5 (1981): 20–38 at 26–27.

13 See O'Neill, *Prose Translation,* 41–44.

14 J. M. Bately, "The Literary Prose of King Alfred's Reign: Translation or Transformation?" in *Old English Prose: Basic Readings,* ed. P. E. Szarmach (New York, 2000), 3–27.

15 For examples, see O'Neill, *Prose Translation,* 46–47. On the differences in numbering between the Latin and Old English verses, see below, pp. 611–12.

16 See the criticisms of M. S. Griffith, "Poetic Language and the Paris Psalter: the Decay of the Old English Tradition," *Anglo-Saxon England* 20 (1991): 167–86; for a more positive view, see Toswell, *The Anglo-Saxon Psalter,* 319–32.

17 See Toswell, *The Anglo-Saxon Psalter,* 310–19.

18 Though with the caveat that the author of the Metrical Psalms might have composed specifically for a lay audience that was still using the outmoded Roman Psalter.

19 See Notes to the Translations at Psalms 67.25, 104.35, 104.36, 105.24, 107.7, and 113.2.

20 See Notes to the Translations at Psalm 140.3.

21 For example, the treatment of onomastica at Psalms 77.14 and 107.6, the latter involving the creation of the ghost place-name, *Metibor;* and misreadings of the Latin, on which see the Index under "Latin Psalms, misreadings of."

22 H. Bartlett, *The Metrical Division of the Paris Psalter, Baltimore* (Baltimore, 1896), 28–40, has useful, though not always accurate, lists of mistranslations, additions, and omissions, from which she concluded (at p. 36) that Psalms 51–104 were "rendered with considerably less accuracy than psalms 104–150."

23 Bartlett, *The Metrical Division,* 36.

24 Other occurrences of appeals to Christ are found at Psalms 108.25 and 118.146.

25 Thus, *on cyrcean folcyes,* in the Cambridge Psalter, ed. K. Wildhagen, *Der Cambridger Psalter,* Bibliothek der angelsächsischen Prosa VII (Hamburg, 1910), 106.

26 Likewise, Psalms 67.24, 133.2, and 134.2.

27 Although Psalm 50 of the Metrical Psalms is absent from the Paris

Psalter, a good portion of it has survived in the so-called Junius Office; see note 5, above.

28 Analyzed in P. P. O'Neill, "Strategies of Translation in the Old English Versions (Prose and Metrical) of the Psalms in the Paris Psalter (Paris, Bibliothèque nationale de France, Fonds latin, 8824)," *Bulletin of the Institute of Oriental and Occidental Studies, Kansai University* 48 (Osaka, 2015): 137–71 at 152–55.

29 This text is neither specifically Benedictine nor substantially an Office, since it lacks the psalm readings required for liturgical use. See Jones, *Shorter Poems,* Appendix B, 284–85, whose nomenclature I follow in referring to this work as the Junius Office.

30 H. D. Meritt, *The construction ἀπὸ κοινοῦ in the Germanic Languages,* Language and Literature, vol. 6, no. 2 (Stanford, 1938), 16.

31 For example, Psalm 21.8, *syððan ic of hire innoðe eode* (since I emerged from her womb); 21.21, *herie hine* (praise him); 32.12, *of his þam wlitegan temple* (from his beautiful temple); 59.7, *min gescy* (my shoes); 117.18, *Drihten ælmihtig* (the almighty Lord); 144.7, *þa miclan geniht* (the great largesse).

32 Following the edition of Edgar (with Kinney), *The Vulgate Bible, Volume III: The Poetical Books, Douay-Rheims Translation.* A useful list of alternative spellings of these onomastica is found on pp. 1177–83.

PROSE PSALMS

Psalm 1

1   Eadig byð se wer þe ne gæð on geþeaht unrihtwisra, ne on þam wege ne stent synfulra, ne on heora wol-bærendum setle ne sitt;

2   ac his willa byð on Godes æ, and ymb his æ he byð smeagende dæges and nihtes.

3   Him byð swa þam treowe þe byð aplantod neah wætera rynum,

4   þæt sylð his wæstmas to rihtre tide; and his leaf and his blæda ne fealwiað ne ne seariað; swa byð þam men þe we ær ymbspræcon: eall him cymð to gode þæt þæt he deð.

5   Ac þa unrihtwisan ne beoð na swylce, ne him eac swa ne limpð; ac hi beoð duste gelicran þonne hit wind toblæwð.

6   Þy ne arisað þa unrihtwisan on domes-dæg, ne þa syn-fullan ne beoð on geþeahte þæra rihtwisena,

7   for þam God wat hwylcne weg þa rihtwisan geearne-don, ac þa unrihtwisan cumað to witum.

Psalm 1

1   [1] Happy is the man who does not enter into the counsels of the wicked, nor share the path of sinners, nor sit in their pestiferous seat;

2   [2] instead, his intent is on God's law, and he continues to meditate on it night and day.

3   [3] It will turn out for him as for the tree planted near watercourses,

4   which yields its fruits at the proper time; and its leaves and its flowers neither grow yellow nor wither; so also for the man whom we have just mentioned: everything that he does will go well for him.

5   [4] But the wicked are not like that, nor will it work out so well for them; instead, they will be more like dust scattered by the wind.

6   [5] Accordingly, the wicked will not rise again on Judgment Day, nor will the sinful be present in the counsel of the just,

7   [6] because God knows what destiny the just have earned, but the wicked will come to grief.

Psalm 2

Ðæs æfteran sealmes capitul is gecweden *Psalmus Dauid,*
þæt ys on Englisc, Dauides sealm, for þæm he is hys sealm
gecweden for þi he seofode on þæm sealme and mænde to
Drihtne be his feondum, ægðer ge inlendum ge utlendum,
and be eallum his earfoðum; and swa deð ælc þæra þe þysne
sealm sincgð be his sylfes feondum; and swa dyde Crist be
Iudeum.

1   Hwy ryð ælc folc, and hwi smeagað hi unnytt?

2   And hwy arisað eorð-cynincgas, and ealdor-menn cumað tosomne wið Gode and wið þam þe he to hlaforde geceas and gesmyrede? Hi cweðað:

3   "Utan tobrecan heora bendas and aweorpan heora
geocu of us."

4   Hwæt forstent heora spræc (cwæð se witega) þeah hi
swa cweðen, for þam se God þe on heofonum ys hig ge-
hyspð, and Drihten hyg gescent;

5   and he clypað to him on his yrre and gedrefð heora
geþeaht.

6   And ic eam, þeah, cincg geset fram Gode ofer his ðone
halgan munt Syon, to þam þæt ic lære his willan and his æ.

7   For þan cwæð Drihten to me: "Þu eart min sunu; nu
todæg ic ðe acende.

8   Bide me, and ic þe sylle þeoda to agnum yrfe, and þinne
anwald ic gebræde ofer ðeoda gemæro,

Psalm 2

The second psalm's heading is entitled *Psalmus Dauid,* that is in English, "David's psalm," and it is called his psalm because he lamented in the psalm and complained to God about his enemies, domestic and foreign, and about all his difficulties; and everyone who recites this psalm does likewise about his own enemies; and so did Christ about the Jews.

1   [1] Why does every nation rage, and why do they make futile plans?

2   [2] And why do earth's kings rise up, and princes band together against God and him whom he chose and anointed as ruler? They declare:

3   [3] "Let us break asunder their fetters and cast off from us their yoke."

4   [4] What use (said the prophet) is their declaration, delivered like this, since God in heaven will mock them, and the Lord will confound them;

5   [5] and he will shout at them in his anger, and upset their plans.

6   [6] But I, however, am appointed by God king over Zion, that holy mountain of his, to teach his will and his law.

7   [7] Therefore the Lord said to me: "You are my son; see! today I have begotten you.

8   [8] Ask me, and I will give you nations as your own inheritance, extending your dominion throughout the boundaries of the nations,

9 and ic gedo þæt þu heora wylst mid isernre gyrde, and hi miht swa eaðe abrecan swa se croccwyrhta mæg ænne croccan."

10 Ongytað nu, kyningas, and leorniað, ge domeras þe ofer eorðan demað:

11 þeowiað Drihtne and ondrædað hine, blissiað on Gode, and ðeah mid ege;

12 onfoð lare þy læs eow God yrre weorðe, and þy læs ge wendon of rihtum wege,

13 for þæm þonne his yrre byð onæled, þonne beoð eadige þa þe nu on hine getrywað.

Psalm 3

Ðysne þriddan sealm Dauid sang þa he fleah Absalon his sunu, and seofode þa yrmðe to Drihtne; swa deþ ælc þæra manna þe þisne sealm singð: his sylfes earfoðu, ægðer ge modes ge lichaman, he seofað to Drihtne; swa dyde Crist þonne he þysne sealm sang: be Iudeum he hine sang and be Iudan Scarioth þe hine læwde. He seofode to Drihtne:

1 Eala, Drihten, hwi synt swa manige minra feonda, þara þe me swencað; for hwi arisað swa mænige wið me? Monige cweðað to minum mode þæt hit næbbe nane hæle æt his Gode.

9   ⁹ and causing you to rule them with an iron rod and have the power to smash them into pieces as easily as a potter smashes a pitcher."

10   ¹⁰ Kings, and you judges who judge throughout the earth, understand now, be instructed:

11   ¹¹ serve the Lord and fear him, rejoice in God, and yet do so in trepidation;

12   ¹² accept discipline lest God become angry with you, and lest you turn from the right way,

13   ¹³ because whenever his anger is kindled, then they who now trust in him will be blessed.

Psalm 3

David sang this third psalm when he fled from his son, Absalom, and lamented that distressing situation to the Lord; so too does everyone who sings this psalm, lamenting to the Lord their own sufferings, spiritual and physical; likewise did Christ, when he recited this psalm, singing about the Jews, and about Judas Iscariot who betrayed him. David complained to the Lord:

1   ² Alas, Lord, why are my enemies who oppress me so numerous; why do so many rise up against me? ³ Many say to my soul that it gets no security from its God.

2   Ac hit nis na swa hy cweðað, ac þu eart butan ælcum tweon min fultum and min wuldor, and þu ahefst upp min heafod.

3   Mid minre stemne ic cleopode to Drihtne, and he me gehyrde of his þam halgan munte.

4   Þa ongan ic slapan, and slep, and eft aras, for ðam þe Drihten me awehte and me upp arærde.

5   For ðam ic me nu na ondræde þusendu folces, þeah hi me utan ymbþringen; ac ðu, Drihten, aris and gedo me halne, for þam þu eart min God.

6   For ðam þu ofsloge ealle þa ðe me wiðerwearde wæron butan gewyrhton, and þara synfulra mægen þu gebryttest,

7   for ðam on ðe ys eall ure hæl and ure tohopa; and ofer þin folc sy þin bletsuncg.

Psalm 4

Þe feorða sealm ys gecweden Dauides sealm and Dauides sang, for ði ælc þæra sealma þe swa gecweden byð—þæt he sy ægðer ge Dauides sealm ge Dauides sancg—ælcne ðæra he sancg be sone mid weorode, ac ða he þysne sealm sancg, þa gealp he and fægnode Godes fultumes wið his feondum; and swa deð ælc welwillende man þe þisne sealm singð; and swa dyde Ezechias þa he wæs ahred æt his feondum; and swa dyde Crist ða he wæs ahred æt Iudeum.

1   Þonne ic cleopode to þe, þonne gehyrdest þu me, Drihten, for ðam þu eart se ðe me gerihtwisast, and on minum earfoðum and nearonessum þu me gerymdest.

2   ⁴ But it is not as they say, for you are certainly my help and glory, and you raise up my head.

3   ⁵ I invoked the Lord with my appeal, and he heard me from his holy mountain.

4   ⁶ Then I began to sleep, and slept, and afterward arose, because the Lord awoke me and raised me up.

5   ⁷ Therefore, I do not now fear even if thousands of people throng about me; but arise, Lord, and keep me safe, because you are my God.

6   ⁸ Because you have struck down all those who were hostile to me without good reason, and have broken the power of sinners,

7   ⁹ so all our salvation and our hope is in you; and may your blessing rest on your people.

Psalm 4

The fourth psalm is called "David's psalm" and "David's canticle," because each psalm so called—being both "David's psalm" and "David's canticle"—he sang with a full voice in choir, but when he sang this present psalm he boasted of, and rejoiced in, God's help against his enemies; and every right-minded person who sings this psalm does likewise; and Hezekiah did likewise when he had been liberated from his enemies; and Christ did too, when he had been liberated from the Jews.

1   ² Lord, you heard me whenever I invoked you, because you are my justifier, and in my difficulties and constraints you cleared a way for me.

2   Gemiltsa me, Drihten, and gehyr min gebed.

3   Eala, manna bearn, hu lange wylle ge beon swa heard-
heorte wið gode, and hwi lufige ge idelnesse and secað leas-
uncga?

4   Wite ge þæt God gemyclade his ðone gehalgodan, and
he me gehyrð þonne ic him to clypige.

5   Þeah hit gebyrige þæt ge on woh yrsien, ne scule ge hit
no þy hraþor þurhteon, þe læs ge syngien; and þæt unriht
þæt ge smeagað on ewerum mode, forlætað and hreowsiað
þæs.

6   Offriað ge mid rihtwisnesse, and bringað þa Gode to lacum, and hopiað to Drihtne.

7   Manig man cwyð: "Hwa tæcð us teala, and hwa sylð us
þa god þe us man gehæt?" And is, þeah, geswutelod ofer us
þin gifu, þeah hi swa ne cweðen:

8   þæt ys, þæt þu sealdest blisse minre heortan, and þin
folc gemicladest, and him sealdest geniht hwætes and wines
and eles and ealra goda, þeah hi his ðe ne ðancien.

9   Ac gedo nu þæt ic mote on þam genihte and on þære
sibbe slapan and me gerestan, for ðam þu, Drihten, synderlice me gesettest on blisse and on tohopan.

2   Lord, have mercy on me, and hear my prayer.

3   ³ O sons of men, how long do you intend to be so impervious to good (and/or God) and why do you love vanity and search out falsehoods?

4   ⁴ Know that God has made his consecrated one great, and will hear me whenever I invoke him.

5   ⁵ Though you may become angry without good reason, nevertheless you should not follow through with it, lest you sin; and the iniquity which you inwardly contemplate, abandon and repent of it.

6   ⁶ Make offerings sincerely, and bring those good deeds as gifts, and trust in the Lord.

7   Many say: "Who will properly guide us and give us the good things promised us?" ⁷ And though they do not admit it, your favor is evident in us:

8   you gladdened my heart ⁸ and made your people great, giving them wheat, wine, oil, and all good things in abundance, although they do not thank you for that.

9   ⁹ And make possible now that I can sleep and rest in that abundance and in that peace, ¹⁰ because you, Lord, have settled me uniquely in joy and hope.

Psalm 5

Ðe fifta sealm ys gecweden Dauides sealm, þone he sang be his sylfes frofre and be herenesse ealra ðæra rihtwisena ðe secað yrfeweardnesse on heofonrice mid Criste, se ys ende ealra ðinga; and ælc mann þe þisne sealm singð, he hine singð be his sylfes frofre; and swa dyde Ezechias, þa he alysed wæs of his mettrumnesse; and swa dyde Crist, þa he alysed wæs fram Iudeum.

1   Drihten, onfoh min word mid þinum earum, and ongyt mine stemne and min gehrop, and ðenc þara worda minra gebeda,

2   for ðam ic gebidde on dægred to ðe; ac gedo þæt þu gehyre min gebed, Drihten.

3   Ic stande on ær-mergen beforan ðe æt gebede and seo þe (þæt is, þæt ic ongite þinne willan butan tweon and eac þone wyrce), for ðam þu eart se ylca God þe nan unriht nelt.

4   Ne mid þe ne wunað se yfel-willenda, ne þa unrihtwisan ne wuniað beforan þinum eagum.

5   Þu hatast ealle þa þe unriht wyrcað and þæt ne forlætað ne his ne hreowsiað, and þu fordest þa þe symle leasinga specað,

6   and þa man-slagan and þa swicolan þu forsyhst.

7   Ic þonne hopiende to þinre þære myclan mild-heortnesse, ic gange to þinum huse, Drihten, and me gebidde to þinum halgan altare, on ðinum ege.

Psalm 5

The fifth psalm is called "David's psalm," which he sang
about his own comforting and to praise all the just who seek
an inheritance in the heavenly kingdom with Christ, who is
the perfection of all things; and everyone who sings this
psalm sings it about his own comforting; and Hezekiah did
likewise, when he had been freed from his illness; and so did
Christ when he had been freed from the Jews.

1   2 Lord, lend your ear to my words, and understand my
voice and cry, 3 and consider my appeal,

2   4 because at dawn I will pray to you; yet deign to hear
my appeal, Lord.

3   5 I will stand before you in prayer in the early morning
and will see you (that is, that I will understand your will with
certainty, and also do it), because you are the same God who
wills no wrong.

4   6 Nor will the wickedly disposed person dwell with you,
or the unjust remain before your sight.

5   7 You hate all those who do evil while refusing to abandon or repent of it, and you will destroy those who constantly lie,

6   and you abhor murderers and deceivers.

7   8 Hoping in your great mercy, however, I will go to your
house, Lord, and worship at your holy altar in awe of you.

8   Drihten, læd me on þine rihtwisnesse fram minra feonda willan; geriht minne weg beforan þinre ansyne (se weg ys min weorc),

9   for ðam on minra feonda muðe is leasuncg, and heora mod is swiðe idel.

10   Heora mod and heora wilnuncg ys swa deop swa grundleas pytt, and heora tungan sprecað symle facn, ac dem him, Drihten.

11   And gedo þæt hy ne mægen don þæt yfel þæt hy þencað and sprecað, ac be þære andefne heora unrihtwisnesse fordrif hi, for þam hy ðe gremiað and þine þeowas, Drihten.

12   And blissian ealle þa þe to ðe hopiað, and fægnian on ecnesse—and þu wuna on him—and fægnian þin, ealle þa þe lufiað þinne naman,

13   for þam þu eart se Drihten þe gebletsast and geblissast rihtwise. Þu us gecoronadest and geweorðadest, and us gescyldst mid þam scylde þinre welwilnesse.

Psalm 6

Dauid sang þysne syxtan sealm be his mettrumnesse and be his earfoðum, and eac be þam ege þæs domes on domes-dæge; and swa deð ælc þæra þe hine singð; and swa dyde Crist, þa he on eorðan wæs, he hine sang be his earfoðum; and eac Ezechias be his untrumnesse.

1   Drihten, ne þrea þu me on þinum yrre, ne on þinre hat-heortnesse ne swenc me.

2   Ac miltsa me, Dryhten, for þam ic eom unhal, and ge-

8   9 Lord, in your justice guide me away from my enemies' evil intent; direct my way in your sight (that way signifies my work),

9   10 because lying lurks in my enemies' mouths, and their minds are exceedingly hollow.

10   11 Their minds (and their desires) are as unfathomable as a bottomless pit, while their tongues always utter falsehoods, but judge them, Lord.

11   And make it so that they cannot do the evil which they contemplate and speak, and expel them according to the extent of their iniquity, because they provoke you and your servants, Lord.

12   12 And let all who trust in you rejoice and be happy forever—and may you reside in them—and let all who love your name rejoice in you,

13   13 because you are the Lord who will bless and gladden the just. You have crowned and honored us, protecting us with the shield of your goodwill.

Psalm 6

David sang this sixth psalm about his weakness and sufferings, and also about the terror of the Judgment Day verdict; and everyone who sings it does likewise; and Christ did likewise when he was on earth, singing it about his sufferings; and Hezekiah also about his illness.

1   2 Lord, do not rebuke me in your anger, or afflict me in your fury.

2   3 Instead, have mercy on me, Lord, because I am sick,

hæl me for þam eall min mægn and eal min ban synt gebrytt and gedrefed, and min sawl and min mod ys swyðe gedrefed.

3   Eala, Drihten, hu lange wylt þu þæt hit on ðam sy? Gehwyrf, la, Drihten, to me and alys mine sawle, and gedo me halne for ðinre mild-heornesse,

4   for ðam þa deadan þe on helle beoð, þin ne gemunan, ne ðe andetað ne ne heriað, swa swa we doð.

5   Ic swince on minre granunge, and ælce niht on minum bedde ic sice and wepe, and hwilum min bedd wæte mid tearum.

6   Mine eagan synt gedrefede for yrre, and ic eom forealdod betweoh eallum minum feondum.

7   Gewitað fram me ealle þa þe unriht wyrcað, for ðam þe Drihten hyrde mine wependan stefne, and God gehyrde mine healsunge, and Drihten onfeng min gebed.

8   Sceamian heora for ði and syn gedrefede ealle mine fynd, and gan hy on earsling and sceamien heora swiðe hrædlice.

Psalm 7

Þysne seofoðan sealm Dauid sang þæ he seofode his ungelimp to Drihtne (þæt wæs þa Absalon his sunu hine adrifen hæfde of ðam rice); þa hine teonode and wyrde Chus Geminis sunu, þa seofode he þæt to Drihtne; and swa deð ælc mann þe þysne sealm singð, mænð his earfoðu to Drihtne; and swa dyde Crist, þa he on eorðan wæs.

1   Drihten, min God, to þe ic hopige; alys me fram eallum þam þe min ehtað, and gefriða me,

2   þæt næfre mine fynd ne gripen mine sawle swa swa leo,

and heal me because all my strength and bones are broken and afflicted, ⁴ and I am greatly agitated in mind and soul.

3   O Lord, how long will you allow that to continue so? ⁵ Lord, in your mercy turn to me, free my soul and heal me,

4   ⁶ because the dead in hell do not think of you, nor will they acknowledge or praise you, as we do.

5   ⁷ I labor in my moaning, and every night I sigh and weep in my bed, sometimes even sprinkling it with tears.

6   ⁸ My eyes are troubled by anger, and I have grown old among all my enemies.

7   ⁹ Depart from me all evildoers, because the Lord has heard my weeping, ¹⁰ and God has listened to my appeal, and the Lord accepted my prayer.

8   ¹¹ May all my enemies be shamed and troubled as a result, and may they retreat and very soon be mortified.

Psalm 7

David sang this seventh psalm when he lamented his misfortunes to the Lord (that happened when his son Absalom had driven him from the kingdom); when Cush, the son of Jemini, abused and cursed him, he lamented that to the Lord; and everyone who sings this psalm does likewise, complaining of their difficulties to the Lord; and Christ did likewise when he lived on earth.

1   ² Lord, my God, in you I trust; free me from all my persecutors, and rescue me,

2   ³ lest my enemies ever seize my soul like a lion, because

for þam ic nat ealles hwa me ahredde and gehæle butan þu wylle.

3   Drihten, min God, gif ic to þisum þe me nu swencað þæs geearnod hæbbe, þæt hi nu doð, oððe ænig unriht wið hi gedon hæbbe,

4   oþþe furðum him gulde yfel wið yfle, swa swa hi hit geworhton, þonne ofslean me mine fynd orwigne—næs þas þe mine frynd beon sceoldon—

5   and secan mine fynd mine sawle and þa gefon, and oftreden on eorðan min lif and minne weorðscipe to duste gewyrcen.

6   Aris, Drihten, on þinum yrre, and ræs on minra feonda mearce, and geweorða þe sylfne þara.

7   Aris, Drihten, to þinum gehate, and do swa swa þu gehete, þæt wæs þæt þu woldest helpan unscyldegum. Gif þu swa dest, þonne cymð swiðe mycel folc to þinum þeowdome,

8   and þu upp astihst and hi mid þe lætst to heofonum. Drihten, dem folcum and dem me.

9   Drihten, dem me æfter minum gewyrhtan, and dem me æfter minre unscæðfulnesse.

10   Geenda nu þæt yfel þæra unrihtwisra, and gerece and geræd þa rihtwisan, þu, Drihten, þe smeast heortan and ædra and manna geþohtas.

11   Mid rihte we secað fultum to þe, Drihten, for ðam þu gehælst þa heortan rihtra geþohta.

12   Þe Drihten þe is rihtwis dema, and strang, and geþyldig, hwæðer he yrsige ælce dæge? Bute ge to him gecyrren, se deofol cwecð his sweord to eow.

13   And he bende his bogan; se is nu gearo to sceotanne. He teohað þæt he scyle sceotan þæt deaðes fæt (þæt synt, þa

I do not quite know who can rescue and save me unless you will.

3   4 Lord, my God, if I have deserved from these tormentors of mine what they are now doing, or have perpetrated any injustice against them,

4   5 or so much as paid them back evil for evil, as they did, then let my true enemies kill me without my resistance — not those who ought to have been my friends —

5   6 and pursue my soul and seize it, and trample my life into the ground, and reduce my dignity to dust.

6   7 Lord, in your anger arise and launch an attack on the borders of my enemies, and exalt yourself at their expense.

7   Lord, rise up as you promised, and act on your pledge, that you would help the innocent. 8 If you do so, then very many people will join your service,

8   and you, ascending, will lead them with you to Heaven. 9 Lord, judge the peoples and me.

9   Lord, judge me according to my merits and my innocence.

10   10 Lord, bring to an end now the evil of the wicked, and direct and advise the just, you who scrutinizes people's hearts, innards, and thoughts.

11   11 We justifiably seek help from you, Lord, because you save the hearts that entertain just thoughts.

12   12 The Lord who is a just judge, and strong, and long-suffering, does he get angry every day? 13 Unless you turn to him, the devil will brandish his sword at you.

13   And he has drawn his bow; it is now ready to shoot. 14 He decides to shoot the vessel of death (that is, the un-

unrihtwisan); he gedeð his flan fyrena þæt he mæge mid sceotan and bærnan þa þe her byrnað on wrænnesse and on unðeawum.

14   He cenð ælc unriht, and hit cymð him sare and his geferum.

15   He adylfð þone pytt, and he hine ontynð, and on þone ylcan befylð.

16   Gehweorfe his sar on his heafod and on his brægn astige his unriht.

17   Ic þonne andette Drihtne æfter his rihtwisnesse and herie his ðone hean naman and lofige.

Psalm 8

Þysne eahteoðan sealm sang Dauid, þa he wundrade Godes wundra, se wylt eallum gesceaftum; and eac he witgode on ðam sealme be þære wuldorlican acennednesse Cristes. He cwæð:

1   Eala, Drihten, ure God, hu wundorlic þin nama ys geond ealle eorðan,

2   for þam ahefen ys þin myclung ofer heofonas; ge furðum of ðæra cilda muðe þe meolc sucað, þu byst hered.

3   Þæt hi doð to bysmore þinum feondum, for ðam þu towyrpest þine fynd and ealle þa þe unrihtwisnesse ladiað and scyldað.

just); he prepares his fiery arrows with which to shoot and set on fire those on earth who are consumed by licentiousness and vices.

14   [15] He gives birth to every kind of wrong, and the outcome will be grievous for him and his companions.

15   [16] He digs and opens a hole and then falls into it.

16   [17] May his sorrow recoil on his head and his iniquity come down on his crown.

17   [18] Then I will acknowledge the Lord for his justice, and praise and glorify his exalted name.

Psalm 8

David sang this eighth psalm when he marveled at the wonders of the God who governs all created things; and also he prophesied in the psalm about Christ's glorious birth. He said:

1   [2] O Lord, our God, how marvelous your name is throughout all the earth,

2   because your greatness is exalted above the heavens; [3] moreover, from the mouth of infants who suckle, you are praised.

3   They give praise as a reproach to your enemies, for you destroy them and all those who excuse and defend iniquity.

4   Ic ongite nu þæt weorc þinra fingra, þæt synd, heofonas and mona and steorran, þa þu astealdest.

5   Drihten, hwæt is se mann, þe þu swa myclum amanst, oþþe hwæt is se mannes sunu, þe þu oftrædlice neosast?

6   Þu hine gedest lytle læssan þonne englas, þu hine gewuldrast and geweorðast, and him sylst heafodgold to mærðe, and þu hine gesetest ofer þin hand-geweorc.

7   Ealle gesceafta þu legst under his fet and under his an-wald: sceap and hryðera and ealle eorðan nytenu,

8   fleogende fuglas, and sæ-fiscas þa farað geond þa sæ-wegas.

9   Drihten, Drihten, ure God, hu wuldorlic þin nama ys geond ealle eorðan.

Psalm 9

On ðam nigoðan sealme Dauid hine gebæd to Drihtne and him þancode þæt his sunu and eac oðre fynd him ne mihton eall þæt yfel don þæt hi him geteohod hæfdon; and on þa yl-can gerad hine singð ælc rihtwis mann be his sylfes feon-dum; and be þam ylcan hine sang Crist, þa Iudeas hine woldan don mare yfel ðonne hig mihton; and swa dyde eac Ezechias, ða his fynd hine ne meahton ateon swa hy woldon.

1   Ic andete Drihtne on ealre minre heortan, and ic bodige ealle ðine wundra,

2   and ic blissige and fægnige and herige þinne naman, ðu hea God,

4   ⁴ Now I understand the work of your fingers, the heavens, moon and stars, which you have established.

5   ⁵ Lord, what are human beings, whom you regard so highly, or what are their descendants, whom you frequently visit?

6   ⁶ You make them a little less than the angels, glorifying and honoring them, and bestowing a golden crown on them as an honor, ⁷ and appointing them over your handiwork.

7   ⁸ All creatures you lay at their feet and under their control: sheep, cattle, and all earth-bound beasts,

8   ⁹ birds soaring in the sky, and fish navigating the ocean's paths.

9   ¹⁰ Lord, Lord, our God, how glorious your name is throughout all the earth.

Psalm 9

In the ninth psalm David prayed to the Lord and thanked him that his son and other enemies besides failed to inflict on him all the harm they had planned for him; and in a similar situation every just person sings it about their own enemies; and Christ sang it about the same situation, when the Jews desired to inflict more harm on him than they could; and Hezekiah too did likewise, when his enemies failed to harm him as they wished to.

1   ² I will praise the Lord with all my heart, and make known all your wonders,

2   ³ and I will be glad and rejoice and praise your name, you exalted God,

3   for ðam þu gehwyrfdest mine fynd underbæc, and hi wæron geuntrumode and forwurdon beforan ðinre ansyne;

4   for ðam þu demst minne dom and mine spræce, and eall for me dydest þæt ic don sceolde; ðu sitst on ðam hean setle, þu ðe symle demst swiðe rihte.

5   Ðu ðreast and bregst þa ðeoda þe us ðreatigað, and ða unrihtwisan forweorðað, and ðu adilgas heora naman on worulda woruld.

6   Seo redelse and þæt geþeaht urra feonda geteorode, ða hi hit endian sceoldan; and heora byrig þu towurpe ealla;

7   and heora gemynd onweg gewat mid þam myclan hlisan, and Drihten þurhwunað on ecnesse.

8   And he gearwað his dom-setl, and he demð ealre eor-þan swyðe emne.

9   He demð folcum mid rihte; he ys geworden frið-stow ðearfendra.

10   And gefultumend þu eart, Drihten, æt ælcere ðearfe, for ðy hopiað to þe ealle þa ðe witan þinne naman,

11   for ðam þu ne forlætst nanne þara þe ðe secð. Heriað for ði Drihten, þone ðe eardað on Sion,

12   and bodiað betweoh folcum his wundru, for ðam he nis na ofergeotol þara gebeda his þearfena, ac he is swyþe ge-myndig heora blod to wrecanne.

13   Gemiltsa me, Drihten, and geseoh mine eaðmetto (hu earmne me habbað gedon mine fynd), for ðam þu eart se ylca God þe me upp ahofe fram deaðes gatum, to þam þæt ic bo-dade eall þin lof on ðam geatum þære burge Hierusalem.

14   Ic fægnie on þinre hælo ðe þu me sylest; and ða ðeoda þe min ehtað syn afæstnode on ðam ylcan earfoðum þe hi me geteohhod hæfdon, and heora fet synt gefangene mid þy ilcan gryne þe hi me gehyd and gehealden hæfdon.

3   ⁴ because you made my enemies retreat, and they were weakened and perished in your sight;

4   ⁵ because you judge my case and my cause, and did for me everything that I should have done; you sit in a high seat, you who consistently judge most fairly.

5   ⁶ You reprove and terrify those people who harass us, and the wicked will perish, and you will blot out their names forever.

6   ⁷ Our enemy's design and plan failed, just when they were about to realize it; and you destroyed all their cities;

7   and their name then disappeared, accompanied by the great report of their downfall, ⁸ but the Lord will endure forever.

8   And he will prepare his judgment seat ⁹ and judge all the earth very fairly.

9   He will judge the peoples with justice; ¹⁰ he has become a place of refuge for the needy.

10   And you, Lord, are a helper in every difficulty, ¹¹ so that all those who know your name have confidence in you,

11   because you will not abandon a single one of those who seek you. ¹² Praise then the Lord who dwells in Zion,

12   and make known his wonders among the peoples, ¹³ because he does not forget the prayers of his needy ones, but is intent on avenging the spilling of their blood.

13   ¹⁴ Lord, have mercy on me, and see my affliction (how wretched my enemies have made me), ¹⁵ because you are the same God who raised me up from death's door, to proclaim your full praise at Jerusalem's gates.

14   ¹⁶ I rejoice in the deliverance you grant me; and my persecutors are trapped in the very tribulations which they had planned for me, and their feet are caught with the same snare which they had concealed and laid for me.

15   For þam byð Drihten cuð on his rihtum domum, and on his hand-geweorce byð gefangen se synfulla;

16   and þa unrihtwisan beoð gehwyrfede to helle, and ælc folc þæra ðe God forgyt,

17   for þam God ne forgyt his ðearfan oð heora ende, ne heora geþyld ne forweorð oþ ende.

18   Aris, Drihten, þy læs se yfel-willenda mæge don þæt he wille, and gedo þæt eallum folcum sy gedemed beforan ðe.

19   Gesete, Drihten, ofer hy sumne anwald þæt hig gelære þæt hy witon þæt hi men synt.

20   Drihten, hwi gewitst þu swa feor fram us, and hwi noldest þu cuman to us to þære tide þe us nyd-þearf wæs?

21   Þonne se unrihtwisa ofermodegað, þonne byð se earma ðearfa onæled and gedrefed and eac geunrotsod—ac weorðon þa unrihtwisan gefangene on þam geþohtum þe hi geþoht habbað—

22   for þam se synfulla byð hered þær he his yfelan willan wyrcð, and hine bletsiað þa yfelan for his yfelan dædum.

23   Se synfulla bysmrað Drihten, and for þære menigu his unrihtes he ne geðencð þæt God hit mæg gewrecan.

24   For þam he ne deð God beforan his modes ansyne, for þam beoð his wegas and his weorc ealneh unclæne.

25   For þam he næfð nan gemynd Godes doma beforan his ansyne, þæt he mæge rixian and wealdan ealra his feonda and don him to yfele þæt þæt he wylle.

26   And he cwyð on his mode: "Ne wyrð þisses næfre nan wending butan mycelre frecennesse minra feonda."

27   His muð byð symle full wyrignessa and bitera worda and facnes and searuwa,

15   [17] For the Lord will be revealed in his just judgments, but the sinner will be ensnared in his own handiwork;

16   [18] and the wicked will be transported to hell, and anyone who neglects God,

17   [19] for God will not forget his needy ones, nor will their patience wane to the very end.

18   [20] Arise, God, so that the wickedly disposed cannot fulfill their wishes, and cause judgment to be passed on all the peoples in your presence.

19   [21] Arrange, Lord, some control over them, teaching them to realize that they are mere mortals.

20   [22] Lord, why do you distance yourself so far from us, and why were you not willing to join us in the time of our need?

21   [23] Whenever the wicked are puffed up, the wretched and needy are inflamed and troubled and made despondent —but let the wicked be ensnared in the schemes which they have devised—

22   [24] because the sinner will be lauded whenever he gets his way, and the wicked bless him for his evil deeds.

23   [25] The sinner insults God, and because of how often he sins, he does not think that God can punish it.

24   [26] Because he does not keep God in mind, his ways and his works are always defiled.

25   So he holds no memory of God's judgments in view, in order that that he can govern and control all his enemies and harm them as he pleases.

26   [27] And he says to himself: "Absent the great threat of my enemies, this situation will never change."

27   [28] His mouth is constantly loaded with curses, spiteful words, deceit, and wiles,

28 and under his tungan byð ealne weg oþera manna sar and geswinc. He syt symle on geþeahte mid þam welegum dygollice to þam þæt he mæge fordon þa unsceðþendan;

29 and þreatað þone earman mid his eagum, and sætað his digollice swa swa leo det of his hole.

30 He sætað þæt he bereafige þone earman and þæs wilnað; and þonne he hine gefangen hafað mid his gryne, þonne genæt he hine; and þonne he hine hæfð gewyldne, þonne aginð he sylf sigan, oððe afylð.

31 He cwæð ær on his mode: "Ne geþencð God þyllices, ac ahwyrfð his eagan þæt he hit næfre ne gesyhð."

32 Aris, Drihten, min God, and ahefe upp þine hand ofer ða unrihtwisan, and ne forgit þone þearfan oð ende.

33 For þam bysmrað se unrihtwisa Drihten, for ðam he cwyð on his mode: "Ne recþ God þeah ic þus do."

34 Gesyhst þu nu (cwæð se witega to Drihtne) hwylc broc and hwylc sar we þoliað and þrowiað? Nu, hit wære cyn þæt þu hit him wræce mid þinre handa. Ic þearfa eom nu to ðe forlæten; þu eart fultumiend þara þe nabbað nawðer ne fæder ne modor.

35 Þu forbrycst þone earm and þæt mægen þæs synfullan for þy, þeah hine hwa ahsode for hwi he swa dyde, þonne ne mihte he hit na gereccan, ne geþafa beon nolde þæt he untela dyde.

36 Drihten rixað on ecnesse on þisse worulde ge on þære toweardan; for þæm weorðað aworpene þa synfullan of ægðrum his rica.

37 Drihten gehyrð þa wilnunga his þearfena, and heora modes gyrnesse gehyrað þine earan.

28   and under his tongue always lies sorrow and affliction for other men. ²⁹ He continually deliberates in secret with the rich to destroy the innocent;

29   ³⁰ and he threatens the poor man with his glance, and lies in wait secretly for him, as the lion does from his den.

30   He waits to seize the poor man, keen for that; and when he has caught him with his snare, ³¹ he will mistreat him; but having subdued him, he himself begins to decline, or collapses.

31   ³² He had already said to himself: "God will not consider such behavior, but will avert his eyes so as never to witness it."

32   ³³ Lord my God, arise, raise up your hand against the wicked, and do not forget the needy to the end.

33   ³⁴ The wicked man insults the Lord because he says to himself: "God does not care about my behavior."

34   ³⁵ Do you see now (said the prophet to the Lord) what kind of affliction and sorrow we suffer and endure? Truly, you would have done well to punish him with your power. I am now entrusted to you as a poor man; you are the helper of orphans.

35   ³⁶ You will break the sinner's arm and strength because, even if he were asked why he behaved so, he could not explain it, nor would he be willing to concede that he had acted badly.

36   ³⁷ The Lord will rule forever in this world and in the next; sinners, therefore, will be cast out from both of his kingdoms.

37   ³⁸ The Lord hears the complaints of his needy ones, and your ears pay attention to the yearnings of their heart.

38   Dem nu, Drihten, þearfe þæs earman and þæs eaðmodan, þæt se awyrgeda ne ece þæt he hine leng myclie ofer
eorðan.

Psalm 10

Ðysne teoþan sealm Dauid sang þa he wæs adrifen on þæt
westen fram Sawle þam cynge, þa his geferan hine lærdon
þæt he hine þær hydde swa þer spearuwa; and swa ylce þa
rihtwisan þe hine singað, hi seofiað be heora feondum,
ægðer ge gesewenlicum ge ungesewenlicum; and swa dyde
Crist be Iudeum, þa he þysne sealm sang.

1   Hwy lære ge me þæt ic fleo geond muntas and geond
westenu swa spearwa, for þam ic getrywe Drihtne?
2   Ic wat, þeah, for þam þe þa synfullan bendað heora bogan and fyllaþ heora coceras mid flanum, to þam þæt hi magon sceotan þa unscyldigan heortan dygollice þonan hi læst
wenað,
3   for þam hi wilniað—þæs þe hi magon—þæt hi toweor-
pen þæt God geteohhad hæfð to wyrcanne. Hwæt dyde ic,
unscyldega, wið hi, oþþe hwæt mæg ic nu don?
4   Drihten ys on his halgan temple, se Drihten se þæs setl
ys on heofenum.
5   His egan lociað on his earman þearfan, his bræwas (þæt
ys, his rihta dom) ahsað manna bearn.

38   [39] Lord, consider now the needs of the destitute and humble, so that the wicked cannot continue to aggrandize themselves throughout the earth.

Psalm 10

David sang this tenth psalm when, driven into the wilderness by King Saul, he was advised by his companions to conceal himself there like a sparrow; and the just who sing it likewise complain about their enemies, seen and unseen; and so did Christ about the Jews, when he sang this psalm.

1   [2] Why do you advise me to flee through mountains and deserts like a sparrow, since I trust in the Lord?

2   [3] I realize, however, that the sinners bend their bows and fill their quivers with arrows to shoot covertly the innocent of heart, from where they least expect it,

3   [4] because they wish to destroy—to the extent that they can—what God decided to make. What did I (guiltless) perpetrate against them, or what can I now do?

4   [5] The Lord resides in his holy temple, that Lord whose seat is in the heavens.

5   His eyes regard the wretched one in need, his eyelids (that is, his just judgment) interrogate humankind.

6   Se ylca Drihten ahsað rihtwise and unrihtwise, þæt heora ægðer secge hwæt he dyde, þæt he him mæge gyldan be heora gewyrhtum, for ðam se þe lufað unriht, he hatað his agene sawle.

7   Drihten onsent manegra cynna witu swa swa ren ofer ða synfullan, and hi gewyrpð mid grine, and he onsent fyr ofer hig and ungemetlice hæto þære sunnan and wolberende windas; mid þyllicum and mid manegum þyllicum beoð heora drinc-fatu gefyldu.

8   For þam God ys swyðe rihtwis, and he lufað rihtwisnesse, and heo byð symle swyðe emn beforan him.

Psalm 11

Þa Dafid þisne endleftan sealm sang, þa seofode he on þam sealme þæt on his dagum sceolde rihtwisnes and wisdom beon swa swiðe alegen; and swa deð ælc rihtwis mann, þonne he þysne sealm singð, þonne mænð he to Drihtne þæt unriht þæt on his dagum bið; and swa dyde Crist þa he hine sang, þa mænde he to Drihtne Iudea ungeleaffulnesse.

1   Gehæl me, Drihten, for þam haligdom is nu on þisum tidum fullneah asprungen, and soðfæstnes ys swyðe gelytlod.

2   Idla spræca hi sprecað to heora nyhstum, facen hi sprecað mid heora weolorum, for þam hi nabbað on heora mode

6   ⁶That same Lord will question the just and the unjust, making each describe what they have done, to requite them according to their merits, because the one who loves iniquity hates his own soul.

7   ⁷God will deliver like rain punishments of many kinds on the sinful, and will catch them with a snare, and he will pour on them fire, the excessive heat of the sun, and pestiferous winds; with many such punishments their drinking cups will be filled.

8   ⁸For God is exceedingly just, and he loves justice, and it will always appear very proper in his sight.

Psalm 11

When David sang this eleventh psalm he lamented that in his time justice and wisdom should be brought so very low; and so does every just man whenever he sings this psalm, lamenting to the Lord the injustice prevailing in his time; and so did Christ when he sang it, complaining to the Lord about the unbelief of the Jews.

1   ²Lord, save me because holiness in these times has now almost died out, and truth is very much belittled.

2   ³They make useless conversation with their neighbors, telling lies with their lips, because what they say by word of

þæt hi on heora muðe sprecað, ac þencað yfel, þeah hi hwilum tela cweðen.

3   Ac Drihten towyrpð ealle þa facnesfullan weoloras, and þa oferspræcan and þa yfel-spræcan tungan.

4   Þa þe teohhiað þæt hi scylen hi sylfe weorðian mid idelre spræce, hy cweðað: "Hwi ne synt we muð-freo? Hu ne moton we sprecan þæt we wyllað? Hwæt ondræde we? Hwylc hlaford mæg us forbeodan urne willan?"

5   Ac Drihten cwyð: "For yrðum þæra wædlena and for granunge þæra þearfena ic arise,

6   and hi sette on mine hælo, and ic do swyðe treowlice ymb hy."

7   Godes word (cwæð Dauid) beoð swiðe soð and swiðe clænu; hy beoð swa hluttur swa þæt seolfor þe byþ seofon siðon amered syþþan se ora adolfen byð.

8   Þu, Drihten, gehælst us and gefreoðast fram heora yfle on ecnesse.

9   Ðeah þa unrihtwisan us utan began on ælce healfe, and heora sy mycle ma þonne ure, þeah þu us tobrædst ongean hy, and wið hi gefriðast.

mouth does not match what they think, and they plan evil, although they sometimes speak smoothly.

3   [4] But the Lord will destroy all those deceitful lips, and those boastful and those malicious tongues.

4   [5] Those who think that they should boost themselves with idle talk say: "Look here! Are we not at liberty to speak? Are we not allowed to say what we like? What are we afraid of? What kind of lord can deny us our whim?"

5   [6] But the Lord will say: "Because of the miseries of the needy and the groaning of the poor I will arise,

6   and nestle them in my security, and work very faithfully on their behalf."

7   [7] God's words (said David) are very true and genuine; they are as unalloyed as silver purified seven times after its ore is dug up.

8   [8] You, Lord, will save and guard us from their wickedness forever.

9   [9] Though the wicked surround us from without on every side, and are far more numerous than we are, still you multiply us against them, and rescue us from them.

Psalm 12

Ða Dafid þysne twelftan sealm sang, þa seofode he to
Drihtne on þam sealme be his feondum, ægþer ge gastlicum
ge lic-hamlicum; and swa deð ælc þæra þe hine singð; and
swa dyde Crist be Iudeum and be deoflum; and swa dyde
Ezechias se cyng be Assiriam, þa hi hine ymbseten hæfdon
on þære byrig.

1   Hu lange wilt þu, Drihten, min forgitan—hwæðer þu
oð minne ende wylle? Oððe hu lange wilt þu ahwyrfan þinne
andwlitan fram me?

2   Hu lange sceal ic settan on mine sawle þis sorhfulle
geþeaht and þis sar æt minre heortan, hwæþer ic ælce dæge
scyle?

3   Hu lange sceal min feond beon uppahafen ofer me? Beseoh to me, Drihten, min God, and gehyr me.

4   Onliht mine eagan, þæt hi næfre ne slapan on swylcum
deaðe,

5   þy læs æfre min feond cweðe, "Ic eom strengra þonne
he."

6   Þa þe me swencað, hy fægniað gif ic onstyred beo; ac ic,
þeah, on þine mild-heortnesse gelyfe.

7   Min heorte blissað on þinre hælo, and ic singe þam
Gode þe me eall god syleð, and lofie þinne naman, þu hehsta
God.

Psalm 12

When David sang this twelfth psalm he complained in it to the Lord about his enemies, spiritual and physical; and so does everyone who sings it; and so did Christ about the Jews and about demons; and so did King Hezekiah about the Assyrians, when they had surrounded him in the city.

1 1 Lord, how long do you intend to forget me—until I die? And how long do you intend to turn away your face from me?

2 2 How long must I harbor in my soul this sad thought and heartfelt sorrow; must I do it every day?

3 3 How long must my enemy be exalted over me? 4 Lord, my God, look favorably on me, and hear me.

4 Enlighten my eyes so that they never sleep in such a death,

5 5 lest my enemy should ever say, "I am stronger than he."

6 Those who afflict me will rejoice if I am agitated; 6 but I, however, will trust in your mercy.

7 My heart will rejoice in your salvation, and I will sing to the God who gives me all good things, and will praise your name, most exalted God.

Psalm 13

Ða Dauid þisne þreotteoðan sealm sang, þa seofode he to
Drihtne on þam sealme þæt æfre on his dagum sceolde
gewurðan swa lytle treowa, and swa lytel wisdom wære on
worulde; and swa deð ælc rihtwis man þe hine nu singð, he
seofað þæt ylce be his tidum; and swa dyde Crist be Iudeum;
and Ezechias be Rapsace, Assyria cyninge.

1   Se unrihtwisa cwyð on his mode: "Nis nan God þe
þis wite oððe wræce." Þonne byð þæt folc for þam cwyde
gewemmed and gescynded on heora won willan.

2   Nis nan þe eallunga wel do—ne forðon anlepe.

3   Drihten locað of heofenum ofer manna bearn, and ha-
wað hwæðer he geseo ænigne þæra þe hine sece oþþe hine
ongite.

4   Ac hi hine fleoð ealle endemes, and secað and lufiað
þæt hy syn idle and unnytte; nis heora furðum an þe eallunga
wel do.

5   Hi synt byrgenum gelice: seo byð utan fæger and innan ful. Heora tungan wyrcaþ mycel facn, þeah hi fægere
sprecon, heora geþeaht and heora willa and heora weorc byð
swylce þære wyrrestan nædran attor, þa mon *aspis* hæt.

6   Ðara muð byð symle full wyrignessa and bitera worda;
heora fet beoð swiðe hraðe blod to ageotanne unþearfes for
yflum willan,

Psalm 13

When David sang this thirteenth psalm he lamented to the Lord that always in his time so few covenants should be made, and that so little wisdom existed in the world; and so does every just person who now sings it, lamenting the same thing about his times; and so did Christ about the Jews; and Hezekiah about Rabshakeh, king of the Assyrians.

1   ¹ The wicked one says in his heart: "There is no God who knows or avenges this." Then the people will be corrupted and defiled in their perverse desire because of that statement.

2   There is no one who can entirely behave well—not even a single person.

3   ² The Lord looks from heaven on humankind, searching for one of them who seeks or recognizes him.

4   ³ But they flee from him all at once, and seek and delight to be vain and idle; not even a single one of them can entirely behave well.

5   They resemble sepulchers: beautiful from without and stinking within. Their tongues work many deceits, though they speak pleasantly, their thoughts, desires and deeds are like the venom of that most deadly serpent called "asp."

6   Their mouths forever overflow with curses and bitter words; their feet are very swift to shed blood needlessly because of malicious tendencies,

7   and heora wegas beoþ symle gedrefede. Hie wilniað
ealle mægne oþera manna unsælþa, and him cymð sylfum
þæt ylce; ne secað hi nane sibbe,

8   ne Godes ege ne byð beforan heora modes eagum. Hwi
ne ongitað ealle þe unriht wyrcað—

9   þa þe wilniað fretan min folc swa ænne hlaf, þa ne clypiað to Gode mid godum weorcum—hwi ne ongitað hi þæt
him cymð, þonne hi læst wenað, ege and ungelimp?

10   Hwy ne ongitað hi þæt God byð mid þam rihtwisran
folce? Hwi gedrefe ge min yrmingæs geþeaht, for þam God
ys min geþeaht?

11   Hwa arist elles of Syon to þam þæt he sylle Israelum
hælo, butan þu, Drihten, þe afyrst hæft-nyd of þinum folce?

12   Blissie nu Iacobes cyn and fægnian Israele.

Psalm 14

Dauid sang þysne feowerteoðan sealm, þa he adrifen wæs of
his earde, wiscte þæt he moste eft to cuman; and swa dyde
Israela folc þa hie on hæft-nyde gelædde wæron of Hierusalem to Babilonia; and swa deð ælc rihtwis man þonne he
þysne sealm singð, wilnað him sumere rot-hwile on þissere
worulde and ecre reste æfter þisum; and swa dyde Crist þa
he hine sang, seofode his earfoðu to Drihtne.

1   Drihten, hwa eardað on þinum temple, oððe hwa mot
hine gerestan on þæm halgan munte?

2   Þa andswarode Drihten þæs witgan mode þurh on-

7   and their ways are always troubled. They wish mightily for misfortunes on others, but that same lot will befall them; they do not seek peace,

8   nor is fear of God present to their minds. ⁴ Why do all those who commit iniquity not understand—

9   they who desire to devour my people like a whole loaf of bread, ⁵ who do not invoke God with good deeds—that terror and misfortune will befall them when they least expect it?

10   ⁶ Why do they not understand that God dwells with a more righteous people? Why do you trouble that counsel of mine, one of no account, since God is my counsel?

11   ⁷ Who else will rise up from Zion to grant deliverance to Israel, but you, Lord, who removes captivity from your people?

12   ⁸ Let Jacob's people now rejoice, and let Israel exult.

Psalm 14

David sang this fourteenth psalm when he was driven out of his country, desiring to be allowed to return to it; and the Israelites did likewise when they were led in captivity from Jerusalem to Babylon; and likewise every just person, whenever he sings this psalm, desires for himself some period of comfort in this world and eternal tranquility in the next; and Christ did likewise when he sang it, lamenting his difficulties to the Lord.

1   ¹ Lord, who will dwell in your temple, or who will be allowed to rest on that holy mountain?

2   ² Then the Lord answered the mind of the prophet

bryrdnesse þæs Halgan Gastes, and cwæð se witga: "Ic wat, þeah ic ahsige, hwa þær eardað: se þe ingæð butan wamme and wyrcð rihtwisnesse,

3   and se þe sprycð rihtwisnesse mid his tungan and næfð nan facn on his mode,

4   ne his nyhstan nan yfel ne deð, ne nan edwit ne under-fehð wið his nyhstan;

5   and se þe þone awyrgdan for nawuht hæfð, and se þe þone rihtwisan weorþað, þone þe Godes ege hæfð;

6   se þe his nyhstan swereð, and hine mid treowum ne beswicð, and se þe his feoh to unrihtum wæstm-sceatte ne syleð, ne nanes feos ne wilnað æt þam unscyldigan onfon.

7   Se þe þus deð, ne wyrð he næfre astyred ne scynd on ecnesse."

Psalm 15

Þone fifteoðan sealm Dauid sang be his earfoðum, ægðer ge modes ge lichaman; and eft swa ilce Ezechias hine sang be his mettrumnesse, wilnode him to Gode sumre frofre; and swa deð ælc rihtwis mann þe hine singð on his earfoðum; and swa dyde Crist þa he hine sang.

1   Gehealde me, Drihten, for þam ic hopige to ðe. Hu ne sæde ic þe, Drihten, þæt þu eart min God, for þam þu me eall þa good sealdest þe ic hæbbe, and þe heora nan nyd-þerf nis eft on me to nimene.

2   Drihten gefylde ealne minne willan and me forgeaf þæt

through the Holy Spirit's inspiration, and the prophet said:
"I know, though I ask, who will dwell there: he who enters
free from blemish and does justice,

3   ³ and he who speaks the truth with his tongue and har-
bors no deceit in his mind,

4   nor does any evil to his neighbor, nor levels any accusation at him;

5   ⁴ and he who regards the malicious as nothing, and he
who honors the just one who possesses the fear of God;

6   the one who swears to his neighbor, while not deceiv-
ing him with assurances of good faith, ⁵ and he who does not
lend his money at an exorbitant rate of interest, or desire to
receive any payment from the innocent.

7   He who so behaves will never be agitated or confounded for all time."

Psalm 15

David sang the fifteenth psalm about his difficulties, mental
and physical; and afterward Hezekiah likewise sang it about
his sickness, desiring from God some relief for himself; and
so does every just person who sings it in their difficulties;
and so did Christ when he sang it.

1   ¹ Lord, may you preserve me, because I trust in you.
² What! Did I not say to you, Lord, that you are my God,
because you gave me all the good things that I own, and you
have no need to take them back from me.

2   ³ The Lord fulfilled my every wish, and deigned to al-

43

ic moste ofercuman þa þeoda þe me ungeðwære wæron, and heora hergas toweorpan æfter minum agnum willan.

3   Heora unmiht and heora untrymð is swiðe gemanifeal-dod; nu swyðe hraðe hi forwurðað.

4   Ne gaderie ic nan folc to unrihtum gewinne, swa swa hi doð, ne ic ne clypige to heora godum, ne to heargum ne ge-bidde mid mine muðe,

5   for þam þu, Drihten, eart se dæl mines yrfes and se calic minre blisse, and þu eart se þe me geedniwodest min rice.

6   Þu gedydest þæt we mætan ure land mid rapum, and min hlyt gefeoll ofer þæt betste, for þam is min land nu foremære and me swyðe unbleo.

7   Ic bletsige þone Drihten þe me sealde andgit. Ac þeah he me þara uterrena gewinna gefreode, þeah winnað wið me þa inran unrihtlustas dæges and nihtes, þæt ic ne eom, þeah, eallunga orsorh.

8   Ic ongite Drihten, and he byð symle beforan þære an-syne mines modes; for þæm he bið symle on minum fultume, þæt ic ne beo eallunga oferswiðed.

9   For þæm þingum min mod is gelustfullod, and ic cyðe þa blisse on minre tungan, and on þæm tohopan ic me syððan gereste,

10   for þæm þu ne forlætst mine sawle ne min mod to helle, ne þinne gehalgodan ne lætst forrotian ne forweorðan.

11   Þu me gedydest lifes wegas cuðe, and gefylst me mid gefean beforan þinre ansyne, for ælc rihtlustbærnes cymð þurh þinne fultum, þæm þe heo cimð on ecnesse.

low me to overcome peoples troublesome to me and destroy their idols, following my own wishes.

3 ⁴ Their weakness and infirmity have greatly increased; very soon now they will die.

4 I will not assemble people for an unjust conflict, as they do, nor will I invoke their gods or worship their idols with my speech,

5 ⁵ because you, Lord, are my inheritance's portion and the cup of my happiness, and the one who has restored to me my kingdom.

6 ⁶ You arranged for us to measure our land with ropes, and my lot fell upon the best, and so I now consider my land splendid and very delightful.

7 ⁷ I will bless the Lord who gave me understanding. But though he freed me from those external conflicts, yet internal, unlawful, desires struggle within me night and day, so that I am not, in fact, entirely free from care.

8 ⁸ I will take note of the Lord, and he will always be present in my mind's eye; so he will always be ready to help me lest I be entirely overcome.

9 ⁹ For those reasons my heart is overjoyed, and I will declare that joy with my tongue, and in that expectation will afterward rest,

10 ¹⁰ because you will not abandon my soul or mind to hell, nor permit the one consecrated to you to decay or perish.

11 You made known to me the ways of life, and will fill me with joy in your presence, because every lawful pleasure comes through your help, to him to whom it comes forever.

Psalm 16

Dauid sang þysne syxteoþan sealm, and hine geornfullice gebæd on þisum sealme to Drihtne, and hine unscyldigne
cyðde wið þa his fynd þe his ehton butan scylde; and swa
doð ealle þa rihtwisan þe þisne sealm singað, ymb þæt ylce
hi hine singað; and swa dyde Crist be Iudeum.

1   Gehyr, Drihten, min gebed and ongit mine rihtwisnesse,

2   and onfoh mid þinum earum min gebed, for þon þu
wast þæt ic butan facne to þe cleopige. Beforan ðe sy se dom
betwuh me and him; geseon mine eagan þone rihtan dom
betwuh us.

3   Þu hæfst afandod min mod, and þu come to me on niht
and me gemettest unrotne, and me sude mid þam fyre mo-
negra earfoða, swa swa gold oþþe seolfor, and þu ne fundest
on me nan unriht wiþ hi.

4   Ne ic furðum nanum menn ne sæde eal þa earfoða þe
hi me dydon; for þam wordum þinra weolora ic geþolode
hearde wegas and manigfald earfoðu.

5 Geriht, Drihten, mine stæpas on þine wegas, þæt ic ne
aslide þær þær ic stæppan scyle.

6   For þam ic clypige symle to þe, for þam þu symle me
gehyrdest. Onhyld nu þine earan to me and gehyr min word.

Psalm 16

David sang this sixteenth psalm, in which he earnestly
prayed to the Lord, declaring himself innocent with respect
to those enemies of his who persecuted him without just
cause; and all the just who sing this psalm do likewise, singing it about the same thing; and so did Christ concerning
the Jews.

1   [1] Lord, hear my prayer, and take note of my just conduct,

2   and listen attentively to my prayer, because you know
that I am invoking you without guile. [2] May the decision between me and them be made in your presence; may my eyes
witness the just verdict between us.

3   [3] You have tested my mettle, and coming to me by
night, you found me troubled, and tried me with the fire of
many sufferings, like gold or silver, but you did not find any
malice in me toward them.

4   [4] Nor did I even mention to anyone all the sufferings
which they have inflicted on me; because of the words of
your lips I endured difficult paths and numerous sufferings.

5   [5] Lord, direct my steps in your ways, lest I falter where
I should advance.

6   [6] I will continuously invoke you, because you have always heard me. Incline now your ears to me and hear my
words.

7   Gewundra nu and geweorða þine mild-heortnesse on me, þu þe symle gehælst þa þe to ðe hopiað, and hi gehyldst wið þa þe winnað wið þinne willan.

8   Geheald me, Drihten, and beorh me, swa swa man byrhð þam æplum on his eagum mid his bræwum; gehyd me under þinra fiðera sceade wið þara unrihtwisena ansyne, þe wilniað þæt hi me fordon.

9   Mine fynd me ymbhringdon utan on ælce healfe, and hi habbað ealle heora fætnesse and heora tohopan and heora weolan swiþe orsorhlice utan bewunden, and sprecað nu for þi swiðe ofer-modlice.

10   Hy habbað me swyðe forsewenlice utan ymbstanden; þa eagan heora modes habbað geteohhad þæt hi me gebygen oð eorðan.

11   Hy sætiað min, and sittað swa gearwe swa seo leo deð to þam þe he gefon wyle, and swa swa his hwelp byð gehyd æt þære sæte.

12   Aris, Drihten, and cum to me ær, ær hie cumen, and gehwyrfe hi fram me, and ahrede mine sawle æt þam unrihtan wisan, and of þære wræce minra feonda alys me mid þinre handa and mid þine mægene.

13   Drihten, gedo þæt heora menigo sy læsse þonne ure feawena nu is, and tostence hi geond eorþan, libbende, of þis lande.

14   Gefyl hie nu mid þære witnunga þe þu lange gehyd hæfdest, and þeah him geteohhod. Weorþen hi swa geðræste mid hungre, þæt hi eton swynen flæsc (þæt Iudeum unalyfedlic ys to etanne) and þæt þæt hi læfon, healdan heora bearnum and heora bearna bearnum.

7   ⁷ Make wonderful now and glorify in me your mercy, you who constantly saves those who maintain confidence in you, protecting them ⁸ against those who strive against your will.

8   Lord, preserve and shield me, as one shields the apple of one's eye with the eyelid; hide me under the shadow of your wings ⁹ from the view of the wicked, who wish to kill me.

9   My enemies surrounded me from without on every side, ¹⁰ and they have securely wrapped up on the outside all their fatness, expectations, and wealth, and consequently now speak very arrogantly.

10   ¹¹ They have surrounded me most contemptuously; in their mind's eye they have determined to abase me to the dirt.

11   ¹² They lie in wait for me, and sit as prepared as the lion for the one he intends to catch, and just like its whelp lying concealed at the place of ambush.

12   ¹³ Lord, arise and come to me first, before they come, and turn them away from me, and save my soul from that wicked leader, ¹⁴ and with your might and power free me from the persecution of my enemies.

13   Lord, bring about that their multitude becomes fewer than our small number is now, and scatter them still living throughout the earth, out of this land.

14   Fill them now with the retribution that you had long concealed, and yet had ordained for them. May they be so afflicted with hunger that they will eat swine's flesh (which is unlawful for Jews to consume) and that what remains will be preserved for their children and their children's children.

15 Ic þonne rihtwis me oðywe beforan þinre ansyne and beo þonne gefylled ealles goodes, þonne me byð æteawed ðin wuldor.

Psalm 17

Dauid sang þysne seofonteoþan sealm lytle ær his ende ymb swyðe lang þæs þe hine God alysed hæfde, ægðer ge æt Sawle ge æt eallum his feondum; and swa deð ælc þæra þe hine singð, þancað Gode his mundbyrde—þonne he hine of hwylcum earfoðum alysed hæfð—oþþe hine oððe þæne þe he hine fore singð; for þæm ylcan hine sang Crist, þonne he alysed wæs fram Iudea ehtnesse.

1 Ic þe lufige, Drihten, for þæm þu eart min mægen; Drihten, þu eart min trymenes and min frið-stow.

2 Þu eart min alysend and min God and min gefultumend; to þe ic hopige.

3 Þu eart min scyldere and se horn minre hælo; þu eart min fultumen. Herigende ic clypige to þe, Drihten, and fram minum feondum ic weorðe ahredd.

4 Me ymbhringdon sar and sorga and granung fulneah oð deað; and geotende stream unrihtwisnessa minra wiðerweardra me gedrefdon.

5 Me ymbhringdon sar and manigfeald witu fulneah anlic

15   15 Justified then, I will show myself before you and will be filled with every good thing, when your glory is revealed to me.

Psalm 17

David sang this seventeenth psalm a little before his death, an exceedingly long time after God had delivered him both from Saul and from all his enemies; and everyone who sings it does the same, thanking God for his protection — whenever he has freed him from any difficulties — either for himself or him on whose behalf he sings it; for the same reason Christ sang it whenever he was freed from persecution by the Jews.

1   2 Lord, I will love you because you are my strength; 3 Lord, you are my support and place of refuge.

2   You are my redeemer, my God and helper; I will hope in you.

3   You are my protector and the horn of my salvation; you are my helper. 4 Lord, I will cry to you in praise and will be saved from my enemies.

4   5 Sorrows, cares, and groaning surrounded me almost to the point of death; and the gushing torrent of my enemies' iniquities troubled me.

5   6 Sorrows and numerous torments almost like those of

helle witum, and deaðes grynu me gefengon; and on eallum minum earfoðum ic clypige to Drihtne, and to minum Gode ic cige.

6   And he gehyrde of his þam halgan temple mine stemne, and min gehrop com beforan his ansyne, and eac on his earan hit eode.

7   And astyred wæs and acwacode seo eorðe minra feonda, and se grundweall þara munta wæs tohrered (þæt is, þæt mægen minra ofer-modena feonda); hy wæron astyrede, for þam him wæs God yrre.

8   For þam astah smec for his yrre and fyr blysede beforan his ansyne;

9   gleda wæron onælde fram him. He onælde heofonas and astah me on fultum, and seo eorðe wæs gesworcen and aðystrod under his fotum.

10   And he astah eft ofer Cherubin, and he fleah; and he fleah ofer winda fiðeru,

11   and let þystru betwuh him and minum feondum, þæt he nære næfre gesewen fram him, and he wæs, þeah, swiðe leoht on his temple. Þa hangode swiðe þystru wæter on þam wolcnum and on þære lyfte,

12   and þa wolcnu urnan swa swa ligetu beforan his ansyne, and he gemengde hagol and fyres gleda,

13   and worhte þunor-rada on heofonum; and se hyhsta sealde his stemne.

14   He sende his strælas, and hi tostencte, and gemanigfealdode his ligeta and gedrefde hig mid þy.

15   And eorðan wæter ut fleowan, and seo eorðe wæs astyred and on manegum stowum gehroren,

16   for þinum þrean and for þinum yrre.

17   Drihten sende of his heanesse and ahredde me æt þam ofer-mætum wæterum,

hell surrounded me, and the snares of death trapped me; [7] and in all my tribulations I will invoke the Lord, and I will call on my God.

6   And he heard my voice from his holy temple, and my cry came before his face and also entered his ears.

7   [8] And my enemies' land was shaken and trembled, and the mountains' foundation was shaken asunder (that is, the power of my arrogant enemies); they were disturbed because God was angry with them.

8   [9] So smoke rose up because of his anger, and fire blazed before his face;

9   coals were kindled by him. [10] He lit up the heavens and descended to help me, and the earth became dark and obscured under his feet.

10   [11] And he arose afterward above the Cherubim and took flight; and he flew above the wings of the winds,

11   [12] and placed darkness between him and my enemies, so that he was never visible to them, and yet he was exceedingly bright in his temple. Then very dark water hung in the clouds and the air,

12   [13] and the clouds scudded like lightning in his sight, and he mixed hail and coals of fire,

13   [14] and produced peals of thunder in the heavens; and the Most High sent out his voice.

14   [15] He hurled his arrows and scattered them, increased his lightning, which troubled them.

15   [16] And the earth's waters flowed out, and the earth was shaken and in many places caved in,

16   because of your rebuke and anger.

17   [17] The Lord sent help from his high place and saved me from the immense waters,

18   and of minum strengestum feondum, and from eallum þam þe me hatedon, for þam hig wæron gestrangode ofer me.

19   Hie me bregdon swiðe swiðlice on þam dagum þe ic geþræsted wæs; and Drihten wæs geworden min scyld, and he me gelædde on rymet of minum nearonessum and gedyde me halne, for þam he me wolde.

20   And he me geald æfter minre rihtwisnesse, and æfter þære unscæðfulnesse minra handa he me geald,

21   for þam ic heold Godes wegas and his bebodu, and ic ne dyde arleaslice ne unhyrsumlice wið minne Drihten.

22   For þam ealle his domas beoð symle beforan minre ansyne, and his rihtwisnessa ic ne awearp fram me,

23   for ði ic weorðe unwemme beforan him and ic me behealde wið min unriht.

24   And me gylt Drihten æfter minre rihtwisnesse and æfter þære unscæðfulnesse minra handa beforan his eagum.

25   Ac beo þu halig, Drihten, wið þa halgan, and unsceðfull wið þa unsceðfullan, and gecoren wið þa gecorenan, and hwyrf þe wið þa forhwyrfdan,

26   for þam ic wat þæt þu symle eadmod folc gehælst, and þa eagan þara ofer-modena ðu geeaðmetst.

27   For þam þu onælest min leoht-fæt, Drihten, min God, onlyht mine þystru.

28   For þam ic weorðe fram þe alysed æt costingum, and þurh mines Godes fultum ic utgange ofer minre burge weall, þeah heo sy utan behringed mid minum feondum.

29   Drihten, min God, unwemme synt þine wegas; Godes word synt amered on fyre; he is gefriþiend ælces þara þe him to hopað.

18   ¹⁸ and from my strongest enemies, and all those who hated me, because they had been fortified more than I.

19   ¹⁹ They had terrified me greatly in those days when I was afflicted; but the Lord became my protector, ²⁰ and led me out of my straits into an expanse and kept me safe, because he wished well for me.

20   ²¹ And he rewarded me according to my justice and the innocence of my hands,

21   ²² because I have observed God's ways and commands, and have not behaved wickedly or disobediently toward my Lord.

22   ²³ Because all his judgments are always in my sight, and I have not rejected his just deeds,

23   ²⁴ I will be spotless in his sight and guard myself against my iniquity.

24   ²⁵ And the Lord will reward me for my justice and the innocence of my hands in his sight.

25   ²⁶ But be holy, Lord, toward the holy, and innocent toward the innocent ²⁷ and distinguished toward the elect, and turn away from the perverted,

26   ²⁸ because I know that you will always save lowly people and humble the eyes of the proud.

27   ²⁹ Lord, my God, since you kindle my lamp, enlighten my darkness.

28   ³⁰ For I will be delivered by you from temptations, and with my God's help I will clamber over the city wall, even if it is surrounded from without by my enemies.

29   ³¹ Lord, my God, your ways are undefiled; God's words are purified in fire; he is the protector of everyone who trusts in him.

30 Hwylc ys god, butan uran Gode, oððe hwylc drihten, butan urum Drihtne?

31 Se God me gegyrde mid mægnum and mid cræftum and gesette mine wegas unwæmme.

32 He gedyde mine fet swa geræde swa swa heorotum, and me gesette ofer heanesse.

33 He gelærde mine handa to gefeohte, and he gedyde mine earmas swa strange swa ærene bogan.

34 And þu, Drihten, sealdest me gescyldnesse þinre hælo, and þin swiðre hand me underfeng and þin lar me getyde.

35 Þu gebræddest mine stæpas under me þæt mine fet ne slideredon.

36 Ic ehte minra feonda, and ic hie gefeng, and ic ne geswac ær hie forwurdon; ic hie gebigde þæt hie ne mihton gestandan ongean me,

37 ac feollon under mine fet. Þu me begyrdest mid mægenum and mid cræftum to wige.

38 Þu gedydest me underþeodde þa þe wið me upp arison, and minra feonda bæc þu onwendest to me, and me hine gesealdest; and þu tostenctest þa þe me hatedon.

39 Hy clypodon, and næs nan þara þe hig gehælde; hy clypodon to heora godum, and hy noldon gehyran.

40 For þam ic hi todælde swa smæle swa swa dust beforan winde, and hi adilgode swa swa wind deð dust on herestrætum.

41 Gefriða me, Drihten, wið þises folces unhyrsumnesse, for þam þu me gesettest him to heafde and eac oðrum ðeodum.

42 And þæt folc me þeowode þæt ic næfre ne cuðe; hy onhyldan heora earan to minum wordum and gehyrdon me.

43 Ac þa ælðeodgan bearn me oft lugon, and þeah hi for-

30   ³² Which one is god, but our God, or which one lord, but our Lord?

31   ³³ That God girded me with strength and power and established my ways as spotless.

32   ³⁴ He made my feet swift just as with the hart, and established me on a height.

33   ³⁵ He instructed my hands for battle and made my arms as strong as a brass bow.

34   ³⁶ And you, Lord, gave me your secure protection, your right hand received me, and your teaching instructed me.

35   ³⁷ You broadened my steps under me so that my feet did not slip.

36   ³⁸ I pursued my enemies and caught them, and I did not desist until they perished; ³⁹ I subdued them so that they could not resist me,

37   but fell under my feet. ⁴⁰ You have girded me with strength and power for war.

38   You made those who rose up against me subject to me, ⁴¹ and you turned my enemy's back to me, and gave him over to me; and you destroyed those who hated me.

39   ⁴² They cried out, but not one of those gods could save them; they called to their gods, but they would not listen.

40   ⁴³ So, I dispersed them as finely as dust before the wind, obliterating them as wind does dust on the highways.

41   ⁴⁴ Lord, protect me from this people's recalcitrance, because you have appointed me as leader over them and also over other peoples.

42   ⁴⁵ And that people whom I had never known served me; they listened attentively to my words and obeyed me.

43   ⁴⁶ But foreign children often lied to me, and although

ealdedon on minum ðeowdome, hy healtodan on heora wegum, for þam hi hyra willum ne heoldon Iudea æ.

44 Min Drihten leofað symle, and he byð symle gebletsad,
and he is upahafen, Drihten, min hælend.

45 Þu eart soð God, þu þe me sealdest þæt ic meahte swylc
wite don minum feondum, and me swylc folc underþydes.

46 Þu eart min alysend fram þam þeodum ðe wið me yr-
siað, and me upp ahefst ofer ða þe arison wið me, and fram
þam unrihtwisan were þu me alysdest.

47 For þam ic ðe andette, Drihten, beforan folcum, and on
þinum naman ic singe sealmas.

48 Gemycla nu, and gemonigfealda þa hælo þæs cynges ðe
ðu gesettest ofer folcum, and do mild-heortnesse þinum
gesmyredan Dauide and his cynne on ecnesse.

Psalm 18

Ðysne eahtateoðan sealm Dafid sang, Gode to þancunga his
mislicra and manigfealdra gesceafta, ðe he gesceop mannum
to ðeowianne — ne for ðy þæt þa men sceoldon him ðeow-
ian. Be þam he cwæð:

1 Heofonas bodiað Godes wuldor, and his hand-geweorc
bodiað þone rodor.

2 Se dæg segð þam oðrum dæge Godes wundru, and seo
niht þære nihte cyð Godes wisdom.

they grew old in my service, they wavered on their paths, because they did not voluntarily observe Jewish law.

44   ^{47} My Lord always lives, and is forever blessed and exalted, the Lord my savior.

45   ^{48} You are the true God, you who granted me power to inflict such punishment on my enemies, and who subjugated such people to me.

46   You are my deliverer from those hostile nations, ^{49} and you will exalt me above those who rose up against me, and you freed me from the wicked man.

47   ^{50} Therefore, I will give praise to you, Lord, in public, and will sing psalms in your name.

48   ^{51} Magnify now, and strengthen the safety of the king whom you appointed over peoples, and show mercy to David, your anointed, and to his progeny forever.

Psalm 18

David sang this eighteenth psalm in thanksgiving to God
for the diverse and numerous creatures which he has made
to serve humankind—not so that humankind should serve
them. On this subject he said:

1   ^{2} The heavens proclaim God's glory, and the works of his hand celebrate the firmament.

2   ^{3} One day announces God's wonders to the next, and the night declares to the coming night God's wisdom.

3   Nis nan folc on eorðan, ne nan mennisc geþeode, þe ne gehyre mistlica Godes gesceafta.

4   Ofer ealle eorðan færð heora stemn, ofer ealle eorðan endas heora word.

5   Drihten timbrede his templ on þære sunnan; seo sunne arist swiðe ær on morgen up, swa swa bryd-guma of his bryd-bure,

6   and heo yrnð swa egeslice on hyre weg, swa swa gigant yrnð on his weg; heo stihð oð þæs heofenes heanesse, and þanon astihð, and swa yrnð ymbutan oð heo eft þyder cymð; ne mæg hine nan man behydan wið hire hæto.

7   Godes æ is swiðe unleahtor-wyrðe, for þæm heo hwyrfð manna mod and heora sawla to Gode; Godes bebod is swiðe getrywe.

8   Godes rihtwisnessa synt swiðe rihta, for ðæm hy geblis-siað manna heortan; Godes bebod is swiðe leoht, hit onliht þa eagan ægþer ge modes ge lichaman.

9   Godes ege is swiðe halig, he þurhwunað a worlda world; Godes domas synt swiðe soðe, hi synt gerihtwisode on him sylfum.

10   Hy synt ma to lufianne þonne gold oððe deor-wurðe gimmas, and hi synt swetran ðonne hunig oððe beo-bread.

11   For þam ðin ðeow hi hylt—on heora gehyldnesse is mænig edlean.

12   Hwa ongyt his uncysta? From þæm ðe me beholen synt, geclænsa me, Drihten, and from ælðeodegum feondum spara me, þinne ðeow, Drihten.

13   Gif mine fynd ne ricsiað ofer me, þonne beo ic un-wemme, and beo geclænsod from þæm mæstum scyldum; ac gif hi me abysgiað, þonne ne mæg ic smeagan mine unscylda, ne eac ðinne willan ne mæg smeagan to wyrcanne.

3   ⁴There is no people on earth, nor any language, which does not hear God's diverse creations.

4   ⁵Their sound travels throughout all the earth, their word throughout all its regions.

5   ⁶The Lord built his temple in the sun; it rises up very early in the morning, like a bridegroom from his bridal chamber,

6   and it speeds as threateningly on its course as a giant runs on his way; ⁷it ascends as far as heaven's summit and from there descends, and so moves quickly in its orbit until it returns there; and no one is able to hide himself from its heat.

7   ⁸God's law is beyond reproach, because it turns people's minds and souls to him; his decree is very faithful.

8   ⁹God's just deeds are exceedingly upright, so they gladden men's hearts; God's command is very clear, enlightening the eyes of soul and body.

9   ¹⁰The fear of God is most holy, and continues forever; God's judgments are exceedingly true, justified in themselves.

10   ¹¹They are to be esteemed more than gold or precious jewels, and are sweeter than honey or bee bread.

11   ¹²Therefore, your servant will observe them—in the keeping of them lies many a reward.

12   ¹³Who recognizes his faults? From those which are hidden from me, purify me, Lord, ¹⁴and from foreign enemies save me, your servant, Lord.

13   If my enemies do not dominate me, then I will be spotless and purified from the most serious faults; but if they harass me, then I will not be able to examine my grievous faults, nor also consider how to do your will.

14 Gif ðu me þonne fram him alyst, ðonne sprece ic þæt
þe licað, and mines modes smeaung byð symle beforan ðinre
ansyne.

15 Drihten, þu eart min fultum and min alysend.

Psalm 19

Dauid sang þysne nigonteoðan sealm, and sæde on ðæm
sealme hu his folc him fore gebæde on his earfoðum; and
eac Ezechias folc gebæd for hine, þa he wæs beseten mid his
feondum on þære byrig; and swa doð ealle cristene men þe
þysne sealm singað, hy hine singað for heora kyningas; and
eac þa apostolas hine sungon be Criste, þa hine man lædde
to rode.

1 Gehyre ðe Drihten on þæm dæge þinra earfoða; gefriðie þe se nama Iacobes Godes,

2 and onsende þe fultum of his þam halgan temple, and
of Sion gehæle ðe.

3 Gemyndig sy Drihten ealra þinra offrunga, and þin
ælmesse sy andfengu.

4 Gylde ðe Drihten æfter ðinum willan, and eall ðin
geðeaht he getrymie,

5 þæt we moton fægnian on ðinre hælo, and on ðæm naman Drihtnes ures Godes we syn gemyclade.

6 Gefylle Drihten eall þin gebedu. Nu we ongitað þæt
Drihten wile gehælan his þone gesmyredan and ðone gehal-

14   [15] If you then free me from them, I will say what pleases you, and the deliberations of my mind will always be present in your sight.

15   Lord, you are my help and my savior.

Psalm 19

David sang this nineteenth psalm, relating in it how his people prayed for him in his tribulations; and also Hezekiah's people prayed for him, when he was besieged by his enemies in the city; and likewise all Christians who sing this psalm do so on behalf of their kings; and also the Apostles sang it about Christ, when he was led to the Cross.

1   [2] May the Lord hear you in the day of your tribulations; may the name of Jacob's God protect you,

2   [3] and send you help from his holy temple, and save you from out of Zion.

3   [4] May the Lord be mindful of all your offerings, and may your alms be acceptable.

4   [5] May the Lord pay you back according to your wishes and strengthen all your plans,

5   [6] so that we can rejoice in your salvation and be magnified in our Lord God's name.

6   [7] May the Lord fulfill all your prayers. Now we know that the Lord intends to save his anointed and consecrated

godan, and he hine gehyrð of his þam halgan heofone; swiðe mihtig is seo hælo his ðære swyðran handa.

7   On ryne-wænum and on horsum ure fynd fægniað, and þæs gilpað; we þonne on þæm naman Drihtnes ures Godes us micliað.

8   Hy synd nu gebundne and hi afeollon, and we soðlice arison and synt uppahafene.

9   Drihten, gehæl urne kyning, and gehyr us on ðæm dæge þe we ðe to clypiað.

Psalm 20

Ðysne twentigoðan sealm Dauid sang be him sylfum; and eac witegode be Ezechie þæm kinge; and ælc folc þe hine singð, hine singð for heora kyning; and ealra mæst Dauid witegode on þam sealme be Criste.

1   Drihten, on ðinum mægene nu blissað ure kyning, and for þinre hælo he fægnað swiðe swiðlice.

2   For ðæm þu him sealdest his modes willan, and þæs þe he mid his weolorum wilnade, þæs þu him ne forwyrndest.

3   Mid þære swetnesse þinra bletsunga þu wære hrædra to his fultume þonne he wende: þu sendest on his heafod kyne-gold mid deor-wyrþum gimmum astæned.

4   He þe bæd langes lifes, and þu hit him sealdest a worlda world.

5   Swiðe micel is his wul . . .

one, and he will hear him from his holy heaven; exceedingly powerful is the safety of his right hand.

7 8 Our enemies glory in chariots and in horses, and boast about it; but we will magnify ourselves in our Lord God's name.

8 9 They are bound now and have fallen, while we, in fact, have risen up and are exalted.

9 10 Lord, save our king, and hear us on the day when we invoke you.

Psalm 20

David sang this twentieth psalm about himself; and he also prophesied about King Hezekiah; and every nation which sings it, does so on behalf of their king; and, most of all, David prophesied in the psalm about Christ.

1 2 Lord, our king will now rejoice in your strength, and because you saved him he will exult exceedingly.

2 3 For you granted him his heart's desire, and what he desired with his lips you did not refuse him.

3 4 By means of the sweetness of your blessings you were more expeditious in helping him than he expected: you placed on his head a crown bejeweled with precious gems.

4 5 He asked you for a long life, and you granted it to him forever.

5 Exceedingly great is his glory . . .

Psalm 21

Ðisne an and twentiguþan sealm Dauid sang, biddende to Dryhtne and seofigende be his earfoðum and be his feondum; and swa deð ælc man þe hine singð, be his feondum he hine singð; and swa dyde Crist be Iudeum.

1   Drihten, Drihten, min God, beseoh to me; hwi forlete þu me swa feor minre hælo?

2   Ic clypige dæges and nihtes to ðe, and andette mine scylda and seofige min ungelimp, and þu hit ne gehyrst; ac ne understand þu hit me to unrihtwisnesse, for ðæm ic þe na ne oðwite þæt þu me ne gehyrst, ac minum agnum scyldum ic hit wite.

3   Ðu wunast on halgum stowum, Drihten, Israela lof; to þe hopedon ure fæderas; hi hopedon to þe, and þu hi alysdest.

4   Hy clypodon to ðe, and hi wurdon for ði gehælde; hi hopedon, and hi þæs ne sceamode.

5   Ic eam wyrme gelicra ðonne men, for þam ic eom worden mannum to leahtrunge and to forsewennesse, and ic eom ut aworpen fram him of heora gesomnunga, swa þer wyrm.

6   Ælc þæra þe me gesyhð, he me forsyhð and onscunað; hi sprecað mid heora welerum and wecgað heora heafdu and cweðað,

Psalm 21

David sang this twenty-first psalm, beseeching the Lord and complaining about his sufferings and his enemies; and everyone who sings it does the same about their enemies; and so did Christ about the Jews.

1   ² Lord, Lord, my God, look favorably on me; why have you abandoned me so far from my salvation?

2   ³ Day and night I call out to you, confess my sins, and lament my misfortunes, but you do not listen to any of it; yet do not consider it as infamy in me, because I certainly do not reproach you for not hearing me, rather, I impute it to my own sins.

3   ⁴ You dwell in holy places, Lord, the praise of Israel; ⁵ our fathers trusted in you; they trusted in you, and you freed them.

4   ⁶ They invoked you, and so they were saved; they hoped, and it brought them no shame.

5   ⁷ I am more like a worm than a human, because I have become a reproach and an object of contempt to people, and I have been cast out by them from their assembly, like a worm.

6   ⁸ Everyone who sees me despises and shuns me; they speak with their mouths and shake their heads, saying,

7   "He hopode to Drihtne, alyse he hine nu he gealp þæt he hine lufode."

8   Drihten, þu eart se þe me gelæddest of minre modor innoðe; þu wære min tohopa, syþþan ic fram minre modor breoston gelæd wæs. Þinre gymenne ic wæs beboden, syððan ic of hire innoðe eode, þu wære min God.

9   Ne gewit þu fram me, for þam me synt earfoðu swyðe neh, and nis nan oþer þe wylle oððe mæge me gehelpan.

10   Me ymbhringdon swiðe mænige calfru (þæt synt, lytle and niwe fynd), and þa fættan fearas me ofsæton (þæt synd, strengran fynd).

11   Hi todydon heora muð ongean me, swa swa leo þonne he geonað and grymetað and gefehð þæt þæt he wyle. Eall min mægen is tostenged and to nauhte worden, swa swa þæt wæter þæt þe byð ut agoten.

12   Min heorte and min mod is gemolten swa þær weax oninnan me,

13   and min mægen ys forsearod, swa swa læmen crocca; and min tunge ys gecleofod to minum gomum, and to deadum duste fulneah mine fynd me geworhton,

14   for ðan me ymbhringdon swiðe mænige hundas, and seo gegaderung þara awyrgedra me ofsæton.

15   Hy þurhdulfon mine handa and mine fet, and gerimdon eall min ban (þæt ys, min mægn); and mine getrywan frynd, þam ic getruwode swa wel swa minum agenum limum,

16   hy min hawodon and me beheoldon, and gedældan him min hrægl and þæt tohlutan.

17   Ac, la, Drihten, ne afyr þinne fultum fram me, ac loca to minre generennesse.

18   Ahrede mine sawle æt heora sweordum, and of þæs hundes handa min lif.

7   [9] "He trusted in the Lord, let him free him, seeing that he boasted that the Lord loved him."

8   [10] Lord, you drew me out of my mother's womb; you have been my hope since I have been weaned from my mother's breasts. [11] I have been committed to your care, since I emerged from her womb, you have been my God.

9   [12] Do not leave me, because tribulations are very near to me, and no one else is willing or able to help me.

10   [13] Calves in great numbers surrounded me (those are insignificant and recent enemies), and fat bulls besieged me (those are more powerful enemies).

11   [14] Their mouths loudly voiced opposition to me, as when a lion opens his mouth, roars, and seizes what he wants. [15] All my strength is diffused and reduced to nothing, just like water poured out on the ground.

12   My heart and mind is melted like wax within me,

13   [16] and my strength is dried up like an earthen pot; my tongue is stuck to my jaws, and my enemies have reduced me almost to lifeless dust,

14   [17] because a great many mastiffs have surrounded me, and a throng of the wicked has besieged me.

15   They pierced my hands and my feet, [18] and they counted all my bones (that is, my strength); and my "trustworthy" friends, whom I trusted as completely as my own body,

16   scrutinized me and stared, [19] and divided for themselves my garment, casting lots for separate pieces of it.

17   [20] Do not remove your help from me, Lord, only look to my protection.

18   [21] Save my soul from their swords, and my life from the mastiff's claw.

19   Gefriða me of þæs leon muðe, and of þam hornum þara anhyrna gefriða me, yrming.

20   Ic þonne bodie þinne naman minum broðrum; on midre heora gesomnunge ic þe herie, and cweþe to him:

21   "Se þe Drihten ondræde, herie hine, eall Iacobes cynn.

22   Ondræde hine eall Israela cynn, for þam he na forsyhð ne ne awyrpð earmra manna gebeda, ne he his andwlitan ne awende fram me, ac þonne ic clypode to him, þonne gehyrde he me."

23   Beforan þe byð min lof on þære myclan cyrcan; ic gylde min gehat Drihtne beforan þam þe hine ondrædað.

24   Þonne etaþ þa þearfan and hi beoð gefyllede, and heriað þonne Drihten þa þe hine secað,

25   and heora heortan onfoð mægene and libbað a worlda world. Þonne gemunan þæt eall eorð-gemæru, and gecyrrað ealle to Drihtne,

26   and gebiddað hy to him ealle þeoda and ælc cynn, for þam ðe Drihtnes synd þa ricu, and he wylt ealra þeoda.

27   Hy etað and hy gebiddað, ealle þa welegan geond þas eorþan; beforan his ansyne cumað ealle þa ðe on eorðan astigað.

28   And min sawl him leofað, and min sæd him þeowað.

29   And hy bodiað Drihten, ure cyn þæt æfter us cymð; and heofonas bodiað his rihtwisnesse þam folcum þe þonne beoð acende þa worhte Drihten.

19   [22] Free me from the lion's mouth, and from the horns of the unicorns free me, a needy person.

20   [23] Then I will proclaim your name to my brothers; in the middle of their assembly I will praise you, while saying to them:

21   [24] "He who fears the Lord, praise him, all Jacob's progeny.

22   [25] Let all Israelites fear him, because he certainly does not despise or reject the prayers of the poor, nor did he turn his face away from me, but whenever I invoked him, he listened."

23   [26] My praise will endure in your presence in the great assembly; I will repay my vows to the Lord before those who fear him.

24   [27] Then the needy will eat and will be satiated, and those who seek him will then praise the Lord,

25   and their hearts will receive strength and live forever. [28] Then all the ends of the earth will remember that, and all humankind will turn to the Lord,

26   and all peoples and every race will worship him, [29] because their kingdoms are the Lord's, and he governs all nations.

27   [30] All the wealthy throughout this earth eat and worship; all those who descend to the grave will enter into his presence.

28   [31] And my soul will live for him, and my descendants will serve him.

29   [32] And our offspring coming after us will proclaim the Lord; and the heavens will proclaim his justice to future generations created by the Lord.

Psalm 22

Dauid sang þysne twa and twenteogeþan sealm, þa he witegode be Israela folces freodome, hu hy sceoldon beon alæd
of Babilonia þeowdome, and hu hi sceoldon Gode þancian
þæra ara þe hi be wege hæfdon hamweardes, and eac be his
agenre gehwyrftnesse of his wræc-siðe; and ælc þæra ðe hine
singð, he þancað Gode his alysnesse of his earfoðum; and
swa dydon þa apostolas and eall þæt cristene folc, Cristes
æriste; and eac þanciað cristene men on þyson sealme heora
alysnesse of heora scyldum æfter fulluhte.

1   Drihten me ræt: ne byð me nanes godes wan; and he me
geset on swyðe good feoh-land,
2   and fedde me be wætera staðum, and min mod gehwyrfde of unrotnesse on gefean.
3   He me gelædde ofer þa wegas rihtwisnesse for his naman.
4   Þeah ic nu gange on midde þa sceade deaðes, ne ondræde ic me nan yfel, for þam þu byst mid me, Drihten.
5   Þin gyrd and þin stæf me afrefredon (þæt is, þin
þreaung and eft þin frefrung).
6   Þu gegearwodest beforan me swiðe bradne beod wið
þara willan þe me hatedon,
7   þu gesmyredest me mid ele min heafod; Drihten, hu
mære þin folc nu is, ælce dæge hit symblað.

Psalm 22

David sang this twenty-second psalm prophesying about the Jewish people's liberation, how they were destined to be led from the Babylonian captivity, and how they would thank God for the favors which they experienced along the way homewards, and also concerning his own return from his journey of exile; and everyone who sings it, thanks God for their liberation from sufferings; and the apostles and all the Christian community did likewise, about Christ's resurrection; and Christians also thank God in this psalm for their liberation from their sins after baptism.

1   [1] The Lord governs me: I will not lack any good thing; [2] and he establishes me in exceedingly fine pastureland,

2   and has fed me by the water's edge, [3] and turned my mind from sadness to joy.

3   He led me over paths of justice because of his name.

4   [4] Even though I should now advance into the middle of death's shadow, I will not fear any evil, because you will be with me, Lord.

5   Your rod and your staff consoled me (that is, your reproofs and afterward your comforting).

6   [5] You made ready in my presence an exceedingly broad table, contrary to the wishes of my haters,

7   you anointed my head for me with oil; Lord, how glorious your people is now, it feasts every day.

8   And folgie me nu þin mild-heortnes ealle dagas mines
lifes,

9   þæt ic mæge wunian on þinum huse swiþe lange tiid oð
lange ylde.

Psalm 23

On þissum þreo and twentigoðan sealme Dauid witegode
and rehte mid hwylcum geearnungum gehwylc man hine
mæg alysan of his earfoðum; and eac he witgode be Cristes
sigefæstnesse, þa þa he on heofonas astah æfter his æriste;
and eac he witgode be him sylfum, hu his ealdor-menn
sceoldon fægnian his cymes of his wræc-siðe.

1   Drihtnes ys eorðe and eall þæt heo mid gefyld is, and
eall mancynn, þe þæron eardað, is Drihtnes.

2   He gesette þa eorþan ofer þære sæ, and ofer ðam eam
he hi gestaðelode.

3   Hwa is þæs wyrðe þæt he astige on Godes munt, oþþe
hwa mot standan on his halgan stowe?

4   He byð þæs wyrðe, þe unscæðfull byð mid his handum
and clæne on his heortan, se þe ne hwyrfð his mod æfter idlum geþohtum and him mid weorcum fulgæð—þeah hi him
on mod cumen—ne nænne að ne swerað to biswice his nyhstan.

8   6 And may your mercy follow me now all the days of my life,

9   so that I can dwell in your house for the longest time into old age.

Psalm 23

In this twenty-third psalm David prophesied and explained what kinds of merits allow all humans to free themselves from their sufferings; and he also prophesied about Christ's triumph, when he ascended to the heavens after his resurrection; and he prophesied about himself as well, that his noblemen would rejoice at his coming from his exile.

1   1 The earth and everything it contains is the Lord's, and all humankind dwelling in it, as well.

2   2 He placed the earth on the sea, on the waters he established it.

3   3 Who is so deserving that he may ascend to God's mountain, or who is allowed to stand in his holy place?

4   4 He will be deserving, who is innocent with his hands and pure of heart, who does not turn his mind to vain thoughts, and carry them out with actions—even if they do enter his mind—or swear an oath to deceive his neighbor.

5   Se þe swylc byð, he onfehð bletsunge fram Gode and miltse æt Drihtne hælende.

6   Þyllic byð þæt cyn þe God secð, and þa þe secað þone andwlitan Iacobes Godes.

7   Undoð nu eower geatu, ge ealdor-men, and onhlidað þa ecan geata, for þan þe ingæð se kyning þe God gewuldrod hæfð and geweorðod. Þa andswarode þæt folc and cwæð:

8   "Hwæt is þes wuldorfæsta kyning? Hit is ure hlaford, strang and mihtig, se þe hæfde anweald on gefeohte."

9   Gedoð nu, ealdor-men, eowru geatu, and onhlidað eow, ge ecan geatu, for þam þær inngæð se kyning þe God gewuldrod hæfð and geweorðod.

10   Hwæt is se gewuldroda kyning? Hit is se wuldorfæsta, se þe God fore wyrcð swylc wundru.

Psalm 24

Dauid sang þysne feower and twentigoðan sealm and hine þæron gebæd, þa he to þære reste becom þe he ær wilnode; and eac he witegode on þam sealme be þæs folces gehwyrf-nesse of heora hæft-nyde, þa hi on Babilonia gehæfte wæron; and swa ylce bi ælcum rihtwisum þonne he ænige reste hæfð æfter his earfoðum; and eac be Criste æfter his æriste.

1   To þe ic hæbbe, Drihten, min mod and mine sawle; Drihten, min God, to þe ic hopige, and ic þæs næfre ne sceamige,

5   5 Such a one will receive God's blessing and mercy from the saving Lord.

6   6 Just so is the generation that seeks God, and those who seek the face of Jacob's God.

7   7 You princes, open now your gates, and reveal the eternal gates, because the king glorified and honored by God will enter. Then that people replied and said:

8   8 "What kind of person is this glorious king? It is our lord, strong and powerful, he who had victory in battle."

9   9 Princes, open now your gates, and you eternal gates, reveal yourselves, because the king glorified and honored by God will enter there.

10   10 What kind of man is that glorified king? It is the majestic one, for whom God performs such wonders.

Psalm 24

David sang this twenty-fourth psalm and in it he prayed,
since he attained to that tranquility which he had desired;
and also he prophesied in the psalm about the people's return from their captivity, when they were prisoners in Babylon; and likewise about the recovery of the just person,
whenever he experiences some tranquility after sufferings;
and also about Christ after his resurrection.

1   1 Lord, to you I will raise my mind and soul; 2 Lord, my God, I will trust in you, and will never be ashamed of that,

2   ne mine fynd me næfre for ðy ne bysmrian; ne nan þæra þe to þe hopað ne wyrð gescended.

3   Scamien heora ealle þa unrihtwisan þe idelnesse wyrcað; Drihten, gedo me þine wegas cuðe, and lær me þine paðas.

4   Geræd me and gerece on þinre soðfæstnesse, and lær me, for þam þu eart, Drihten, min hælend; ælce dæge ic anbidige þines fultumes.

5   Gemun, Drihten, þinra miltsunga and þinre mildheortnesse, þe fram fruman worlde wæs.

6   Þa scylda mines iugoðhades ne gemun þu, Drihten, ne huru þa þe ic ungewisses geworhte (þæt synt, þa þe ic wende þæt nan scyld nære), ac for þinre myclan mild-heortnesse beo þu min gemyndig, Drihten.

7   For þinre godnesse, Drihten, þu eart swete and wynsum and eac rihtwis.

8   For þam gesette God æ scyldiendum on heora wegum, and geriht þa manðwæran on domum, and him getæceð his wegas.

9   Ealle Godes wegas syndon mild-heortnes and rihtwisnes ælcum þæra þe his æ secað and his bebodu lufiað.

10   Drihten, for þinum naman beo þu forgifende mina synna, for þy hi synt swyðe mycele.

11   Swa hwylc mann swa Drihten ondræt, he him geset þa æ, and him sylð þæt geþeaht on þone weg þe heora ægðrum licað, ge Gode ge eac þam men.

12   His sawl hi gerest softe on monegum goodum, and his sæd on ece yrfeweardnesse gesit eorðan.

13   Drihten is mægen and cræft ælces þæra þe hine ondræt, and he him getæcð eallum his willan.

2   ³ nor should my enemies ever deride me because of that; nor will anyone who trusts in you be confounded.

3   ⁴ Let all the wicked who do vain things be ashamed of themselves; Lord, make known to me your ways, and teach me your paths.

4   ⁵ Direct and guide me in your truth, and teach me, since you are my savior, Lord; every day I expect your help.

5   ⁶ Lord, be mindful of your mercies and compassion, which has existed from the world's beginning.

6   ⁷ Lord, do not remember my youthful sins, nor indeed those that I committed unwittingly (that is, things which I thought did not constitute sin), but for your great mercy's sake be mindful of me, Lord.

7   Lord, because of your goodness ⁸ you are pleasant, agreeable, and also just.

8   So, God established a law for sinners in their ways, ⁹ and he will direct the meek in judgments, teaching them his ways.

9   ¹⁰ All God's ways are mercy and justice for every seeker of his law and lover of his commands.

10   ¹¹ Lord, for your name's sake, forgive my sins, since they are exceedingly serious.

11   ¹² For whoever fears him, the Lord will establish that law, and will counsel him on the path that will please both God and him.

12   ¹³ His soul will dwell without disturbance in many good things, and his children will possess the earth in an eternal inheritance.

13   ¹⁴ The Lord is the strength and power of everyone who fears him, and will teach all of them his will.

14   Symle lociað mine eagan to Gode, for þam he alysð mine fet of gryne.

15   Geloca to me, Drihten, and gemiltsa me, for þam ic eom ana forlæten, yrming.

16   And þa earfoðu minre heortan synd swyðe tobræd and gemanigfealdod; gedo for þi, Drihten, þæt þu me gefriðie æt minre nyd-þearfe.

17   Geseoh mine eaðmetto and mine earfoða, and forgif ealle mine scylda.

18   And geseoh eac mine fynd, for þam hi synt swyþe gemanigfealdode; and geseoh hu unrihtlice hi me hatiað.

19   Geheald mine sawle, and gefriða me, þæt me ne sceamie þæs þe ic to þe clypige.

20   Þa unsceðfullan and þa rihtwisan, þa þe begangað, coman to me, wendon þæt me sceolde cuman sum fultum and sum frofor fram þe, for þam ic symle þæs anbidode and wilnode and wende æt þe, Drihten.

21   Gefriða me, Drihten, Israela God, of eallum minum nearonessum.

14 ¹⁵ My eyes will constantly look to God, because he will free my feet from the snare.

15 ¹⁶ Lord, take care of me and have mercy on me, because I am abandoned, a wretch.

16 ¹⁷ And the worries of my heart are greatly enlarged and multiplied; so, Lord, free me from my distress.

17 ¹⁸ Witness my abjection and troubles, and forgive all my sins.

18 ¹⁹ And regard also my enemies, how they are greatly multiplied; and see how unjustly they hate me.

19 ²⁰ Preserve my soul and free me, so that I may not be ashamed of invoking you.

20 ²¹ The innocent and the just, those who worship you, came to me, thinking that to me would come some help and some support from you, because I always expected, desired, and anticipated it from you, Lord.

21 ²² Lord, God of Israel, rescue me from all my difficulties.

Psalm 25

Dauid sang þisne fif and twentigoðan sealm be his unscyldi-
nesse wið his sunu and wið his geþeahteras, þe hine on woh
lærdan; and eac he witgode on þam sealme be þære unscyl-
dignesse Israela folces wið Asirie, þa hi hy læddan on hæft-
nyd to Babilonia; and eac swa ylce ælc rihtwis man þe hine
singð, he hine singð be him sylfum and be þam þe hine unscyldigne dreccað; and swa dyde eac Crist be Iudeum.

1   Dem me, Drihten, for þam ic eom unscyldig wið þas
mine fynd, and ic hopige to Drihtne, and ic ne weorðe for þi
geuntrumod.

2   Fanda min, Drihten, and smea mine geþohtas,

3   for þan þin mild-heortnes ys beforan minum eagum,
and ic symle tilode mid rihtwisnesse þe and him to licianne.

4   Ne sæt ic na on þære samnunge idelra manna and un-
nytra, ne ic in eode on þæt geþeaht unriht-wyrcendra;

5   ac ic hatode þa gesamnunge unrihtwisra, for þam ic
næfre ne teolade sittan on anum willan mid þam arleasum.

6   Ac ic wilnode symle þæt ic aðwoge mine handa betwuh
þam unscæððigum (þæt is, þæt ic wære unscyldig betwuh
him), þæt ic meahte hweorfan ymb þinne þone halgan alter,
Drihten,

7   and þær gehyran þa stemne þines lofes, and þæt ic
mæge cyþan eall þin wundru.

8   Drihten, ic lufode þone wlite þines huses and þa stowe
þines wuldorfæstan temples.

Psalm 25

David sang this twenty-fifth psalm about his innocence toward his son and his own counselors who wrongly advised him; and he also prophesied about the innocence of the Israelites toward the Assyrians, when the latter led them in captivity to Babylon; and likewise every just person who sings it does so about himself and those who afflict him while innocent; and so did Christ also about the Jews.

1   ¹ Lord, judge me, because I am guiltless toward these enemies of mine, and trusting in the Lord, I will not become weak.

2   ² Lord, test me, and examine my thoughts,

3   ³ because your mercy is before my eyes, and I have always honestly striven to please you and them.

4   ⁴ I did not sit in the assemblies of vain and idle men, nor did I enter into the counsel of wrongdoers;

5   ⁵ on the contrary, I hated their assembly and so never attempted to sit with shared resolve among the impious.

6   ⁶ Indeed, I constantly wished to purify my hands among the innocent (that is, to be guiltless among them), so that I could circle your holy altar, Lord,

7   ⁷ and there hear the sound of praise raised to you, and declare all your wonders.

8   ⁸ Lord, I have loved the beautiful appearance of your house and the site of your glorious temple.

9 Ac ne forleos mine sawle ongemang þam arleasum, ne min lif betwuh þam man-slagum, þæra handa and þæra weorc syndon fulle unrihtwisnesse ...

Psalm 26

... oran w ... and eac he witegode on þam sealme be Eze-chie þam cyning, hu he scolde gode þancian þære blisse þe he hæfde; and swa ylce deð ælc þæra þe hine singð, oððe for hine sylfne oððe for oðerne, Gode he þancað þære blisse þe he hæfð; and eac witegode on þam sealme be Criste, hu he sceolde beon alysed.

1 Drihten is min onlyhtend and min hælend; hwæt þearf ic ondrædan?

2 Drihten is scyldend mines lifes; hwy sceal ic beon afærd?

3 Þonne me to genealæhton mine fynd me to derianne, swylce hi woldon fretan min flæsc, þa þe me swencton, hi wæron sylfe geuntrumode and gefeollon.

4 Þeah hi nu gyt wyrcen getruman and scyld-ridan wið me, ne byð min heorte nawuht afæred; þeah hi arisan on-gean me to feohtanne, to þam Gode ic hopie þe me ær ge-freode.

5 ... and geseon Godes willan, and þone ongitan; and he me gefriðie on his þam halgan temple.

9   ⁹ But do not destroy my soul among the wicked, nor my life among those killers ¹⁰ whose hands and deeds are full of iniquity . . .

Psalm 26

. . . and he also prophesied in the psalm about King Hezekiah, how he was destined to thank God for the joy which he experienced; and likewise does everyone who sings it, either for themselves or for another person, thanking God for the joy which they experience; and he also prophesied in the psalm about Christ, how he was destined to be liberated.

1   ¹ The Lord is the one who enlightens and saves me; whom need I fear?

2   The Lord is the protector of my life; of whom will I be afraid?

3   ² When my enemies approached me to inflict harm, as if they desired to devour my flesh, those tormentors were themselves weakened and they fell.

4   ³ Even if they still employ troops and phalanxes against me, my heart will certainly not be dismayed; even if they rise up to fight against me, I will trust in the God who previously freed me.

5   ⁴ . . . and recognize God's will and understand it; and may he protect me in his holy temple.

6   For þam he me gehydde on his temple; on þam yflan dagum he me gefriðode on þam sceade his geteldes and his temples, and he me ahof upp on heane stan,

7   and huru nu hæfð min heafod upp ahafen ofer mine fynd, for þæm ic ymbhweorfe þin þæt halige tempel, Drihten, and þær offrige on þinum huse þa offrunga . . . ; sangas ic singe, and secge Gode lof.

8   Gehyr, Drihten, mine stefne, mid þære ic clypige to þe; gemiltsa me and gehyr me.

9   To þe cwyð min heorte: "Ic sohte þine ansyne; ic sece gyt symle, Drihten."

10   Ne awend þu þine ansyne fram me, ne þe næfre yrringa acyr fram þinum þeowe.

11   Þu eart min fultumend, Drihten, ne forlæt me, ne ne forseoh me, Drihten, min hælend.

12   For þam min fæder and min modor me forleton, ac Drihten me ne forlet.

13   Gesete me æ, Drihten, on þinum wege, and gerece me on rihtne pæð fore minum feondum,

14   and ne syle me to þara modes willan þe min ehtað, for ðam arison ongean me lease gewitnessa, and heora leasung wæs gecyrred to heom sylfum.

15   Ic gelyfe þæt ic geseo Godes good on libbendra lande. Hopa nu, min mod, to Drihtne, and gebid his willan, and do esnlice, and gestaþela and gestranga þine heortan, and geþola Drihtnes willan.

6   5 For he hid me in his temple; in the evil days he protected me in his tabernacle and temple's shelter, 6 and raised me up on a high rock,

7   and truly he has now raised up my head above my enemies, therefore I will circle your holy temple, Lord, and there in your house offer those sacrifices . . . ; I will sing psalms, and give praise to God.

8   7 Lord, hear my voice, with which I cry to you; have mercy on me and hear me.

9   8 My heart says to you: "I searched for your face; I will continue to search, Lord."

10   9 Do not turn away your face from me, nor in anger ever turn away from your servant.

11   Lord, you are my helper, do not abandon or despise me, Lord, my savior.

12   10 For my father and my mother have abandoned me, but the Lord did not.

13   11 Lord, establish for me a law in your way, and direct me in a just path because of my enemies,

14   12 and do not surrender me to the whim of my persecutors, for false witnesses have risen up against me, but their falsehood was turned back on themselves.

15   13 I believe that I will see God's bounty in the land of the living. 14 My spirit, trust now in the Lord, await his will, act manfully, fortify and strengthen your heart, and endure the Lord's will.

Psalm 27

Dauid sang þisne seofon and twentigoþan sealm, on þæm
sealme he wæs cleopiende to Drihtne, wilnode þæt he hine
arette and gefriðode wiþ eallum earfoðum, ægðer ge modes
ge lichaman, and wið ealle his fynd gescylde, ge wið ge-
sewene ge wið ungesewene; and eac Ezehias on þam ylcan
sealme hine gebæd þæt hine God alysde, ægðer ge æt his
mettrumnesse ge æt his feondum, swa he þa dyde; and þæs
ylcan wilnað ælc þe hine singð, oþþe for hine sylfne oððe for
oþerne; and swa ylce dyde Crist, þa þa he þysne sealm sang.

1   To þe ic hopige, Drihten, min God; ne swuga, ac dem
and miltsa me; gif þu swa ne dest, þonne beo ic gelicost þam
þe afylð on pytt.

2   Ac gehyr þa stemne mines gebedes, for þam ic nu to þe
clypige and mine handa upp hebbe to þinum þam halgan
temple.

3   Ne syle me, ne ne send mid þam synfullan, and mid þam
unrihtwyrcendum ne forleos me,

4   ne me ne fordo mid þam þe luflice sprecað to heora
nyhstum and habbað, þeah, facn on heora heortan.

5   Ic wat þæt þu sylst him edlean be heora gewyrhtum,
and æfter þam unrihte þe hi an swincað, þu heom gyldest.

6   Ðu heom sylst edlean, for þam hy ne ongitað þin weorc
ne þa ne geseoð.

Psalm 27

David sang this twenty-seventh psalm, in which he invoked
the Lord, desiring that he should comfort and free him
from all sufferings, both mental and physical, and that he
should protect him against all his enemies, both visible and
invisible; and also Hezekiah in the same psalm prayed that
God would free him both from his illness and from his enemies, as he subsequently did; and everyone who sings it desires the same thing, either for himself or for another; and
Christ did likewise when he sang this psalm.

1   ^{1} Lord, my God, in you I trust; do not be silent, but
judge and have mercy on me; if you do not do so, then I will
become very like him who falls into a pit.

2   ^{2} But hear the sound of my supplication, because I now
invoke you and raise up my hands to your holy temple.

3   ^{3} Do not hand me over or consign me to sinners, and do
not ruin me with evildoers,

4   or undo me with those who, while speaking amiably to
their neighbors, harbor deceit in their hearts.

5   ^{4} I know that you will render retribution to them just as
they deserve, and you will punish them in proportion to the
injustice at which they labor.

6   You will repay them, ^{5} because they do not understand
or consider your works.

7   Þu hi towyrpst and hi eft ne getimbrast; gebletsod sy
Drihten, for þam þe he gehyrde þa stemne mines gebedes.

8   Drihten is min fultumend and min gescyldend; on hine
gehyht min heorte, and he me gefultumað.

9   Drihten is strengo his folces and gescyldend þære hælo
his gesmyredan.

10   Gehæl, Drihten, þin folc, and gebletsa þin yrfe-land,
and gerece þa þe þæron eardiað, and hi upp ahefe on ecnesse.

Psalm 28

Ðysne eahta and twentigoðan sealm Dauid sang bebeo-
dende þam folce þæt hi gelæston heora gehat and heora
ælmesan sealdon Gode for swa myclum gifum swa he him
geaf; and he witegode eac þæt ylce be Ezechie, þe lange
æfter him wæs, þæt he sceolde þæt ylce don þonne he alysed
wære æt Asirium and eac æt his mettrumnesse; and eac swa
ilce he witegode be eallum þam þe æfter him gebrocode
wæron and eft arette, þæt hi eac þæs Gode þancodon æfter
heora bysne; and eac he witegode be Criste, þæt he sceolde
beon alysed æt Iudeum. He cwæð:

1   Ge Godes bearn, bringað eow sylfe Gode, and bringað
him eac eowera ramma bearn.

2   And bringað eac Drihtne wuldor and weorðmynd, and
bringað wuldor Drihtnes naman,

7   You will destroy them and will not resuscitate them;
⁶ blessed be the Lord, because he heard the sound of my appeal.

8   ⁷ The Lord is my helper and protector; my heart will trust in him, and he will help me.

9   ⁸ The Lord is the strength of his people and protector of his anointed one's security.

10   ⁹ Lord, save your people, and bless the land which you have given them as an inheritance, and direct those who dwell in it, and exalt them forever.

Psalm 28

David sang this twenty-eighth psalm, commanding the people to fulfill their vows and make votive offerings to God for such great gifts as he gave them; and he also prophesied the same about Hezekiah, who lived long after him, that he was destined to do the same when he was freed from the Assyrians and also from his illness; and also he prophesied in the same way about all those coming after him who were afflicted and afterward comforted, that they also would thank God for that after their predecessors' example; and also he prophesied about Christ, that he was destined to be freed from the Jews. David said:

1   ¹ You children of God, bring yourselves and also your rams' offspring to God.

2   ² And bring also glory and honor to the Lord, and glory to the Lord's name,

3   and gebiddað eow to Gode on his halgan healle. Godes
word is ofer wætrum, and hy gehæft; he is mægen-þrymmes
God and he þunrað ofer manegum wæterum and mycelum.

4   Godes word is on mycelum mægene and mycelu þing
deð.

5   Þæs Godes word brycþ cedor-treowu, and symle se
God brycð þa hean ceder-treowu on Libano, þam myclan
munte (þa treowa tacniað ofermodra manna anweald).
Drihten forbrycð and forbryt þa myclan ceder-treowu,
emne swa þa lytlan onwæstmas. Þa owæstmas beoð swa
mycle and swa fægere swa swa þees deores bearn þe *unicornus* hatte.

6   Godes word adwæscð fyres lig; Drihten ahrysode þa
westan eorðan and astyrede þa westan stowe þe is gehaten
Cades.

7   And he gedyde þæt þa fynd flugan swa heortas, and he
onwreah þa eorðan þe ær wæs oferþeaht mid feondum. Cu-
mon nu for þi ealle to his temple and secgon him þæs lof.

8   Drihten us gedyde þæt we moston buian æfter þam
folce; se Drihten is ure kyning, se sitt on ecnesse ofer us.

9   Drihten sylþ his folce mægen, and gebletsað his folc on
sibbe.

3   and worship God in his holy palace. ³ God's word rests above the waters and controls them; he, the God of majesty, thunders over many and mighty waters.

4   ⁴ God's word is present in great power and does great things.

5   ⁵ God's word shatters cedar trees, and that same God constantly shatters the lofty cedar trees on Lebanon, the great mountain (the trees signify the power of arrogant men). ⁶ The Lord will crush and dash into pieces the mighty cedar trees, even as he does the tender shoots. Those shoots are as great and as beautiful as the offspring of the animal called "unicornus."

6   ⁷ God's word quenches the fire's flame; ⁸ the Lord shook the deserted earth and convulsed that uninhabited place called Cades.

7   ⁹ And he caused those enemies to flee like harts, and he denuded the earth which was previously thick with enemies. Let all, therefore, come now to his temple and praise him for that.

8   ¹⁰ The Lord arranged that we could live on after that people; the Lord is our king, ruling forever over us.

9   ¹¹ The Lord will fortify his people and bless them with peace.

Psalm 29

Dauid sang þysne nigan and twentigoþan sealm þam Gode
þe hine alysde æt his feondum and æt eallum earfoðum; and
þæt ylce he witgode be Ezechie þæt he sceolde þæt ylce don
þonne he alysed wære æt Assirium and æt his metrumnesse;
and þæt ylce he witegode be ælcum rihtwison men þe þysne
sealm singð oþþe for hine sylfne oþþe for oðerne, Gode to
þancunge þære blisse þe he þonne hæfð; and eac he witegode on þam sealme be Criste, hu he sceolde alysed beon,
ægðer ge fram Iudeum ge of ðy deaðe.

1   Ic fægnige, Drihten, and þe herige, for þam þu me ge-
friðadest, and þu ne lete mine fynd min fægnian.

2   Drihten, min God, ic clypode to þe, and þu me gehældest, and atuge mine sawle of neolnessum and of helle, and
me gehældest fram þæra geferscipe þe feollon on pytt.

3   Heriað nu Drihten ealle his halige, and andetað þæt gemynd his halignesse,

4   for þam open wracu ys on his yrsunga, and soð lif on
þam þæt man wrece his willan.

5   Þeah we wepon on æfen, he gedeð þæt we hlihhað on
morgen.

6   Ic cwæð on minum wlencum and on minre orsorhnesse: "Ne wyrð þises næfre nan wendincg,"

7   for þam þu me sealdest on ðinum goodan willan wlite
and mægen; þa awendest þu þinne andwlitan fram me, þa
wearð ic sona gedrefed.

Psalm 29

David sang this twenty-ninth psalm to the God who had freed him from his enemies and all tribulations; and he prophesied about Hezekiah that he would do the same when he was freed from the Assyrians and from his illness; and he prophesied the same about each of the just who sing this psalm either on their own behalf or for another, in thanksgiving to God for the joy which they then experience; and also he prophesied in that psalm about Christ, how he would be freed, both from the Jews and from death.

1   2 Lord, I will rejoice and praise you because you protected me, and did not allow my enemies to exult over me.

2   3 Lord, my God, I invoked you, and you healed me, 4 and brought my soul out from the lower regions and from hell, and saved me from the company of those who have fallen into that pit.

3   5 Praise the Lord now, all his holy ones, and acknowledge the memory of his holiness,

4   6 for there is manifest vengeance in his anger, but true life in fulfilling his will.

5   Even if we weep in the evening, he will cause us to laugh in the morning.

6   7 In my pride and insouciance, I boasted: "This will never change,"

7   8 because in your benevolence you gave me beauty and strength; but when you turned away your face from me, I immediately became troubled.

8   Þa clypode ic eft to þe and gebæd me to minum Drihtne and cwæð: "Drihten, hu nyt is þe min slæge, oþþe min cwalu, oððe min rotung on byrgenne?

9   Hwæðer þe þæt dust herige on þære byrgene, oþþe hwæðer hit cyðe þine rihtwisnesse?"

10   Þa gehyrde Drihten þa word and gemildsade me, he wearð me to fultume.

11   Drihten, þu gehwyrfdest minne heaf and mine seo-funga me to gefean, þu totære min wite-hrægl, and þu me begyrdst mid gefean; for þam hit ys cyn þæt min wuldor and min gylp þe herige, þæt ic ne wurðe gedrefed.

12   Drihten, min God, on ecnesse ic þe herige.

Psalm 30

Dauid sang þysne þrittigoðan sealm, gebiddende to Drihtne
for his ham-cyme of þam wræce and of þam earfoðan þe he
þa on wæs; and eac he witgode be þære wræce þe æfter him
wurðan sceolde þam folce (þæt wæs, þa hi to Babilonia
gelædde wæron), he witgode þæt hi sceoldon gebiddan on
þa ylcan wisan þe he dyde, and hyra ungelimp þær seofian
swa he dyde; and eac he witegode be ælcum rihtwison menn
þe sealmas singð, awþer oþþe for hine sylfne oððe for
oðerne mann þara þe geswenced byð, awðer oþþe on mode
oþþe on lichaman; and he witegode eac be Criste, þæt he
hine sceolde swa gebiddan wið þam earfoðum þe Iudas him
dydon.

1   To þe ic hopige, Drihten, ne gesceamað me næfre þæs;
on þinre rihtwisnesse alys me and gefriða me.

8 ⁹ Then I invoked you again, begging my Lord, and said:
¹⁰ "Lord, of what use to you is my death, or destruction, or my rotting in a sepulcher?

9 Will the dust praise you in the sepulcher, or will it declare your justice?"

10 ¹¹ Then the Lord heard those words, and taking pity on me, he became my helper.

11 ¹² Lord, you changed my mourning and complaining into joy, you tore up my sackcloth and you gird me with happiness; ¹³ it is only right then that my glory and boasting should serve to praise you, and so I will not be confounded.

12 Lord, my God, I will praise you forever.

Psalm 30

David sang this thirtieth psalm, entreating the Lord for his homecoming from the exile and troubles which beset him then; and also he prophesied about the exile which would befall the Jewish people after his time (that was, when they were led in captivity to Babylon), foretelling that they would pray in the same manner as he did, and lament their misfortune in that place, as he did; and also he prophesied about the just person who sings psalms, either for himself or for another person afflicted either in mind or in body; and he prophesied also about Christ, that he would petition in the same way against the sufferings which the Jews inflicted on him.

1 ² Lord, in you I trust, I will never be ashamed of it; in your justice free and deliver me.

2   Onhyld to me þine earan, and efste þæt þu me gefriðie.

3   And beo min God and min gefriðiend, and beo min frið-stow and gedo me halne,

4   for þam þu eart min trymnes and min gebeorh, and on þinum naman ic þe healsige þæt þu beo min lad-þeow and me fede,

5   and alæd me of þysum grynum þe her gehydde synt beforan me, for þam þu eart min gescyldend, Drihten; an þine handa ic befæste mine sawle.

6   Þu me ahreddest, Drihten, rihtwisnesse God. Þu hatodest þa þe beeodon idelnesse and eac þa þe unnyt worhton.

7   Ic þonne symle hopige to Drihtne, and fægnie and wynsumige and blissige on þinre mild-heortnesse,

8   for þam þu gesawe mine eadmodnesse, and þu gedydest hale æt nyd-þearfe mine sawle, and me ne clemdes on minra feonda handa,

9   ac asettest mine fet on swyðe brad land. Gemiltsa me nu, Drihten, for þam ic swince.

10   Mine eagan wæron gedrefede and afærde for þinum yrre, and eac swa ilce min mod and min maga,

11   for þam fullneah on þam sare geteorode and geendode min lif, and min gear wæron on sicetunga and on gestæne;

12   and geuntrumod wæs for wædle and for yrmðum min mægen, and min ban wæron gedrefedu and fullneah forod.

13   Ofer ealle mine fynd ic eom geworden to edwite, and minum neah-geburum swiðost; ic eom worden him to ege and eallum þam þe me cunnon.

14   Þa þe me gesawon, hi me flugon. Fulneah ic afeoll swa swa se þe byð dead on his heortan and on his mode, and ic wæs swylce forloren fæt and tobrocen,

2   [3] Be all ears to me, and hasten to free me.

3   And be my God, protector, and place of refuge, and make me safe,

4   [4] because you are my support and defense, and in your name I beg you to become my guide and feed me,

5   [5] and lead me out of these snares concealed here in front of me, because you are my protector, Lord; [6] to your hands I entrust my soul.

6   Lord, God of justice, you saved me. [7] You hated those who cultivated idleness and also those who did purposeless things.

7   I, however, will always trust in the Lord, [8] and exult, rejoice, and be happy in your mercy,

8   because you noticed my humility and kept my soul safe from trouble, [9] and did not enclose me in my enemy's grasp,

9   but placed my feet, instead, in an exceedingly spacious land. [10] Lord, have mercy on me now, because I am distressed.

10   My eyes were troubled and dismayed because of your anger, and so too my mind and innards,

11   [11] because from that grief my life very nearly failed and came to an end, and my years were passed in sighing and groaning;

12   and my strength was weakened by want and misery, and my bones were afflicted and almost broken.

13   [12] I have become a reproach to all my enemies, and my neighbors especially; I have become an object of fear to them and all who know me.

14   Those who saw me, ran from me. [13] I almost fell down, like someone numb in heart and mind, and I was like a pot abandoned and shattered,

15   for þam ic gehyrde manegra manna edwit, þe me ymbutan budon,

16   and swa hwær swa hi hi gegaderodon ealle togædere, to þam þæt hy þeahtodon hu hi mihton geniman mine sawle.

17   And ic, þeah, Drihten, to þe hopode and sæde þæt þu wære min God; on þinum handum synd þa lenga minra tida.

18   Alys me and gefriða me of minra feonda handum and fram þam þe min ehtað,

19   and onliht þinne andwlitan ofer þinne þeow, and gedo me halne for þinre mild-heortnesse, and gedo þæt me ne gesceamige, for þam ic cleopode to þe.

20   Ac, þeah, sceal gescamian þa unrihtwisan, and hi beoð gelæd to helle; and adumbiað þa facnfullan weoloras, þa þe sprecað wið þone rihtwisan unriht on heora ofermettum and on heora leahtrunga.

21   Eala, Drihten, hu micel and hu manigfeald is seo mycelnes þinre swetnesse þe þu hæfst gehyd and gehealden þam þe þe ondrædað; þa swetnesse þu him ne lætst næfre aspringan nanum þæra þe to þe hopað beforan manna bearnum.

22   Þu hi gehydst and gehyldst hale and orsorge, ægðer ge modes ge lichaman, butan ælcere gedrefednesse þe menn þrowiað.

23   Þu hi gescyldst on þinum temple wið ælcere tungan leahtrunge.

24   Gebletsod sy Drihten, for þam he swa wuldorlice gecydde his mild-heortnesse me on þære fæstan byrig.

25   Ic cwæð on minre fyrhto þæt ic wære aworpen of þinra eagena ansyne,

26   and þu þa for þi gehyrdest þa stemne minra gebeda, þa ic to þe cliopode.

15   14 because I heard the insults of many people who lived around me,

16   and wherever they all gathered together to plan how to grab my soul.

17   15 Yet I trusted, however, in you, Lord, and declared that you were my God; 16 in your hands is the duration of my allotted time.

18   17 Deliver and free me from the hands of my enemies and from those who persecute me,

19   and make your face shine on your servant, and secure me in your mercy,18 and ensure that I am not confounded, because I invoked you.

20   But the wicked, however, are destined to be put to shame, and they will be led to hell; 19 and those deceitful lips, which in their arrogance and contempt utter wicked things against the just, will become dumb.

21   20 O Lord, how great and how varied is the abundance of your sweetness, which you have hidden and concealed for those who fear you; you will never allow that sweetness to fail anyone who trusts in you in the people's sight.

22   21 You will hide them and keep them sound and secure both in mind and body, free from every disturbance that humans suffer.

23   You will protect them in your temple against the insults of every tongue.

24   22 Blessed be the Lord, because he made known his mercy to me so gloriously in that fortified city.

25   23 I said in my fear that I was rejected from your sight,

26   and because of that you listened then to my appeals, when I invoked you.

27   Lufiað nu for þan Drihten, ealle his halgan, for þam
rihtwisnesse God lufiað and secð, and forgylt be fullan ælcum þe ofermetto doð.

28   Ac doð esnlice, and gestrangiað eowere heortan and eower mod, ælc þæra þe to Gode hopige.

Psalm 31

Dauid sang þisne an and þrittigoðan sealm, wundriende
þære unaseccgendlican gesælignesse þæra manna þe him
God forgifð ealle heora scylda and him ælc geswinc aferþ,
swa swa he him oft dyde; and he witgode eac be Ezechie, hu
he sceolde wundrian þære myclan mild-heortnesse þe he
him oft forgeaf, ægðer ge on his hælo ge on his alysnesse æt
his feondum; and swa ylce he witgode be ælcum godum men
þe him God swa ymb dyde, and he ætwat eac him sylfum,
þæt he ne hreowsode his synna ær he hæfde witnunga; and
he witgode eac be Criste, þæt he swa ylce wolde herian
swylce menn.

1   Eadige beoð þa þe him beoð heora unrihtwisnessa for-
gifene and heora synna beoð behelede.

2   Eadig byð se wer þe him God ne oðwit his scylda, ne on
his mode ne byð facen.

3   For þam þe ic sugode and hæl mine scylda, eal min ban
and min mægen forealdode; þa ongan ic clypian ealne dæg,

27 ²⁴ So, let all his holy ones now love the Lord, because God loves and seeks truth, but he will repay in full all who act arrogantly.

28 ²⁵ And let everyone who trusts in God act manfully, and fortify your heart and soul.

Psalm 31

David sang this thirty-first psalm, marveling at the indescribable happiness of those whom God absolves of all their sins, and from whom he removes every hardship, just as he often did for him; and he prophesied also about Hezekiah, how he would marvel at the magnanimous mercy which God often accorded him, both in healing him and liberating him from his enemies; and likewise he prophesied about every virtuous person toward whom God so behaved, and he also reproached himself for not repenting of his sins until he experienced punishments; and he prophesied also about Christ, that he likewise would praise such people.

1 ¹ Blessed are those whose iniquities are forgiven and whose sins are covered up.

2 ² Blessed is the one to whom God imputes no guilt, and who does not inwardly harbor deceit.

3 ³ Because I was silent and concealed my guilt, all my bones and strength became enfeebled with age; then I began to call out all day,

4   for þam ægðer ge on dæg ge on niht wæs swyðe hefig ofer me þin hand and þin yrre; ic wæs gehwyrfed on ælce yrmðe swylce me wære se hrycg forbrocen.

5   Ic þa gedyde mine scylda þe swyþe cuþe, and min un-riht ic na ne helede wið þe.

6   Þa cwæð ic on minum mode þæt ic wolde andettan and stælan ongean me sylfne mine scylda, and þa Gode andetan; and þu me þa forgeafe þæt unriht minra scylda.

7   For þam gebiddað ealle halige to þe on tilne timan; for þæm þonne and for eallum heora goodum dædum ne ge-nealæcð him na þæt flod þæra myclena wæterena (þæt synt, þas andweardan earfoþa and eac þa toweardan).

8   Þu eart min gebeorh-stow on minum earfoþum, þa me habbað utan behringed; ac þu þe eart min frefrend, ahrede me æt þam þe me habbað utan bestanden.

9   Þa andswarode God þam witegan þurh þæne Halgan Gast and cwæð: "Ic þe sylle andgit and þe getæce þone weg þe þu onsteppan scealt, and ic locie to þe mid minum eagum.

10   Ne beo ge na swylce hors and mulas, on þam nis nan andgit,

11   þæra cin-ban þu scealt mid bridle and mid caman to þe geteon"; swa ylce þu scealt þa men þe heora gelican beoð, for þam hi elles ne genealæceað þinum willan.

12   Swiþe manifealde synt synfulra manna swingelan, ac þa þe to Gode hopiað beoð ymbhringde mid swyþe manegre mild-heortnesse.

13   Blissiað for þæm on Gode and wynsumiað, ge riht-wisan, and fægniað and wuldriað, ealra riht-willenda heor-tan.

4   ⁴ because both during the day and at night your power and anger were exceedingly heavy upon me; in every distress I was contorted as if my back had been broken.

5   ⁵ Then I made known fully to you my guilt, and did not conceal my transgressions from you.

6   I said then inwardly that I would confess and declare my guilt, and acknowledge it to God; and after that you forgave me the wrong of my sins.

7   ⁶ So, all the holy ones will pray to you at the proper time; then in consideration of that and all their good deeds, the flood of mighty waters will surely not reach them (that is, these present tribulations and future ones also).

8   ⁷ You are my place of refuge in the tribulations which have circumscribed me from without; and you who are my comforter, save me from those who have surrounded me from without.

9   ⁸ Then God, through the Holy Spirit, answered the prophet, declaring: "I will grant you understanding, and will teach you the path on which you should walk, and my eyes will focus on you.

10   ⁹ Do not be like horses and mules, which completely lack understanding,

11   whose jaws you must pull to you with bridle and bit"; so you should treat their human counterparts, because otherwise they will not adhere to your will.

12   ¹⁰ The sufferings of sinful people will be exceedingly numerous, but those who trust in God will be surrounded with very many acts of mercy.

13   ¹¹ Rejoice, therefore, you just, in God, and make merry, and let the hearts of all the sincerely disposed exult and be happy.

Psalm 32

Dauid sang þisne twa and þrittigoþan sealm, herigende Drihten and him þanciende þæt he hine swa wundorlice of eallum his earfoþum gefriðode, and hine swa weorðlice gesette ofer his rice; and eac he lærde on þam sealme ealle men þæt hi sceoldon Gode þancian ealra þæra gooda þe he him dyde; and he witgode eac be Ezechie þæt he sceolde þæt ylce don þonne he alysed wære of his earfoþum; and be ælcum þæra þe þysne sealm singð; and eac be Criste he witgode þæt he sceolde æfter his æriste ealle men þæt ylce læran.

1   Blissiað, ge rihtwisan, on Godes gifum; rihte hit gerist þæt hine ealle riht-willende emnlice herian.

2   Heriað hine mid hearpum and on þære tyn-strengean hearpan.

3   Singað him niwne sang, and heriað hine swyþe wel mid heare stemne,

4   for þæm his word synd swyþe riht and ealle his weorc synt getreowe.

5   He lufað mild-heortnesse and rihte domas, mid his mild-heortnesse he gefylð ealle eorðan; mid his worde synt getrymede heofonas, and þurh þone gast his muðes synt eall heofona mægn.

6   He gegaderode eall sæ-wætru tosomne swylce hi wæron on anum cylle; he gesette þone garsecg on his gold-horde.

7   Ondræde hine eall eorðe; fram him beoð onstyred ealle gesceafta and ealle þa þe on eorðan buiað.

Psalm 32

David sang this thirty-second psalm, praising the Lord and thanking him because he so miraculously freed him from all his troubles, and so honorably appointed him over his kingdom; and also he urged all people to thank God for all the good things which he did for them; and he prophesied also about Hezekiah, that he was destined to do the same, whenever he was freed from his difficulties; and he prophesied about everyone who sings this psalm; and he prophesied also about Christ, that after his resurrection he would teach the same thing to all people.

1   1 Rejoice, you just, in God's gifts; it is truly fitting that all rightly disposed people praise him simultaneously.

2   2 Praise him with harps and on the ten-stringed lyre.

3   3 Sing to him a new song, and praise him most fervently with a strong voice,

4   4 because his words are exceedingly just, and all his works are reliable.

5   5 He loves mercy and just judgments, he fills all the earth with his mercy; 6 the heavens are set in order through his word, and through the spirit from his mouth all the powers of the heavens exist.

6   7 He collected all the waters of the sea as if they belonged in a single vessel; he placed the ocean in his treasury.

7   8 Fear him all the earth; all creatures and all dwelling on earth are stirred by him.

8　For þæm he cwæð his willan, þa wæs he geworden; he bebead his willan, þa wæron ealle gesceafta gesceapene.

9　Se Drihten tostencð þa geþeaht yfel-willendra kynna, and he forsyhð þa geþohtas þara folca, and eac yfelra ealdor-manna geþeaht he forsyhð.

10　Ac Godes geþeaht wunað on ecnesse, and geþoht his modes a weorulda weoruld.

11　Eala, eadig byþ þæt kynn þe swylc god byð heora God, and eadig byð þæt folc þe se Drihten gecyst him to yrfe-weardnesse.

12　Drihten locað of heofonum and gesihð eall manna bearn, of his þam wlitegan temple, he wlit ofer ealle þa þe ealre eorðan ymb-hwyrft buiað,

13　for þam he gesceop heora heortan, ælces synderlice, and he ongit heora ealra weorc.

14　Ne wyrð nan kyning næfre gehæled þurh his agen mæ-gen, ne se gigant ne wyrð na gehæled on þære mycelnesse his mægenes.

15　Þi byð swiðe dysig se þe getruwað on his horses swift-nesse, for þæm hit is swiðe leas tohopa, for þæm nawþer ne ðam horse ne þæm ræde-men ne wyrð geborgen of his ag-num cræftum.

16　Symle beoð Godes eagan open ofer þa ðe hine on-drædað, and ofer þa þe hopiað to his mild-heortnesse, for þam þæt he gefriðie heora sawla fram deaðe and hi fede on hungres tide.

17　Hopiað nu to Drihtne ure sawla, for þam he ys ure frið-igend and ure gescyldend, and on hine blissiað ure heortan and to his halgan naman we hopiað.

18　Sy, Drihten, þin mild-heortnes ofer us, swa swa we ge-hyhtað on þe.

8   9 Because he uttered his wish, it was then fulfilled; he issued his command, and after that all created things came into being.

9   10 The Lord scatters the counsels of the wickedly disposed generations and spurns the people's plans, as well as the counsel of evil princes.

10   11 But God's counsel endures forever, and the intent of his mind forever.

11   12 Ah! Blessed is the people for whom such a god is their God, and blessed is the nation which that Lord chooses as his inheritance.

12   13 The Lord looks from the heavens and sees all humankind's children, 14 from his beautiful temple, he regards all those who inhabit the whole earth's environs,

13   15 because he created their hearts, each one individually, and he understands the works of them all.

14   16 No king will ever be saved through his own power, nor will the giant by the greatness of his strength.

15   17 He who trusts in his horse's speed is extremely foolish then, because that is a very false hope, since neither horse nor rider will be protected by their own abilities.

16   18 God's eyes are always receptive to those who fear him and trust in his mercy, 19 in order that he may free their souls from death and feed them in time of famine.

17   20 Let our souls now trust in the Lord, because he is our helper and protector, 21 and in him our hearts rejoice, and in his holy name we hope.

18   22 Lord, may your mercy dwell with us, according as we hope in you.

Psalm 33

Dauid sang þysne þreo and þrittigoðan sealm, gehatende
Drihtne þæt he hine symle wolde bletsian for þæm gifum þe
he him geaf, and he wilnode on þæm sealme þæt him God
sende his god-cundne engel on his fultum; and he lærde eac
on þæm sealme ælcne man þe æfter him wære, þæt he þæt
ylce dyde; and he witgode eac on þæm sealme be Ezechie
þam kincge, þæt he sceolde þæt ylce don æfter þam sige þe
he hæfde wið Assirium; and þæt ylce he witgode be Criste,
þæt he þæt ylce don wolde and eac oðre læran.

1   Ic bletsige Drihten on ælce tid, symle byð his lof on minum muðe.

2   On Gode byð geherod min sawl. Gehyren þæt þa manþwæran and blissien for þy.

3   Micliað Drihten mid me, and upp ahebben we his naman betwuh us.

4   Ic sohte Drihten and he me gehyrde, and of eallum minum earfoðum he me gefriðode.

5   Cumað nu to him and genealæcað him; and he eow onliht, and eowerne andwlitan na ne gesceamað.

6   Þes þearfa clepode to Drihtne, and Drihten hine gehyrde, and of eallum his earfoþum he hine alysde.

7   Onsende he his engel ymbutan þa þe hine ondrædað,
þæt he hi gefriðige, swa he me dyde.

8   Fandiað nu, þonne ongite ge þæt Drihten is swyðe
sefte; eadig byð se wer þe to him cleopað.

Psalm 33

David sang this thirty-third psalm, promising the Lord that he would constantly bless him for the gifts which he gave him, and he desired in that psalm that God send him his heavenly angel to help him; and in that psalm he also advised everyone who lived after him to do the same; and he also prophesied in the psalm about King Hezekiah, that he was destined to do the same after the victory which he gained against the Assyrians; and he prophesied about Christ that he would do the same and teach it to others.

1   2 I will bless the Lord at all times, his praise will always be in my mouth.

2   3 In God my soul will be praised. Let the meek hear that and rejoice because of it.

3   4 Extol the Lord with me, and let us exalt his name among us.

4   5 I sought the Lord, and he heard me, and freed me from all my sufferings.

5   6 Advance now toward him and approach him; he will enlighten you, and your countenance will not be abashed.

6   7 This poor man called to the Lord, who heard and freed him from all his sufferings.

7   8 May he send his angel to encircle those who fear him, rescuing them, as he did me.

8   9 Taste now, and then discover that the Lord is exceedingly sweet; the one who invokes him is blessed.

9 Ondrædon hine ealle his halige, for þæm þæm ne byð nanes goodes wana þe hine ondrædað.

10 Þa welegan wædledon and eodon biddende, and hi hingrode, ac þa þe God seceað ne aspringeð him nan good.

11 Cumað nu, bearn, and gehyrað me; ic eow lære Godes ege.

12 Se þe libban wylle, and wilnige þæt he geseo goode dagas, gehyre hwæt ic secge.

13 Forbeode his tungan ælc yfel and his weolorum, þæt hi ne sprecon nan facn.

14 Onwende hine fram yfele and wyrce good, sece sibbe and folgie þære,

15 for þæm Godes eagan beoð ofer þa rihtwisan ontynde, and eac his earan to heora gebedum.

16 Ac Godes andwlita and his yrre byð ofer þa þe yfel wyrcað, to þæm þæt he forleose heora gemynd ofer eorðan.

17 Þa rihtwisan cleopodon, and Drihten hi gehyrde, and of eallum hiora earfoðum he hi alysde.

18 Swiþe neah is Drihten þam þe beoð gedrefede on heora heortum, and þa eaðmodan on heora gaste he gehælð.

19 Monigu synt earfoðu þara rihtwisena, and of eallum þæm hi alysð Drihten.

20 Drihten gehylt eall heora ban (þæt ys, eall heora mægen), þæt heora ne wyrð furðon an tobrocen.

21 Ac þæra synfullena dead byð se wyrsta, and þa þe þone rihtwisan hatiað, þa agyltað.

22 Drihten gefriðað þa sawla his þeowa, and ne forlæt nænne þæra þe him to hopað.

9   ^{10} Let all his holy ones fear him, because those who do will not lack for anything good.

10   ^{11} The rich suffered want, went begging, and were hungry, but for those who seek God no good will be lacking.

11   ^{12} Come now, children, and hear me; I will teach you the fear of God.

12   ^{13} Let the one who wishes to enjoy life and experience good days, listen to what I say.

13   ^{14} Let him deny his tongue and lips every evil, so that they do not say anything deceitful.

14   ^{15} Let that one turn away from evil and do good, seek peace and pursue it,

15   ^{16} because God's eyes are open to the just, and his ears also to their appeals.

16   ^{17} But God's face and his anger are directed at those who do evil, to annihilate the memory of them on earth.

17   ^{18} The just cried out, and the Lord heard and freed them from all their sufferings.

18   ^{19} The Lord is exceedingly close to those troubled of heart, and will save the humble in spirit.

19   ^{20} Many are the tribulations of the just, but from all of them the Lord will free them.

20   ^{21} The Lord will guard all their bones (that is, all their strength), so that not even a single one of them will be broken.

21   ^{22} But the death of evildoers is the most awful, and those who hate the just will be judged guilty.

22   ^{23} The Lord will rescue the souls of his servants, and will not forsake a single one who trusts in him.

Psalm 34

Dauid sang þysne feower and þrittigoþan sealm, siofigende
to Drihtne his yrmða, tealde his ungelimp and hu he hine
gebæd to Gode þæt he him gearode; and eac he witegode on
þam ilcan sealme þæt ylce be ælcum rihtwison menn þe
þysne sealm sunge, oððe for hine sylfne oþþe for oþerne
mann, þæt he sceolde þæs ylcan wilnian; and eac he witgode
be Criste þæt he wolde þæt ylce don þonne he come. Ma
witgiende þonne wyrgende oððe wilniende:

1   Dem me, Drihten, and þæm þe me swencað; feoht wið
þa þe wið me feohtað,

2   and gefoh wæpn and scyld, and aris me to fultume.

3   Geteoh þin sweord and cum ongean hy, and beluc heora
wegas mid þinum sweorde, þara þe min ehtað; cweð to
minre sawle: "Ne ondræd þu þe: ic eom þin hælo, and ic þe
gehealde."

4   Geleahtrode syn mine fynd, and sceamien heora þa þa
secað mine sawle to fordonne.

5   Syn hi gecyrde on earsling and scamien heora, þa þe me
ðenceað yfeles.

6   Syn hi tostencte swa swa dust beforan winde, and
Godes engel hi geþræste.

7   Syn heora wegas þystre and slidore, and Godes engel
heora ehte,

8   for þam hi butan gewyrhtum teldedon gryne and þa ge-
hyddon, to þam þæt hi woldan me an gefon; and idle hi
wæron, þa hi me tældon.

Psalm 34

David sang this thirty-fourth psalm, lamenting his miseries to the Lord, recounting his misfortune and how he beseeched God to show him compassion; and in the same psalm he also prophesied the same thing about every just person who might sing this psalm, either on their own behalf or for someone else, that they would desire the same; and he also prophesied that Christ would do the same when he came. More in prophecy than condemning or wishing, David sang:

1 ¹ Lord, judge me and my tormenters; attack those who attack me,

2 ² and grab weapons and shield, and rise up to help me.

3 ³ Draw your sword and advance against them, and with it block the paths of my pursuers; say to my soul: "Do not be afraid: I am your salvation and will protect you."

4 ⁴ May my enemies be disgraced, and may they who attempt to destroy my soul be confounded.

5 May they be turned backward and put to shame, those who plan evil for me.

6 ⁵ May they be scattered like dust before the wind, and may God's angel afflict them.

7 ⁶ May their ways be dark and slippery, and may God's angel pursue them,

8 ⁷ because without just cause they spread a snare and concealed it to trap me in it; but they failed, when they slandered me.

9 Gefon hi þa grynu þe wið hy beheled synt, and eac þa þe hi wið me beheled hæfdon.

10 Þonne blissað min sawl and min mod on Drihtne, and hit byð gelust-fullod on his hælo.

11 Eall min ban (þæt is, min mægen) cwyð: "Eala, Drihten, hwa is ðin gelica, for þam þu generest þone earman of þæs strengran anwealde, and þone wædlan and þone þearfan ahredst æt þæm þe hine swencað."

12 Þonne wið me arison lease gewitan and stældon on me þæt ic nawþer ne nyste ne ne worhte; ac guldon me yfel wið gode and woldon me gedon unwæstmbærne swa swa se þe butan ælcum yrfe-wearde byð.

13 Ic, þa þa hi me swa hefige wæron, dyde me wite-hrægl an, and gebigde min mod to fæstenne, and min gebedo wendon eft to me on minne agene bosm, for þam heora nolde onfon se dema, þe ic hi to sende.

14 And ic, þeah, þeah hi me swa hefige wæron, hy lufode and him tilode to licianne and to cwemanne, swa swa minum nyhstum oððe minum breðer; and hy me gedydon swa un-rotne and swa wependne swa se byð þone þe he lufað.

15 Hy wæron bliðe wið me on heora gebærum, and þeah on heora mode hi blissedon micle swyðor on minum unge-limpe; and hi comon ongean me and gegaderodon swyðe manega swingellan ofer me, and ic nyste hwæt hi me witon.

16 And hy wurdon, þeah, tostencte, and hy, þeah, þæs na ne hreowsedon; ac fandodon eft min and bysmredon me mid ælcere bysmrunga, and grisbitedon mid heora toþum ongean me.

17 And þa cwæð ic: "Drihten, hwænne gesyhst þu þis, oððe hwænne gefriðast þu mine sawle wið heora yfelum dæ-dum, oþþe hwænne ahredst mine angan sawle æt þæm leoum?"

9   8 May snares hidden from them catch them, and those also which they concealed from me.

10   9 Then my soul and mind will rejoice in the Lord, and it will fully delight in his safety.

11   10 All my bones (that is, my strength) will say: "Ah! Lord, who is your equal, since you deliver the poor from the stronger person's power, and you save the needy and the poor from their tormentors."

12   11 Then false witnesses rose up against me, accusing me of things that I neither knew nor committed; 12 indeed, they paid me back evil for good, and desired to make me barren like an heirless person.

13   13 When these people thus became oppressive to me, I put on sackcloth, and humbled my mind with fasting, but my prayers turned back on me into my own heart, because the judge to whom I directed them refused to accept them.

14   14 As for me, even though those people were oppressive to me, I loved them and strove to please and delight them, like my neighbors or my brother; yet they made me as dejected and sad as one is after a loved one.

15   15 They were cheerful to me in their conduct, and yet inwardly they rejoiced much in my misfortune; and they advanced against me, assembling a great many afflictions for me, and I had no idea what they accused me of.

16   16 However, they were scattered, yet they had absolutely no regrets about that; in fact, they again tested and derided me with every kind of insult, and gnashed their teeth at me.

17   17 And after that I said: "Lord, when will you notice this, or free my soul from their vile actions, or when will you rescue my unique soul from the lions?"

18 Gif þu me æfre alyst, ic þe andette on mycelre gesamnunge and þe þær herige,

19 for þæm þæt mine fynd ne blissien æfter me, þa þe winnað mid unrihte ongean me and me hatiað butan scylde, and
wincettað mid heora eagum betwuh him.

20 Þeah hi gesibsumlice hwilum wið me sprecen, hy
þenceað, þeah, swiðe facenlice.

21 Hy geopenodon ealneh heora muð for leahtre, to þæm
þæt hi me bysmredon, and cwædon: "Hit is la ful good þæt
æfre ure eagan moston geseon þæt we wilnodon." Nu þu gesyhst, Drihten, hwæt hy doð; ne geþafa þu hit leng, ne gewit
fram me.

22 Aris, Drihten, and beseoh to me, and geseoh hu unscyldig ic eom wið þa þe min ehtað; Drihten, min God, aris to
minum þinge and to minre þearfe.

23 Drihten, Drihten, min God, dem me æfter þinre mild-
heortnesse, þæt mine fynd ne gefeon mines ungelimpes, ne
hy cweþan on heora mode, "Wel la wel is urum modum," ne
hy ne cweðen, "We hine frætan."

24 Ac sceamien hy heora, and him eac ondrædon—ægðer
endemes—þa þe fægniað mines ungelimpes. Beslepen hi on
hy bysmor, and gegyrion hy mid sceame, þa ofer-sprecan þe
me yfel cweðað.

25 Fægnien þa and blissien þa þe willon me þancian minre
rihtwisnesse, and þa þe symle cweðað, "Gemyclad sy
Drihten," and þa þe willon sibbe wið his ðeow.

26 Þonne smeað min tunge þine rihtwisnesse, and ealne dæg
þin lof.

18   18 If you ever release me, I will acknowledge you in the great assembly and praise you there,

19   19 so that my enemies may not gloat over me, those who unjustly contend with me and hate me without good reason, and wink among themselves.

20   20 Though they sometimes speak amicably to me, yet they think very deceitfully.

21   21 They continually opened their mouths in scornful laughter to insult me, and said: "Indeed, it is good that our eyes ever got to see what we wanted." 22 Now you see, Lord, what they are up to; do not tolerate it any longer, do not leave me.

22   23 Lord, rise up and observe me, and see how innocent I am toward my persecutors; Lord, my God, rise up for my cause and my need.

23   24 Lord, Lord, my God, judge me by your mercy, lest my enemies rejoice at my misfortune, 25 or in their hearts say, "It is fine, truly fine to our way of thinking," or, "We have devoured him."

24   26 Instead, let those who enjoy my misfortune be ashamed of themselves and terrified also—both at once. Let them cover themselves with disgrace and dress themselves with shame, those excessive talkers, who say evil things to me.

25   27 After that let those rejoice and be happy who wish to thank me for my upright conduct, and those who constantly say "May the Lord be magnified," and those who desire peace for his servant.

26   28 Then my tongue will consider your justice, and all day long your praise.

Psalm 35

Dauid sang þysne fif and þrittigoðan sealm, þa he wæs afly-
med fram Sawle, on þa ylcan tiid þe he genam his ceac and
his spere on his getelde on niht to tacne þæt he inne mid
him slæpendum wæs; and swa deð ælc þæra þe þysne sealm
singð for his earfoþum; and swa dyde Crist þa he hine sang
for þam earfoðum þe Iudas him dydon.

1   Se unrihtwisa cwyþ on his mode þæt he wylle syngian,
for þam Godes ege nis beforan his eagum,

2   for þæm he deð swiðe facenlice beforan his ansyne, ac
his unriht and his feoung wurð, þeah, swiðe open.

3   Þa word his muðes beoð unriht and facen; he nyle ongitan þæt he cunne wel don; unriht he byð smeagende on his
cliofan.

4   He stent on ælcum yflum wege, ne hatað he nan yfel.

5   Drihten, þin mild-heortnes is on heofonum, and þin
rihtwisnes is upp oð þa wolcnu.

6   Þin rihtwisnes is swa heah swa þa heofonlican muntas,
and þine domas synt swa deope swa swa æfgrynde oþþe seo
deoposte sæ.

7   Menn and nytenu þu gehælst, Drihten; hu wundorlice
þu gemanigfealdodest þine mild-heortnesse, Drihten.

8   Manna bearn soðlice symle hopiað to þæm sceade þinra
fiðera, and hy beoð oferdrencte on þære genihte þines huses,
and on þære æ þines willan þu hy drencst,

Psalm 35

David sang this thirty-fifth psalm when he was banished by Saul, on that same occasion when he removed that king's pitcher and spear from his tent at night as a sign that he had been present inside with him as he was sleeping; and so does everyone who sings this psalm because of tribulations; and so did Christ when he sang it on account of the tribulations which the Jews inflicted on him.

1 2 The unjust person says within himself that he will sin, because fear of God is absent from his sight,

2 3 so he acts very deceitfully in God's sight, but his iniquity and hostility are exceedingly obvious nevertheless.

3 4 The words of his mouth are made up of iniquity and guile; he is unwilling to recognize that he knows how to behave well; 5 he plots iniquity in his bedchamber.

4 He takes his stand on every evil path, he does not hate any evil.

5 6 Lord, your mercy exists in the heavens and your justice is on high, extending to the clouds.

6 7 Your justice is as high as the heavenly mountains, and your judgments are as profound as an abyss or the deepest sea.

7 Lord, you will save humans and beasts; 8 how marvelously you have multiplied your mercies, Lord.

8 Humankind will truly have confidence always in the shelter of your wings, 9 and they will be inebriated with the plenty of your house, and from the torrent of your benevolence you will give them drink,

9   for þæm mid þe is lifes wylle, and of þinum leohte we beoð onlihte.

10   Læt forð þine mild-heortnesse þam þe þe witon, and þine rihtwisnesse þam þæ synt rihtes modes.

11   Ne læt þu me oftredan þa ofer-modan under heora fotum, and þara synfullena handa me na ne styrien,

12   ac under heora fet and under heora handa gefeallen ealle þa þe unriht wyrcen and him þæt licað; hy synt aworpene, þæt hi ne ma . . .

Psalm 36

Dauid sang þysne syx and þritigoðan sealm, on þæm he lærde ealle geleaffulle þæt hy ne onhyredon þam yfel-willendum, þeah him þuhte þæt hi gesælige and orsorge wæron, for þæm hyra orsorgnes swiðe hraðe aspringð; and ælc þæra ðe gyt þysne sealm singð, be þam ylcan he hine singð; and eac Crist þæt ylce lærde and witgode, þonne he þysne sealm sang.

1   Ne wundrie ge þæra yfel-willendra and þæra orsorgra, ne him na ne onhyriað, ne eow ne ofþince þeah eow ne sy swa swa him þam þe unriht wyrcað,

2   for þæm swyþe hraþe forseariað swa fileðe, and hy gefeallað swiðe hrædlice swa swa wyrta leaf, oþþe blostman.

9   10 because in you is the fountain of life, and by your light we will be enlightened.

10   11 Extend your mercy to those who know you, and your justice to those of upright disposition.

11   12 Do not allow the proud to trample me under their feet, and may the sinners' hands not disturb me,

12   13 instead, let all those who commit iniquity and take pleasure in it fall under their control and their power; they are cast out, so that they . . .

Psalm 36

David sang this thirty-sixth psalm in which he advised all believers not to emulate the wickedly disposed, even though it seemed to them that those people were blessed and prosperous, since their prosperity will fail very quickly; and everyone who still sings this psalm does so about the same thing; and also Christ advised and foretold the same thing, when he sang this psalm.

1   1 Do not admire the evilly disposed and the prosperous, nor imitate them, nor feel aggrieved that things do not work out for you as they do for those who do wrong,

2   2 because they will wither very quickly like hay, and they will fall to their destruction very swiftly like the leaves of herbs, or like blossoms.

3   Ac þu, hopa to Drihtne and do good, and buwa eorðan, and fed þe on hyre welum,

4   and blissa on Drihtne; þonne syleð he þe þæt þu bidst on þinum mode.

5   Onwreoh Gode þine wegas and hopa to him; he þe gedeð fultum

6   and he gedeð þine rihtwisnesse mannum swa sweotole swa sunnan, and þinne dom he gedeð swa sweotolne swa sunne byð to middes dæges.

7   Beo þu Gode under-þyd and halsa hine, and ne onhyre þam þe byð orsorh on his wege, and wyrcð, þeah, unriht.

8   Forlæt yrre and hat-heortnesse; ne bysna þe be nanum þæra þe yfel don,

9   for þæm þa þe yfel doð and þæt ne betað, hy beoð awyrtwalode of eorþan; ac þa þe to Gode hopiað and his fultumes anbidiað, hy gesittað on yrfe-weardnesse eorþan.

10   Gebid ane lytle hwile, þonne ne byð se synfulla; þeah þu þonne sece his stowe, þonne ne findst þu hy.

11   Ac þa manþwæran gesittað eorþan and fægniað þære myclan sibbe.

12   Se synfulla sætað þæs rihtwisan and gristbatað mid his toþum ongean hine, ac Drihten hine gebysmrað, for þam he gesyhð hu hraðe his ende cymð.

13   Þa synfullan teoð heora sweord and bendað heora bogan to þæm þæt hi mægon besyrian þone earman and þone wædlan, and þurhsceotan þa unscæðfullan heortan,

14   ac heora sweord gað innon heora heortan, and heora bogan forberstað.

15   Betere ys þam rihtwisan lytel þonne þam synfullan mycel wela,

3   ³ But as for you, trust in the Lord, and do right, inhabit the earth and feed yourself on its riches,

4   ⁴ and be happy in the Lord; then he will grant you what you ask for in your heart.

5   ⁵ Reveal to God your ways and trust in him; he will provide help for you,

6   ⁶ and will make your justice as transparent to men as the sun, and your judgment as clear as the midday sun.

7   ⁷ Be subject to God and appeal to him, and do not imitate the one who prospers in his career, and perpetrates injustice, however.

8   ⁸ Abandon rage and fury; do not model yourself on any evildoer,

9   ⁹ because those who do evil and do not make amends for it, will be eradicated from the earth; but those who trust in God and wait hopefully for his help will possess the earth by inheritance.

10   ¹⁰ Wait for a short while, and the sinner will no longer exist; though you then seek his location, you will not find it.

11   ¹¹ But the meek will possess the earth and will rejoice in abundant peace.

12   ¹² The sinner will lie in wait for the upright person and will gnash his teeth at him, ¹³ but the Lord will mock him, because he foresees how swiftly his death will come.

13   ¹⁴ The sinners will draw their swords and stretch their bows so as to ensnare the poor and the needy, and transfix the innocent of heart,

14   ¹⁵ but their swords will enter their own hearts, and their bows will snap.

15   ¹⁶ To the just man a little is better than great wealth to the sinner,

16 for þam se earm and þæt mægen þæra synfulra byð forbrocen, ac Drihten gestrangað þa rihtwisan.

17 For þæm he wat þa wegas þæra unsceðfulra, and heora
yrfeweardnes byð on ecnesse.

18 Ne gesceamað hy na on þære yflan tide, ac on hungres
tide hy beoð gefyllede, þonne þa synfullan forweorðað.

19 Þa Godes fynd, swiþe hraðe þæs þe hy beoð gearode
and upp ahefene, beoð gedwæscte swa ðer smec.

20 Æfre borgiað þa synfullan, and næfre ne gyldað; þa rihtwisan syllað ægþer ge to borge ge to gife.

21 Þa þe God bletsiað beoð eorðan yrfe-weardas, and þa
þe hine wyrgeað forweorðað.

22 Fram Gode byð gereht se weg þæs rihtwisan, and hine
lyst his wega and his weorca swiðe.

23 And þeah se rihtwisa afealle, ne wyrð he gebrysed, ne
his nan ban tobrocen, for þam God gefehð his hand and hine
upp arærð.

24 Ic wæs geo geong, and nu ic ealdige, and ne geseah ic
næfre rihtwisne man forlætenne, ne his sæd þæt wære hlafes
wædla.

25 Ac se rihtwisa ælce dæge miltsað, and syleð oþrum to
borge, and his sæd byð on bletsunge on genihte.

26 Gecyr for þæm fram yfele and do good, þonne wunast
þu on weorulda weorld,

27 for þam God lufað ryhte domas, and ne forlæt næfre
his halge, ac he gehylt hy on ecnesse.

28 He witnað þa scyldigan, and þæt sæd þæra unrihtwisra
forwyrð.

29 Þa rihtwisan gesittað eorðan on yrfe-weardnesse, and
hy buiað on hyre a weorulda weoruld.

16   17 because the arm and strength of sinners will be broken, but the Lord will fortify the just.

17   18 For he knows the ways of the innocent, and their inheritance will endure forever.

18   19 They will not be confounded in the evil time, instead they will be satiated in time of famine, 20 while sinners perish.

19   Then God's enemies, very soon after they are honored and exalted, will be extinguished like smoke.

20   21 The wicked constantly borrow, but never pay their debts; the just give, both on loan and as presents.

21   22 Those who bless God will be the earth's inheritors, and those who curse him will perish.

22   23 The way of the just will be directed by God, and he will be pleased mightily by that one's ways and works.

23   24 And though the just person should fall down, he will not be bruised, nor any bone of his broken, because God will catch his arm and raise him up.

24   25 I was once young, and now I am growing old, yet I have never seen a just man abandoned, nor descendants of his who lacked bread.

25   26 Indeed, the just man takes pity every day on others, and lends to them, for which his descendants will be blessed with plenty.

26   27 Turn away, then, from evil and do good, then you will live for ever and ever,

27   28 because God loves just judgments, and will never abandon his holy ones, but will keep them safe forever.

28   He will punish the guilty, and the descendants of the wicked will perish.

29   29 The just will possess the earth by inheritance and will dwell in it, for ever and ever.

30 Se muð þæs rihtwisan smeað wisdom, and his tunge sprycð rihte domas.

31 Seo æ his Godes bið on his heortan, and ne aslit his fot.

32 Se synfulla hawaþ symle þæs rihtwisan, and secð hine to fordonne, ac Drihten hine ne forlæt on his handa to þam þæt he hine mæge fordon; and Drihten demð hym bæm.

33 Gebid Drihtnes and heald his bebodu, and he þe upp ahefð to þæm þæt þu bust eorðan; and þu gesyhst hwær þa synfullan forweorðað.

34 Ic geseah þone unrihtwisan swiðe up ahafenne, swa swa sum ceder-treow on Libanus munte,

35 and ic þa þanon for and eft ðyder com, þonne næs he; and ic acsode æfter him and hine sohte, and hine ne funde, ne furþum þa stowe, þe ic hine ær on geseah, gecnawan ne mihte.

36 Heald for ðy rihtwisnesse and efnesse, for þæm se gesibsuma læfð symle yrfe-weard æfter him,

37 ac þa unrihtwisan symle forweorþað ealle ætsomne mid hyra yrfe-weardum.

38 Ac seo hæl þæra rihtwisena cymeð symle fram Gode, and he byð heora gescyldend on geswinces tide;

39 and Drihten him gefultumað and hy alysð, and hy ahret æt þam synfullum, and hy gedeð hale, for þæm hy hopiað to him.

30 ³⁰ The just person's mouth will ruminate on wisdom, and his tongue will pronounce just judgments.

31 ³¹ God's law resides in his heart, and his foot will not slip.

32 ³² The sinner constantly watches the just person, seeking to destroy him, ³³ but the Lord will not surrender him into that one's hands for his destruction; moreover, the Lord will judge them both.

33 ³⁴ Place your hope in the Lord and observe his commands, and he will exalt you, so that you will inhabit the earth; moreover, you will witness where the sinners will perish.

34 ³⁵ I saw the wicked one greatly exalted, just like some cedar tree on Mount Lebanon,

35 ³⁶ and I then journeyed from that place and afterward came back there, and by then he had vanished; and I asked after him and looked for him, and did not find him, nor could I even recognize the place where I previously saw him.

36 ³⁷ So, maintain justice and fairness, because the peaceable person always leaves an heir behind,

37 ³⁸ but the wicked will always perish, all together with their heirs.

38 ³⁹ And the salvation of the just always comes from God, and he is their protector in time of trouble;

39 ⁴⁰ and the Lord will help and deliver them, rescuing them from sinners and keeping them safe, because they hope in him.

Psalm 37

Dauid sang þysne seofon and þrittigoðan sealm, andettende
Drihtne his scylde, and seofigende his ungelimp þæt he ær
mid his scyldum geearnode, and he eac healsode Drihten on
ðæm sealme þæt he hine on swylcum earfeðum ne lete his
life geendian; and he witegode eac be Ezechie þam kyncge
þæt he sceolde þæt ylce don on his earfoðum; and eac be ælcum þæra þe þysne sealm sunge, oþþe for hine sylfne oððe
for oðerne man, he witgode þæt he sceolde þæt ilce mænan
and eac þæt ylce gemetan; and eac be Criste he witegode,
þæt he wolde þæt ylce don.

1   Drihten, ne þrea þu me, ne ne þrafa on þinum yrre, ne
on þinre hat-heortnesse ne witna ðu me,

2   for þam þine flana synt afæstnad on me (þæt synt, þa
earfoðu þe ic nu þolie), and þu gestrangodes þine handa ofer
me.

3   Nis nan hælo on minum flæsce for þære andweardnesse
þines yrres, ne nan sib ne nan rest nis minum banum beforan
þære ansyne minra synna,

4   for þæm min unriht me hlypð nu ofer heafod, and swa
swa hefig byrðen hy synt gehefegode ofer me.

5   Mina wunda rotedan and fuledon for minum dysige.

6   Ic eom swiðe earm geworden, and ic eom fulneah gebiged to ende; ælce dæge ic gange inn unrot.

Psalm 37

David sang this thirty-seventh psalm, confessing his sin to the Lord and lamenting his misfortunes which he had previously merited by his sins, and he also begged the Lord not to allow his life to end in such tribulations; and he prophesied also about King Hezekiah that he was destined to do the same in his tribulations; and also concerning everyone who sang this psalm either for themselves or for another person, he foretold that each was destined to relate and also to experience the same; and also he prophesied that Christ would do the same.

1   [2] Lord, do not reprove or rebuke me in your anger, nor punish me in your fury,

2   [3] for your arrows are stuck fast in me (those are the tribulations which I now endure), and you have tightened your grip on me.

3   [4] My body is unhealthy because of the immediacy of your anger, nor is there any peace or rest for my bones, confronted by the image of my sins,

4   [5] for my crimes now mount over my head, and just like a heavy load they are weighing on me.

5   [6] My wounds putrefied and festered because of my folly.

6   [7] I am become very wretched, and I am almost bowed down to the point of death; every day I enter, dejected.

7   For þæm eall min lichama is full flæsclicra lusta, for þam nis nan hælo on minum flæsce.

8   Ac ic eom gesæged and gehnæged and swiðe geeaðmed, and ic grymetige and stene swiþe swiðlice mid ealle mode; Drihten, Drihten, þu wast nu eall hwæs ic wilnie, eall hit ys beforan ðe, and min granung þe nis na forholen.

9   Min heorte is gedrefed and min mod oninnan me, for þæm min mægen and min strengo and min cræft me hæfð forlæten, and þæt leoht and seo scearpnes minra eagena, þe ic ær hæfde, nis nu mid me swa swa ic hy geo hæfde.

10   Mine frynd and mine magas and mine neah-geburas synt nu gemengde wið mine fynd, and standað nu mid him ongean me, and synt me nu toweardes; and þa þe me nyhst wæran, þa ic orsorgost wæs, standað me nu swiðe feor,

11   and wyrceað woh, þa þe me hefigiað and mine sawle seceað, hu hy magon yfel don, sprecað idelnesse and smeagað facn ælce dæge.

12   Ic þonne, swa swa deaf, dyde swylce ic hit ne gehyrde, and swugode, swa swa se dumba þe næfre his muð ne ontynð.

13   Ic wæs geworden swylce se mann þe nanwuht ne gehyrð, ne on his muðe næfð nane riht-andsware.

14   For þam ic hopode to þe, Drihten, and cwæð to þe: "Gehyr ðis, Drihten, and andswara him."

15   For þæm ic symle bæd þæt næfre mine fynd ne gefægen æfter me, þy læs hi mægen sprecan ungemetlico word ongean me, gif hy geseon þæt mine fet slidrien.

16   For þæm ic eom nu to swingellan gearu, and min sar ys symle beforan me,

17   for þæm ic andette Gode min unriht, and ic þence ymbe mine synna.

7   8 Because my whole body suffers a surfeit of carnal desires, my flesh is not healthy.

8   9 And I am laid low, cast down, and exceedingly humiliated, so I will roar and groan vehemently with my whole being; 10 Lord, Lord, you know now all that I long for, it is all on view to you, and my groaning is not concealed from you.

9   11 My heart and spirit are disturbed within me, because my power, strength, and might have abandoned me, and that light and keenness of vision, which I previously enjoyed, is not mine now, as I once possessed it.

10   12 My friends, kinsmen, and neighbors have now joined up with my enemies, and stand with them against me, and are now opposed to me; and those who were closest to me, when I was most prosperous, now stand very far removed from me,

11   13 and they commit violence, those who oppress me and seek my soul, probing how they can inflict evil, speaking falsehoods and plotting deceit every day.

12   14 Yet I, as though deaf, acted as if I did not hear it, and was silent, like a dumb person who never opens his mouth.

13   15 I became like the man who hears nothing, nor has any retort ready on his lips.

14   16 For I trusted in you, Lord, and said to you: "Hear this, Lord, and answer them."

15   17 For I have constantly requested that my enemies never gloat over me, lest they speak intemperate words against me, should they see my feet slipping.

16   18 Because I am now prepared for affliction, and my sorrow is always before me,

17   19 I will confess my iniquity to God, and reflect on my sins.

18 Gyt libbað mine fynd and synt strengran þonne ic, and
synt swiðe gemanigfealdode þa þe me mid unrihte hatiað.

19 Þa ðe me gyldað yfel mid goode, hy me tælað for þy ic
sece riht.

20 Ne forlæt me, Drihten, min God, ne ne gewit fram me,
ac beseoh me to fultume, Drihten God, min hælend.

Psalm 38

Dauid sang þysne eahta and þrittigoþan sealm seofigende to
Drihtne mid hu manegum unrotnessum he wæs ofðrycced
under Sawle; on þæm sealme he lærde and tælde ealle men
þe worulde welan gaderiað mid unrihte, and nytan hwam hi
hine læfað; and eac he witgode þæt ælc þæra þæt ylce don
sceolde, þe þysne sealm æfter him sunge; and eac he witgode
be Criste, þæt he wolde seofian swa ylce his nearonesse þe
he hæfde under Iudeum; and eac on æfteweardum þæm
sealme he wilnode ealra swiðost þæt him God sealde sume
frofre and sume rot-hwile on þysan andweardum life ær his
ende.

6 . . . ælces libbendes mannes mægen and anwald is
idelnes; and swa þeah ælc man hæfð Godes anlicnesse on
him, þeah hit idel sy þæt hy mid gedrefde synt:

18 ²⁰ My enemies still live, stronger than I, and those who unjustly hate me are greatly multiplied.

19 ²¹ Those who repay me evil for good slander me because I seek justice.

20 ²² Lord, my God, do not abandon me, or depart from me, ²³ but look favorably on me with help, Lord God, my savior.

Psalm 38

David sang this thirty-eighth psalm, complaining to the Lord about how many troubles he was oppressed by under Saul; in the psalm he admonished and rebuked all those who accumulate worldly wealth unjustly, yet not knowing to whom they will leave it; and he also prophesied that everyone who sang this psalm after him was destined to do the same; and also he prophesied about Christ, that he would likewise lament the anxiety which he experienced under the Jews; and also in the latter part of the psalm David desired most of all that God grant him some comfort and some period of ease in this present life before his death.

6 ⁶ . . . every living person's might and power is vanity; ⁷ and yet each person has God's image within, although what they worry about is worthless:

7   þæt ys, þæt hy gaderiað feoh, and nyton hwam hy hyt gadriað. Hwæt ys þonne min tohopa, hwæs anbidie ic butan þin, Drihten, for þam mid þe is eall min æht.

8   Ac of eallum minum unrihtwisnessum gefriða me. Þu me sealdest to bysmrianne þam unrihtwisan;

9   þa geswugode ic and ne ondyde na minne muð, for þæm ic ongeat þæt þu hit geðafodest. Ac awend nu fram me þine witnunga, for þam ic eom nu geteorod for þæm; for þære strenge þinra handa and þinre þreaunga ic geteorode on þære þrowunga.

10   Ælcne man þu þreast for his agenre scylde and gedest þæt he aswint on his mode and wyrð swa tedre swa swa gange-wifran nett,

11   for þam byð ælc man gedrefed and abysgod on idlum sorgum and on ymb-hogum. Drihten, gehyr min gebed and mine healsunga, onfoh mid þinum earum minne wop and mine tearas, ne swuga wið me, ac andswara me mid þine fultume,

12   for þam ic eom nifara hider on eorþan beforan ðe, and ælðeodig, swa swa ealle mine fæderas wæran.

13   Forlæt me nu, Drihten, to sumre rot-hwile on þisse weorulde, ær ic hire swa of gewite, þæt ic eft an ne sy.

7   that is, to accumulate wealth, although they do not know for whom they are accumulating it. ⁸ What is my hope then, for whom do I wait but you, Lord, because all my possessions are with you.

8   ⁹ But deliver me from all my iniquities. You handed me over to be insulted by the wicked;

9   ¹⁰ I fell silent then and did not open my mouth at all, because I realized that you had permitted it. ¹¹ But remove now from me your punishments, because I am worn out by them; ¹² because of the strength of your hands and your reproof, I was exhausted by that suffering.

10   You rebuke each person for his individual sin, making him languish in spirit and become as fragile as a spider's web,

11   for every man is troubled and preoccupied with vain cares and anxieties. ¹³ Lord, hear my prayer and appeals, listen to my crying and tears, do not be silent, but answer me with your help,

12   because I am a stranger here on earth in your sight, and an exile, as all my ancestors were.

13   ¹⁴ Lord, grant me now some period of ease in this world, before I take my leave of it with no prospect of my return.

Psalm 39

Dauid sang þysne nigan and þritigoþan sealm, gylpende on þam sealme þæt he nauht idel nære, þa he anbidode Godes fultumes, for þam he on þæm ærran sealme ahsode God hwæt his anbid wære oððe hwæs he anbidode; and eac he witgode be þam gehæftan folce on Babylonia þæt hy sceoldon þone ylcan sealm singan and þæt ylce seofian, and eft fægnian þonne hy on genere wæron, and þysne sealm singan swa he dyde; and swa ylce gebyreð ælcum cristnum men þas twegen sealmas to singanne: þonne ærran on his earfoðum and þone æftran syþþan he genered byð; and þæt ylce he witgode be Criste, þæt he wolde be þam ylcan þas sealmas singan, ægðer ge be þam earfoðum þe him Iudeas dydon ge eft be his alysnesse.

1   Næs ic on nauht idlum anbide, þeah hit me lang anbid þuhte þa ða ic anbidode Godes fultumes, for þam he beseah wið min and gehyrde min gebed and alædde me fram þam pytte ælcra yrmða, and of þam duste and of þam drosnum ælces ðeowdomes and ælcere hæft-nyde.

2   And he asette mine fet on swiðe heanne stan (þæt ys, on swyðe heah setl and on swyðe fæstne anweald), and he gerihte mine stæpas, and sende on minne muð niwne sang (þæt is, lof-sang urum Gode).

Psalm 39

David sang this thirty-ninth psalm, boasting in the psalm
that he was by no means wasting his time when he waited
for God's help, since in the previous psalm he had asked
God what his expectations should be, or for whom he
should be waiting; and also he prophesied about how the
captive people in Babylon were destined to sing the same
psalm and lament the same thing, and afterward rejoice
when they found a safe place, and sing this psalm as he did;
and likewise it is fitting for every Christian to sing these two
psalms: the former in their tribulations and the latter after
they are rescued; and he prophesied the same thing about
Christ, that he would sing these psalms about the same
things, both the sufferings which the Jews inflicted on him
and his subsequent deliverance.

1   2 I did not entertain idle expectations, though it
seemed to me a long wait when I awaited God's help, because he looked favorably on me, 3 and heard my prayer,
leading me out of the pit of all miseries, and from the dust
and dregs of every kind of servitude and slavery.

2   And he placed my feet on a very high stone (that is, on a
very high seat and with very secure control), and directed
my steps, 4 and put in my mouth a new song (that is, a song
of praise to our God).

3   Manege geseoð hu þu hæfst ymbe us gedon, and for þy to þe hopiað and þe ondrædað.

4   Eadig byð se wer þe his tohopa byð to swylcum Drihtne and ne locað næfre to idelnesse ne to leasungum ne to dysige.

5   Drihten, min God, þu gemanigfealdodest þin wundru and þine geðohtas (þæt ys, þin weorc); nis nan þæra þe þe gelic seo.

6   Ic spræc and þæt sæde, for ðam hy wæran gemanigfealdode ofer ælc gerim; noldest þu na ofrunga and oflatan nane, ac hyrsumnesse þu me bebude for ofrunga.

7   Ne bud þu me na ælmesan to syllanne for minum synnum, þa þa ic hy næfde, ac ic cwæð, "Ic eom gearu, ic cume and sylle þæt þu ær bebude" (þæt ys, hyrsumness).

8   On forewardre þyssere bec ys awriten be me, and eac on manegum oþrum, þæt ic sceolde þinne willan wyrcan, and swa ic eac wylle don. Drihten, min God, ic hæfde geteohhod, and gyt hæbbe, þæt ic scyle healdan þine æ symle on minre heortan.

9   Ic cyðe þine rihtwisnesse on micelre gesamnunge, and minum weolorum ic ne forbeode, ac bebeode þæt hy þæt sprecon symle.

10   Drihten, þu wast þæt ic ne ahydde on minum mode þine rihtwisnesse, ac þine soðfæstnesse and þine hælo ic sæde.

11   Ne ahydde ic na þine mild-heortnesse and þine rihtwisnesse on myclum gemotum.

12   Ac ne do þu, Drihten, þæt þin mild-heortnes sy me afyrred, for þam þin mild-heortnes and þin soðfæstnes me symle underfengon.

3   Many will see how you have acted toward us, and because of that will trust in you and be in awe of you.

4   [5] Blessed is the man whose hope rests in such a Lord, and who does not ever look to vanity, deceits, or folly.

5   [6] Lord, my God, you multiplied your wonders and thoughts (that is, your works); not one of them compares to you.

6   I spoke and said that, because those works were multiplied beyond all reckoning; [7] you did not desire offerings at all or any oblation, instead, you enjoined obedience on me in place of offerings.

7   You did not command me to give alms, when I did not possess them, in recompense for my sins, [8] so, I said, "I am ready, I will come and will give what you previously demanded" (that is, obedience).

8   In the front of this book, and also in many others, it is written down about me [9] that I should do your will, and so I intend to do. Lord, my God, I had determined, and still have, that I must always observe your law in my heart.

9   [10] I will declare your justice in the great assembly, while not restraining my lips, and will enjoin them to repeat that constantly.

10   Lord, you know [11] that I did not hide your justice in my heart; rather, I declared your truth and your salvation.

11   I certainly did not at all conceal your mercy and your justice in the great councils.

12   [12] But, Lord, do not cause your mercy to be removed from me, because it and your truth have always supported me.

13 For þam me ymbhringde manig yfel, þæra nis nan rim, me gefengan mine agene unrihtwisnessa, and ic hy ne meahte geseon ne ongytan.

14 Mine fynd wæran gemanigfealdode, þæt heora wæs ma þonne hæra on minum heafde; and min heorte and min mod me forleton, to þam þæt ic me nyste næne ræd.

15 Ac licige þe nu, Dryhten, ic þe bidde, þæt þu me arige, and ne lata þu to minum fultume.

16 Sceamien hiora and ondræden him endemes, þa þe ehtað mine sawle, and hy teohhiað me to afyrranne.

17 Syn hy gehwyrfde underbæc and ondræden him, þa þe me yfeles unnon.

18 Beren hi swiðe raþe heora agene scame, þa þe cweþað be me, þonne me hwylc ungelimp becymð, "Is þæt la well!"

19 Blissien þa and fægnien, þa þe þinne willan seceað, and cweðen þa þe hopiað to þinre hælo, "Gemyclad sy se Drihten þe swylc deð."

20 Ic eom yrming and þearfa, and þeah Dryhten min gymð.

21 Þu, Drihten, eart min friðiend and min gefultumend and min gescyldend; Drihten, min God, ne yld nu þæt þu me arie.

13   13 For many evils, countless in number, surrounded me, my own iniquities have trapped me, and I was not able to see or recognize them.

14   My enemies were multiplied, so that there was more of them than hairs on my head; and my heart and spirit abandoned me to the point that I lacked a course of action for myself.

15   14 But may it please you now, Lord, I beseech you, to spare me, and do not delay in helping me.

16   15 Let them be ashamed of themselves and be afraid all at once, who pursue my soul even as they resolve to remove me.

17   Let them be turned backward and become fearful, those who wish me evil.

18   16 May they very quickly carry their own shame, who say about me, when any misfortune befalls me, "Ha! That is good!"

19   17 Let those who seek your will be happy then, and rejoice, and let those who trust in your salvation say, "May the Lord who does such things be magnified."

20   18 I am a wretched and needy person, and yet the Lord takes care of me.

21   Lord, you are my defender, helper, and protector; Lord, my God, do not delay in showing me mercy.

Psalm 40

Dauid sang þysne feowertigoðan sealm be his earfoðum, and
eft be þam fultume þe he hæfde fram Gode, and he sæde
eac on þam sealme hu he hæfde afandod ægðer ge his frynd
ge his fynd on his earfoðum and on his ungelimpe; and eac
he witgode be Ezechie cincge þe æfter him beon sceolde,
þæt him sceolde þæt ylce beon; and eac be ælcum crisnum
men he witgode þæt ylce, þara þe ærest on earfoðum byð
and eft on eðnesse; and eac be Criste he witgode on þæm
sealme and be Iudeum, hu hy hine swencton, and hu hine
God eft arette.

1   Eadig bið se þe ongyt þæs þearfan and þæs wædlan, and
him þonne gefultumað gif hine to onhagað; gif hine ne onhagað, þonne ne licað him, þeah, his earfoðu; þone gefriþað
Drihten on swylcum dæge swylce him swylc yfel becymð.
2   Drihten hine gehylt and hine geliffæst and gedeð hine
gesæligne on eorðan, and ne sylð hine na on his feonda
handa and anweald.
3   Drihten him bringð fultum to his bedde, þe he an lið,
and eall his bedd he onwent of untrumnesse to trymðe.
4   Ic cweðe, Drihten, to þe: "Gemildsa me and gehæl
mine sawle, for ðon ic gesyngode wið þe."
5   Mine fynd me cwædon yfel and wilnodon, and spræcon

Psalm 40

David sang this fortieth psalm about his sufferings, and later
about the help which he received from God, and he also
mentioned in the psalm how in his sufferings and misfortune he had discovered both his friends and his enemies;
and also he prophesied about King Hezekiah, who was destined to come after him, that the same thing would happen
to him; and also he prophesied the same about every Christian who at first lives in sufferings and afterward in comfort;
and also he prophesied about Christ and about the Jews,
how they would afflict him, and how God afterward would
comfort him.

1   2 Blessed is the one who is aware of the poor and the
needy, and then helps them if he has the means; if he does
not have the means, then at least he does not take pleasure
in their sufferings; such a one the Lord will protect at whatever time a similar evil befalls him.

2   3 The Lord will preserve him, keep him alive, and make
him happy on earth, and will not surrender him into his enemies' hands and control.

3   4 The Lord will bring help to him on his sickbed, and
will transform his bed completely from sickness to strength.

4   5 I will say to you, Lord, "Have mercy on me and heal
my soul, because I have sinned against you."

5   6 My enemies spoke (and desired) evil things about me,

betwuh him and cwædon: "Hwonne ær he beo dead, oþþe hwænne his nama aspringe?"

6   And þeah hy þæs lyste, þeah hy eodon in to me and fandodon min and seofodon min sar.

7   And þonne hy ut eodon from me, þonne worhton hy heora gemot, and wæran ealle anspræce þonne hy me leahtrodon and læðdon.

8   Ealle mine fynd, hy þonne gegaderodon ongean me and þohton me yfeles, and spræcon me yfeles and spræcon un-riht wið me, and cwædon on bysmor:

9   "Nis him nan lað, he reste hine; eaðe he mæg arisan, þeah he slape and liccete untrymnesse"; ge furðon þa spræ-con þæt ylce mid him, þe ic betst truwode, and þa þe ær æton and druncon mid me.

10 Þu, þonne, Drihten, nu gemiltsa me and arære me to þam þæt ic him mæge forgyldan þæs lean.

11 Þonne ongyte ic on þam þæt þu me lufast, gif nan minra feonda ne fægnað mines ungelimpes.

12 Þu me underfenge for minre unsceðfulnesse and me gestrangodest beforan þinre ansyne on ecnesse.

13 Gebletsod sy se Drihten, Israela God, on weorulda weoruld; sy swa!

and talked among themselves, saying, "How soon before he dies, or when will his name perish?"

6   7 And although they wished for that, they came in to see me, nevertheless, and examined me, lamenting my pain.

7   And when they went out from me, they assembled their council, 8 and were unanimous in calumniating and speaking ill of me.

8   All my enemies then came together against me and plotted harm for me, and spoke evil of me, 9 and said unjust things about me, and declared derisively:

9   "He suffers no pain, he is just resting; he can easily get up, although he sleeps and feigns sickness"; 10 and even they whom I most trusted, and they who previously ate and drank in my company, joined them in saying the same thing.

10   11 But you, Lord, have pity on me now and restore me so that I can recompense them for that.

11   12 I will know then that you love me, when none of my enemies will rejoice at my misfortune.

12   13 You supported me on account of my innocence and strengthened me in your sight forever.

13   14 Blessed be that Lord, the God of Israel, for ever and ever; so be it!

Psalm 41

Dauid sang þysne an and feowertigoþan sealm, þa he wilnode to hys eðle to cumanne of his wræcsiðe; and þæt ilce
he witgode be Israela folce gehæftum on Babilonia, þæt hy
sceoldon þæt ylce don; and eac he witgode be ælcum cristnum men, þara þe geswenced wære, oþþe on mode oððe on
lichaman, and þonne wilnode ægðer ge þyses lifes frofre ge
þæs toweardan; and eac be Criste and be Iudeum he witgode, hu he wilnode þæt he wurde gedæled wið hy and wið
heora yfelnesse.

1   Swa heort wilnað to wætre þonne he werig byð oþþe
ofþyrst, swa wilnað min sawl and min mod to þe, Drihten.

2   Mine sawle þyrst and lyst þæt heo mæge cuman to
Gode, for þam he is se libbenda wylle. Eala, Dryhten,
hwænne gewyrð þæt, þæt ic cume and ætywe beforan Godes
ansyne?

3   Me wæran mine tearas for hlafas, ægþer ge on dæg ge
on niht, þonne ic gehyrde mine fynd cweþan: "Hwær is þin
God þe þu to hopast?"

4   Ac þonne gemunde ic þine ærran gyfa, and gestaðelode
on me mine sawle, for þy ic geare wiste þæt ic sceolde cuman for Godes mild-heortnesse to þam wundorlican temple
(þæt ys, Godes hus); þyder ic sceal cuman mid mycelre wyn-
sumnesse stemne and mid andetnesse, swylce symblendra
sweg byð and bliðra.

Psalm 41

David sang this forty-first psalm when he desired to return from exile to his homeland; and he prophesied the same thing about the people of Israel held captive in Babylon, that they were destined to do the same; and also he prophesied about every Christian troubled either in mind or body, and wishing then for consolation both in this life and the next; and also he prophesied about Christ and the Jews, that he would wish to be separated from them and from their wickedness.

1   2 As the hart desires to come to water, whenever it is weary or thirsty, so my soul and spirit desire to come to you, Lord.

2   3 My soul thirsts and desires permission to come to God, because he is the living well. O Lord, when will my coming and appearing in God's presence happen?

3   4 For me tears took the place of bread, both night and day, whenever I heard my enemies say, "Where is your God in whom you trust?"

4   5 But then I remembered your former gifts, and fortified my soul within, because I realized for sure that, because of God's mercy, I would come to that wonderful temple (that is, God's house); I shall come there with an acknowledging cry of great exultation, like the noise of revelers and those rejoicing.

5   For hwi eart þu þonne unrot, min sawl and min mod; hwi gedrefe gyt me?

6   Hopa to Drihtne, for þam ic hine gyt andette, for þam he ys min hælend and min God.

7   Wið me sylfne wæs min sawl and min mod gebolgen and gedrefed; for þæm ic eom gemyndig þin, Drihten, be Iordane staðe, and on þam lytlan cnolle þe Ermon hatte.

8   Seo neolnes cliopað to þære neolnesse, and heo oncwyð for þære stemne eorðan wæter-ædra (þæt ys, þin yrre); eall heah witu and hefug coman to me, and þine yþa me oferfleo-won.

9   On dæg bebead God his mild-heortnesse cuman to me, me to gefriþianne wið þyssum yrmðum, and on niht he us bebead þæt we sceoldon singan his sang.

10   Mid me beoð symble gearo gebedu to þam Gode þe me libbendne þanon gelædde. Ic cweðe to þam Gode: "Þu eart min andfengend;

11   hwy forgits þu min, and hwi awyrpst þu me fram þe, oððe hwy lætst þu me gan þus unrotne, þonne me mysceað mine fynd,

12   and þonne hy tobrecað eall min ban, and þonne me hyspað þa þe me swencað, and huru swiðost þonne hy cweðað ælce dæge: 'Hwær ys þin God?'"

13   For hwy eart þu unrot, min mod and min sawl, and hwy gedrefst þu me?

14   Hopa to Drihtne, for þam ic gyt hine andette, for þam he is min hælend and min God.

5   ⁶ Why then are you sad, my soul and mind; why do you trouble me still?

6   Trust in the Lord, for I will continue to praise him, because he is my savior ⁷ and my God.

7   My soul and spirit were angered and disturbed against myself; so, Lord, I remember you by Jordan's banks and on the little hilltop called Hermon.

8   ⁸ Deep calls to deep, and it responds as the roar of earth's cataracts (that is, your anger); all kinds of great and grievous punishments befell me, and your waves flooded me.

9   ⁹ In the daytime God commanded his mercy to come to me, to free me from these miseries, and at night he commanded us to sing his song.

10   I will always have ready prayers for the God who led me, still living, from there. ¹⁰ I will say to that God: "You are my defender;

11   why do you neglect me and cast me off from you, or why do you tolerate my wandering about in this sad state, whenever my enemies afflict me,

12   ¹¹ and break all my bones in pieces, and when my tormenters taunt me, and especially when they say daily: 'Where is your God?'"

13   ¹² Why are you sad, my mind and soul, and why do you trouble me?

14   Trust in the Lord, for I will continue to praise him, because he is my savior and my God.

Psalm 42

Dauid sang þysne tu and feowertigoþan sealm, and healsode
God on þyssum sealme þæt he demde betwuh him and his
feondum þe nane æ Godes ne heoldon; and he eac witgode
be þam gehæftan folce on Babylonia, þæt hy sceoldon þæt
ylce don; and be ælcum cristnum menn þe þysne sealm
singð, he witgode þæt hy hine sceoldan be þam ylcan singan;
and eac Crist be Iudeum.

1   Dem me, Dryhten, and do sum toscead betwuh me and
unrihtwisum folce, and from facenfullum menn and unrihtwisum gefriða me,

2   for þam þu eart min God and min mægen. For hwy
awyrpst þu me, and hwi lætst þu me gan unrotne, þonne
mine fynd me drecceað?

3   Send þin leoht and þine soðfæstnesse, þa me geo-geara
læddon, þæt hy me nu gyt gelædan to þinum halgan munte,
inon þin halge templ,

4   þæt ic þonne gange to þinum altere and to þam Gode
þe me bliðne gedyde on minum geogoðhade.

5   Ic þe andette, Dryhten, mid sange and mid hearpan.
Hwy eart þu unrot, min sawl, oþþe hwi gedrefest þu me?

6   Hopa to Drihtne, for þam ic hine gyt andette, for þam
þu eart, God, min hælend and min Dryhten.

Psalm 42

David sang this forty-second psalm, beseeching God in this psalm to judge between him and his enemies, who did not observe any of God's law; and he also prophesied about the captive people in Babylon, that they were destined to do the same; and he prophesied about every Christian who sings this psalm, that they were destined to sing it about the same thing; and also Christ about the Jews.

1   1 Judge me, Lord, and make some distinction between me and the wicked, and deliver me from the deceitful and the wicked,

2   2 because you are my God and my strength. Why do you cast me off, and why do you tolerate my wandering about in this sad state, whenever my enemies afflict me?

3   3 Send your light and truth, which formerly led me, to ensure that they continue to lead me to your holy mountain, into your holy temple,

4   4 so that I may then proceed to your altar and to the God who made me cheerful in my youth.

5   Lord, I will give praise to you with song and harp. 5 My soul, why are you sad, or why do you trouble me?

6   Trust in the Lord, for I will continue to praise him, because you, God, are my savior and my Lord.

Psalm 43

Dauid sang þysne þreo and feowertigoðan sealm, seofigende
his earfoþa, and myngode þæra gyfa þe he his fædrum and
his fore-gengum sealde and hiora eaforum gehet; and eac
seofode þæt him þuhte þæt hy God on ðam tidum swa
hrædlice ne gehyrde swa he his fore-gengan dyde; and eac he
witgode on þam sealme be Mathathia and be his sunum (þa
we Machabeas hatað), þæt hy sceoldon þæt ylce seofian on
hiora earfoðum under Antiochus þam kynge; and eac he
witgode be ælcum cristnum men þe to Gode hopað, þæt he
sceolde þæt ylce don; and eac be Criste, þæt he wolde þæt
ylce don be Iudeum.

1   Drihten, we gehyrdon mid urum earum and ure fæderas
hit us sædon

2   þa weorc þe þu worhtest on hiora dagum and on hiora
fore-gengena dagum:

3   þæt wæs, þæt þin hand towearp þæ elðeodegan folc
and plantode and tydrede ure fore-gengan; þu swenctest þa
elðeodgan folc and hy awurpe.

4   Ne geeodon ure fore-gengan na ðas eorðan mid sweorda
ecgum, ne hy mid þy ne geheoldon, ne heora earmas hy ne
geheoldon ne ne gehældon,

5   ac þin swiðre hand and þin earm and þæt leoht þines
andwlitan, for þam hy þe þa licodon, and þe licode mid him
to beonne.

Psalm 43

David sang this forty-third psalm, lamenting his sufferings,
and he recalled the gifts that God gave to his forefathers
and ancestors and promised to their offspring; and also he
lamented that it seemed to him that God at that time did
not listen to them as promptly as he did to their predecessors; and also he prophesied in the psalm about Mattathias
and his sons (whom we call the Maccabees), that they were
destined to lament the same thing in their difficulties under
King Antiochus; and also he prophesied about every Christian who trusts in God, that they would do the same; and
also that Christ would do the same in relation to the Jews.

1   2 Lord, we heard with our own ears and our fathers related to us

2   the deeds you performed in their days and in their forefathers' days:

3   3 that your hand destroyed the alien peoples and
planted and propagated our forefathers; you harassed those
gentiles and expelled them.

4   4 Our forefathers by no means subdued this land by the
sword's edge, nor did they maintain it by the same means,
nor did the strength of their arms protect or save it,

5   rather, it was your right hand and arm and the light of
your face, because the people at that time pleased you, and
you enjoyed dwelling among them.

6   Hu ne eart þu min cyning and min Drihten, swa ylce swa þu hiora wære, þu þe bebude hælo cuman to Iacobes cynne?

7   Þurh þe we beþurscon ure fynd and awindwedan, and for þinum naman we forsawan þa þe stodon ongean us.

8   Ne getruwode ic næfre on minne bogan, ne min sweord me ne gefriðode ne ne gehælde.

9   Ac þu us ahreddest æt þam þe ure ehton, and þa ðe us hatedon þu gebysmrodest.

10   And we þa heredon God ælce dæge, and we wæron eac geherede fram oþrum þeodum for his weorcum, and his naman we andettað a weoruld,

11   þeah þu, Drihten, us nu adrifen hæbbe fram þe and us gebysmrod, and mid us ne fare on fyrd, swa þu geo dydest.

12   Ac þu hæfst nu us gehwyrfde on bæclincg and us forsewenran gedone þonne ure fynd, and þa þe us hatiað, hy us gegripað and him sylfum gehrespað.

13   Þu us geþafodest him to metsianne swa swa sceap, and þu us tostenctest geond manega þeoda.

14   Þu us bebohtest and bewrixledest, and nan folc mid us ne gehwyrfdest.

15   Þu us gesettest to edwite and to bysmre urum neah-geburum, and to hleahtre and to forsewennesse eallum þam þe us ymbsittað.

16   Þu hæfst us gedon to eald-spræce, þæt oðra þeoda nyton hwæt hy elles sprecon buton ure bysmer, and wecg-geað heora heafod ongean us on heora gesamnuncge.

17   Ælce dæge byð min sceamu beforan me and ongean me, and mid minum bysmre ic eom bewrogen,

6 ⁵ Surely are you not my king and my Lord, just as you were theirs, the one who decreed impending salvation for Jacob's tribe?

7 ⁶ Because of you we thoroughly thrashed and winnowed our enemies, and because of your name we despised those who opposed us.

8 ⁷ I never trusted in my bow, nor did my sword deliver or save me.

9 ⁸ But you freed us from those who persecuted us, and confounded those who hated us.

10 ⁹ And thereafter we praised God every day, and we were, in turn, praised by other peoples on account of his deeds, and we will acknowledge his name for ever,

11 ¹⁰ even though you, Lord, have now driven us from you and confounded us, and do not march on campaign with us, as you formerly did.

12 ¹¹ On the contrary, you have now turned us backward in retreat, and made us more despised than our enemies, and those who hate us lay hold of us and plunder at their whim.

13 ¹² You allowed us like sheep to become fodder for them, and you scattered us throughout many peoples.

14 ¹³ You sold us into slavery and bartered us, yet did not exchange any people for us.

15 ¹⁴ You set us up as a reproach and disgrace to our neighbors, and an object of laughter and derision to all those around us.

16 ¹⁵ You have made us a byword, so that other peoples do not know what else to say about us except insults, while they shake their heads at us in their assembly.

17 ¹⁶ Every day my shame is before and in front of me, and I am enveloped by my humiliation,

18   for þara stemne þe me hyspað and tælað, and for þara ansyne þe min ehtað.

19   Eall þas earfoðu becoman ofer us, and ne forgeate we, þeah, na þe, ne þæt woh ne worhton, þæt we þine æ forleten, ne ure mod ne eode on bæclincg fram þe.

20   And þeah þu geþafodest þæt ure stæpas wendon of þinum wege, for þam þu woldest us geeaðmedan on þære stowe ure unrotnesse, þær we wæron bewrigene mid deaþes sceade.

21   Gif we ofer-geotole wæron Drihtnes naman, ures Godes, and gif we ure handa upp hofon to oþrum gode,

22   hu ne wræce hit þonne God, for þan he wat ealle dygelnessa ælcere heortan?

23   For þam we beoð ælce dæge for ðe geswencte; hy teohhiað us him to snædincg-sceapum.

24   Aris, Drihten, for hwi slæpst þu? Aris, and ne drif us fram þe oð urne ende.

25   For hwi wendst þu þinne andwlitan fram us, oððe hwy forgytst þu ure yrmða and ure geswinc?

26   For þam synt nu fullneah to duste gelæd ure sawla, and ure wamb lið on þære eorðan.

27   Aris, Drihten, and gefultuma us, and alys us for þinum naman.

18   ¹⁷ caused by their comments of reproach and slander against me, and the look of my persecutors.

19   ¹⁸ All these tribulations came down on us, and yet we did not forget you at all, nor commit the error of abandoning your law, ¹⁹ nor did our hearts pull back from you.

20   And yet you allowed our steps to turn from your path, ²⁰ because you wished to humiliate us in the place of our troubles, where we were covered by the shadow of death.

21   ²¹ If we had been forgetful of the name of the Lord our God, and if we had lifted up our hands to another god,

22   ²² would not God, surely, have avenged that then, since he knows all the heart's secrets?

23   For we are afflicted every day because of you; they consider us as sheep for slaughter.

24   ²³ Arise, Lord, why do you sleep? Arise, and do not expel us from you to our destruction.

25   ²⁴ Why do you turn your face from us, or why are you oblivious to our miseries and tribulations?

26   ²⁵ For our souls are almost pulled down to the dirt now, and our bellies lie on the earth.

27   ²⁶ Lord, arise and help us, and free us for your name's sake.

Psalm 44

Dauid witgode on þissum feower and feowertigoþan sealme, þa he wæs oferdrenct mid þy Halgan Gaste, and on eallum þam sealme he spræc ymb Fæder and ymb Sunu and ymb þa halgan gesamnuncga cristenra manna geond ealre eorðan. Sona on þam forman ferse, se Fæder spræc þurh Dauid be Cristes acennesse and cwæð:

1   "Min heorte bealcet good word (þæt ys, good Godes bearn); þæm cyncge ic befæste anweald ofer eall min weorc.
2   Min tunge ys gelicost þæs writeres feþere þe hraðost writ" (þæt ys, Crist, se ys word and tunge God-Fæder, þurh hine synt ealle þincg geworht).
3   He ys fægrostes andwlitan ofer eall manna bearn; geondgotene synt þine weleras mid Godes gyfe,
4   for þam þe gebletsode God on ecnesse. Gyrd nu þin sweord ofer þin þeoh, þu mihtiga (þæt ys, gastlicu lar seo ys on ðam godspelle, seo ys scearpre þonne æni sweord).
5   Geheald nu þinne wlite and þine fægernesse, and cum orsorg, and rixsa,
6   for þinre soðfæstnesse and for þinre ryhtwisnesse, þe gelæt swyðe wundorlice þin seo swyþre hand and þin agen anweald to þæm.

Psalm 44

David prophesied in this forty-fourth psalm, when he was intoxicated by the Holy Spirit, and all through the psalm he spoke about the Father and the Son and about the blessed congregations of Christians throughout all the earth. Immediately in the first verse, the Father spoke through David about Christ's incarnation, saying:

1   2 "My heart will utter a noble word (that is, the most virtuous Son of God); to that king I will entrust power over all my works.

2   My tongue is very like the scribe's pen that writes with greatest speed" (that is, Christ, who is the word and tongue of God the Father, all things are created by him).

3   3 He is most beautiful, beyond all the sons of men in appearance; your lips are suffused with God's grace,

4   because God has blessed you forever. 4 Gird now your sword on your thigh, you mighty one (that is, the spiritual teaching present in the gospel, which is keener than any sword).

5   5 Maintain now your beauty and your comeliness, and advance in prosperity, and rule,

6   because of your truth and justice, your right hand and your own power will lead you most marvelously to them.

7   Þina flana synt swyþe scearpa on þam heortum þinra
feonda; folc gefeallað under ðe (þæt ys, þæt hy oþer twega
oþþe an andetnesse gefeallað oþþe on helle).

8   Þin setl is, Drihten, on weorulda weoruld; swiðe ryht is
seo cyne-gyrd þines rices, seo gerecð ælcne mann oþþe to þinum willan oððe to wite.

9   Þu lufodest rihtwisnesse and hatodest unryhtwisnesse,
for þam þe gesmyrede Dryhten, þin God, mid þam ele blisse
ofer ealle oþre menn.

10   Myrre and gutta and cassia dropiað of þinum claðum
and of þinum elpan-bænenum husum on þæm þe gelufiað
cynincga dohtor, þa þær wuniað for þinre lufan and for
þinre weorðunga. (Þa wyrt-gemang tacniað mistlicu mægen
Cristes, and þæt hrægl tacnað Cristes lichaman, and þa
elpan-bænenan hus tacniað rihtwisra manna heortan; þara
kynincga dohtor tacniað rihtwisra manna sawla.)

11   And þær stent cwen þe on þa swyðran hand, mid golde
getuncode, and mid ælcere mislicre fægernesse gegyred
(þæt ys, eall cristnu gesamnung).

12   Gehyr nu, min dohtor (þæt ys, seo gesamnuncg cristnes
folces), geseoh, and onhyld þin eare, and forgit and alæt þin
folc (þæt synd, yfel-willende menn and unðeawas) and þæt
hus and þone hired þines leasan fæder (þæt ys, deofol),

13   for þam se cyncg wilnað þines wlites. For þam he ys
Drihten, þin God, gebide þe to him and weorþa hine; and
swa ylce doð eac þa dohtor þære welegan byrig Tyrig: hi hine
weorðiað mid gyfum (þæt synt, þa sawla þe beoð gewelgoda
mid goodum geearnuncgum).

7　⁶ Your arrows are exceedingly sharp in your enemies' hearts; people will fall under you (that is, that they will either apply themselves to acknowledging you, or fall into hell).

8　⁷ Lord, your throne exists for ever and ever; perfectly upright is the scepter of your kingdom, which directs every man either to your will or to punishment.

9　⁸ You have loved justice and hated iniquity, so the Lord, your God, anointed you with the oil of gladness in preference to all others.

10　⁹ Myrrh, stacte, and cassia drip from your clothes and your ivory houses where ¹⁰ the kings' daughters delight in you, those who dwell there in love and veneration of you. (Those spices signify the diverse powers of Christ, and the garment signifies Christ's body, and the ivory houses signify the hearts of just men; the daughters of the kings signify the souls of just men.)

11　And the queen stands there on your right hand, arrayed in a brocaded dress and decked with every possible kind of ornament (that is, the whole christian congregation).

12　¹¹ My daughter (that is, the assembly of christian people), hear, look, and listen, and forget and renounce your people (that is, evilly disposed people and the vices) and the house, with its household, of your false father (that is, the devil),

13　¹² because the king desires your beauty. Since he is the Lord, your God, worship and honor him; ¹³ and the daughters of the wealthy city of Tyre will also do likewise: they will honor him with gifts (that is, those souls endowed with meritorious deeds).

14   Gif þu þus dest, þonne weorðiað þe ealle þa welegastan
on ælcum folce, and habbað him þæt to mæstum gylpe þæt
hy geseon kyninga dohtra inne mid him,

15   utan beslepte and gegyrede mid eallum mislicum
hrægla wlitum and mid gyldnum fnasum (þæt synt, mistlica
geearnunga ful-fremedra manna).

16   Eala, kynincg, hwæt, þe beoð broht manega mædenu,
and æfter þam þære seo nyhste, þe we ær ymbespræcon;
mid blisse and mid fægnuncge hy bioð gelædde into þinum
temple (þæt synt, þa sawla þe heora mægðhad gehealdað,
and þa hreowsiendan, and þa þe gewitnode beoð for hiora
scyldum, oþþe heora willum oððe heora unwillum).

17   For þinum fædrum þe bioð acennedu bearn (þæt synt,
apostolas wið þam heah-fædrum and wið witgum), and þu
hy gesetst to ealdor-mannum ofer ealle eorþan,

18   and hy beoð gemyndige þines naman, Dryhten, on ælcere cneorisse.

19   And þonne for þy þe andett ælc folc on ecnesse and on
weorulda weoruld.

14   If you so conduct yourself, then all the wealthiest people will honor you, [14] and will have as their greatest boast that they get to see the kings' daughters inside among them,

15   [15] clothed and covered on the outside with every kind of elaborate clothing and with golden fringes (that is, the diverse merits of perfectly virtuous people).

16   O king! Many virgins will be brought to you, and following them the female companion of her whom we previously spoke about; [16] they will be led into your temple with joy and with rejoicing (that is, those souls who preserve their virginity, and those who are doing penance, and those who are punished for their sins, either willingly or unwillingly).

17   [17] In place of your ancestors, children will be born to you (that is, the apostles with the patriarchs and prophets), and you will appoint them as leaders over all the earth,

18   [18] and they will be mindful of your name, Lord, in every generation.

19   And so every people will then acknowledge you, for ever and ever.

Psalm 45

Dauid sang þysne fif and feowertigoþan sealm, þanciende
Gode þæt he hine oft alysde of manegum earfoðum; and eac
he witgode þæt þæt ylce sceoldon don þa men, þa þe twa
scira hatte (þæt ys, Iude and Beniamin), þæt hy sceoldon
þam Gode þancian þe hy gefriðode fram þære ymbseten-
nesse and fram þære heregunge þara twega kynincga, Facces, Rumeles suna, and Rasses, Syria cyncges—næs þæt na
gedon for þæs cynincges geearnuncga Achats, ac for Godes
mild-heortnesse and for his yldrena gewyrhtum hit gewearð
þæt þa twegen kyningas wæron adrifene fram Assyria cynge;
and eac þæt ylce he witgode be ælcum rihtwisum menn þe
ærest geswenced byð and eft gearod; and eac be Criste and
be Iudeum he witgode þæt ylce.

1   Dryhten ys ure gebeorh and ure mægen and ure fultumend on earfoðum þa us swiðe swiðlice oft on becomon.
2   For þam we us ne ondrædað, þeah eall eorðe sy gedrefedu, and þeah þa muntas syn aworpene on midde þa sæ.
3   Ure fynd coman swa egeslice to us þæt us ðuhte for þam
geþune þæt sio eorþe eall cwacode; and hy wæron, þeah,
sona afærde fram Gode swyþor þonne we, and þa up ahafenan kynincgas swa þær muntas wæron eac gedrefde for þæs
Godes strenge.

Psalm 45

David sang this forty-fifth psalm, thanking God for having often rescued him from numerous troubles; and also he prophesied that those men after whom the two tribes were named (that is, Judah and Benjamin) were destined to do the same, thanking the God who liberated them from the siege and from the ravaging of the two kings, Pekah the son of Remaliah, and Rezin, king of Syria—that was not done in consideration of the supposed merits of King Ahaz, but because of God's mercy and the merits of Ahaz's ancestors it came about that those two kings were expelled by the Assyrian king; and David also prophesied the same thing about every just person who at first is afflicted, and afterward shown mercy; and also he prophesied the same about Christ and about the Jews.

1   ² The Lord is our refuge, strength, and helper in the troubles that have often befallen us most intensely.

2   ³ We will not be afraid, then, even if all the earth is disturbed and the mountains thrown into the middle of the sea.

3   ⁴ Our enemies advanced on us so threateningly that it seemed to us, on account of the noise, that the earth entirely shook; and yet they were soon struck by God with terror more intensely than we, and because of God's strength those exalted kings were also agitated like the mountains.

4   Þa wæs geblissod seo Godes burh on Hierusalem for
þam cyme þæs scures þe hy geclæsnode; se hyhsta gehalgode
his templ inon þære byrig; for þam ne wyrð seo burh næfre
onwend, þa hwile þe God byð unonwendedlic on hire midle.

5   God hyre gehealp swyþe ær on morgen, and gedrefed
wæron þa elðeodgan folc, and hiora rice wæs gehnæged; se
hyhsta sende his word, and gehwyrfed wæs ure land and ure
folc to beteran, and hi and heora land to wyrsan.

6   Drihten, mægena God, ys mid us, and ure andfengend
is Iacobes God.

7   Cumað and gesioð Godes weorc and his wundru, þe he
wyrcð ofer eorðan.

8   He afierð fram us ælc gefeoht ut ofer ure land-gemæru,
and forbrycð ura feonda bogan, and eall heora wæpn gebryt,
and heora scyldas forbærnð. Þa andswarode God þæs witgan mode and cwæð eft þurh þone witgan:

9   "Geæmetgiað eow nu and gesioð þæt ic eom ana God,
and me nu up ahebbe ofer ða elðeodegan folc, and eac on
þysum folce ic beo nu up ahæfen."

10   Dryhten, mægena God, ys mid us, and ure andfengend
ys Iacobes God.

4   ⁵ Then God's city in Jerusalem was gladdened by the coming of the rainstorm which cleansed it; the Most High sanctified his temple within the city; ⁶ as a result, that city will never be moved while God remains immovable at its center.

5   God came to its help very early in the morning, ⁷ and the foreign peoples were disturbed, and their kingdom was subdued; the Most High uttered his words, and our land and people was changed for the better, but they and their land for the worse.

6   ⁸ The Lord, the God of hosts, is on our side, and our defender is Jacob's God.

7   ⁹ Come and see God's works and wonders, which he performs throughout the earth.

8   ¹⁰ He removes every battle from us out beyond our borders, and breaks our enemies' bows, and smashes all their weapons, and burns their shields. Then God answered the mind of the prophet, and through him once more said:

9   ¹¹ "Relax now, and see that I alone am God, and I will exalt myself now over those foreign peoples, and will also be exalted now in this people."

10   ¹² The Lord, the God of hosts, is on our side, and our defender is Jacob's God.

Psalm 46

Dauid sang þysne syx and feowertigoþan sealm and lærde on
þam sealme ealle þeoda þæt hy heredon þone God mid him,
mid ælcum þæra cræftum þe man God mid herian mihte,
þone God þe hine swa arlice gefriðode on eallum his earfoðum, and ealle his fynd gebrytte; and eac he witgode be
Machabeum, þæt hy sceoldon þæt ylce don, þa hy alysde
wæron æt elðeodegum folcum; and eac he witgode be ælcum ryhtwisum, geswenctum and eft alysdum; and eac be
Criste and be Iudeum.

1   Wepað nu and heofað, eall orlegu folc, for þam ure
God eow hæfð ofercumen; and eac, ge Israhela, hebbað upp
eowre handa and fægniað, and myrgað Gode mid wynsumre
stemne,

2   for þam he ys swyþe heah God and swyþe andrysnlic,
and swiþe micel cynincg ofer ealle oðre godas.

3   He us underþeodde ure folc, and orlega þeoda he alede
under ure fet.

4   He us geceas him to yrfe-weardnesse and Iacobes cynn,
þæt he lufode.

5   Drihten astah mid wynsume sange and mid bymena
stemne.

6   Ac singað urum Gode and heriað hine; singað, singað,
and heriað urne cyning; singað, and heriað hine,

Psalm 46

David sang this forty-sixth psalm, in which he advised all nations to praise God with him, using all the skills with which God can be praised, the God who so mercifully delivered him in all his troubles, and smashed all his enemies; and also he prophesied about the Maccabees, that they were destined to do the same, when they were delivered from foreign peoples; and also he prophesied about every just person who suffered and afterward was delivered; and also about Christ and the Jews.

1   ² All you hostile peoples, lament now and grieve, because our God has overcome you; and moreover, you Israelites, lift up your hands and exult and rejoice in God with a triumphant voice,

2   ³ because he is an exceedingly exalted and awe-inspiring God, and a very great king above all other gods.

3   ⁴ He made our own peoples subject to us, and he subdued hostile nations under our feet.

4   ⁵ He chose us as his inheritance and Jacob's tribe, which he loved.

5   ⁶ The Lord ascended to the accompaniment of joyous song and the sound of trumpets.

6   ⁷ Sing to our God and praise him; sing, sing, and praise our king; sing, and praise him,

7   for þam he ys God and cynincg ealre eorðan; singað and heriað hine wislice.

8   Dryhten rixað ofer eall cynrynu; Drihten sit ofer his ðam halgan setle.

9   Þa ealdor-men ealre eorðan becumað to Abrahames Gode, and beoð him underðydde, for þam he oferswiðde þa strangan kynincgas ofer eorðan, þa þe wæron up ahæfene swa þas godas.

Psalm 47

Dauid sang þysne seofon and feowertigoþan sealm, mycli-
ende þone wundorlican sige Godes, þe he þa (and oftor ær)
dyde, hu hrædlice he oferswiðde swa ofermode kyningas;
and eac he lærde ælcne man þe geswære wære and ofercumen and eft gefriðod, þæt he swa ylce Gode þancode and
his anweald herede; and þæt ylce he witgode be Criste, þæt
he þæt ylce sceolde cweðan to his Fæder æfter ðære æriste.

1   Mycel ys se Drihten ure God, and swyþe to herianne on þære byrig ures Drihtnes and on his þam halgan munte.

2   He tobrædde blisse ofer ealle ure eorþan; sio mycle burh þæs myclan kyninges is aset on þa norðhealfe þæs muntes Syon.

3   Se God ys cuð on þære byrig, for þam he hire symle ful-tumað.

7   ^{8} because he is God and king of all the earth; sing and praise him skillfully.

8   ^{9} The Lord rules over all nations; he sits on his holy throne.

9   ^{10} The princes of the whole world will come to Abraham's God, and will be subject to him, because he has overcome the strong kings throughout the earth, who had been exalted like these gods.

Psalm 47

David sang this forty-seventh psalm, extolling God's wonderful victory gained at that time (and even more often before), when he swiftly overpowered such arrogant kings; and also he advised everyone who was oppressed and subjugated and afterward liberated, likewise to thank God and praise his power; and he prophesied the same about Christ, that he would say the same thing to his Father after the resurrection.

1   ^{2} Great is the Lord our God, and to be praised exceedingly in our Lord's city and on his holy mountain.

2   ^{3} He spread joy throughout all our land; the great king's grand city is founded on the north side of Mount Zion.

3   ^{4} That God is manifest in the city, because he constantly supports it.

4   Eala, hwæt, ge sawon hu egeslice gegaderode wæron eorð-kyningas, and hu hi togædere comon.

5   And sona swa hi gesawon Godes wundru, hy wæron wundriende and wæran gedrefde, and wæran styriende and onwende, for þam ege and fyrhto þe hi gegripon,

6   for þam him com swa hrædlic sar and wracu swa þam cennendan wife cymð færlic sar; and hy wæron gebrytte swa hrædlice swa swa hradu yst windes scip tobrycð on þam san- dum, neah þære byrig þe Tarsit hatte (seo is on þam lande þe Cilicia hatte).

7   Swa swa we geo-geare hyrdon þæt God dyde be urum fæderum, swa we geseoð nu þæt he deð be us on þæs Godes byrig, þe myclu wundru wyrcð, þæt ys, on ures Godes byrig, þe he gestaþelode on ecnesse.

8   We onfoð, Drihten, þinre mild-heortnesse on middum þinum temple.

9   Swa swa þin nama is tobræd and gemyclad geond ealle eorðan, swa ys eac þin lof; þin swiðre hand is full riht- wisnesse.

10   Blissie nu Syon se munt, and fægnie Iudea cyn, for þi- num domum, Drihten.

11   Hweorfað ymb Sion and gað ofer þone weall Hierusa- lem and ymbutan, heriað God mid ælces cynnes heringe, and lufiað hine, and secgað his wundru on þam torrum and on þam wig-husum þære byrig; and fæstniað eower mod on his wundrum, and dælað hire weorðias swiðe rihte, and secgað swylc wundru eowrum gingrum, þæt hy hy mægen eft secgan of cynne on cynn,

12   for þam he is ure God on ecnesse and on weorulda wor- uld, and he ræt us and recð on weorulda weorld.

4   ⁵ Behold! You saw how threateningly kings of the earth were assembled, and how they came together.

5   ⁶ But as soon as they witnessed God's wonders, they were amazed and disturbed, agitated and overturned, ⁷ by the terror and dread that seized them,

6   because pains and suffering came on them, as sudden as unexpected pangs on a woman in childbirth; ⁸ and they were broken in pieces, as abruptly as a fast-moving storm breaks asunder a ship on the sands, near the city called Tarshish (it is located in the country which is called Cilicia).

7   ⁹ Just as we heard what God did for our ancestors long ago, so we see now what he does for us in the city of that God who works great wonders, that is, in the city of our God, which he established forever.

8   ¹⁰ We receive, Lord, your mercy in the middle of your temple.

9   ¹¹ Just as your name is broadcast and magnified throughout all the earth, so is your praise also; your right hand is full of justice.

10   ¹² Let Mount Zion rejoice now, and Juda's people exult because of your judgments, Lord.

11   ¹³ Go around Zion and over and around Jerusalem's walls, praise God with the tribute of every tribe, and love him, and declare his wonders in the city's towers and fortifications; ¹⁴ and fix your minds on his wonders, and portion out its dwellings very fairly, and relate such wonders to your children, so that they can retell them from generation to generation,

12   ¹⁵ because he is our God, for ever and ever, and he will govern and rule us, for ever and ever.

Psalm 48

Dauid sang þysne eahta and feowertigoðan sealm, on þam he lærde ealle men, ge on his dagum ge æfter his dagum, þæt hy hy upp ne ahofen for heora welum, and þæt hy ongeaton þæt hi ne mihton þa welan mid him lædan heonon of weorulde, and eac he lærde þæt þa ðearfan hy ne forðohton, ne ne wenden þæt God heora ne rohte; and eac he witgode þæt ealle rihtwise menn sceoldon þæt ylce læran; and eac þæt Crist wolde þæt ylce læran þonne he come.

1   Gehyrað nu þas word, ealle þeoda, and onfoð heora mid eowrum earum, ealle þa þe eorðan buiað,

2   and ealle þa þe þæron acende synt, and eall manna bearn, ægðer ge welige ge heane.

3   Min muð wile sprecan wisdom and seo smeaung minre heortan fore-þancolnesse.

4   Ic onhylde min earan to þam bispellum þæs ðe me innan lærð, and ic secge on þys sealme hwæs ic wylle ascian,

5   and hwæt ic ondræde on þæm yflan dagum, þæt is, unrihtwisnes minra hoa and ealles mines flæsces, sio me hæfð utan behringced.

6   Ongitan nu, þa þe truwiað heora agenum mægene and þære mycelnesse hiora speda gylpað and wuldrað:

Psalm 48

David sang this forty-eight psalm, in which he advised all
people, both in and after his time, not to puff themselves up
on account of their wealth, and to understand that they
could not carry it with them from this world, and he also ex-
horted the needy not to despair, or think that God did not
care about them; and also he prophesied that all just people
would teach the same thing; and also that Christ would
teach the same when he came.

1   2 All peoples, hear these words now, and let all you who
inhabit the earth lend an ear to them,

2   3 and all who are born here, and all humankind, both
wealthy and poor.

3   4 My mouth will speak wisdom, and my heart will express thoughts about the future.

4   5 I will listen carefully to the parables of that message
which instructs me inwardly, and declare in this psalm what
I intend to investigate,

5   6 and what I fear in the evil days, that is, the iniquity
of my heels and all my flesh, which has encircled me from
without.

6   7 Let those who trust in their own power, boasting and
glorying in the abundance of their riches, now understand:

7   þæt nan broðor oþres sawle nele alysan of helle, ne ne mæg (þeah he wylle), gif he sylf nanwuht nyle, ne ne deð to goode þa hwile þe he her byð. Gylde for þy him sylf and alyse his sawle þa hwyle ðe he her sy, for þam se broðor oþþe nyle oððe ne mæg, gif he sylf na ne onginð to tilianne þæt he þæt weorð agife to alysnesse his sawle. Ac þæt ys wyrse þæt fullneah ælc mann þæs tiolað fram þæm anginne his lifes oþ þæne ende, hu he on ecnesse swincan mæge,

8   and næfð nænne forðanc be his deaðe, þonne he gesyhð þa welegan and þa weoruld-wisan sweltan. Se unwisa and se dysega forweorþað him ætsamne,

9   and læfað fremdum heora æhte. (Þeah hy gesibbe hæbben, hy beð him swyðe fremde, þonne hi nan good æfter him ne doð.) Ac heora byrgen byð heora hus on ecnesse,

10   and heora geteld of cynne on cynn; and hi nemnað hiora land and hiora tunas be heora naman.

11   Þa hwile þe mon on are and on anwealde byð, næfð he fullneah nan andgyt nanes goodes; ac onhyred dysegum neatum, swa hi eac beoð him swyðe gelice.

12   Ac þes weg, and þeos orsorgnes þyses andweardan lifes, him fet witu on þam toweardan, for þam heo on last tiliað to cwemanne Gode and mannum mid wordum næs mid weorcum, ne furþum gearone willan nabbað to þam weorce.

13   Mid swylcum monnum byð hell gefylled swa swa fald mid sceapum, and se deað hy forswylcð on ecnesse.

7   [8] that no brother is willing to free the soul of another brother from hell, nor is able (even if he wanted to), if that second brother himself does not desire it at all, or fails to behave morally while he lives on earth. [9] So, let the latter make compensation for himself and save his soul, while he lives on earth, because the first brother either is unwilling, or unable, if he himself does not begin to attempt to pay the price for his soul's redemption. But even worse is that almost everyone seeks, from birth to death, [10] the means whereby he can perpetually toil at work,

8   [11] entertaining no consideration of his own demise, when he witnesses the wealthy and the worldly-wise die. The foolish and the insouciant will perish simultaneously,

9   leaving their possessions to strangers. (Although they may have relatives, the latter will be very much strangers to them, since they do nothing beneficial for them.) [12] Moreover, their sepulcher will be their house forever,

10   and their tabernacle from generation to generation; and their descendants will rename their lands and their towns with their own names.

11   [13] As long as people live in distinction and power, they have almost no understanding of what is good; instead, they imitate senseless beasts, so that they too become very like beasts.

12   [14] But this conduct, and the prosperity of this present life, will produce punishments for them in the next, because ultimately they try to please God and man with words not with deeds, nor do they even bring a ready will to that task.

13   [15] With such people is hell filled, just as an enclosure with sheep, and death will devour them forever.

14 And sona on þam ylcan morgene þa rihtwisan heora wealdað, and hyra fultum and hyra anweald forealdað on helle, for þæm hy beoð adrifene of heora wuldre.

15 Ac God, þeah, alyst mine sawle of helle handa, þeah ic þyder cume, þonne he me underfehð.

16 Ne wundrige ge na, ne ne andgiað on þone welegan, þeah he welig seo geworden, and þeah gemanigfealdod sy þæt wuldor his huses,

17 for þam þe he ðyder ne læt þæt eall mid him, þonne he heonan færþ, ne hit him æfter þyder ne færeð.

18 For þæm he hæfde his heofon-rice her on eorðan, þa him nanes willan næs forwyrnd her, ne nanes lustes on þysse weorulde, for þam he nyste him nænne þanc, ne Gode ne mannum, þæs ðe him man sealde (syððan he hit hæfde), butan þa ane hwile þe hit him man sealde,

19 for þam he færð þær his fore-gengan beoð, þæt is, to helle, þær he næfre nan leoht ne gesyhð.

20 Ac þas spræce ne ongit na swylc mann, þonne he byð on welan and on weorðscipe, and onhyreð þonne dysegum neatum, and byð him swiðe gelic geworden.

14 And on that same morning, with no delay, the just will dominate them, and their support and power will deteriorate in hell, because they will be removed from their glory.

15 [16] Despite that, God will rescue my soul from the power of hell, although I should come there, he will then gather me up.

16 [17] Do not admire or be at all envious of the rich person, even if he has acquired wealth and the splendor of his house is magnified,

17 [18] because he will not carry all that wealth with him to the other side, when he journeys from here, nor will it travel after him there.

18 [19] Because he enjoyed his paradise here on earth, during which time no desire or inclination was denied him in this world, and because he did not feel any gratitude toward either God or man for what was given to him (once he possessed it), except for that single occasion when it was given to him,

19 [20] as a result he will journey where his predecessors dwell, that is, to hell, where he will never see light.

20 [21] But a person of such disposition does not understand this speech at all, living as he does in wealth and honor, yet imitating insensate beasts, so that he is become very like them.

Psalm 49

Dauid sang þysne nigen and feowertigoðan sealm be ægrum tocyme Cristes; on þam sealme he cydde hu egeslice Crist þreatode Iudeas and ealle heora gelican þe þæt ylce doð þæt hy dydon, for þam hy sealdon ælmesan and ofredon Gode heora nytenu, næs hy sylfe.

1   Dryhtna Drihten wæs sprecende þæt he wolde cuman to eorðan (swa he eft dyde), and cliopode eorðlice men to geleafan.

2   Fram sunnan up-gange oð hire setl-gang, of Sion aras se wlite his andwlitan.

3   And eft cymð se ylca God swiðe openlice (þæt ys, ure God), and he þonne naht ne swugað.

4   Fyr byrnð for his ansyne and ymb hine utan strange stormas.

5   And he cleopað to þæm heofone, hæt hine þæt he hine fealde swa swa boc; and he bebyt þære eorðan þæt heo todæle hyre folc,

6   and gegadrie on þa swyðran hand his halgan, þa þe heoldon his bebodu ofer ælcere offrunga.

7   Heofonas bodiað his rihtwisnesse, for þam se God is demend, and þonne cwyð to him:

8   "Gehyrað nu, min folc; ic sprece to eow Israelum, and ic eow secge soðlice, for þam ic eom Drihten eower God.

Psalm 49

David sang this forty-ninth psalm about both of Christ's comings; in it he made known how sternly Christ threatened the Jews and all those like them who do the same thing which they did, for they gave alms and sacrificed to God their beasts, not themselves.

1   [1] The Lord of lords said that he would come to the earth (as he subsequently did), and summoned earth's people to belief.

2   From the rising of the sun until its setting, [2] the beauty of his face rose up out of Zion.

3   [3] And the same God (that is, our God) will come again very openly, and then he will not be silent at all.

4   Fire will burn before him and powerful storms around him.

5   [4] And he will invoke the sky, commanding it to fold itself like a book; and he will order the earth to separate its inhabitants,

6   [5] and to gather on the right hand his holy ones, those who observed his commands above every other kind of offering.

7   [6] The heavens will declare his justice, because that God is judge, and will then say to them:

8   [7] "Listen now, my people; to you Israelites I will speak, and do so truthfully, because I am the Lord your God.

9   Ne þreage ic eow na æfter offrunga, for ðam eowra offrunga synt symle beforan minre ansyne.

10   Ne onfo ic na of eowrum huse cealfas, ne of eowrum
heordum buccan,

11   for þam min synt ealra wuda wildeor, and ealra duna
ceap and nytenu, and oxan;

12   ic can ealle heofones fugelas, and eall eorþan wlite is
mid me.

13   Gif me hingreð, ne seofige ic þæt na to eow, for ðam
min is eall earðan ymb-hwyrft and eall hyre innuncg.

14   Wene ge þæt ic ete þæra fearra flæsc, oþþe þara buc-
cena blod drince?

15   Ac ofriað Gode þa offrunge lofes, and gyldað þam hyh-
stan eower gehat,

16   and cleopiað to me on þam dagum eowra earfoða;
þonne gefriðie ic eow, and ge weorðiað me."

17   Ac to þam synfullan cwyð God: "For hwy bodast þu
mine rihtwisnesse, oððe for hwy onfehst þu on þinne fulan
muð mine æ,

18   for þæm þu hatodest symle leornunga and forwurpe
min word symle underbæc fram þe?

19   Gif þu gesawe þeof, þu urne mid him, næs na ongean
hine; and þu dydest þe to þam woh-hæmendum.

20   Þin muð wæs symle ful unrihtes, and þin tunge ontynde
facn.

21   Þu sæte ongean þinne broðor and tældest hine, and
worhtest wrohte betwuh þe and þinre modor suna oðrum.

22   Eall þis yfel þu dydest, and ic swugode and þolode
swylce ic hit nyste; þu ræswedest swiðe unryhte þæt ic wære
þin gelica, swylce ic ne meahte þe forgyldan swylces edlean.

9   ⁸ By no means will I reprove you about offerings, since they are always before me.

10   ⁹ I will not accept calves from your house, nor he-goats from your herds,

11   ¹⁰ since the wild animals of all the woods, and the cattle and animals of all the hills, and the oxen are already mine;

12   ¹¹ I know all the birds of the sky, and the earth's entire beauty resides in me.

13   ¹² If I am hungry, I do not complain at all about that to you, because all the earth's compass and contents are mine.

14   ¹³ Do you really think that I would eat the flesh of those bulls, or drink the blood of those he-goats?

15   ¹⁴ Instead, offer to God the offering of praise, and fulfill your vows to the Most High,

16   ¹⁵ and invoke me in the time of your troubles; I will deliver you then, and you will honor me."

17   ¹⁶ But to sinners God will say: "Why do you proclaim my justice, or why do you accept my law with your foul mouths,

18   ¹⁷ seeing that you have always hated instruction and constantly tossed my words backward away from you?

19   ¹⁸ If you saw a thief, you would run with him, not away from him; moreover, you gave yourselves over to adulterers.

20   ¹⁹ Your mouth was constantly spilling over with iniquity, and your tongue revealed deceits.

21   ²⁰ You sat in opposition to your brother and slandered him, and caused strife between you and another son of your mother.

22   ²¹ You perpetrated all this evil, yet I was silent and patient, as if unaware of it; you very unjustly supposed that I was like you, as if I was incapable of exacting suitable retribution from you.

23   Ic þe þreage nu, and stæle beforan þe, and þe cyðe eal
þas yflu." Gehyrað nu ðiss and ongytað ealle þa þe Godes
forgytað, þy læs he eow gegripe, for þam nys nan oþer þe
eow mæge gefriðian of his handa:

24   "seo ofrung lofes me licað swiðost and me eac swyðost
weorþað, and on þære offrunga is se rihtwisa weg." On þære
ic getæce Godes hælo eallum þam þe swa doð.

Psalm 50

Dauid sang þysne fiftigoðan sealm, hreowsiende for ðam
ærendum þe Nathan se witga him sæde, þæt wæs þæt he
hæfde gesyngod wið Ureus þone Cyðþiscan, þa he hine
beswac for his wifes þingum, þære nama wæs Bersabe; and
heac he witgode on þam sealme be Israela folce, hu hy
sceoldon hreowsian hyra hæft-nyd on Babilonia; and eac be
Sancte Paule þam apostole; and be ælcum rihtwisum men he
witgode, hu hy sceoldon syngian and eft hreowsian. He
cwæð:

1   Miltsa me, Drihten, æfter þinre mycelan mild-
heortnesse,

2   and æfter þære menigu þinra mild-heortnessa, adilega
mine unrihtwisnessa.

23   I will reprove you now, and make accusations against you, and reveal to you all these evil doings." ²² Those who are oblivious of God, listen now, and understand this advice, lest he seize you, because there is no one else who can free you from his grip:

24   ²³ "the offering of praise pleases me most and also honors me most, and in that lies the upright way." In that kind of sacrifice I will teach God's salvation to all those who so behave.

Psalm 50

David sang this fiftieth psalm, repenting on account of the message which Nathan the prophet announced to him, which was that he had sinned against Uriah the Hittite, when he betrayed him on account of his wife, whose name was Bathsheba; and also he prophesied about the people of Israel, how they would regret their captivity in Babylon; and also about Saint Paul the apostle; and he prophesied about every just person, that they would sin and afterward repent. He said:

1   ³ Have mercy on me, Lord, in your great compassion,

2   and in the abundance of your mercies, blot out my iniquities.

3   And aðweah me clænran from minum unrihtwisnessum þonne ic ær ðysse scylde wæs, and of þysse scamleasan scylde geclænsa me,

4   for þam mine unryhtwisnessa ic ongyte, and mina synna beoð symle beforan me on minum gemynde.

5   Wið þe ænne ic gesyngode, and ic dyde yfel beforan ðe; wið þe ænne ic sceal þæt betan, for þæm þu ana eart rihtwis and oferswiðest ealle þonne ðu demst.

6   Nis hit nan wundor þeah þu sy god and ic yfel, for ðam þu wast þæt ic wæs mid unrihtwisnesse onfangen, and min modor me gebær mid synne.

7   Ic wat þæt þu symle lufast rihtwisnesse and me sealdest mænega gyfa ðines wisdomes (þa gyfa synt beheleda and uncuþa manegum oðrum).

8   Ac bespreng me nu mid þinum haligdome swa swa mid ysopon, þæt ic beo geclænsod; and aðweah me þæt ic sy hwitra þonne snaw.

9   Syle minre gehyrnesse gefean and blisse, þæt ic gehyre þæt ic wylle, and eac oðre gehyron be me þæt þæt ic wilnige, swa swa hy ær gehyrdon þæt þæt ic nolde, þæt þonne mæge unrote mod blissian . . .

3   ⁴ And wash me cleaner from my iniquities than I was before this sin, and cleanse me of this scandalous sin,

4   ⁵ because I recognize my iniquities, and my sins are always before me in my mind.

5   ⁶ Against you alone I have sinned, and I did evil in your sight; to you alone I must make amends for that, because you alone are just and will dominate all people when you judge.

6   ⁷ No wonder you are perfect and I evil, since, as you know, I was conceived in iniquity, and my mother gave birth to me in sin.

7   ⁸ I know that you always love justice and have given me many gifts from the store of your wisdom (those gifts are concealed from and unknown to many others).

8   ⁹ But sprinkle me now with your holiness as with hyssop, so that I may be cleansed; and wash me, so that I will become whiter than snow.

9   ¹⁰ Grant to my hearing joy and gladness, so that I may hear what I desire, and also others may hear about me what I desire, just as they previously heard what I did not desire to hear, so that my troubled heart can then rejoice . . .

METRICAL PSALMS

Psalm 51

6   . . . fore ænigre   egesan næfde,
ne him fultum þær   fæstne gelyfde;
ac he on his welan spede   wræste getruwode,
and on idel gylp   ealra geornost.

7   Ic þonne swa ele-beam   up weaxende
on Godes huse   ece gewene
and on milde mod   mines Drihtnes,
and me þæt to worulde   wat to helpe.

8   Ic þe andette   awa to feore
on þære worulde   ðe þu geworhtest her,
for þan þu eart se gooda,   gleaw on gesyhðe,
þe þinne held curan,   þara haligra.

Psalm 52

1   On his heortan cwæð   unhydig sum,
ungleawlice,   þætte God nære;
heo onsceoniendlice   syndon gewordene,
and heora willan   wraðe besmitene.

2   Næs þa god-doend,   se þe god wiste,
ne an furðum   ealra wære.

Psalm 51

6   9 . . . he entertained no fear of anything, nor did he believe in steadfast help for himself at that time; instead, he firmly trusted in the abundance of his wealth and in vain boasting, altogether most eagerly.

7   10 I, however, like a flourishing olive tree, trust perpetually in God's house and my Lord's merciful spirit, knowing that it will be my support forever.

8   11 I will acknowledge you always and forever in the world which you created here, because you are the virtuous one, wise in the sight of the holy ones who have chosen your protection.

Psalm 52

1   1 A certain foolish man imprudently said in his heart that there was no God; 2 these people have become abominable, and their intentions defiled by cruelty.

2   At that time there was no one who did good, who was conscious of good, not even a single one out of all of them.

3   Þa of heofenum beseah   halig Drihten
ofer manna bearn   hwæðer his mihta ða
andgyt ænig   ealra hæfde,
oððe God wolde   georne secan.

4   Ealle heo on ane   idelnesse
symle besegan;   þa wæs soð nan mann
þe god wolde   georne wyrcan,
ne an furþum   ealra wære.

5   Ac ge þæs ealle ne magon   andgyt habban,
þe unrihtes   elne wyrceað
and min folc fretað   swa fælne hlaf;
ne hio God wyllað   georne ciegan;
þær hio forhtigað   frecnes egesan
æniges ne þurfon.

6   For þam manna ban   mihtig Drihten
liste tosceadeð   þa him liciað;
beoð þa gehyrwede   þe forhycggeað God.

7   Hwylc Israela   ece hælu
syleð of Sione,   nymðe sylfa God,
þonne he his folc   fægere alyseð
of hæft-nyde,   halig Drihten?

8   Þonne Iacob byð   on glædum sælum,
and Israelas   ealle bliðe.

3   ³ Then the holy Lord looked down from heaven on humankind to see whether any one of them had then any understanding of his powers, or earnestly desired to seek God.

4   ⁴ All of them continually sank into the same vacuity; at that time no just person lived who keenly desired to do good, not even a single one of all of them.

5   ⁵ But all of you, who blatantly perpetrate evil and devour my people like fine bread, are incapable of understanding that; ⁶ nor do they wish to invoke God earnestly; they are afraid where they have no good reason to fear any danger.

6   So, the mighty Lord skillfully scatters the bones of those who indulge themselves; they will be despised because they reject God.

7   ⁷ Who from Zion will grant eternal salvation to the Israelites, except God himself, the holy Lord, when he kindly releases his people from captivity?

8   Then Jacob will live in happy times, and all Israel be joyful.

Psalm 53

1   On þinum þam haligan naman,   gedo me halne,
                                                      God;
    alys me fram laðum   þurh þin leofe mægen.

2   God, min gebed   gearuwe gehyre,
    and earum onfoh   min agen word,

3   for þam me fremde oft   facne gestodon;
    sohtan mine sawle   swiðe strange,
    and na heom God setton   gleawne on gesyhðe.

4   Efne, me þonne God   gleawe fultumeð;
    is andfengea   ece Drihten
    sawle minre,   he me swican ne wile.

5   Afyr me fæcne yfel   feonda minra,
    and hi soðfæst toweorp   syððan wide.

6   Ic ðe lustum   lace cweme,
    and naman þinne   niode swylce
    geara andette,   for ðon ic hine goodne wat.

7   For þon þu me alysdest,   lifes Ealdor,
    of earfoðum   eallum symble,
    ealle mine fynd   eagum ofersawe.

Psalm 53

1   ³ God, in your holy name, save me; release me from enemies through your respected power.

2   ⁴ God, hear my prayer promptly, and give ear to my very words,

3   ⁵ because strangers have often attacked me deceitfully; exceedingly powerful people sought my soul, and they did not keep a wise God in their sight.

4   ⁶ Truly! God will ably help me then; the eternal Lord is my soul's support, he will not deceive me.

5   ⁷ Remove from me the treacherous evil of my enemies, and afterward in your justice dissipate them widely.

6   ⁸ I will gladly please you with an offering, and promptly acknowledge your name also, because I know it to be good.

7   ⁹ For you, Lord of life, constantly freed me from all tribulations, you kept an eye on my enemies.

Psalm 54

1 Gehyr min gebed,   halig Drihten;
ne forseoh æfre   sariges bene;
beheald me holdlice   and gehyr me eac.

2 Grimme ic eom begangen,   forðon ic gnornige
and me forhtige   feondes stefne
and fyrenfulra   fæcne niðas,

3 for ðam me on sah   unrihtes feala;
wurdon me þa on yrre   yfele and hefige.

4 Ys me on hreðre heah   heorte gedrefed,
and me fealleð   on fyrhtu deaðes.

5 Egsa me and fyrhtu   ealne forcwomon,
and me beþeahton   þeostru nið-grim.

6 Ic þa on mode cwæð: "Hwa me sealde
to fleogenne   fiðeru swa culfran,
and ic þonne ricene   reste syððan?"

7 Efne, ic feor gewite,   fleame dæle,
—and on westene   wunode lange—
bide þæs beornes   þe me bete eft
modes mindom   and mægenes hreoh.

8 Hat nu todælan,   Drihten usser,
heora geðeode   geond þas woruld wide,
for ðon ic þær on unriht   oft locade,
and wiðer-cwyda   wearn gehyrde;
drugon þæt on burgum   dæges and nihtes.

Psalm 54

1   2 Holy Lord, hear my prayer, never despise the request of the one who grieves; 3 faithfully keep watch over me and hear me also.

2   I am sorely afflicted, so I lament and am made fearful 4 by the enemy's clamor and the treacherous hostility of sinners,

3   for many an injustice has befallen me; in their anger they became malicious and burdensome to me then.

4   5 My heart is troubled exceedingly within me, and dread of death descends on me.

5   6 Terror and fear took hold of me all over, and stark darkness enveloped me.

6   7 Then I said to myself: "Who gave me wings to fly like a dove, so that I might then quickly rest afterward?"

7   8 Truly! I will go far, engage in flight—for I have long lived in the desert—9 I will await that hero who will afterward heal within me the lack of mental courage and agitation induced by violence.

8   10 Our Lord, command now that their languages be scattered widely throughout this world, because there I have often observed injustice, and listened to a cacophony of contradictions; they carried out that activity in cities, 11 day and night.

9 Þunie him gewinnes wearn   ofer wealles hrof,
   and heom on midle wese   man and inwit,
   and unsoðfæstnys   ealle wealde.

10 Næfre on his weorþige   wea aspringe,
   mearce man-sceat,   man inwides;
   for þon gif me min feond   fæcne wyrgeð,
   ic þæt abere   bliðe mode.

11 Þeah þe þa ealle   ðe me a feodon,
   wordum wyrigen   and wearn sprecan,
   ic me wið heora hete   hyde sneome.

12 Þu eart se man   þe me wære
   on anmede,   and æghwæs cuð
   latteow lustum;   and wyt gelome eac
   æton swetne mete   samed ætgædere,
   and on Godes huse   gangan swylce
   mid geþeahtunge   þine and mine.

13 Hi ofer cume   unþinged deað;
   astigon heo on helle   heonan lifigende,

14 for ðam on heora gast-husum   is gramlic inwit,
   and on hiora midle   man inwit-stæf.

15 Ic soðlice   to sylfum Drihtne
   cleopode on corðre,   and me cuðlice
   gehyrde   hælend Drihten.

16 Ic on æfenne,   eac on mergenne
   and on midne dæg,   mægene sæcge
   and bodie   þæt þu bliðe me
   mine stefne   stiðe gehyre.

9   May a heap of trouble for them be lifted up over the rampart's summit, and may wickedness and deceit be present in their midst, [12] and injustice dominate all of them.

10   May misfortune never cease on its street, usury in its territory, the injustice of deceit; [13] so, even if my enemy curses me exceedingly, I will happily endure that.

11   Although all those who perpetually hate me should curse me with their words and utter reproaches, I may quickly hide myself from their hate.

12   [14] You are the one who was in accord with me, and in every respect a pleasantly familiar leader; [15] and we two also frequently ate sweet food together, and likewise walked in God's house in mutual agreement.

13   [16] May sudden death come upon them; still alive, may they go from here down into hell,

14   because cruel deceit dwells in their guesthouses, and wicked malice in their midst.

15   [17] I cried out sincerely to the same Lord from a crowd, and the savior Lord kindly heard me.

16   [18] In the evening, in the morning and at midday also, I will forcefully declare and announce that you will for my sake gladly and effectively hear my voice.

17   A ðu symle   sawle mine
lustum alyse,   laðum wiðferige,
for ðon me manige ymb   mægene syrewað.

18   Þæt gehyreð God   and hi gehyneð eac,
þe ær worulde wæs   and nu wunað ece.

19   Nis him onwendednes   on woruld-life,
ne him Godes fyrhtu   georne ondrædað.
Heo besmitað   swylce his sylfes
þa gewitnesse,   þær hi woh fremedon;
for ðon hi synt on yrre   ut adælde,
ne hi sylfe wel   geseon æfre,
for ðon hit wæs his heortan   gehygde neah.

20   Hi word hira   wel gesmyredon
ele anlicast,   eft gewurdon
on gescot-feohta   scearpe garas.

21   Sete on Drihten   þin soð gehygd;
he þe butan fracoðum   fedeð syððan.

22   Ne syleð he soðfæstum   syððan to feore
þæt him yþende mod   innan hreðre;
ðu arlease   ealle gelædest
on soðe forwyrd   seaðes deopes.

23   Se blod-hreowa wer   bealu-inwites
fæcne gefylled,   ne fæger lif
on middum feore   gemeteð ahwær;
ic me on minne Drihten   deorne getreowige.

17   ¹⁹ May you willingly redeem my soul always and ever, rescuing it from odious people, because many have lain snares mightily around me.

18   ²⁰ God will hear that prayer and humble them too, he who existed before the world and now lives eternally.

19   During this earthly life, they make no change, nor do they seriously entertain a fear of God. ²¹ When they perpetrated iniquity, they also defile his very covenant; ²² consequently, they are cut off in his anger, nor are they themselves ever regarded positively, because that contract was close to the thought of his heart.

20   They skillfully smoothed their words like oil, which afterward became sharp javelins in spear battles.

21   ²³ Confide your true thoughts to the Lord; he will then feed you without insult.

22   He will never after impart to the just person that wavering disposition within his heart; ²⁴ you will lead all the wicked into the deep pit's true destruction.

23   The bloodthirsty person filled with the guile of malicious deceit, will not find in his lifetime a pleasant existence anywhere; but I will trust myself to my beloved Lord.

Psalm 55

1 Miltsa me Drihten,   for ðon me man tredeð,
and me ealne dæg   mid unrihte
fynd onfeohtað   þurh facen-searu,

2 and me fæcne tredað   feondas mine;
doð þæt ealne dæg   fram ær-mergene.

3 For ðon monige synd   ðe to me feohtað,
wene ic me wraðe to ðe,   wuldres Drihten.

4 Ic Wealdend-God   wordum herige,
and on God swylce   georne gelyfe,
þæt minre spræce   sped folgie
æghwæs ealne dæg;   eac ic swylce
on God Drihten   gearewe gewene;
nis me ege mannes   for ahwæðer.

5 Hwæt, me ealne dæg   mine agen word
sylfne socon,   swyþe oncuðon;
and wiðer me   wæran georne
on yfel heora geðeaht   ealle onwende.

6 On eardiað, þa ðe swa þenceað
þæt heo gehyden   hælun mine;
swa min sawl bad   þæt ðu swylce heo
for nahwæðer   nowiht hæle;
on yrre þu folc   eall geðreatast.

7 Ic nu leofum Gode   lif min secge,
sette on ðinre gesyhðe   sarige tearas,
swa ic ðe on gehate   hæfde geneahhige.

Psalm 55

1   [2] Lord, have pity on me, because people trample on me, and enemies unjustly assault me all day by means of treachery,

2   [3] and my enemies tread maliciously on me; all day, [4] from early morning, they do that.

3   Because many oppose me, I expect my support from you, Lord of glory.

4   [5] I will praise the sovereign God with words, and also eagerly believe in God, so that success in every form accompanies my speech all day; moreover, I will also trust entirely in the Lord God; I have no fear of anyone on any account.

5   [6] They disparaged me all day long, excessively reviled my very own words; and all their plans were sharply perverted into evil against me.

6   [7] There they dwell, those who thus plot to conceal my heels; so my soul anticipated [8] that you also would not save them on any account; you will afflict all that people in your anger.

7   [9] Now I will relate my life to that beloved God, will shed mournful tears in your sight, just as I frequently promised you.

8   Þonne on hinderling   hweorfað mine
     feondas fæcne,   ðonne ic me freoðu to ðe
     wordum wilnige;   ic wat and can,
     þæt þu min God   gleawe wære.

9   Ic on God min word   georne herige,
     and on God swylce   georne gelyfe;
     and ic ealne dæg   ecne Drihten
     wordum weorðige,   ne me wiht an siteð
     egesan awiht   æniges mannes.

10   On me synd, mihtig God,   þæt ic þe min gehat
     on herenesse   hyldo gylde,
     for þon ðu mine sawle   of swylt-deaðes
     laþum wiðlæddest,   dydest lof stunde,
     aweredest mine eagan   wraðum tearum,
     and mine fet   fæle beweredest,
     þæt ic gearewe   Gode licode
     on lifigendra   leohte eallum.

Psalm 56

1   Miltsa min, God,   and me milde weorð,
     for þon min sawel on þe   swyðe getryweð,
     and ic on fægerum scuan   fiðera ðinra
     gewicie,   oð þæt gewite forð
     and unriht me   eall beglide.

2   Heonan ic cleopige   to Heah-Gode
     and to Wealdend-Gode,   ðe me wel dyde.

8   10 Whenever I ask in words for protection for myself from you, my treacherous enemies will turn backward; I know and understand that you were truly my God.

9   11 I will eagerly shower my words of praise on God, and also earnestly believe in him; and all day I will honor the eternal Lord with my words, nor will the slightest fear of anyone weigh on me at all.

10   12 Mighty God, on me lies the obligation to fulfill my vow to you to praise your protection, 13 because you rescued my soul from the agonies of death, provided protection at once, shielded my eyes from bitter tears, and faithfully guarded my feet, so that I could readily please God in the full light of the living.

Psalm 56

1   2 God, have pity on me and be kind to me, because my soul trusts mightily in you, and I nestle in the pleasant protection of your wings, until wickedness departs and fully passes me by.

2   3 From now on I will invoke the supreme God and the sovereign deity who treated me well.

3   He þa of heofenum   hider onsende
þe me alysde,   laþum wiðferede,
sealde on edwit   þe me ær trædan.

4   Sende mihtig God   his milde gehigd
and his soðfæst mod   samod ætgædere,
and mine sawle   sona alysde
of leon hwelpum   reðe gemanan;
wæs ic slæpende,   sare gedrefed.

5   Synd me manna bearn   mihtigum toðum
wæpen-strælas,   þa me wundedon;
wæron hyra tungan getale   teonan gehwylcre
and to yfele gehwam   ungemet scearpe.

6   Ahefe þe ofer heofenas,   halig Drihten;
is wuldur ðin   wide and side
ofer ðas eorþan   ealle mære.

7   Fotum heo minum   fæcne grine
grame gearwodon,   and geornlice
mine sawle   swyðe onbigdon.

8   Hi deopne seað   dulfon widne,
þær ic eagum   on locade,
and hi on ðone ylcan   eft gefeollan.

9   Gearo is min heorte   þæt ic Gode cweme
gearo is min heorte   þæt ic Gode swylce
sealmas singe,   soð-word sprece.

10   Aris, wuldur min,   wyn-*psalterium;*
and ic on ær-mergene   eac arise,
and min hearpe   herige Drihten.

3   [4] He then sent to this world from the heavens the one who redeemed me, rescued me from misfortunes, gave over to disgrace those who formerly trampled me.

4   That mighty God sent his compassionate forethought and his trustworthy purpose, both together, [5] and he at once rescued my soul from lion cubs, bloodthirsty bands; I was sleeping, sorely troubled.

5   The children of humankind with their powerful teeth are the arms and arrows that wounded me; their tongues were quick to every kind of injury and exceedingly sharp for any kind of evildoing.

6   [6] Holy Lord, raise yourself up above the heavens; your glory is famed far and wide throughout all this earth.

7   [7] With malice they prepared treacherous snares for my feet, and in their eagerness severely subdued my soul.

8   They dug a pit deep and wide, which I viewed with my own eyes, but afterward they fell into the same pit.

9   [8] My heart is ready to please God, and it is ready also to sing psalms to him, speaking words of truth.

10   [9] Rise up, my glory, a joyful psaltery, and I will too arise in the early morning, and my harp will praise the Lord.

11   Ic þe on folcum   frine Drihten
ecne andete;   eac geond þeode
sealmas singe   swiðe geneahhige,

12   for ðon þin mild-heortnes is   mycel wið
heofenas,
is ðin soðfæstnes   swylce wið wolcnum.

13   Ahafen þu eart ofer heofenas,   halig Drihten;
is ofer ealle   eorðan swylce
þines wuldres wlite   wide and side.

Psalm 57

1   Gif ge soð sprecan   symble wyllen,
demað manna bearn   domum rihtum.

2   Eft ge on heortan   hogedon inwit,
worhton wraðe;   for þan ðæs wite eft
on eowre handa   hefige geeode.

3   Ge firenfulle   fremde wurdon,
syððan hi on worlde   wæron acende,
and heo on life   lyge-word spæcon.

4   Yrre heom becume   anlic nædran,
ða aspide   ylde nemnað;
seo hi deafe deð,   dytteð hyre earan,
þæt heo nele gehyran   heah-galdor sum
þæt snotre men   singað wið attrum.

11   10 I will acknowledge you, noble and eternal Lord, among the nations; I will also sing psalms very frequently among the people,

12   11 because your mercy is great, extending to the heavens, your truth likewise as far as the clouds.

13   12 Holy Lord, you are exalted above the heavens; the splendor of your glory likewise is present over all the earth, far and wide.

Psalm 57

1   2 If you wish to speak the truth always, judge humankind with fair verdicts.

2   3 Once more you contemplated iniquity in your hearts, behaved cruelly; accordingly, punishment for that fell heavily upon you once more.

3   4 After they were born into the world, the wicked became alienated, and they told lies all during their lives.

4   5 May anger befall them, like that of the serpent which people call an asp; it makes itself deaf, it stops up its ears, 6 lest it hear some charm that skillful men chant against venom.

5   God heora toðas   grame gescæneð
þa hi on muðe   mycle habbað;
tolyseð leona mægen   lungre Drihten.

6   Ac hi forweorðan   wætere gelicost,
þonne hit yrnende   eorðe forswelgeð;
swa his bogan bendeð,   oðþæt bitere eft
adl on seteð,   swa his geearnuncg byð.

7   Swa weax melteð,   gif hit byð wearmum neah
fyre gefæstnad,   swa heo feallað on þæt;
hi sunnan ne geseoð   syððan æfre.

8   Ær ðon eowre treowu   telgum blowe,
wæstmum weaxe,   ær him wol becimeð,
þæt heo beoð on yrre   ealle forswelgene.

9   Soðfæst blissað,   þonne he sið ongan,
hu þa arleasan   ealle forweorðað;
and his handa ðwehð   on hæþenra
and þæra fyrenfulra   fæcnum blode.

10   And þonne man cweþeð   on his mod-sefan:
"Þis is wæstm   wises and goodes,
þe his soðfæst weorc   symble læste;
hi on eorðan God   ealle gedemeð."

Psalm 58

1   Ahrede me, halig God,   hefiges niðes
feonda minra,   ðe me feohtað to;
alys me fram laðum   þe me lungre on
risan willað,   nymðe þu me ræd geofe.

5   7 God will fiercely break the great teeth in their mouths; the Lord will quickly diffuse the power of lions.

6   8 But may they come to nothing, like water still running when the earth absorbs it; so, he bends his bow until sickness again bitterly oppresses him, as he deserves.

7   9 Just as wax melts if it is placed near a warm fire, so they will fall into that fire; they will never afterward see the sun.

8   10 Before your trees bloom with shoots, flourish with fruits, a pestilence will come on them, so that they will be completely swallowed up in his anger.

9   11 The righteous man will rejoice, whenever he sees ahead that the wicked utterly perish; and he will wash his hands in the treacherous blood of heathens and the wicked.

10   12 And then people will say to themselves: "This is the reward for the wise and virtuous person who has continually performed God's just works; God fully judges them here on earth."

Psalm 58

1   2 Holy Lord, deliver me from the burdensome hostility of my enemies, those who contend with me; release me from hateful people who will quickly rise up against me, unless you give me counsel.

2   Genere me fram niþe   naht-fremmendra,
    þe her unrihtes   ealle wyrceað;
    and me wið blod-hreowes weres   bealuwe
                         gehæle,

3   þi nu mine sawle,   swiþe bysige,
    feondas mine   fæcne ofþryhtun,
    and me strange eac   stundum ongunnon;
    ne me unrihtes on   awiht wistan,
    ne ic firene eac   fremde Drihtne.

4   Gif ic on unriht bearn,   ic þæs eft geswac;
    on minne gean-ryne,   aris ðu, Drihten, nu,
    and ðu sylfa gesyhst,   þæt ic swa dyde;
    þu eart mægena God,   mihtig Drihten,
    and Israela God   æghwær æt þearfe.

5   Beheald holdlice,   hu þu hraðe wylle
    geneosian   niða bearna
    ealra ðeoda   æghwær landes;
    ne þu hweðere on mode   milde weorðest
    eallum ðe unriht   elne wyrceað.

6   Hi æt æfene eft   in gecyrrað,
    þonne hy heardne   hungor þoliað,
    swa hundas ymbgað   hwommas ceastre.

7   Efne, hi habbað on muðe   milde spræce,
    is him on welerum   wrað sweord and scearp.

8   Þonne gehyreð hwylc,   hwæt hyra hyge seceð?
    And ðu hi, Drihten, dest   deope to bysmre,
    nafast þu for awiht   ealle þeoda.

2   ³ Redeem me from the evildoers' hate, those who unreservedly practice injustice on earth; and save me from the wickedness of the bloodthirsty one,

3   ⁴ because now my enemies, exceptionally diligent, cunningly oppressed my soul, and the powerful also fiercely attacked me; ⁵ nor could they impute to me any kind of iniquity, nor did I also commit any wrong against the Lord.

4   If I was involved in evil, I desisted from it afterward; ⁶ Lord, arise now to meet me, and you will see for yourself that I behaved so; mighty Lord, you are the God of hosts and entirely Israel's God in its difficulty.

5   Kindly witness how you will promptly visit the human race, all its peoples in every place; however, you will not be mildly disposed toward all those who fiercely perpetrate injustice.

6   ⁷ In the evening when they suffer cruel hunger, they will turn back in, just like dogs prowling the city corners.

7   ⁸ Indeed! They maintain polite speech in their mouths, yet they have a hostile and sharp sword on their lips.

8   Who, then, will hear what their minds seek? ⁹ But you, Lord, will humiliate them deeply, you will treat all nations as nothing.

9   Ic mine strengðe on ðe   strange gehealde,
for ðon þu me, God, eart   geara andfencgea,
and mild-heortnes   mines Drihtnes
me fægere becom   þær me wæs freondes þearf.

10   Min se goda God, ætyw me   þin agen good
for minum feondum,   þe me feale syndun;
ne do hy to deadan,   þy læs hi dollice
þinre æ geban   anforlæton.

11   Ac þu hi wide todrif   þurh þines wordes
                       mægen,
and hi wraðe toweorp,   wealdend min Drihten.

12   Ys hyra muðes scyld   man-worda feala,
ða hi mid welerum   wraðe aspræcan;
wærun hi on ofer-hygde   ealle gescende,
þa hi on lige   lange feredon;
for ðon hi on ende   yrre forgripeð,
and hi syþþan ne beoð   samod ætgædere.

13   Syððan hi wisslice witon   þætte wealdeð God
ofer middan-geard   manna cynnes,
and ealra eac   eorðan gemæru.

14   Hi on æfenne   eft gecyrrað,
and heardne eac   hungor ðoliað,
swa hundas ymbgað   hwommas ceastre.

15   Efne, hi to æte   ut gewitað,
þær hi towrecene   wide hweorfað;
gif hi fulle ne beoð,   fela gnorniað.

16   Ic þonne ðine strengþu   stundum singe
and ðin milde mod   morgena gehwylce,

9   [10] I will firmly entrust my strength to you, because for me you, God, are a ready defender, [11] and my Lord's compassion happily befell me when I needed a friend.

10   [12] Excellent God of mine, reveal to me your own good things in the sight of my enemies, who are numerous against me; do not put them to death lest they rashly disregard the decrees of your law.

11   Instead, disperse them widely with the power of your word, and put an end to them harshly, my Lord and ruler.

12   [13] The guilt in their mouths is the many wicked words which they perversely utter with their lips; in their arrogance they were totally confounded, when they engaged for a long time in lying; [14] as a result, anger will finally overwhelm them, and they will no longer continue together.

13   Later they will certainly come to understand that God reigns over humankind's world, even to the extremities of the earth.

14   [15] In the evening they will turn back again, while also enduring biting hunger, like dogs prowling the city corners.

15   [16] Indeed! They will venture out to eat, where, scattered widely, they will roam; if they do not have their fill, they will complain much.

16   [17] As for me, I will sing from time to time of your strength and of your compassionate soul each morning,

17   for ðon þu min andfengea   æghwær wære,
and ic helpe æt ðe   hæfde symble
þonne me costunge   cnysedon geneahhige.
Þu eart fultum min,   ic ðe fela singe,

18   for ðon þu me, God, eart   geara andfengea
and mild-heortnes,   mihtig Drihten.

Psalm 59

1   Þu us todrife,   Drihten user,
and us towurpe   geond wer-þeoda;
yrre us wurde   and eft milde.

2   Eorðan ðu onhrerdest,   ealle gedrefdest;
hæl hyre wunde,   nu heo ahrered is.

3   Feala ðu ætywdest   folce ðinum
heardra wisan,   and hi hraþe æfter
mid wynsume   wine drenctest.

4   Þu becnuncge   beorhte sealdest
þam þe ege ðinne   elne healdað,
þæt hi him gebeorgen   bogan and stræle;
and wæron alysede   leofe þine.

5   Do me þin seo swyðre hand   symle halne;
gehyr me, halig God.   Hwæt, ðu holdlice
on ðinre halignesse   her aspræce:
"And ic blissie   ba gedæle,
Sicimam et Conuallem, ða samod wæron
on Metiboris   mihtum spedige.

17 because you were my defender everywhere, and I constantly obtained your help whenever trials very much pressed on me. [18] You are my help to whom I will sing copiously,

18 because you, God, mighty Lord, are a ready defender and source of compassion for me.

Psalm 59

1 [3] God of ours, you scattered and devastated us throughout the nations; you became angry with us, and afterward compassionate.

2 [4] You disturbed the earth, troubled it all over; now that it is shaken, heal its injuries.

3 [5] You exposed your people to many kinds of hardship, but soon after you inebriated them with wine that induces merriment.

4 [6] You gave a clear warning to those who strongly maintain feelings of awe for you, to guard themselves from bow and arrow; and your beloved ones were saved.

5 [7] Let that right hand of yours make me safe always; holy God, hear me. [8] Behold! In your sanctuary here on earth, may you graciously declare: "And I will make glad both regions, Shechem and Convallem, which coexisted in Metiboris, prosperous with power.

6   Min is Galaad,   gleaw Mannases
      and Effrem ys   æðele strengþu
      heafdes mines   her on foldan.

7   Cyninc ys me   Iuda cuð;
      is me Moab   mines hyhtes hwer,
      and ic aðenige eac   on Idumea,
      min gescy sende,   and me syððan gedo
      Allophilas   ealle gewylde."

8   Hwylc gelædeð me   leofran on ceastre
      weallum beworhte;   hwa wyle swylce me
      in Idumea   eac gelædan?

9   Ac ne eart þu se sylfa God   ðe us swa drife?
      Ne ga ðu us on mægene,   mihtig Drihten.

10   Syle us nu on earfoðum   æðelne fultum,
      for ðon hælu byð   her on eorðan
      manna gehwylces   mægene idel.

11   Us sceal mægenes gemet   mihtig Drihten
      soðfæst syllan,   and he sona mæg
      ure fynd gedon   fracoþe to nahte.

Psalm 60

1   Gehyr, halig God,   hraþe mine bene;
      beheald mine gebed   holde mode;
      nu ic of eorðan   ut-gemærum

6   ⁹ Gilead is mine, and wise Manasseh and Ephraim is the noble strength of my head here on earth.

7   Renowned Judah is my king; ¹⁰ Moab is the vessel of my hope, and I will expand also into Edom, advance my shoes, and afterward make Allophilas totally subservient to me."

8   ¹¹ Who will conduct me to a more pleasant city enclosed by walls; likewise, who will also lead me into Edom?

9   ¹² But are you not the same God who expelled us so? Mighty Lord, do not advance on us with force.

10   ¹³ Grant us now precious help in our difficulties, because the security of humankind on earth is powerless.

11   ¹⁴ The mighty and trustworthy Lord shall grant us an abundance of power, and he can immediately reduce our wicked enemies to nothing.

Psalm 60

1 ² Holy God, hasten to hear my prayer; regard my request favorably; ³ I call on you now from the earth's extremities,

cleopige to þe,   nu me caru beateð
heard æt heortan,   help min nu þa;
ahefe me holdlice   on halne stan.

2   Þu me gelæddest   mid lufan hyhte;
wære me se stranga tor,   stið wið feondum.

3   Ic eardige   awa to feore
on ðinum sele-gesceote;   þær me softe byð,
þær ic beo fægere beþeaht   fiðerum ðinum.

4   For ðon ðu gehyrdest,   halig Drihten,
hu min gebed to ðe   beorhte eode;
yrfe þu sealdest   anra gehwylcum,
se þe naman ðinne   þurh neod forhtað.

5   Dæg byð ofer dæge,   þær byð gedefe cynincg;
beoð his winter eac   wynnum iced,
oð þone dæg þe he   on Drihtnes sceal
on ansyne   andweard gangan,
and þær to worlde   wunian ece.

6   Hwylc seceð þæt   þe soðfæst byð?
Swa ic naman ðinum   neode singe,
þæt ic min gehat   her agylde
of dæge on dæg,   swa hit gedefe wese.

Psalm 61

1   Ic mine sawle   symble wylle
full gleawlice   Gode underþeodan;
æt him is hælu min   her eall gelancg.

seeing that anxiety presses hard on my heart, help me right now; graciously raise me up onto a secure boulder.

2   You guided me [4] with the expectation of your love; you were for me a strong tower, firm against enemies.

3   [5] I will dwell for ever and ever in your tabernacle; wherever I am gently protected by your wings I will remain undisturbed.

4   [6] For you, Holy Lord, heard that my prayer clearly reached you; you bestowed an inheritance on each individual who in need fears your name.

5   [7] Where there is a proper king, one day blends into the next; his years, moreover, will be enhanced with joys, until that day when he must enter into the Lord's presence and sight, [8] and there dwell forever, eternally.

6   Who will seek what is truthful? [9] So I will diligently sing to your name **so** that I can render my vows from day to day on this earth, as it should be.

Psalm 61

1   [2] I resolve always to subject my soul most ardently to God; my well-being in this world is totally dependent on him.

2 Hwæt, he is God min and gearu hælend;
  is he fultum min, ic ne forhtige wiht.

3 Đonne ge mid mane men ongunnon,
  ealle ge ða to deadan dædun sona,
  swa ge awurpon wah of stofne.

4 Swa ge mine are ealle þohton
  wraðe toweorpan; wide urnon
  þurstige muðe, þæne bletsadan,
  and ðone wyrgedan wraðe mid heortan.

5 Hwæðere ic me soðe, sawle mine,
  to Gode hæfde georne geðeoded;
  he minre geðylde þingum wealdeð.

6 Hwæt, he is God min and gleaw hælend
  and fultum is; ne mæg ic hine ahwær befleon.

7 On Gode standeð min gearu hælu
  and wuldor min and wyn mycel;
  me is halig hyht on hine swylce.

8 Hycge him halig folc hælu to Drihtne;
  doð eowre heortan hige hale and clæne,
  for ðon eow God standeð, georne on fultum.

9 Hwæðere ge, manna bearn, manes unlyt
  wyrceað on wægum, and woh doð,
  and eow beswicað sylfe oftast,
  þær ge idel gylp on þam ilcan fremmað.

10 Nellað ge gewenan welan unrihte,
  oþþe to reaflace ræda þencean.

2   ³ Listen! He is my God and a ready savior; he is my help, I will fear nothing.

3   ⁴ Whenever you people viciously attacked men, you put them all to death without delay, as if you were toppling a wall from its foundation.

4   ⁵ In the same way you thoroughly planned how to destroy my honor cruelly; running here and there with thirsty mouths, you blessed him, but angrily cursed him in your hearts.

5   ⁶ I, however, had truly subjected myself, my soul, sincerely to God; he purposefully controls my patience.

6   ⁷ He is my God and wise savior, and help; I cannot flee anywhere from him.

7   ⁸ In God resides my ready salvation and my glory and great joy; likewise my sacred trust is in him.

8   ⁹ You devout people, hope in him, salvation from the Lord; make the intent of your hearts wholesome and pure, because God stands firm for you, eager to help.

9   ¹⁰ You, children of humankind, however, commit grievous sin in your conduct, and do wrong, and deceive yourselves very often, when you make vain boasts about that.

10   ¹¹ Do not trust in unlawful wealth, or devise plans for acquiring booty.

11 Þeah þe eow wealan to   wearnum flowen,
    nyllan ge eow on heortan þa   hige staðelian;
    æne ic God spræcan   gearuwe gehyrde,
    and þæt treowe ongeat,   tidum gemeldad:

12 "Miht is Drihtnes   ofer middangeard,
    and him þæs to worlde   wuldor stande
    and mild-heortness,   þæt he manna gehwam
    æfter his agenum   earnungum demeð,
    efne swa he wyrceð   on world-life."

Psalm 62

1 God min, God min,   ic þe gearuwe to
   æt leohte gehwam   lustum wacie.

2 Min sawl on ðe   swyðe þyrsteð,
   and min flæsc on ðe   fæste getreoweð.

3 On westene,   and on wege swylce,
   and on wæter-flodum,   wene ic swiðe,
   þæt ic ðe on halgum   her ætywe,
   þæt ic þin wuldur and mægen   wis sceawige.

4 Ys þin milde mod   micele betere
   þonne þis læne lif   þe we lifiað on;
   weleras ðe mine   wynnum heriað.

5 Swa ic ðe on minum life   lustum bletsige,
   and ic on naman þinum   neode swylce
   mine handa þwea   halgum gelome.

6 Ys sawl min   swetes gefylled,
   swa seo fætte gelynd   fægeres smeoruwes;

11 Even though riches should flow in profusion to you, do not fix your heart's intent on those things; 12 I distinctly heard God speak once, and recognized that utterance as trustworthy, announced at regular times:

12 "To the Lord belongs power over the earth 13 and, in virtue of that, may glory and mercy abide in him forever, so that he will judge every human being according to his particular merits, just as he behaves in this life."

Psalm 62

1 2 My God, my God, at each dawn I watch for you eagerly and with pleasure.

2 My soul thirsts for you exceedingly, and my flesh firmly trusts in you.

3 3 In the desert, on the road, and in floods also, I earnestly anticipate appearing before you here on earth among the holy ones, so that, now wise, I can witness your glory and power.

4 4 Your gentle disposition is much superior to this fleeting world that we live in; my lips will joyfully praise you.

5 5 So I will gladly bless you in my lifetime, and in your name will also diligently purify my hands with the holy ones frequently.

6 6 My soul is filled with sweetness, like the finest fat of

weleras mine   wynnum swylce
þinne naman nu ða   neode heriað.

7   Swa ic þin gemynd   on mod-sefan
on minre reste   rihte begange,
and on ærmergen on ðe   eac gewene,
for ðon þu me on fultum   fæste gestode.

8   Ic beo fægere beþeaht   fiðerum þinum,
and hiht on ðon   hæbbe georne,
for ðon min sawl on ðe   soðe getreoweþ;
me ðin seo swiðre onfencg   symble æt ðearfe.

9   For ðon hi on idel   ealle syððan
sohton synlice   sawle mine,
and geond eorð-scræfu   eodon geneahhe;
nu hi wæran geseald   under sweordes hand,
syndon fracuðe nu   foxes dælas.

10   Kynincg sceal on Drihtne   clæne blisse
hluttre habban,   and hine heriað eac
ealle þa ðe on hine   aðas sweriað,
for þon synt gemyrde   muðas ealle
þa unriht sprecað   ahwær landes.

Psalm 63

1   Gehyr min gebed,   halig Drihten,
nu me costunge   cnyssað geneahhe;
and wið egesan   yfeles feondes
mine sawle gescyld   symle æt þearfe.

rich lard; my lips also will diligently praise your name right now with pleasure.

7   [7] So I will fittingly recall your memory as I lie on my bed, and I will also think of you in the early morning, [8] because you steadily remained a support to me.

8   I will be comfortably protected by your wings, and I eagerly experience joy in that, [9] because my soul truly trusts in you; your right hand has always sustained me in necessity,

9   [10] For all of them afterward sinfully pursued my soul in vain, and frequently crawled through earthen caves; [11] now that they have been handed over to the sword's edge, they will soon serve as disgusting helpings for the fox.

10   [12] The king will experience the purest joy in the Lord, and all those who make vows to him will also praise him, because the mouths of all scandalmongers anywhere in the land will be blocked up.

Psalm 63

1   [2] Holy Lord, hear, my prayer, now that tribulations frequently overwhelm me; and protect my soul always in difficulty against the terror of a malevolent enemy.

2   Þu me oft aweredest   wyrigra gemotes
    and fram þære menegeo   þe man woldon
    and unrihte   æghwær fremman.

3   Þa heora tungan teoð   teonan gehwylce
    sweorde efen-scearpe,   and heora swiðne
                                    bogan,
    and unscyldige mid þy   scotian þenceað.

4   Hi hine samnuncga   scearpum strelum
    on scotiað;   egsan ne habbað,
    ac hi mid wraðum   wordum trymmað
    and sare sprecað,   "Hwa gesyhð usic?"

5   Swa hi smeagað oft   swiðost unriht,
    and on þam ilcan   eft forweorðað,
    þær hi mamriað   man and unriht.

6   Gangeð man manig,   modig on heortan,
    oðþæt hine ahefeð   hælend Drihten.

7   Syndon hyra wita   scytelum cilda
    æghwæs onlicost,   ne him awiht þon ma
    heora tungan nu   teonan on sittað.

8   Ealle synd gedrefede   þe hi on sioð;
    sceal him manna gehwylc   man ondrædan,
    and weorc Godes   wide mærsian,
    and his weorc ongitan   mid wisdome.

9   Se soðfæsta   symble on Drihten
    blissað baldlice,   bote geweneð;
    and hine heriað eac   heortan clæne.

2   3 You frequently shielded me from the assembly of the wicked and the multitude who wished to perpetrate evils and iniquities in any way possible.

3   4 Then they will extend their tongues, as sharp as any sword for inflicting every sort of injury, as well as their powerful bow, 5 and by that means they plan to shoot the innocent.

4   6 They will let fly at him suddenly with sharp arrows; they will have no fear, but will fortify themselves with angry words and declare sourly, "Who will see us?"

5   7 So they often plan the most grievous wrongs, but they will afterward perish in that very same endeavor, when they devise crime and injustice.

6   Many a one proceeds, proud of heart, 8 until the savior Lord raises him up then.

7   The woundings they inflict are altogether like the darts of children, 9 nor do their tongues abuse others now any the more grievously.

8   All who view them are troubled; 10 everyone should fear evil, proclaim God's operations widely, and understand them by means of wisdom.

9   11 The righteous person will always rejoice confidently in the Lord, expecting relief; and the pure of heart will also praise him.

Psalm 64

1   Þe gedafenað,   Drihten user,
     þæt þe man on Sion   swyðe herige,
     and on Hierusalem   gylde and gehate.

2   Gehyr min gebed,   halig Drihten,
     for ðe sceal ælc flæsc   forð siðian.

3   Synfulra word   swyþe ofer usic
     fræcne foran;   þu gefultuma
     urum misdædum,   mihta wealdend.

4   He weorðeð eadig,   se þe hine ece God
     cystum geceoseð   and hine clæne hefeð,
     and on his earduncg-stowum   eardað syððan.

5   Ealle we ðin hus   ecum godum
     fægere fyllað;   fæste is þin templ,
     ece and wræclic,   awa to feore.

6   Gehyr us, hælend God,   þu eart hyht ealra
     þe on ðysse eorðan   utan syndon,
     oþþe feor on sæ   foldum wuniað.

7   Þinre mihte sculon   muntas hyran;
     swylce þu gedrefest   deope wælas
     þæt beoð ormætum   yþa hlude,
     and hi uneaðe mæg   ænig aræfnan.

8   Þeoda him ondrædað   þinne egesan,
     þe eard nymað   utan landes;
     for þinum wundrum   forhte weorðað.

Psalm 64

1   [2] Lord of ours, it is fitting for you to be fervently praised in Zion, and rendered homage and vows in Jerusalem.

2   [3] Holy Lord, hear my prayer, since all flesh is destined to travel on to you.

3   [4] The words of sinners came over us very violently; mighty ruler, forgive our evil deeds.

4   [5] He is blessed whom the eternal God in his generosity will choose and fully raise up, and who will afterward reside in his dwelling places.

5   All of us will elegantly fill your house with enduring good things; your temple is secure, eternal, and [6] extraordinary, for ever and ever.

6   Savior God, hear us, you are the hope of all those living round about on this earth, or dwelling in lands far out in the sea.

7   [7] The mountains are compelled to obey your power; [8] you disturb deep oceans also, so that the waves are excessively loud, and one can scarcely endure them.

8   [9] Those peoples who occupy distant lands will be in awe of your fearsomeness; they will be afraid because of your marvels.

9   Ær-morgenes gancg   wið æfen-tid,
ealle þa deman   Drihten healdeð;
eorðan ðu gefyllest   eceum wæstmum,
þæt heo welig weorþeð   wera cneorissum.

10   Beoð Godes streamas   gode wætere
fæste gefylde,   þanan feorh-nere
findað fold-buend,   swa him fægere oft
gegearewadest,   God lifigende.

11   Wæter yrnende   wæstme tyddrað;
mænige on moldan   manna cynnes
on cneorisse   cende weorðað,
and blissiað,   blowað and growað
þurh dropunge   deawes and renes.

12   Þonne þu geares hring   mid gyfe bletsast,
and þine fremsumnesse wylt   folcum dælan,
þonne beoð þine feldas   fylde mid wæstmum,

13   þonne on wæstmum   weorðað mæsted,
and mid wynn-grafe   weaxað geswiru.

14   Hi beoð gegyrede   godre wulle,
eowde sceapum;   cumað eadilic
wæstm on wangas   weorðlic on hwætum;
þonne hi cynlice to ðe   cleopiað sona
and þe þonne lustum   lofe þanciað.

9   From the early morning's end until evening, the Lord
will control all the judges; [10] you will fill the earth with constant fruits, so that it will become fecund for the generations.

10   God's rivers are brimming with pure water, in which
earth's inhabitants will find essential nourishment, such as
the living God has often graciously provided for them.

11   [11] The running waters produce fruits; multitudes of humankind are propagated on earth in their time, and they
will rejoice, grow, and flourish by means of falling dew and
rain.

12   [12] Whenever you bless the yearly cycle with your benevolence, and wish to distribute your largesse to the people, your fields will be filled with crops,

13   [13] and will be fattened with fruits, and the hills will
flourish with pleasant groves.

14   [14] They are clothed with fine wool from the sheep of
the flock; abundant crops will come to the plains, fertile in
grains; then they will rightly invoke you at once and thank
you then with profuse praise.

Psalm 65

1 Ealle eorð-buend ecne Drihten
wordum wislicum wide herian,
and his naman secgeað neode mid sealmum,
and him wuldres lof wide syllað.

2 And Gode secgeað hu his þa goodan weorc
syndon wundorlice wide geond eorðan,
and eac on menigeo mægenes þines,
þine feondas þe fæcne leogað.

3 Geweorðie wuldres Ealdor
eall ðeos eorþe, ecne Drihten,
and þe singe eac, secge geneahhie
þæt þin nama is ofer eall niða bearn,
se hehsta hæleþa cynnes.

4 Cumað nu and geseoð hu cyme weorc
Drihten worhte; synt his domas eac
swiþe egeslice ofer eall ylda bearn.

5 He mæg onwendan wætera ðryðe,
þæt þas deopan sæ drige weorðað;
and þa strangan mæg streamas swylce
gefeterian, þæt þu mid fote miht
on treddian eorðan gelice.

6 His mægen wealdeð ofer eall manna cyn
on ecnesse, awa to feore,
and he ofer ealle þeode eagum wliteð;
þa hine on yrre æghwær gebringað,
ne beoð þa on him sylfum syððan ahafene.

Psalm 65

1   ¹ All inhabitants of the earth praise the eternal Lord far and wide with crafted words, ² and eagerly say his name with psalms, and widely convey to him acknowledgment of his glory.

2   ³ And declare to God how those excellent works of his are gloriously present widely throughout the earth, and how, moreover, in the enormity of your power, your enemies basely lie to you.

3   ⁴ Let all this earth worship the prince of glory, the eternal Lord, and sing to you also, declare frequently that your name, the most exalted over the human race, surpasses all humankind.

4   ⁵ Come now and see what glorious works the Lord has made; his judgments on all humankind are also exceedingly terrifying.

5   ⁶ He has the power to transform the force of the waters, so that those deep seas will be dried up; and he can likewise bind those powerful rivers, so that you can be traverse them on foot like dry land.

6   ⁷ His power dominates all humankind, forever to eternity, and with his eyes he observes all peoples; those who in any way provoke him to anger will not be puffed up in themselves afterward.

7 Bletsigen þeoda   bliþe mode,
   ealle eorð-buend,   ecne Drihten,
   and mid stefne lof   strang asecgean.

8 He mine sawle   sette to life;
   ne læteð mine fet   laðe hreran.

9 Ure costade God   clæne fyre,
   soðe dome,   swa man seolfor deð
   þonne man hit aseoðeð   swyðe mid fyre.

10 Þu us on grame swylce   gryne gelæddest,
   and us bealuwa fela   on bæce standeð;
   settest us mænige eac   men ofer heafod.

11 We þuruh fyr farað   and þuruh floda þrym,
   and ðu us on colnesse   clæne gelæddest.

12 Ic on þin hus   halig gange,
   and þær tidum þe   tifer onsecge;
   þær ic min gehat   mid hyge gylde,
   þæt mine weleras ær   wise gedældan.

13 Þas ic mid muðe aspræc   mine æt þearfe,
   þær me costunge   cnyssedan geneahhe,
   þæt ic ðe on tifrum   teala forgulde
   ealle þa gehat   þe ic æfre her
   mid minum welerum   wis todælde.

14 Gehyrað me   and her cumað:
   ic eow mid soþe   secgean wylle,
   gif ge Godes egesan   georne habbað,
   hu mycel he dyde   minre sawle.

15 Þuruh his mihte ic   muðe cleopige,
   oþþe mine tungan   tidum blissade.

7   8 Let the peoples, all the inhabitants of earth, bless the eternal Lord cheerfully, and call out forceful praise with their voices.

8   9 He assigned life to my soul, he does not allow my feet to be agitated by hostility.

9   10 God tested us with pure fire, with true discernment, just as silver is when it is intensely refined in the furnace.

10   11 You led us into suffering as if into a snare, and many torments stalk us; 12 you also positioned many people to dominate us.

11   We move through fire and through a torrent of floods, and you guided us perfectly to refreshment.

12   13 I will enter into your holy dwelling, and there regularly offer sacrifice to you; in that place I will purposefully render the vows, 14 which my lips prudently uttered before.

13   Those vows I declared with my mouth in my time of trouble, when tribulations often oppressed me, 15 promising that I would properly make good to you in offerings all the wise promises that I ever expressed with my lips on earth.

14   16 Listen to me and come here; I will declare truthfully to you, if you earnestly maintain fear of God, how much he did for my soul.

15   17 Through his power I call out with my mouth, and with my tongue I rejoiced at appropriate times.

16   Gif ic me unrihtes oncneow   awiht on heortan,
ne wite me þæt,   Wealdend-Drihten.

17   For ðon me gehyrde   hælend Drihten,
and minre stefne beheold   strange bene.

18   Drihten si gebletsad,   þe he ne dyde æfre
nymðe he mine bene   bealde gehyrde,
ne his milde mod   me dyde fremde.

Psalm 66

1   Miltsa us, mihtig Drihten,   and us on mode eac
gebletsa nu;   beorhte leohte
þinne andwlitan,   and us on mode weorð
þuruh þine mycelnesse   milde and bliðe;

2   and we þæs on eorðan   andgyt habbað,
ure wegas wide   geond þas wer-ðeode
on þinre hælo   healdan motan.

3   Folc þe andette;   þu eart fæle God,
and þe andetten   ealle þeoda.

4   Hæbbe þæs gefean   folca æghwylc,
and blissien   bealde þeoda,
þæs þe þu hi on rihtum   rædum demest,
and eorð-buende   ealle healdest.

5   Folc þe andetten,   fælne Drihten,
and þe andetten   ealle þeoda.

16   18 If I have identified within my heart any trace of evil, do not impute that to me, sovereign Lord.

17   19 For the savior Lord heard me, and heeded the fervent petition of my voice.

18   20 May the Lord be blessed, because he never did anything but boldly hear my prayer, nor did his kind heart behave coldly toward me.

Psalm 66

1   2 Mighty Lord, have pity on us and likewise bless our minds at this time; brightly illuminate your face, and through your greatness make us kind and happy in disposition;

2   3 and we here on earth will afterward grasp that we may in your saving help observe our way of life widely throughout those other peoples.

3   4 May the people acknowledge you; you are the faithful God, and may all peoples acknowledge you.

4   5 May each of the peoples experience that joy, and may the nations boldly rejoice, because you judge them with just deliberations, and you direct all humankind on earth.

5   6 May the peoples acknowledge you, faithful Lord, and all nations acknowledge you.

6   Ge him eorðe syleð   æþele wæstme;
    gebletsige us   bliðe Drihten,
    and user God   eac bletsige;
    hæbbe his egesan eall   eorþan gemæru.

Psalm 67

1   Arise God,   ricene weorðe
    his feonda gehwylc   fæste toworpen;
    fleoð his ansyne,   þa þe hine feodan ær.

2   Rece hi gelicast   ricene geteoriað;
    swa fram fyre weax   floweð and mylteð,
    swa þa fyrenfullan   frecne forweorðað.
    Habbað soðfæste   symbel ece,

3   hi ansyne   ecean Drihtnes
    habbað beorhtlice   blisse and sibbe.

4   Singað soðum Gode   sealmas geneahhige,
    and his naman swylce   neode heriað;
    doð siðfæt þæs   seftne and rihtne,
    þe he sylfa astah   ofer sunnan up,
    þam is to naman   nemned Drihten.

5   Wesað ge on his gesyhþe   symble bliðe,
    and on his ansyne wesan   ealle gedrefde,
    þa þe wydewum syn   wraðe æt dome,
    oþþe steop-cildum wesen   strange fæderas.

6   7 And the earth will give them excellent crops; kind Lord, bless us, 8 and may our God also bestow a blessing; may all the ends of the earth maintain their fear of him.

Psalm 67

1   2 Let God arise, let each of his enemies be firmly overthrown at once; those who had hated him flee from his sight.

2   3 They will quickly fade very like smoke; and as wax melts and flows by the agency of fire, so the wicked will perish horribly. 4 The just will enjoy an eternal feast,

3   they will gloriously experience the sight of the eternal Lord in joy and peace.

4   5 Sing psalms frequently to the true God, and likewise diligently praise his name; make pleasant and straight the path of that one who himself ascended above the sun, who goes by the name of Lord.

5   Always be happy in his presence, and in his sight let those be thoroughly troubled, 6 who behave cruelly in their verdicts against widows, and are severe fathers to orphans.

6   Drihten is on his stowe,   dema halig,
se þe eardian deð   anes modes,
and on hiora huse   healdeð blisse;

7   se þe on his mægenes   mihte gelædeð,
þæt he þa gehæftan   hæleð sniome,
and þa to yrre beoð   ealle gecigde
and eardiað   on eorð-scræfum.

8   Þonne God gangeð   for his þæt gleawe folc,
oððe geond westena   wide ferað,
þanon eorðe byð   eall onhrered.

9   For ansyne   ecean Drihtnes
heofenas droppetað; hrusan forhtiað
for Israela Godes   egesan þrymme.

10   Wilsumne regn   wolcen brincgeð,
and þonne ascadeð God   sundor-yrfe;
eall þu þa gefremest   þurh þine fæste miht.

11   Þine wihte on þam   wynnum lifiað;
þu þin swete good   sealdest þearfum.

12   God gifeð gleaw word   god-spellendum,
syleð him modes mægen,   se þe is mihtig
                            kynincg
and wlites wealdend;   oft weorðlic reaf
on huse men   her gedælað.

13   Gif ge slæpað   samod on *clero,*
fiðeru beoþ culfran   fægeres seolfres,
and hire bæc scineð   beorhtan golde.

14   Þonne hi se heofonlica kynincg   her toscadeð,
syþþan hi on Selmon   snawe weorðað.

6   The Lord is present in his place, [7] the venerable judge who makes them live together in unanimity, and maintains joy in their house;

7   he who leads in the power of his might, so that he speedily rescues the captives and those who are thoroughly provoked to anger and live in caves.

8   [8] Then God advances for the sake of that wise people of his, and furthermore he journeys widely throughout the deserts, [9] whereupon the earth will be shaken to its foundations.

9   The heavens will begin to fall before the eternal Lord's face; the earth will tremble with fear in the presence of the awesome power of Israel's God.

10   [10] The sky will produce spontaneous rain, and God will set aside then a separate inheritance; you will accomplish all that through your disciplined power.

11   [11] Your creatures will pass their lives in those joys; you bestowed your pleasant advantages on the needy.

12   [12] To those who proclaim good news, God will impart wise words, will bestow strength of purpose on them, [13] he who is mighty king and ruler in splendor; people on earth often distribute valuable spoils in the house.

13   [14] If you sleep together among the clergy, the dove's wings will be of shining silver, and its back radiant with gleaming gold.

14   [15] Whenever the heavenly king separates them on earth, they afterward become whitened with snow in Zalmon.

15 Gebeorh Godes   bringeð to genihte
    wæstme weorðlice   and wel þicce.

16 For þon ge onfoð   fægerum beorge,
    þær ge to genihte   geniomað wæstme;
    se is Wealdend-Gode   wel liciendlic
    on þam wið ende   eardað Drihten.

17 Wærun Godes cræta   gegearwedra
    tyn þusendo,   geteled rime,
    mænigfeald þusend   mod-blissiendra.

18 Drihten is on þam   dædum spedig:
    on heanesse astah,   hæft-ned lædde
    þa on hæft-nede   hwile micele
    lange lifdon,   and wæs lac-geofa
    ofer middan-geard   manna bearnum.

19 Ne magon þær eard niman   ungeleafe menn;
    wese of dæge on dæg   Drihten usser,
    se goda God,   georne gebletsad.

20 Sylle us gesundne   siðfæt, Drihten,
    ure Hælend-God   helpe usser,
    and us æt deaðe eac   Drihten gehealde.

21 Hwæðere Wealdend-God   wið-hycgendra
    heafdas feonda   her gescæneð,
    and he tofylleð   feaxes scadan
    þe her on scyldum   swærum eodon.

22 "Of Basan," cwæð   bealde Drihten,
    "ic me on sæ deopre   sniome onwende,
    oþ þæt þin fot weorðe   fæste on blode.

15 ¹⁶ God's mountain produces valuable, and extremely plentiful, foods in abundance.

16 ¹⁷ So you will receive a pleasant mountain where you will obtain harvests in abundance; that mountain on which the Lord will live to the end is highly pleasing to the sovereign God.

17 ¹⁸ There were ten thousand of God's equipped chariots, reckoned by counting, multiple thousands of people rejoicing.

18 God is successful in these actions: ¹⁹ he ascended on high, took captive those who for ages had lived long in captivity, and became a generous giver of gifts to humankind throughout the earth.

19 Unbelievers were not able to take up residence there; ²⁰ may our Lord, that excellent God, be diligently blessed from day to day.

20 Lord, give us a safe passage, help us, our savior God, ²¹ and may the Lord also protect us at the moment of death.

21 ²² The sovereign God, however, will shatter, the heads of scornful enemies on earth, and he will smite in pieces the long-haired crowns of those who traveled the earth in grave sin.

22 ²³ "From Bashan," said the Lord confidently, "I will navigate quickly to the deep sea, ²⁴ until your foot is steeped in blood.

23   Hundes tungan   habbað feondas,
      from þam þine gangas   wæron gesewene."
      Wærun Godes mines   gangas rihte,
      soðes kynincges   symble on halgum.

24   Þyder ealdor-men   ofstum coman,
      and gegaderade   gleowe sungon
      on þæra manna   midle geongra
      on *tympanis*   togenum strengum;
      and on ciricean   Crist, Drihten God,
      bealde bletsige   bearn Israela.

25   Þær Benniamines synt   bearn on geogoðe,
      and ealdor-menn   eac of Iudan
      (þe latteow wæs   forð þara leoda),
      and ealdras eac   of Zabulone
      and Neptalim   niode swylce.

26   Bebeod þinum mægene,   þu eart mihtig God,
      and þin weorc on us   mid wisdome
      getryme on þinum temple   tidum gehalgod,
      þæt ys on Hierusalem,   þyder ðe gyfe lædað
      of feorwegum   foldan kynincgas.

27   On wuda þu wildeor   wordum þreatast
      and fearra gemot   under folcum;
      ne beoð ut fram þe   æfre atynde,
      þa þe seolfres beoð   since gecoste.

28   Toweorp þu þa ðeoda . . .

23   Those enemies, [25] by whom your movements were observed, have the tongues of hounds." The steps of my God, the true king perpetually dwelling in holy places, were straight.

24   [26] The leaders came there in haste, and as a united choir they sang joyously among the young men playing on timbrels accompanied by drawn strings; [27] and may Christ, the Lord God, boldly bless the children of Israel in their assembly.

25   [28] Present there are Benjamin's children in their youth, and also the leaders from Judah (which continued to be the head of the tribes), and likewise eagerly also the elders of Zebulun and Naphtali.

26   [29] Summon your power, you are the mighty God, and wisely confirm your operations among us, [30] in your temple , sanctified at regular times, that is, in Jerusalem, to which kings bring you gifts from the four corners of the earth.

27   [31] With your words you threaten the wild beasts in the woods and the gathering of bulls among the people's cows; those who are proved with a hoard of silver will never be excluded from you.

28   Scatter those peoples . . .

Psalm 68

1 Do me halne, God,   for þon hreoh wæter
to minum feore inn   floweð and gangeð;
eom ic on lame oflegd,   hafað lytle sped.

2 Com ic on sæs hricg,   þær me sealt wæter,
hreoh and hopig,   holme besencte.

3 Þær ic werig-mod   wann and cleopode,
þæt me grame syndan   goman hase;
byð me æt þam earon   eagon wiðgangen,
hwæðere ic on God minne   gearewe gewene.

4 Hiora is mycle ma   þonne ic me hæbbe
on heafde nu   hæra feaxes
þe me earwunga   ealle feogeað.

5 Ofer me syndon   þa þe me ehton,
fæstum folmum   forð gestrangad
feondas mine;   and ic forð agef,
unrihtlice,   þa þe ic ne reafude ær.

6 Þu wast, wuldres God,   þæt ic eom unwis
                                    hyges;
ne wæren þe bemiðene   mine scylde.

7 Ne sceolon æt me   ænige habban
sceame sceandlice   þe þines siðes her
ful bealdlice   bidað, Drihten,
þu eart mægena God;   ne sceal æt me
ænige unare   ahwær findan,
þe ðe Israela God   ahwær seceað.

Psalm 68

1   ² Save me, God, because stormy waters wash and surge into my soul; ³ I am mired in mud which has little traction.

2   I came to the summit of the sea, where salt water, tempestuous and surging, submerged me in brine.

3   ⁴ There, sad of soul, I labored and called out, so that my throat became painfully hoarse; my eyes are failing me from those waves, though I readily hope in my God.

4   ⁵ Those who absolutely hate me for no reason are far more numerous than the hairs now in my head.

5   My enemies, who have persecuted me with firm hands, are further strengthened over me; so that I continued to hand over, unfairly, those things that I had not taken by force.

6   ⁶ God of glory, you know that I am hasty of thought; let not my faults be concealed from you.

7   ⁷ Those who await with full confidence your arrival on earth should not have to endure ignominious disgrace because of me, Lord, you are the God of armies; those who seek you, God of Israel, should not have to encounter at any time dishonor anywhere on my account.

8   For þon ic edwit for þe   oft aræfnade,
and me hleor-sceame   hearde becwoman;
and ic framþe wearð   fæderen-broðrum,
wæs unmæge gyst   modor-cildum,

9   for þon me þines huses   heard ellen-wod
æt ormæte;   and me eac fela
þinra edwita   on gefeollon.

10   Þonne ic minum feore   fæsten gesette,
eall hi me þæt on edwit   eft oncyrdan.

11   Gif ic mine gewæda   on wite-hrægl
cyme cyrde,   cwædan hi syþþan
þæt ic him wæfer-syn   wære eallum.

12   Me wiðerwearde   wæron ealle,
þa him sæton   sundor on portum;
spræcon me wraðe   þa þe win druncon.

13   Ic þonne min gebed   to þe, mihtig Drihten,
tidum sende   teala liciendlic;
and þu me þonne on mænigeo   miltsa þinra
gehyre me hlutre,   hælu þine.

14   Alys me of lame,   þe læs ic weorþe lange fæst,
and me feondum afyrr,   frea ælmihtig;
ado me of deope   deorces wæteres,
þe læs me besencen   sealte flodas.

15   Ne me huru forswelge   sæ-grundes deop,
ne me se seað   supe mid muðe.

16   Gehyr, Drihten, me,   for þon gedefe is
þin milde mod   mannum fremsum,

8   8 For I have often endured opprobrium for your sake, and loss of face has grievously befallen me; 9 and I have become a stranger to brothers on my father's side, I was an alien unrelated to the children of our common mother,

9   10 because strong zeal for your house inordinately consumed me; and many of the reproaches meant for you also landed on me.

10   11 Whenever I applied my soul to fasting, they totally twisted that into a slander of me.

11   12 If I changed my elegant clothing into sackcloth, they would afterward say that I was making an exhibition of myself to them all.

12   13 They were all hostile to me when they sat apart at the gates; those who drank wine addressed me aggressively.

13   14 I, however, will address my pleasingly phrased prayer to you regularly, mighty Lord; and in the abundance of your mercy may you then fully hear me, the object of your salvation.

14   15 Free me from the mire, lest I become stuck for a long time, and distance me from enemies, almighty ruler; release me from the abyss of murky water, 16 lest sea surges submerge me.

15   Truly, let neither the depth of the seafloor swallow me up, nor the pit's maw absorb me.

16   17 Lord, hear me because your gentle spirit is well dis-

and for mænigeo   miltsa þinra
geseoh on me   swylce, Drihten;

17   ne acyr þu æfre fram þinum cnihte   þin clæne
                                    gesyhð,
for þan me feondas to   feohtað geneahhe;
gehyr me hrædlice   and me help freme.

18   Beheald mine sawle   and hi hrædlice
alys and wiðfere   laþum feondum.

19   . . . ar scame;
for þinre ansyne   ealle syndon
þe feondas me   fæcne wurdon.

20   Min heorte gebad   hearm-edwit feala,
and yrmðu mænig   eac aræfnede;
næfde eorla þæs   ænig sorge;
frefrend ic sohte,   findan ic ne mihte.

21   Hi minne mete   mengdan wið geallan,
and þa gedrugadne   drenctan mid ecede.

22   Wese heora beod fore him   wended on grine,
and on edlean yfel   and on æwisce.

23   Syn hiora eagan   eac adimmad,
þæt hi geseon ne magon   syþþan awiht;
weorðe heora bæc swylce   abeged eac.

24   Ageot ofer hi   þin þæt grame yrre,
and æbylignes eac   yrres þines,
hi forgripe   gram-hicgende.

25   Wese wic heora   weste and idel,
ne on heora eðele ne sy   þinc on-eardiendes;

posed and kind to people, and in accord with your many mercies look on me also, Lord;

17 18 do not ever turn away your perfect face from your servant, because enemies often fight against me; listen to me promptly and help me.

18 19 Regard my soul, and quickly release and redeem it from odious enemies.

19 . . . 21 all who were treacherous enemies to me are present before your sight.

20 My heart anticipated many a grievous reproach, while it also endured many hardships; not one person felt sorrow for that; I sought a comforter, but could not find one.

21 22 They mixed my food with gall, and then in my parched state plied me with vinegar.

22 23 Let their table in front of them be changed into a snare, and an unlucky reward, and something shameful.

23 24 Let their eyes also be dimmed, so that afterward they cannot see anything; in the same way let their backs also be contorted.

24 25 Pour on them that fierce wrath of yours, and let the fierce fury of your rage also grab them.

25 26 Let their dwelling become useless and desolate, nor may any sign of occupancy remain in their homeland;

26   for þon hi ealra   ehtan ongunnon,
ðe þu him earfoðu   ænig geafe,
and me wean ecton   minra wunda sar.

27   Asete him þa unriht to   þe hi geearnedan
and mid unrihte   ær geworhton;
and hi on þin soðfæst weorc   syþþan ne gangan.

28   Syn hi adilgad   of gedefra eac
þæra lifigendra   leofra bocum;
ne wesen hi mid soðfæstum   syþþan awritene.

29   Ic me sylfa eam   sarig þearfa,
and me andwlita onfeng   ecean Drihtnes,
se me holdlice   hælde sona.

30   Nu ic naman Drihtnes   neode herige
and hine mid lof-sange   læde swylce.

31   Ic þam leofan Gode   licie swyþor
þonne æðele cealf,   þeah þe him upp aga
horn on heafde   oððe hearde cleo.

32   Geseoð þæt and gefeoð,   sarie þearfan,
seceað Drihten   and eower sawl leofað,

33   for þam þa þearfendan   þriste Drihten
gehyreð holdlice;   nyle he gehæfte eac
on heora neode   na forhycgan.

34   Herige hine swylce   heofen and eorðe,
side sæ-flodas   and þa him syndon on,

35   for þon Sione God   symble hæleð;
beoð mænige byrig   mid Iudeum
eft getimbrade,   þær hi eard nimað.

26   27 because they began to persecute all those on whom you had inflicted any hardships, and they increased the pain of my wounds with misfortune.

27   28 Set on them the evils they have earned and flagrantly perpetrated before; and after that let them not enter into your truthful works.

28   29 May they be also wiped off the books of the living, upright and much loved; let them not be recorded among the just afterward.

29   30 I myself am sorrowful and destitute, but the eternal Lord's favor received me, it graciously healed me with no delay.

30   31 Now I will eagerly praise the Lord's name and also spread it with a canticle.

31   32 I will please that beloved God more tellingly than the offering of a splendid calf, even one with horns or sturdy hooves.

32   33 You sorrowing poor, observe that and rejoice, seek the Lord and your soul will live,

33   34 because the Lord will boldly and faithfully listen to those in need; also, he will certainly not reject captives in their necessity.

34   35 Let heaven and earth also praise him, the vast oceans and whatever creatures belong in them,

35   36 because God will always save Zion; many towns will be rebuilt among Judah's tribe, wherever they take up residence.

36   Þær hi yrfe-stol   eft gesittað,
and hiora eþel begytað   esnas Drihtenes,
and his naman   neode lufiað,
þær eardiað   awa to feore.

Psalm 69

1   Wes, Drihten God,   deore fultum;
beheald, Drihten, me   and me hraðe syþþan
gefultuma   æt feorh-þearfe.

2   Þonne beoð gescende   and scame dreogað,
þa þe mine fynd   fæcne wæron
and mine sawle   sohton mid niðe;

3   hi on hinderlincg   hweorfað and cyrrað.
Ealle hiora scamien,   þe me yfel hogedon;

4   and heora æfstu eac   ealle sceamien,
þe me word cwædon,   "Weg la, weg la!"

5   Habban þa mid wynne   weorðe blisse,
þa þe secean   symble Drihten,
and symble cweðen,   "Sy þin miht, Drihten,"
and þine hælu   holde lufigean.

6   Ic eom wædla   and world-þearfa;
gefultuma me, God,   frea ælmihtig.

7   Þu me fultum eart   fæste, Drihten,
eart alysend min;   ne lata þu awiht.

36 ³⁷ Where the Lord's servants reestablish the ancestral seat, and take possession of their native land, and earnestly cherish his name, there they will dwell for ever and ever.

Psalm 69

1 ² Lord God, be a precious help; Lord, look at me and in my extreme need, help me immediately after.

2 ³ Those who were my treacherous enemies and spitefully sought my soul will then be confounded and suffer shame;

3 ⁴ they will turn back and depart. May all of them who planned evil for me be put to shame;

4 and likewise let all those be ashamed of their malice, who said to me the words, "Alas, alas!"

5 ⁵ May they experience then well-deserved happiness with joy who always seek the Lord, and constantly say, "May your power endure, Lord," and faithfully cherish your salvation.

6 ⁶ I am needy and poor in worldly goods; help me, God, almighty ruler;

7 Lord, you are my steady helper, you are my liberator; do not delay at all.

Psalm 70

1   Ic on þe, God Drihten,   gearuwe gewene;
    ne weorðe ic on ealdre   æfre gescended;
    þu me sniome alys   þuruh þine þa swiþeran
                                            miht.

2   Ahyld me þin eare to   holde mode,
    and me lustum alys,   and me lungre weorð
    on God Drihten   georne þeccend
    and on trume stowe,   þær þu me teala hæle;

3   for þon þu me, God, wære   geara trymmend,
    freoða fultumiend.   Alys me feondum nu,
    and me of folmum afere   firen-wyrcendra
    þe þine æ   efnan nellað;
    syndon unrihtes   ealle wyrcende.

4   For þon þu me eart fæle geþyld   fæste, Drihten,
    wære me on geoguðe hyht,   gleaw æt frymðe.

5   Ic of modur hrife   mund-byrd on þe
    þriste hæfde;   þu eart þeccend min;
    on þe ic singge nu   symble and geneahhie.

6   Ic eom swa fore-beacen   folce manegum,
    and þu me eart fultum strang   fæste æt þearfe.

7   Sy min muð and min mod   mægene gefylled,
    þæt ic þin lof mæge   lustum singan,
    and wuldur þin   wide mærsian,
    and þe ealne dæg   æghwær herian.

Psalm 70

1   [1] Lord God, I readily hope in you; may I never, ever, be confounded; [2] free me quickly through the power of your right hand.

2   Incline your ear to me with gracious intent, and gladly free me, [3] and let there be at once a protector for me truly in the Lord God and in a secure place, where you may justifiably save me;

3   for you were readily my support, a guarantor of security. [4] Free me now from enemies, and remove me from the hands of sinners who refuse to fulfill your law; they are altogether perpetrators of iniquity.

4   [5] For you are entirely a trusty source of patience for me, Lord, you were my youthful hope, wise from the beginning.

5   [6] From my mother's womb I confidently enjoyed secure protection from you, you are my defender; I will now sing to you constantly and profusely.

6   [7] I am like a puzzle to many people, yet you are entirely my strong support in trouble.

7   [8] May my mouth and soul be filled with strength, so that I can enthusiastically sing your praises, and widely proclaim your glory, and praise you in every way all day long.

8   Ne aweorp þu me,   wuldres Ealdor,
þonne me ylde tid   on gesige;
þonne me mægen and mod   mylte on hreðre,
ne forlæt þu me,   lifiende God.

9   Oft me feala cwædon   feondas yfele,
and sætendan   sawle minre,
and on anre geþeaht   eodan togædere.

10   Cweþað cuðlice: "Wuton cunnian,
hwænne hine God læte   swa swa gymeleasne;
þonne we hine forgripen   and his geara ehtan,
syþþan he ne hæbbe   helpend ænne."

11   Ne ofgif þu me huru,   God ælmihtig;
beseoh þu me, soð God,   symble on fultum.

12   Beoð gedrecte   eac gescende
þa mine sawle ær   swyþust tældun;
byð þam scand and sceamu   þe me syrwedan
                yfel.

13   Ic me symble on God   swiðost getreowige;
ofer eall þin lof   lengest hihte.

14   Min muð sægeð   þine mægen-spede
and þin soðfæst weorc   swyþust mæreð,
sægeð þe ealne dæg   ece hælu.

15   For þon ic ne ongeat   grame ceapunga;
ac ic on þine þa myclan   mihte gange.

16   Ic þine soðfæstnesse geman   symble, Drihten.
Þu me ara, God,   ærest lærdest
of geoguðhade,   nu ic eom gomel wintrum.

8   9 Lord of glory, do not cast me out, when old age descends on me; living God, do not abandon me, when strength and resolve melt within me.

9   10 All too often enemies spoke to me maliciously, and lay in ambush for my soul, and came together in joint counsel.

10   11 They openly declare: "Let us find out when God will abandon him like a stray; then we may seize him and easily harass him, since he will lack any helper."

11   12 Almighty God, truly do not desert me; true God, look favorably on me with help always.

12   13 Let those who had most severely reviled my soul be destroyed and confounded; shame and confusion will befall those who planned evil for me.

13   14 Always I will trust exceedingly in God; for the longest time I have added to your praise.

14   15 My mouth will declare the abundance of your strength and make known especially your righteous works, will proclaim to you your eternal salvation all day long.

15   For I did not understand unfriendly transactions; 16 yet, I will come under the influence of that great power of yours.

16   Lord, I will always remember your justice. 17 You, God, first taught me from my youth acts of kindness, but now I am advanced in years. I declared your exalted glory always,

A ic wundor þin   weorþlic sægde,
and ic þæt wið oryldu   awa fremme;
ne forlæt þu me,   lifigende God,

17   oð ðæt ic þines earmes   eall asecge
stiþe strencðe   þisse cneorisse,
eallum þam teohhe,   þe nu toweard ys,

18   þines mihtes þrym,   and þæt mære soð,
þæt ðu on heofenum, God,   heah geworhtest,
wundur wræclicu;   nis þe, wuldres cyning,
ænig æfre gelic,   ece Drihten.

19   Oft þu me ætywdest   earfoðes feala
on costunge   cuðra manna,
and me yfela feala   oft oncnyssedest;
þonne þu yrre þin   eft oncyrdest,
and me of neowelnesse eft   neoðan alysdest
þysse eorðan,   þe we on buiað.

20   Ðær þu þin soðfæst weorc   sniome tobræddest,
þonne þu gehwyrfdest   and hulpe min,
and me getrymedest,   þæt ic teala mihte;
for þon ic þe andette,   ece Drihten,
and þe on sealm-fatum   singe be hearpan,
Israela God,   ece and halig.

21   Mine weleras gefeoð,   wynnum lofiað,
þonne ic þe singe,   sigora wealdend,
and min sawl eac,   þa þu sylf lysdest.

22   Swylce min tunge   tidum mærde
þin soðfæst weorc;   scende wæron ealle
þe me yfel to   ær gesohton.

[18] and will continue doing so into extreme old age; living God, do not desert me,

17   until I fully declare the resolute strength of your arm to this generation, to all that company still to come,

18   the force of your might, [19] and that renowned justice which you, God, fulfilled high in the heavens, extraordinary things; king of glory, eternal Lord, there is no one like you, ever.

19   [20] Through the testing of well-known people you often revealed to me many tribulations, and often afflicted me with multiple evils; you then reversed your anger later on, and released me again from the nether region of this earth, in which we live.

20   [21] There you swiftly multiplied your just actions, whenever you turned around and helped me, and strengthened me, so that I was effectively in control; [22] so, I will acknowledge you, eternal Lord, and sing to you on psalteries to the accompaniment of the harp, God of Israel, holy and eternal.

21   [23] Whenever I sing to you, ruler of victories, my lips will rejoice, joyfully give praise, and my soul also, which you yourself freed.

22   [24] My tongue likewise glorified your just works regularly; those who previously attempted to do me evil were utterly confounded.

Psalm 71

1   Syle dom þinne,   Drihten, kyninge;
    suna cynincges syle,   þæt he soð healde.

2   Dem þu þin folc   deore mid soðe,
    heald þine þearfan   holde mid dome;

3   onfon beorgas eac   beorhtre sibbe,
    on þinum folce   fægere blisse,
    and geswyru eac   soþum dædum.

4   On his soðfæstnesse   swylce demeð
    on folce   fyrhte þearfan;
    swylce he þearfena bearn   þriste hæleð.

5   He þa herm-cweðend   hyneð and bygeð,
    se mid sunnan wunað   swylce mid monan,
    þurh ealra worulda woruld   wunað him ece.

6   He þonne astigeð   swa se stranga ren
    fealleð on flys her,   and swa fæger dropa
    þe on þas eorðan   upon dreopað.

7   On his agenum dagum   ypped weorðeþ
    syb, soðfæstnes   swiðe genihtsum,
    oþþæt byð ahafen   hluttor mona.

8   He þonne wealdeð   wera cneorissum,
    be sæ tweonum   sidum ricum,
    and fram stream-racum   styreð him eallum
    oþ þysse eorðan   utgemæru.

Psalm 71

1   ² Lord, deliver your verdict to the king; give it to the king's son, so that he may maintain truth.

2   Judge your people affectionately with truth, graciously rule your needy ones with discernment;

3   ³ let the mountains too receive radiant peace, gratifying joy for your people, and the hills also true deeds.

4   ⁴ In his justice he will likewise judge the apprehensive and destitute among the people; he will audaciously save the children of the needy also.

5   He will then abase and humiliate slanderers, ⁵ he who dwells with the sun and also the moon, dwells with them eternally for ever and ever.

6   ⁶ He will then descend like the heavy rain falling on the fleece here, and like a pleasant shower which rains upon this earth from above.

7   ⁷ In his own days peace will spring up, justice exceedingly plentiful, until the clear moon will be elevated.

8   ⁸ He will then dominate the generations of people, vast territories between the seas, and he will disturb all of them, from the channels to the extremities of this earth.

9 Hine Sigelwearas seceað ealle,
and his feondas foldan liccigeað.

10 Cumað of Tharsis tires eadige,
and of ea-landum utan kynincgas;
þa him eard-gyfu æðele bringað
of Arabia, eac of Saba;
ealle him leoda lacum cwemað.

11 Hine weorðiað worulde kyningas
þa on eorð-wege ealle syndan;
ealle þeoda hine weorðiað georne,

12 for þon he alyseð lungre þearfan,
þæt him se welega ne mæg wiht onsittan,
and þæne wædlan, þe on worulde næfð
ahwær elles ænigne fultum.

13 He helpeð þearfan, swylce eac wædlan,
and he þearfigendra sawla gehæleð.

14 He of man-sceatte and of mane eac
sniome hiora sawle softe alysde;
ys his nama for him neode gebyrhted.

15 He lyfað leodum, him byð lungre seald
of Arabia gold eorlas lædað;
hine weorþiað wera cneoressa
and hine ealne dæg eac bletsiað.

16 Þonne æðele getrym eorðan weardað,
bið se beorht ahafen ofer beorgas up;
ofer Libanum licgeað his yþa,
and on burgum beoþ blostmum fægere,
swa on eorðan heg ute on lande.

9   9 All the Ethiopians will seek him, and his enemies will grovel on the ground.

10   10 Those favored with fame will come from Tarshish, and kings from distant islands; they will bring to him choice local gifts from Arabia and Seba also; all the peoples will please him with gifts.

11   11 The kings of the world, all who live on earth, will worship him; all the peoples will eagerly pay him homage,

12   12 because he will quickly free the indigent one, and the poor one who lacks help anywhere else in the world, so that the rich person cannot oppress him at all.

13   13 He will help the needy and the poor also, and he will save the souls of the destitute.

14   14 Promptly and calmly he freed their souls from the evil of usury and from iniquity also; his name is ardently blazoned before them.

15   15 He will live for the peoples, gold from Arabia is promptly given to him, noblemen bring it; generations will worship him and also bless him all day.

16   16 Then the glorious firmament will protect the earth, that brilliance will be raised up above the mountains; his waves will flow over Lebanon, and in the towns the fruit trees will be adorned with blossoms, as is earth's grass in the open countryside.

17   Þonne byð his nama   ofer eall niða bearn
and to widan feore   weorðeð gebletsod;
ær sunnan his nama   soðfæst standeð;
byð his setl ær   swylce þonne mona.

18   And him byð eorþan cynn   eall gebletsad,
ealle hine þeoda   þriste heriað.

19   Wese Israhela   ece Drihten
and hiora sylfra God   symble gebletsad,
se þe wundor mycel   wyrceð ana;
si his mihta nama   niode gebletsad
on ecnesse   awa to worlde;

20   and þeos eorðe si   eall gefylled
þurh his wuldres miht.   Wese swa! wese swa!

Psalm 72

1   Hu god is ece God   mid Israhelum,
þam þe mid heortan   hycgeað rihte;
me fornean syndon   losode nu ða
ealle on foldan   fota gangas,

2   for þon ic fæstlice   fyren-wyrcende
oft elnade.   Noldun earme mid him
sibbe secean,   sohton fyrene.

3   For þon hira deaðes byð   deorc ende-stæf,
ne heora wites bið   wislic trymnes,

17   [17] His name will be present then to all humankind and will be blessed for all eternity; firm in truth, his name is present before the sun; his seat likewise exists at a time before the moon did.

18   And in him all humankind will be blessed, all peoples will boldly praise him.

19   [18] May the eternal Lord of the Israelites and their very own God be blessed always, he who alone works great marvels; [19] let his mighty name be blessed earnestly, for ever and ever;

20   and may this earth be replenished entirely through the power of his majesty. So be it! So be it!

Psalm 72

1   [1] How good is the eternal God to those Israelites who think rightly in their hearts; [2] all my footsteps on the ground almost failed just now,

2   [3] because I often stubbornly imitated evildoers. The wretches did not want to reconcile with him, instead they pursued sin.

3   [4] For the final stage of their dying is obscure, nor is the burden of their suffering certain,

4   ne synd hi on miclum   manna gewinnum,
    and hi mid manna ne beoð   mægene
                           beswungene,

5   for þon hi oferhygd nam   ungemete swyþe,
    þurh þæt hira unriht wearð   eall untyned.

6   Þanon forð becom   fæcne unriht,
    swa swa hit of gelynde   lungre cwome;
    and hi on heortan   hogedon and þohton,
    hu hi fyrmest   facen and unriht
    on hean huse   hraðost acwædon.

7   Hwæt, hi on heofon setton   hyge hyra muþes,
    and hira tungan   tugon ofer eorðan.

8   (For þon min folc hider   fægere hweorfeð,
    þær hi fulle dagas   findað sona.)

9   And þonne cwædon: "Hu weorðeð þis cuð
                           Gode,
    oþþe þeos gewitness   weorðeþ on heagum?"

10   Þi nu fyrenfulle   foldan æhta
    and þysse worulde welan   wynnum namon.

11   Þa ic on mode cwæð   minum sona:
    "Þeah þe ic on me ingcan   ænne ne wiste,
    hu ic mine heortan   heolde mid soðe,
    and mine handa þwoh,   þær ic hete nyste,
    and ic wæs ealne dæg   eac geswungen,
    wæs me leaw-finger   be leohtne dæg."

12   Gif ic sylf cwæde   and sæcge eac,
    "Swa þe bearn weorðað   geboren syþþan,
    þa ylcan ic   ær foreteode,"

4   5 nor do they share in the common struggles of human-kind, and they will not be afflicted by the power of others,

5   6 consequently, arrogance beyond bounds took hold of them, through which their iniquity was fully revealed.

6   7 From then on their vile iniquity emerged, as if it issued suddenly from fat; 8 and they contemplated and considered in their hearts how to express in an eminent house their deceit and iniquity most thoroughly and expeditiously.

7   9 They planted their spoken reflections in heaven, and their tongues roamed the earth.

8   10 (Because of this, my people will fittingly return here, where they will soon find fullness of days.)

9   11 And then they said: "How will this become known to God, or this evidence extend to high places"?

10   12 As a result, the wicked have now jubilantly taken possession of earth's goods and this world's wealth.

11   13 Then I at once said to myself: "Although not aware of any cause for complaint about how I truthfully controlled my heart, and although I washed my hands, even when I felt no spite, 14 yet I too was scourged all day, for me there was the finger of accusation in full daylight."

12   15 Even if I myself were to speak, and announce, "So, children will be born to you afterward, for whom I have already predestined the same fate,"

13 ic þæs wende, þæt ic mid wisdome
  full gleawlice ongitan mihte,
  hu þis gewinn wolde gangan,
  oþ þæt ic on his hus halig gange,
  and ic þa nehstan ongite neode syþþan.

14 Hwæðere þu him for inwite yfel befæle,
  awurpe hi wraðe, þa hi wendan ær
  þæt hi wæron alysde laðum wiðferede.

15 Nu syndon hi gewordene wraðe tolysde,
  and semninga sneome forwurdon
  for unrihte þe hi ær dydon,
  swa fram slæpe hwylc swærum arise.

16 And hi on byrig Drihtnes bealde habbað
  hiora ansyne, and þu hi eaðe miht
  to nawihte forniman sneome.

17 Ys minre heortan hige hluttor and clæne;
  wærun mine ædra ealle tolysde,
  and ic to nawihte eom nyde gebiged,
  swa ic þæt be owihte ær ne wiste.

18 Ic eom anlic mid þe anum neate,
  and ic symble mid þe syþþan hwæðere.

19 Þu mine swyþran hand sylfa gename,
  and me mid þinon willan well gelæddest,
  and me þa mid wuldres welan gename.

20 Hwæt mæg me wiðerhabban on heofon-rice;
  hwæt wolde ic fram þe wyrcean ofer eorþan?

13   [16] I thought that with well-considered wisdom I could understand how this struggle would resolve itself, [17] until such time as I should enter into his holy house, and afterward earnestly understand the most recent turn of events.

14   [18] Nevertheless, because of their deceit, you gave them over to evil and cast them down angrily, when they had already imagined that they were delivered, saved from misfortunes.

15   [19] Now they are become horribly desolated, and they perished all at once because of their previous depravity, [20] like someone who rises from oppressive sleep.

16   And they audaciously maintain their idolatrous images in the Lord's city, yet you could easily reduce them to nothing in an instant.

17   [21] The thought of my heart is pure and clean; my feelings were totally numbed, [22] and I am reduced to nothing by distress, as if I had not realized that at all.

18   [23] In your company I am like an animal, and yet I will be with you always in the hereafter.

19   [24] You personally took my right hand, and by your will guided me perfectly, and then you took possession of me in an abundance of glory.

20   [25] What can resist me in the heavenly kingdom; what did I wish to be done by you on earth?

21   Me is heorte and flæsc   hearde geteorad;
      ys me heortan gehygd   hyldu Drihtnes
      and ece dæl   awa to worulde.

22   For þan þa forweorþað,   þe hira wynne to þe
      habban noldan,   ne heora hyge settan;
      huru þu forleosest   þa forhealdað þe.

23   Min is ætfele   mihtigum Drihtne;
      good is swylce   þæt ic on God Drihten
      minne hiht sette,   healde fæste.

24   And ic eall þin lof   eft asecge
      Sione dohtrum   on hire sylfre durum.

Psalm 73

1   For hwan þu us, ece God,   æfre woldest
     æt ende fram þe   ahwær drifan?
     Is þin yrre strang   and egesa mycel
     ofer þin agen   eowde sceapa.

2   Gemun þin mann-weorod,   þæt þu, mihtig
                                              God,
     æt fruman ærest   fægere geworhtest.

3   Þu þines yrfes   æþele gyrde
     sylfa alysdest   and Sione byrig,
     on þam ilcan þu   eard gename;
     hefe þu þine handa   and hyn hiora oferhygd.

276

21   [26] My heart and flesh are severely exhausted; my heart's desire is the Lord's protection and an eternal inheritance forever.

22   [27] For they will perish who refuse to accept their joy from you, or set their heart on you; indeed, you will ruin those who ignore you.

23   [28] It is my lot to cleave to a mighty Lord; it is good also that I set my hope in the Lord God, and firmly maintain it.

24   And I will once again make known all your praises to the daughters of Zion, within its own doors.

Psalm 73

1   [1] Eternal God, why would you ever drive us away from you forever? Hovering over your own flock of sheep is your fierce anger and great terror.

2   [2] Mighty God, remember your congregation, which in the very beginning you graciously created.

3   You yourself freed the noble scepter of your inheritance and Zion's citadel, where you took up residence; [3] raise up your hands and crush their arrogance. Cruel enemies

Feala wyrgnessa   wraðe feondas
þinum þam halgum   hefige brohtan;
gylpað gram-hydige,   þa þin geo ehtan
and on þinra wica   wuniað midle.

4   Settan hiora tacen;   soþe ne ongeaton,
swa hi on wege   wyrcean sceoldon
wundor-beacen,   swa hi on wudu dydan.

5   Hi mid æxum duru   elne curfan,
and mid twy-ecgum   teoledan georne
þæt hi mid adesan   ealle towurpan.

6   Þa hi þæt þin fægere hus   fyre forbærndan
and on eorð-stede   eac gewemdan,
þæt þinum naman gewearþ   niode cenned.

7   Cwædan on heortan: "Wutan cuman ealle
and ure magas mid us;   wutun þyder gemot
habban
and symbel-dagas   swylce Drihtnes
on eorð-wege   ealle towurpan.

8   Ne we sweotul tacen   us geseoð ænig,
ne we on ænige wisan   witegan habbað
þæt us andgytes ma   æfre secgen."

9   Wilt þu hu lange,   Wealdend-Drihten,
edwit þolian   yfelum feondum,
and naman þinne   nu bysmriað
þa wiþer-weardan   wraþe wið ende?

10   For hwan awendest þu   wuldres ansyne
æfre fram us   eac þa swyðran hand
of þinum sceate   sylfa wið ende?

harshly brought down much abuse on your holy ones; ⁴ those hostile people boast, who formerly hated you, and dwell in the heart of your fortresses.

4   They set up their symbols; ⁵ they truly did not understand how they were destined to fashion a strange symbol on the way, as they did in the forest.

5   ⁶ They forcefully hacked doors with hatchets, and with two-edged axes and strove mightily to destroy everything with the adze.

6   ⁷ Then they burned down that splendid house of yours, and on earth also profaned what had been piously attributed to your name.

7   ⁸ They said in their hearts: "Let us all assemble, and our kinsmen with us; let us hold an assembly there and also totally abolish on earth the Lord's festive days.

8   ⁹ Nor do we see any divine portent that is clear to us, nor do we have prophets who can ever in any way announce a better understanding to us."

9   ¹⁰ Sovereign Lord, how long are you willing to put up with abuse from those wicked enemies, and will those perverse people now maliciously besmirch your name for all time?

10   ¹¹ Why do you ever turn away from us your glorious face and that right hand from out of your own bosom, for all time?

11   Usser God kynincg,   geara þu worhtest,
      ær woruld wære,   wise hælu
      on þisse eorþan   efen-midre.

12   Þu on þines mægenes   mihte spedum
      sæ gesettest;   swylce gebræce
      þæt dracan heafod   deope wætere.

13   Þu þæs myclan dracan   mihtum forcome,
      and his þæt hearde   heafod gescændest,
      sealdest Siglhearwum   syððan to mose.

14   Þu sylfa eac   toslite wyllas
      and hlynnende   hlude streamas
      on Æthane   ealle adrigdest.

15   Þu dæg settest   and deorce niht;
      swylce þu gesettest   sunnan and monan;
      ealle þu geworhtest   eorðan gemæru,
      sumor þu and lencten   swylce geworhtest.

16   Wes þu gemyndig   manna bearna,
      þæra gesceafta   þe þu gesceope ðe;
      fynd ætwitað   fæcne Drihtne,
      unwis folc ne wat   þinne wyrðne naman.

17   Ne syle þu unscyldigra   sawla deorum,
      þe þe andettað   earme þearfan;
      þara þu on ealdre ne forgit,   ece Drihten.

18   Geseoh þu nu sylfa, God,   soð is gecyðed:
      nu þin gewitnes ys   wel gefylled,
      hu deorce beoð   dagas on eorðan
      þam þe unrihtes   æghwær wyrceað.

11   12 God, our king, in former times before the world came into being, you created providential security in this earth's very center.

12   13 With the might of your power, you quickly established the sea; likewise, you crushed the dragon's head in deep water.

13   14 You overcame that powerful dragon's might, and crushed that hard head of his, giving it afterward to the Ethiopians as food.

14   15 You yourself also destroyed the wells, and totally dried up the loud, roaring, torrents in Ethan.

15   16 You established the day and the dark night; you also positioned the sun and moon; 17 you marked all the earth's boundaries, summer and spring you also created.

16   18 Be mindful of humankind, those creatures which you created for yourself; enemies maliciously reproach the Lord, an ignorant people does not know your worthy name.

17   19 Do not surrender to wild beasts the souls of the innocent, those wretched poor who acknowledge you; do not forget them forever, eternal Lord.

18   20 God, see now for yourself that the reality is revealed: now that your covenant is satisfactorily fulfilled, how uncertain are the days on earth for those who commit injustice everywhere.

19   Ne byð se eadmoda   æfre gecyrred;
     þeah þe wædla   and þearfa, he wyle
     naman þinne   neode herian.

20   Aris, Drihten God,   dem þine nu
     ealde intingan;   eac wes gemyndig
     hu þe unwise   edwita fela
     þurh ealne dæg   oft aspræcon.

21   Ne forgit huru   godra manna
     soðra stefna   þa þe seceað þe;
     fyll þa oferhydigan   ða ðe feogeað þe,
     and eft to þe   ealle stigað.

Psalm 74

1   We þe andettað,   ecne Drihten,
     and þe andettað   ealle þeoda
     and naman þinne   neode ciegen.

2   Ic þin wundur eall   wræclic sæcge,
     swa ic fæstlicast mæg   befon wordum,
     and eac soð   symble deme.

3   Eorðe is gemolten   and hire eardend mid;
     ic þonne hire swyre   symble getrymme.

4   Ic to yflum cwæð   oft nalæs seldan:
     "Nelle ge unriht   ænig fremman
     and agyltan,"   —þæt hi ne gulpan þæs—

19   ²¹ The humble person will never be turned away; though poor and destitute, that one will eagerly praise your name.

20   ²² Lord God, arise and judge now your long-standing causes; be mindful also that the ignorant frequently utter many insulting comments about you all day long.

21   ²³ Indeed, do not forget the genuine cries of the virtuous who seek you; kill the arrogant who hate you, and afterward all will ascend to you.

Psalm 74

1   ² We will acknowledge you, eternal Lord, and all the peoples will praise you and eagerly invoke your name.

2   I will declare all your extraordinary wonders ³ as reliably as I can frame words, and I will also render just judgments always.

3   ⁴ The earth with its inhabitants is dissolved; I, however, will continuously strengthen its pillars.

4   ⁵ Very often I said to the wicked, "Do not plan to do any wicked deed, and to sin,"—lest they boast of it—

5 "ne ahebbað ge to hea eowre hyge-þancas,
  ne ge wið Gode æfre gram-word sprecan."

6 For þon eastan ne cymeð gumena ænig,
  ne of west-wegum wera cneorissa,
  ne of þissum westum widum morum.
  For þon him is dema Drihten sylfa,

7 sumne he gehyneð, sumne ahefeð sniome,
  for þon se wines steap on waldendes handa
  fægere gefylled is; þæs onfehð þe he ann.

8 Þonne he of þysum on þæt þonne oncerreð,
  nyle he þa dærstan him don unbryce,
  for þam sculon ealle drincan synfulle,
  þa on þysse foldan fyrene wyrceað.
  Ic þonne worulde gefean wynnum healde,
  and Iacobes Gode georne singe.

9 Ealra fyrenfulra fyhte-hornas
  ic bealdlice gebrece sniome;
  swyþe beoð ahafene þa soðfæstan.

Psalm 75

1 God wæs geara cuð mid Iudeum,
  and his æþele nama mid Israelum.

2 Is on sibbe his stow soþe behealden,
  and he on Sione swylce eardað.

5   6 "and do not raise too high your ambitions, nor ever utter angry words against God."

6   7 For nobody will come from the east, nor any peoples from the west, nor from these deserts with their vast mountains. 8 Because God himself is their judge,

7   he puts down one, and quickly raises up another, 9 for the beaker of wine in the ruler's hand is full to overflowing; and that one receives it to whom God is pleased to grant it.

8   Whenever he tilts the beaker from this one to that one, he will be sure to make the dregs serve his purpose; and so, all sinners who commit iniquities on this earth are forced to drink. 10 I, however, will gladly hold on to the world's pleasures, and eagerly sing to the God of Jacob.

9   11 I will boldly smash the battle horns of all the wicked quickly; the just will be greatly exalted.

Psalm 75

1   2 God was famed among the Jews from long ago, his eminent name among the Israelites.

2   3 His place is truly inhabited peacefully, and he also dwells on Zion.

3   Þær he horn-bogan   hearde gebendeð,
and sweord and sceld   æt gescot-feohta.

4   Þu wræclice   wundrum onlyhtest
fram þam eceum hider   æðelum beorgum.
Ealle synt yrre,   þa þe unwise
heora heortan hige   healdað mid dysige,
hi slæp hiora   swæfun unmurne;
ne þær wiht fundan   þa þe welan sohtan,
þæs þe hi on handum   hæfdan godes.

5   For þinre þrea   þriste ongunnon,
Iacobes God,   georne slepan,
þa þe on horsum   hwilon wæron.
Is þin egesa mycel: hwylc mæg æfre þe,
gif þu yrre byst,   ahwær wiðstandan?

6   Þonne þu of heofenum dom   hider on eorþan
mid gescote sendest,   þonne hio swyþe beofað.
Ðonne to dome   Drihten ariseð
þæt he on eorðan do   ealle hale
þe he mild-heorte   meteð and findeð.

7   For þon ðe mannes geþoht   mægen andetteð,
and þonne þa lafe   lustum þence,
þæt ic þe symbel-dæg   sette and gyrwe.

8   Gehatað nu Drihtne,   and him hraðe gyldað
eowrum þam godan   Gode georne;
ealle þe on ymb-hwyrfte   ahwær syndan,
him gyfe bringen   gode and clæne.

9   To þam egsan sceal   æghwylc habban,
þe wera gastum   wealdeð and healdeð;
eorð-cynincgum   se ege standeð.

3   [4] There he tightly bends the horn-shaped bow, as well as sword and shield, in missile battles.

4   [5] From those noble, enduring mountains on this side you shine strangely and marvelously. [6] All those who foolishly follow the reckless thoughts of their hearts are confused; they slept their undisturbed sleep; nor did they who sought wealth find there anything of what they previously had of valuables in their possession.

5   [7] God of Jacob, because of your rebuke, they boldly began to sleep soundly, they who were previously on horses. [8] Great is the fear you excite: who can ever in any way withstand you if you are angry?

6   [9] Whenever you hurl a judgment from the heavens down here on the earth, it trembles exceedingly. [10] Then the Lord rises up in judgment to make safe all those he finds and discovers to be compassionate.

7   [11] For the human mind will acknowledge your power, and then gladly ponder what remains, so that I may arrange and prepare a day of celebration for you.

8   [12] Make a promise now to the Lord, and promptly pay homage to him with zeal, that incomparable God of yours; let all who are present anywhere round about, bring him gifts of quality and purity.

9   Everyone should be in awe of that one [13] who controls and rules human souls; the kings of the earth stand in awe.

Psalm 76

1   Ic mid stefne ongann   styrman to Drihtne,
    and he me gehyrde   and beheold sona.

2   Ic on earfoð-dæge   ecne Drihten
    sohte mid handum   swyþe geneahhe,
    and ic on niht for him   neode eode;
    næs ic on þam siðe   beswicen awiht.

3   And ic swiðe wiðsoc   sawle minre
    fælre frofre;   þa ic fæste God
    gemyndgade,   þær ic hæfde mæstne hiht.

4   Swyðe ic begangen wæs,   and min sylfes gast
    wæs hwonlice   ormod worden;
    wæron eagan mine   eac mid wæcceum
    werded swyþe,   ne spræc ic worda feala.

5   Þa ic ealde dagas   eft geþohte,
    hæfde me ece gear   ealle on mode.

6   Ic þa mid heortan ongann   hycggean nihtes;
    wæs min gast on me   georne gebysgad.

7   Þa ic sylfa cwæð: "Ic to soðe wat,
    nele þis ece God   æfre toweorpan,
    ne us witnian   for his wel-dædum,
    oððe wiþ ende   æfre to worulde,
    his milde mod   mannum afyrran
    on woruld-life   wera cneorissum.

8   Ne byð æfre God   ungemyndig
    þæt he miltsige   manna cynne,

288

Psalm 76

1   2 Loudly I began to invoke the Lord, and he heard me and soon paid heed.

2   3 On a difficult day I sought very earnestly the eternal Lord with outstretched hands, and at night I entered eagerly into his presence; nor was I in the least deceived in that course of action.

3   Yet I vehemently denied true help to my soul; 4 when I diligently remembered God, then I experienced the greatest hope.

4   I was exceedingly preoccupied, and my very soul became somewhat despondent; 5 also my eyes were seriously blurred with vigils, I spoke few words.

5   6 Then I again thought on days of old, I entertained fully in my mind the eternal years.

6   7 I began then to commune with my heart at night; my soul within was seriously preoccupied.

7   8 Then I myself said: "I know for a fact that this eternal God, because of his kind actions, would never want to cast off or punish us, 9 or ever, to the end, withdraw from humankind in this world his compassionate disposition toward them.

8   10 God will never forget to take pity on humankind, nor

oþþe on yrre æfre wille
his milde mod mannum dyrnan."

9 And ic selfa cwæð: "Nu ic sona ongann
þas geunwendnes wenan ærest
þara hean handa haligan Drihtnes,
weorca wræclicra worda gemyndig,
þæt he æt fruman wundor fæger geworhte."

10 Þa ic metegian ongan mænigra weorca:
hu ic me on eallum þam eaðust geheolde;
on eallum þinum weorcum ic wæs smeagende,
swylce ic on þinum gehylde sylf begangen.

11 Ys weruda God on wege halgum;
hwylc is mihtig god butan ure se mæra God?
Þu eart ana God þe æghwylc miht
wundor gewyrcean on woruld-life.

12 Eft þu þine mihte mænige cyðdest
folcum on foldan; þu wiðferedes eac
Israhela bearn of Ægyptum.

13 Hwæt, þe, wuldres God, wæter sceawedon,
and þe gesawon sealte yþa;
forhte wurdan flodas gedrefde,
wæs sweg micel sealtera wætera.

14 Sealdon weorðlice wolcnas stefne
þurh þine stræle strange foran;
wæs þunurrad-stefn strang on hweole.

15 Þonne ligette lixan cwoman,
eall ymb-hwyrft eorðan onhrerdan.

will he ever wish in anger to suppress his compassionate regard for them."

9   [11] And I myself said: "Now I have begun first of all to consider the matter of this immutability of the exalted one, the holy Lord's deeds, [12] recalling the words that produced marvelous works, mindful that he created glorious wonders at the beginning."

10   [13] Then I began to meditate on your many works: how in all those I very readily restrained myself; I continued to ponder all your works, also I myself was devoted to your observances.

11   [14] The God of hosts belongs on a holy path; who else is a mighty god but that glorious God of ours? [15] You are the only God who is capable of creating this world's every wonder.

12   Later you gave many demonstrations of your power to the people on earth; [16] you also liberated the children of Israel from Egypt.

13   [17] The waters scrutinized you, God of glory, and the salty waves observed you; the depths were troubled by fear, [18] there was a mighty roar of sea waters.

14   The stately clouds projected sound forward through your powerful arrow, [19] the sound of thunder was violent in its rolling.

15   Then lightning came flashing, thoroughly disturbing the earth's environment.

16   Wærun wegas þine   on widne sæ,
and þine stige   ofer strang wæter;
ne bið þær eþe þin spor   on to findanne.

17   Folc þin ðu feredest   swa fæle sceap
þurh Moyses   mihtige handa
and Aarones,   ealle gesunde.

Psalm 77

1   Geheald þu, min folc,   mine fæste æ,
ahyldað eowre earan,   þæt ge holdlice
mines muðes word   mihte gehyran.

2   Ic on anlicnessum   ærest ontyne
mines sylfes muð,   secggean onginne
þa on world-ricum   wæron æt frymðe;

3   ealle þa we oncneowan,   cuð ongeaton,
and ure fæderas us   æror sægdon.

4   Noldan hi þa swiðe   heora synna dyrnan;
ac ylda gehwylc   oðrum cyðde.

5   Sægdon lof symble   leofum Drihtne
and his þa myclan miht,   mænigu wundur
þa he geworhte   wera cneorissum.

6   He aweahte   gewitnesse
on Iacobe   goode and strange,
and Israhelum   æ gesette,

16   ²⁰ Your ways were in the spacious sea, and your paths upon powerful waters; your track will not be easily discovered therein.

17   ²¹ You led your people like trusty sheep, absolutely unharmed, through the mighty hands of Moses and Aaron.

Psalm 77

1   ¹ My people, pay heed to my immutable law, incline your ears so that you may devoutly hear with all your might the words of my mouth.

2   ² I will first open my own mouth in parables, will begin to relate those things which existed at the beginning of the world;

3   ³ all those things we understood, knew for a fact, and our ancestors previously told them to us.

4   ⁴ They certainly did not wish much to conceal their sins at that time; rather, each age made them known to the next.

5   They continuously gave praise to the beloved Lord and those great powers of his, the many marvels which he performed for humankind.

6   ⁵ He revived in Jacob a covenant, effective and constant, and established a law for the Israelites,

7   þa he fæste bebead   fæderum ussum
     þæt hi heora bearnum   budun and sægdun,
     and cinn oðrum   cyðden and mærden.

8   Gif bearn wære   geboren þam fæder,
     him sceolde se yldra   eall gesæcgan,

9   þæt hi gleawne hiht   to Gode hæfdan,
     and his weorðlicu   weorc gemundon,
     and Godes bebodu   georne heoldan.

10   Ne wesen hi on facne   fæderum gelice;
     þæt wæs earfoð-cynn   yrre and reðe,
     næfdon heora heortan   hige gestaðelod;
     nis to wenanne   þætte wolde God
     hiora gasta mid him   gyman awiht.

11   Effremes bearn   ærest ongunnan
     of bogan stræle   bitere sendan,
     þæs hi on wiges dæge   wendon æfter.

12   Ne heoldan hi   halgan Drihtnes
     gewitnesse,   ne his weorca æ
     awiht wislice   woldan begangan.

13   Ealra god-dæda hi   forgiten hæfdon,
     and þara wundra,   þe he worhte ær,
     þara heora yldran   on locadan.

14   He on Ægypta   agenum lande
     him worhte fore   wundur mære
     and on Campotanea   eac mid soðe.

15   He sæ toslat,   sealte yþa
     gefæstnade,   and hi foran þurh.

7   which he sternly commanded our fathers to proclaim and relate to their children, and the generations to declare and make known to the next.

8   If a son was born to a father, the latter was obliged to relate all those things to him,

9   [7] namely, that they were to maintain a prudent hope in God, and keep in mind his noble works, and earnestly observe God's commands.

10   [8] They should not be deceitful like their ancestors; that was a depraved generation, perverse and cruel, which had not strengthened the disposition of their hearts; it is not to be expected that God would in any way maintain their souls in his safekeeping.

11   [9] The children of Ephraim first began to shoot sharp arrows from their bows, although they turned back on the day of battle.

12   [10] They did not observe the holy Lord's covenant, nor were they at all willing to observe prudently the law of his creations.

13   [11] They had forgotten all the good works and the marvels he once performed, [12] which their ancestors had witnessed.

14   He had worked great wonders in their presence in the land assigned to them in Egypt and indeed in Campotanea also.

15   [13] He divided the sea, bound the salty waves, and they passed through.

16   Him wisode   wolcen unlytel
      daga æghwylce,   swa hit Drihten het,
      and him ealle niht   oðer beacen,
      fyres leoma,   folc-nede heold.

17   He on westene   wide ædran
      him of stane let,   strange burnan.

18   Of þam wæter cwoman   weorude to helpe,
      swyþe wynlice   wætera þryðe.

19   Þa hi hira firene   furþur ehtan,
      and hine on yrre   eft gebrohtan,
      heora heafod-weard   holdne on lande.

20   Hi þa on heortan   hogedon to niðe
      and geornlice   Godes costadan,
      bædan hiora feorum   foddur geafe,
      and gramlice   be Gode spræcan:
      "Ac we þæs ne wenað   þæt us witig God
      mæge bringan to   beod gegearwod
      on þisum westene   widum and sidum,

21   þeah þe he of stane   streamas lete,
      wæter on willan,   wynnum flowan.

22   Ne we hwæðere wenað   þæt he wihte mæge
      mid hlafe þis folc   her afedan."

23   Syþþan þæt gehyrde   halig Drihten,
      he ylde þa gyt   and eft gespræc;
      wæs gegleded fyr   on Iacobe,
      and his yrre barn   on Israhelas,

16 ¹⁴ A huge cloud guided them each day, just as the Lord directed it, and for them all night another sign, the glare of fire, sustained that people in their need.

17 ¹⁵ In the desert he released for them from a rock wide watercourses, powerful streams.

18 ¹⁶ As a relief to that company waters issued from that rock, an exceedingly pleasant surge of waters.

19 ¹⁷ Later they added to their vices even more, and once more provoked him, their chief and loyal protector on earth.

20 ¹⁸ They then contemplated malice in their hearts and eagerly tempted God, demanding that he provide sustenance to save them, ¹⁹ and they spoke sharply about God as follows: "But, we do not expect that the wise God is able to bring us to a prepared table in this desert extending far and wide,

21 ²⁰ even though he caused streams, welling water, to flow pleasingly from a rock.

22 Nor do we expect, still, that he can at all provision this people here with bread."

23 ²¹ After the holy Lord heard that, he still held back, but later responded; fire was kindled against Jacob, and God's anger burned against the Israelites,

24   for þon þe hi ne woldon   wordum Drihtnes
lustum gelyfan,   lare forhogedon.

25   Het he þa widan duru   wolcen ontynan
hea of heofenum   and hider rignan
manna to mose   manna cynne;
sealde him heofenes hlaf   hider on foldan,
and engla hlaf   æton mancynn,
and hwætenne   hæfdon to genihte.

26   And awehte þa   windas of heofenum,
Auster ærest   and þa Affricum.

27   Him þa eac feoll ufan   flæsc to genihte;
swa sand sæs   oððe þiss swearte dust
coman gefiðrade   fugelas swylce,

28   and on middan þa wic   manige feollan,
and ymb hiora sele-gescotu   swiðe geneahhe.

29   Swiðe ætan   and sade wurdan,
and hiora lusta   lifdan hwile;
næron hi bescyrede   sceattes willan.

30   Þa gyt hi on muðe   heora mete hæfdon,
þa him on becwom   yrre Drihtnes,
and heora mænige   mane swultan;
æðele Israhela   eac forwurdan.

31   In eallum hi þissum   ihtan synne
and noldan his wundrum   wel gelyfan.

32   Hi heora dagena tid   dædun idle,
and heora geara gancg   eac unnytte.

24   22 because they were not willing to believe gladly in the Lord's words, they despised his teaching.

25   23 He ordered the wide doors in the heavens above to reveal the clouds 24 and to rain down here manna as food for humankind; he gave them the bread of heaven here on earth, 25 and humankind ate the bread of angels, enjoying that wheaten food in abundance.

26   26 And then from the heavens he stirred up winds, first Auster and then Africus.

27   27 Moreover, flesh for the people also dropped then from above in abundance; like the sands of the sea or the dusky powder of this earth, feathered birds arrived also,

28   28 and many fell in the middle of the camp, and very abundantly so around their tents.

29   29 The people ate voraciously and were sated, and for a time gave free rein to their appetites; 30 they were not deprived of the desire for material things.

30   They still had their food in their mouths 31 when the Lord's anger came down on them, and many of them died in sin; Israel's nobility perished too.

31   32 In all these events they added to their sin by refusing to truly believe in his miracles.

32   33 They passed the course of their days in frivolity, and the progress of their years just as uselessly.

33 Þonne he hi sare sloh,   þonne hi sohton hine,
    and ær leohte to him   lustum cwoman.

34 Syððan hi ongeaton   þæt wæs God heora
    fæle fultum,   freond æt þearfe;
    wæs hea God   heora alysend.

35 Hi hine lufedan   lease muðe;
    ne þæs on heortan   hogedan awiht.

36 Næs him on hreðre   heorte clæne,
    ne hi on gewitnesse   wisne hæfdon,
    on hiora fyrhþe   fæstne geleafan.

37 He þonne is mild-heort   and man-ðwære
    hiora fyren-dædum,   nolde hi to flymum gedon.

38 He þa manige fram him   man-gewyrhtan
    yrre awende;   eall ne wolde
    þurh hatne hyge   hæleðum cyþan.

39 And he gemunde   þæt hi wæran moldan and
                                            flæsc,
    gast gangende,   næs se geon-cer eft.

40 Hi hine on westenne   wordum and dædum
    on yrre mod   eft gebrohtan,
    aweahtan hine on eorðan   oft butan wætere.

41 Oft hi grimlice   Godes costodan,
    and Israhela God   eac abulgan.

42 Na gemynd hæfdan   hu his seo mycle hand
    on gewin-dæge   werede and ferede.

33   ³⁴ Whenever he harshly struck them, they sought him, and willingly came to him before daylight.

34   ³⁵ Afterward, they recognized that God was their faithful help, a friend in need; the high God became their redeemer.

35   ³⁶ They expressed love for him with false speech, nor did they at all consider that in their hearts.

36   ³⁷ They did not have a pure heart within, nor did they in their fear retain a sure belief in the covenant, a firm faith.

37   ³⁸ He, however, is gentle and compassionate toward their evil deeds, he did not wish to make outcasts of them.

38   He turned away from him in his anger those numerous perpetrators of evil; he did not wish to vent all his anger at humankind in the heat of passion.

39   ³⁹ And he remembered that they were dust and flesh, spirits on the move, for whom there was no second encounter.

40   ⁴⁰ In the desert by word and deed, they again put him in an angry mood, often inciting him in that parched land.

41   ⁴¹ Many times they severely tested God, and even provoked the Lord of Israel.

42   ⁴² They had no memory of how that powerful hand of his protected and carried them along in time of trouble.

43   He Ægypti   egesan geþywde,
mid feala tacna   and fore-beacna
in Campotaneos;   þæt wæs cuð werum.

44   Þær he wæter-streamas   wende to blode;
ne meahte wæter drincan   wihta ænig.

45   Sette him heard wite   hundes fleogan,
and hi ætan eac   yfle tostan,
hæfdan hi eallunga   ut aworpen.

46   Sealde erucan,   yfelan wyrme,
let hiora wyrta   wæstme forslitan,
and hiora gram gewinn   hæfdan gærs-hoppan.

47   Heora win-geardas   wraþe hægle
nede fornam;   nænig moste
heora hrorra hrim   æpla gedigean.

48   Sealde heora neat eac   swylce hæglum,
and heora æhta   ealle fyre.

49   He æbyligðe on hi   bitter and yrre,
sarlic sende   oð sawl-hord,
and þæt wið yfele   englas sende.

50   He him weg worhte   wraðan yrres,
ne he heora sawlum dead   swiðe ne sparude;
and heora neat   nið-cwealm forswealh.

51   He þa on þam folce   frum-bearna gehwylc
on Ægiptum   eall acwealde,
and frum-wæstme   folce Chames.

43   [43] He oppressed the Egyptians with fear, with many signs and portents in Campotaneos; that much was evident to everyone.

44   [44] There he converted streams to blood; nobody was able to drink that water.

45   [45] He laid upon them the harsh punishment of dog flies, and horrible frogs also devoured them, they utterly destroyed them.

46   [46] He sent *eruca,* by means of a vile insect, allowing it to devour the fruit of their plants, while locusts appropriated the fruits of their hard work.

47   [47] He utterly destroyed their vineyards with vicious hailstones; none of their hardy fruits were able to survive the hoar frost.

48   [48] Their animals likewise he gave over to hailstones, and all their possessions to fire.

49   [49] He directed sharp indignation and anger at them, painful to their very soul, and delivered that through malevolent angels.

50   [50] He beat a path of fierce anger to them, nor did he very much spare their souls from death; while a brutal pestilence consumed their cattle.

51   [51] He then struck down completely every firstborn among the people of Egypt, and the firstborn from the race of Ham.

52 Þa he his folc genam swa fæle sceap,
   lædde geliccast leofe eowde
   þurh westenas, wegas uncuðe,

53 and he hi on hihte holdre lædde;
   næs him on fyrhtu feondes egsa,
   ac ealle þa yþa fornamon.

54 He hi þa gelædde on leofre byrig
   and haligre, ða his hand begeat.

55 And he manige for him mære þeode
   awearp of wicum, sealde him weste land,
   þæt hi mid tane getugan rihte.

56 Þa Israelas æhte gesætan
   hrores folces, þa hi heanne God
   gebysmredan, noldon his bebodu
   fæste healdan.

57 Hi awendan aweg, nalæs wel dydan,
   swa heora fæderas beforan heoldan,
   and on wiðer-mede wendan and cyrdan.

58 Swa hi his yrre oft aweahtan,
   þonne hi oferhydig up ahofan,
   and him woh godu worhtan and grofun.

59 Þa þæt gehyrde halig Drihten,
   he hi forhogode, and hraðe syþþan
   Israhela cynn egsan geðyde.

60 And he þa swa Selome wiðsoc snytru-huse,
   wæs his agen hus, þær he eard genam
   ær mid mannum, mihtig hæfde.

52   ^{52} Then he gathered up his people like trusty sheep, guiding them like a favored flock through deserts, unfamiliar paths,

53   ^{53} and leading them with favorable expectations; for them fear of the enemy was not a source of terror, for waves engulfed all of them.

54   ^{54} Then he guided them to a citadel, beloved and holy, which his power had won.

55   And for their sakes he ejected many eminent peoples from their dwellings, giving the vacated territory to the Israelites, which they lawfully took control of by casting lots.

56   ^{55} When the Israelites occupied the land of a strong people, ^{56} they insulted the high God, refusing to observe his commandments faithfully.

57   ^{57} They went off track, they did not act well at all, just as their fathers had previously behaved, and they inclined and turned to depravity.

58   ^{58} So they frequently stirred up his anger, when they exalted their pride and shaped and carved for themselves idols.

59   ^{59} When holy Lord heard of that, he spurned them, and soon afterward he oppressed the Israelites with terror.

60   ^{60} And so he abandoned Shiloh then, the house of wisdom, which was his proper dwelling, where he had lived among humankind, maintained his power,

61　He hi þa on hæft-nyd　hean gesealde,
　　and heora fæger folc　on feondes hand.

62　Sealde þa his swæs folc　sweorde under ecge,
　　and his yrfe eac　eall forhogode.

63　Heora geoguðe eac　grimme lige
　　fyr fæðmade,　fæmnan ne wæran
　　geonge begrette,　þeah ðe hi grame swultan.

64　Wæran sacerdas heora　sweordum abrotene,
　　ne þæt heora widwan　wepan mostan.

65　Þa wearð aweaht　Wealdend-Drihten,
　　swa he slæpende　softe reste,
　　oððe swa weorð man　wine druncen.

66　He þa his feondas sloh,　and him ætfæste eac
　　ece edwit,　awa to feore.

67　And he georne wiðsoc　Iosepes huse,
　　ne þon ær geceas　Effremes cynn;
　　ac he geceas Iudan him,　geswæs frum-cynn
　　on Sione byrig,　þær him wæs symble leof.

68　He þa an-hornan　ealra gelicast
　　his halige hus　her on eorðan
　　getimbrade;　het ðæt teala syððan
　　on world-rice　wunian ece.

69　And him ða Dauid geceas　deorne esne,
　　and genam hine æt eowde　ute be sceapum,
　　fostur feormade,　he him onfencg hraðe.

61 ⁶¹ He then gave them over to abject captivity, and their fine folk into enemy hands.

62 ⁶² He surrendered his beloved people then to the sword's edge, and totally scorned his inheritance as well.

63 ⁶³ Fire too engulfed their youth with biting flames, their young women were not mourned, even though they died cruelly.

64 ⁶⁴ Their priests were slain by the sword, nor were their widows allowed to lament that.

65 ⁶⁵ Then the sovereign Lord was aroused, as if he had been gently resting in sleep, or like a man who is drunk on wine.

66 ⁶⁶ Then he killed his enemies, and also attached to them a perpetual reproach, for ever and ever.

67 ⁶⁷ And he studiously spurned the house of Joseph, nor did he any sooner choose the house of Ephraim; ⁶⁸ rather, he selected for himself Judah, a beloved tribe in the citadel of Zion, a place which he always loved.

68 ⁶⁹ He then built here on earth his holy sanctuary, of all things most like a unicorn; he rightly promised afterward that it should endure forever in this world.

69 ⁷⁰ And then he chose for himself David as his beloved servant, and plucked him out from a flock of sheep, fed and nurtured him, promptly took him on.

70   He þonne fedeð   folc Iacobes
and Israhela   yrfe-lafe.

71   And he hi þonne butan facne   fedeð syþþan,
and his folmum syþþan   hi forð lædeð.

Psalm 78

1   Comon on ðin yrfe,   ece Drihten,
fremde þeode,   þa þin fæle hus,
ealh haligne   yfele gewemdan.

2   Settan Hierusalem   samod anlicast
swa in æppel-bearu   ane cytan;
swylce hi setton   swylt þinum esnum,
sealdon flæsc heora   fuglum to mose,
haligra lic   hundum and deorum.

3   Hi þara bearna blod   on byrig leton,
swa man gute wæter   ymb Hierusalem;
blodige lagan,   nahtan byrgendas.

4   We synd gewordene   wera cneorissum,
eallum edwit-stæf   ymb-sittendum,
þe us ahwær neah   nu ða syndon.

5   Hu wilt þu, wuldres God,   wrað yrre þin
on ende fram us   æfre oncyrran?
Is nu onbærned   biter þin yrre
on ðinum folce   fyre hatre.

70   71 He will then nourish Jacob's people and the remnants of Israel's inheritance.

71   72 And then he will feed them with no malice, and afterward with his hands will lead them forth.

Psalm 78

1   1 Eternal Lord, alien peoples have entered into your inheritance, those who sacrilegiously defiled your beloved dwelling, the holy temple.

2   At the same time they set up Jerusalem like a storage shed in an orchard; 2 they also put to death your servants, abandoning their corpses to the birds as carrion, the bodies of the holy ones to dogs and wild animals.

3   3 They spilled the blood of children in the city, as if water were poured out around Jerusalem; the dead lay there in their blood, lacking gravediggers to bury them.

4   4 We are become a reproach to all humankind, to all those living around us, who are located anywhere near us just now.

5   5 God of glory, will you ever remove from us your fierce anger for all time? Your sharp anger is now inflamed hotter than fire against your people.

6 Ageot yrre þin on þæt rice
and on cneow-magas þe ne cunnan ðe,
ne naman þinne neode cigeað.

7 For þon hi Iacob geara ætan,
and his wic-stede westan gelome.

8 Ne gemune þu to oft, mihta wealdend,
ealdra unrihta þe we oft fremedon;
ac we hraðe begytan hyldo ðine
for þon we ðearfende þearle syndon.

9 Gefultuma us, frea ælmihtig,
and alys us, lifigende God;
weorð urum synnum sefte and milde
for naman þinum neode and aare,

10 þy læs æfre cweðan oðre þeoda,
hæðene herigeas, "Hwær com eower halig
               God?"
and us þæt on eagum oftust worpen,
þær manna wese mæst ætgædere.

11 Wrec agen blod esna þinra,
þæt wæs sarlice agoten, þær þu gesawe to;
geonge for ðe gnornendra care
þara þe on feterum fæste wæran.

12 Æfter ðines earmes æðelum mægene
gegang þa deaða bearn þe hi demað nu.

13 Gyld nu gram-hydigum, swa hi geearnedan,
on sceat hiora seofonfealde wrace,
for þon hi edwit on þe ealle hæfdon.

6 ⁶ Pour out your fury against that kingdom and against kinsmen who do not know you, nor earnestly call out your name.

7 ⁷ For they consumed Jacob in times past, and frequently ravaged his dwelling place.

8 ⁸ Ruler of power, do not recall too often the old iniquities which we often perpetrated; rather, let us promptly receive your favor because we are sorely in need of it.

9 ⁹ Almighty ruler, living God, assist and release us; for your name's sake be gentle and compassionate about our sins, with diligence and mercy,

10 ¹⁰ lest other peoples, heathen hordes, ever say, "Where did your holy God go?" and pose that question very often before us, where the greatest number of people congregate.

11 Avenge the very blood of your servants, which was cruelly spilled, to which you were witness; ¹¹ let the sorrow of those grieving, who were tightly bound in chains, come before you.

12 By the glorious power of your arm, take possession of the dead people's children on whom they are now passing judgment.

13 ¹² Render now sevenfold punishment to hostile people in their vitals, just as they have deserved, because they held you thoroughly in contempt.

14   We þin folc wærun   and fæle sceap
   eowdes þines;   we ðe andettað,
   and þe to worulde   wuldur sæcgeað,
   and þe on worulda woruld   wordum heriað.

Psalm 79

1   Þu þe Israela   æðelum cynne
   reccest and rædest,   ðu nu recene beheald,
   þu ðe Ioseph swa sceap   gramum wiðlæddest.

2   Ðu ðe sylfa nu   sittest ofer cherubin,
   æteow fore Effraim,   eac Mannasse
   and Beniamin,   nu we biddað þe.

3   Awece þine mihte   and mid wuldre cum,
   and us hale do   her on eorðan.

4   Gehweorf us, mægena God,   and us mildne
                           æteow
   þinne andwlitan;   ealle we beoð hale.

5   Eala ðu, mægena God,   mære Drihten,
   hu lange yrsast þu   on þines esnes gebed?
   Tyhstð us and fedest   teara hlafe,
   and us drincan gifest   deorcum tearum
   manna gehwylcum   on gemet rihtes.

6   Þu us asettest   on sar-cwide
   urum neah-mannum;   nu we cunnion,
   hu us mid fraceðum   fynd bysmriað.

14 ¹³ We were your people and the trusty sheep of your flock; we will acknowledge you and declare your praise forever, and will extol you eternally in words.

Psalm 79

1 ² You who controls and guides the noble tribe of Israel pay attention at once, you who led away Joseph from his enemies like a sheep.

2 You yourself, who now sits enthroned above the Cherubim, ³ appear before Ephraim, and Manasseh and Benjamin, we beg you now.

3 Stir up your might, and advance in glory, and save us here on earth.

4 ⁴ God of hosts, turn us around, and reveal to us your gentle face; we will all be saved.

5 ⁵ Alas, God of hosts, eminent Lord, how long will you be angry with your servant's prayer? ⁶ You will feed and instruct us with the bread of tears, and will dispense in proper measure to us, to each person, a draft with gloomy tears.

6 ⁷ You established us as a pathetic byword to our neighbors; now we may discover how our enemies deride us with vile behavior.

7   Gehweorf us, mægena God,   and us mildne æteow
    þinne andwlitan;   ealle we beoð hale.

8   Þu of Ægyptum   ut alæddest
    wræstne win-geard;   wurpe þeode
    and þone ylcan ðær   eft asettest.

9   Þu him weg beforan   worhtest rihtne,
    and his wyrtruman   wræstne settest,
    þanon eorðe wearð   eall gefylled.

10   His se brada scua   beorgas þeahte,
    and his tanas astigun   Godes cedder-beam.

11   Ealle þa telgan   ðe him of hlidað,
    þu æt sæ-streamas   sealte gebræddest,
    and hi to flodas   forð aweaxað.

12   Forhwan þu towurpe   weall-fæsten his?
    Wealdeð his win-byrig   eall þæt on wege færð.

13   Hine utan of wuda   eoferas wrotað,
    and wilde deor   westað and frettað.

14   Gehweorf nu, mægena God,   milde and spedig,
    þine ansyne   ufan of heofenum;
    gewite and beseoh   win-geard þisne,
    þæt he mid rihte   ræde gange,
    þæne ðin seo swiðre   sette æt frymðe;
    and ofer mannes sunu,   þe þu his mihte ær
    under ðe getrymedest,   tires wealdend.

15   Fyr onbærneð,   folm þurhdelfeð;
    fram ansyne   egsan ðines
    ealle þa on ealdre   yfele forweorðað.

7   8 God of hosts, turn us around, and reveal to us your gentle face; we will all be saved.

8   9 You transplanted an excellent vineyard from Egypt; you cast out the gentiles and reestablished that same vineyard in their land.

9   10 You furrowed in advance a proper path for it, and established its excellent rootstock, by which the earth was totally filled.

10   11 Its broad shadow covered mountains, while its branches ascended God's cedar tree.

11   12 You extended as far as salty seawaters all the boughs that come forth from it, and they will grow steadily toward the rivers.

12   13 Why did you break down its fence? Every creature that passes by takes control of its walled vineyard.

13   14 Boars emerging from the wood root it up, and wild animals ravage and devour it.

14   15 God of hosts, gentle yet powerful, turn now your face from the heavens above; 16 glorious ruler, guard and watch over this vineyard, which that right hand of yours established at the beginning, so that with proper guidance it may prosper; and watch over humankind whose power, subject to you, you previously confirmed.

15   17 Fire consumes it, a hand digs through it; all those will always be mortally destroyed by the sight of your terror.

16   Si þin seo swiðre hand   ofer soðne wer
and ofer mannes sunu;   þu his mihta ðe
geagnadest,   ealle getrymedest,
weoruda Drihten,   ne gewitað we fram ðe.

17   Ac þu us wel cwica,   wealdend mihtig,
we naman þinne   neode cigeað.

18   Gehweorf us, mægena . . .

Psalm 80

8   . . . gif þu, Israhel, a wylt   elne gehyran.

9   Gif þu, Israhel,   me anum gehyrst,
ne byð god on þe   niwe gemeted,
ne þu fremedne god   sylfa gebiddest.

10   Ic eom þin God,   ðe geara þe
of Ægypta   eorþan alædde.

11   Ontyn þinne muð,   and ic hine teala fylle.
Nele min folc mine stefne   æfre gehyran,
ne me Israhel behealdan   holde mode.

12   Ac hi lifian het   lustum heortena,
swa him leofust wæs,   leode þeodum,
æfter hiora willum   wynnum miclum.

13   Þær min agen folc,   Israhela cynn,
me mid gehygde   hyran cuðan,

16   ¹⁸ Let that right hand of yours rest upon the just man and the son of man; you appropriated his powers for yourself, strengthened all of them, Lord of hosts, ¹⁹ we will not depart from you.

17   Only make us come fully alive, mighty ruler, and we will call out your name eagerly.

18   ²⁰ Turn us around . . .

Psalm 80

8   . . . ⁹ if you, Israel, are willing to listen always with resolve.

9   ¹⁰ If you, Israel, will listen to me only, a newly minted god will not reside among you, nor will you yourself worship an alien deity.

10   ¹¹ I am your God, who in former days led you out of the land of Egypt.

11   Open wide your mouth, and I will fill it well. ¹² My people are reluctant ever to listen to my voice, nor is Israel willing to heed me with a devout disposition.

12   ¹³ And I bid them live by their heart's desires in unhindered pleasures, just as it pleased them most, the peoples of the nation.

13   ¹⁴ If my own people, Israel's kindred, had known how to

oþþe on wegas mine   woldan gangan,
þonne ic hiora fynd   fylde and hynde,
and þæt mycle mægen   minra handa
heora ehtendas   ealle fornam.

14   Him fynd Godes   fæcne leogað;
byð hiora yfele tid   awa to feore.

15   He hi fedde   mid fætre lynde,
hwæte and hunige,   þæt him halig God
sealde of stane,   oþ þæt hi sæde wæron.

Psalm 81

1   God mihtig stod   godum on gemange,
and he hi on midle   mægene tosceadeð:

2   "Hu lange deme ge   domas unrihte,
and ge onfoð ansyna   synn-wyrcendra?

3   Demað steop-cildum   domas soðe
and eadmedum   eac þæt sylfe,
wædlum and ðearfum,   wel soðfæstum;

4   ge of firenfulra   fæcnum handum
þearfan and wædlan   þriste alysað."

5   Ne ongeatan hi   ne geara wistan,
ac hi on ðystrum   þrage eodan;
ealle abeofedan   eorðan staþelas.

listen to me thoughtfully, or had been willing to walk in my ways, 15 then I could have cut down and crushed their enemies, and that powerful strength of my hands would have entirely devastated their persecutors.

14   16 God's enemies will maliciously deceive them; their time of misery will endure forever.

15   17 He fed them with the choicest of rich food, with wheat and honey, which holy God supplied to them from a rock, until they were sated.

Psalm 81

1   1 Mighty God stood among the gods, and in their midst he forcefully distinguishes between them, saying:

2   2 "How long will you render false judgments and listen favorably to practicing sinners?

3   3 Render just verdicts for orphans and the same also for the lowly, the poor, and the needy, the truly righteous;

4   4 and decisively release the poor and the needy from the cunning grasp of evildoers."

5   5 They did not perceive or clearly understand, but for a long time walked in darkness; all the foundations of the earth shook.

6   Ic ærest cwæð: "Ge synd uppe godu,
      ealle uphea   and æðele bearn,

7   ge þonne sweltað   samod mid mannum,
      swa ealdor-mann   an gefealleð."

8   Aris Drihten nu,   dem eorð-ware,
      for þan þu eart erfe-weard   ealra ðeoda.

Psalm 82

1   Hwylc is þe gelic,   ece Drihten?
      Ne swiga ðu   ne þe sylfne bewere,

2   for þon þine feond   fæcne forwurdan,
      þa ðe fæste ær   feodan, Drihten,
      and heora heafod wið þe   hofan swiðe.

3   Hi on ðinum folce him   facen geswipere
      syredan and feredan,   and to swice hogedon;
      and ehtunga   ealle hæfdon,
      hu hi þine halgan   her yfeladan.

4   Cwædan cuðlice: "Wutun cuman ealle
      and hi towyrpan   geond wer-þeoda,
      þæt ne sy gemyndig   manna ænig,
      hu Israhela naman   ænig nemne."

5   For þon hi an geþeaht   ealle ymbsætan,
      and gewitnesse wið þe   wise gesettan.

6   6 At first I said: "you are gods on high, all of you elevated and noble offspring,

7   7 yet you will die along with humans, just as the ruler will drop dead."

8   8 Lord, arise now, judge the inhabitants of earth, because you will be the guardian of all the peoples.

Psalm 82

1   2 Eternal Lord, who is like you? Do not be silent or restrain yourself,

2   3 for your enemies have utterly perished in disgrace, those who had consistently hated you, and forcefully raised their heads against you, Lord.

3   4 They cunningly plotted and contrived treachery against your people, and contemplated treachery; and fully deliberated about how to harm your holy ones on earth.

4   5 They said openly: "Let us all come and scatter them throughout the nations, so that nobody will remember that anyone invoked Israel's name."

5   6 So they unanimously decided on a single plan, and cleverly prepared testimony against you.

6   Sele-gesceotu synd   onsægd in Idumea
and Ismæhelita,   eac synt Moabes,
Ammon and Ammalech,   Agareni,
swylce Gebal   and grame manige
fremde þeoda mid eardiendum   folce on
                                  Tyrum.

7   Cwom samod mid ðam   swylce Assur;
ealle on wegum   æghwær syndon
on leod-stefnum   Loðes bearnum.

8   Do him nu swa ðu dydest   dagum Madiane
and Sisare,   swylce Iabin;
ealle þa namon   Ændor wylle
and Cisone   clæne hlimme,
wurdan þa earme   eorþan to meohxe.

9   Sete heora ealdor-menn   swa ðu Oreb dydest,
Zeb and Zebee   and Salmanaa,
and heora ealdrum   eallum swylce;
ealle þa on an   ær gecwædon,
þæt hi halignesse Godes   her gesettan.

10   Sete hi nu, min God,   samod anlice
swa se wægnes hweol   oþþe windes healm,
and swa færincga   fyr wudu byrneð,
oððe swa lig freteð   lungre mor-hæð.

11   Swa þu hi on yrre   ehtest and drefest
þæt hi on hrernesse   hraþe forweorðað.

12   Gedo þæt hiora ansyn   awa sceamige,
þonne hi naman þinne   neode seceað.

6   7 The tents have come down among the Edomites and Ishmaelites, likewise, those of Moab, Ammon and Amalek, the Hagarenes, 8 Gebal and many hostile gentiles, along with Tyre's inhabitants.

7   9 The Assyrian also joined forces with them; they are all on the highways everywhere in companionable clamor with Lot's offspring.

8   10 Deal with them now as you did in the days of Midian and Sisera and Jabin also; 11 the spring of Endor and the clear torrent of Kishon carried off all of them, those wretches became dung for the soil.

9   12 Dispose of their princes as you did Oreb and Zeeb and Zebah and Zalmunna, and all their elders also; 13 all of them in unison once declared that they would take possession of God's sanctuary on this earth.

10   14 My God, dispose of them now just like the wheel of a wagon, or straw before the wind, 15 and as a fire suddenly burns up a wood, or a flame quickly consumes heather on the moor.

11   16 You will so persecute and harass them in anger that they will quickly perish in the commotion.

12   17 Ensure that their faces will always be filled with shame, whenever they eagerly seek your name.

13 Ealle beoð georette   eac gescende,
    and on weoruld-life   weorþað gedrefde,
    þonne hi naman þinne   neode seceað.

14 Þu ana eart   ofer ealle heah
    eorð-buende,   ece Drihten.

.

Psalm 83

1   Synd me wic þine   weorðe and leofe,
    mægena Drihten;   a ic on mode þæs
    willum hæfde   þet ic him wunude onn.

2   Heorte min and flæsc   hyhtað georne
    on þone lifigendan   leofan Drihten;
    him eac spedlice   spearuwa hus begyteð,
    and tidlice   turtle nistlað,
    þær hio afedeð   fugelas geonge.

3   Wærun wig-bedu þin,   weoruda Drihten;
    þu eart Drihten min   and deore cynincg.

4   Eadige weorðað   þa þe eardiað
    on þinum husum,   halig Drihten,
    and þe on worulda woruld,   wealdend, heriað.

5   Þæt byð eadig wer   se þe him oðerne
    fultum ne seceð   nymþe fælne God,
    and þæt on heortan   hige healdeð fæste,
    geseteð him þæt sylfe   on ðisse sargan dene,

324

13   [18] All of them will be confounded and put to shame, and they will be troubled in their lifetime, whenever they eagerly seek your name.

14   [19] You alone, eternal God, are on high above all earth's inhabitants.

Psalm 83

1   [2] Lord of hosts, your dwellings are precious and dear to me; [3] I have always willingly entertained the thought of living in them.

2   My heart and my flesh eagerly yearn for that beloved living God; [4] the sparrow also successfully obtains a home for itself, and the turtledove opportunely nests where she feeds her nestlings.

3   God of hosts, those dwellings were your altars; you are my Lord and beloved king.

4   [5] They are blessed who dwell in your houses, and who will praise you, holy Lord and ruler, for ever and ever.

5   [6] He is a happy man who does not seek any other help for himself except a trustworthy God, and firmly maintains that trust in the recesses of his heart, [7] proposing the like for those in this sorrowful valley, when the grief of tears op-

þær hi teara   teonan cnyssað,
on þam sylfan stede   þe þu him settest her.

6   Brohte him bletsunge,   se ðe him beorhte æ
soðe sette;   syþþan eodan
of mægene on mægen;   þær wæs miht gesawen
on Sion-beorge   soðes Drihtnes.

7   Gehyr min gebed,   halig Drihten;
þu eart mære God,   mildum earum,
and Iacobes   God se mæra.

8   Beseoh Drihten nu,   scyldend usser,
oncnaw onsyne   cristes þines.

9   Betere is micle   to gebidanne
anne dæg mid þe   þonne oðera
on þeod-stefnum   þusend mæla.

10   Ic me þæs wyrce,   and wel ceose
þæt ic hean gange   on hus Godes,
þonne ic on fyrenfulra   folce eardige.

11   For þon God lufað   geornast ealles
þæt man si mild-heort   mode soðfæst,
þonne him God gyfeð   gyfe and wuldur.

12   Nele God æfre   gode bedælan,
þa ðe heortan gehygd   healdað clæne;
þæt bið eadig mann,   se þe him ecean Godes
to mund-byrde   miht gestreoneð.

presses them, in that same place which you established for them on this earth.

6   [8] He who truly established an excellent law for them, bestowed a blessing on them; afterward they went from strength to strength; the power of the true God was manifested there on Mount Zion.

7   [9] Holy Lord, hear my prayer; you are the glorious God, a compassionate listener and the splendid God of Jacob.

8   [10] Lord, our protector, look now, observe the face of your anointed one.

9   [11] Much better to worship in your company for a single day than spend a thousand other occasions among the clamor of the people.

10   I will effect that, and make a wise choice to enter into the exalted house of God rather than dwell among a multitude of sinners.

11   [12] For God loves best of all for people to be compassionate and truthful in disposition, he bestows then grace and glory on them.

12   [13] God will never deprive of good things those who keep their heart's intention innocent; he is a happy man who gains as protection for himself the eternal God's power.

Psalm 84

1   Þu bletsadest,   bliðe Drihten,
foldan fæle,   and afyrdest eac
of Iacobe   þa graman hæftned.

2   Unriht þu forlete   eallum þinum folce,
and heora fyrene   fæste hæle.

3   Eall þu þin yrre   eðre gedydest;
na ðu ure gyltas   egsan gewræce.

4   Gehweorf us hraðe,   hælend Drihten,
and þin yrre fram us   eac oncyrre,
þæt ðu us ne weorðe   wrað on mode.

5   Ne wrec þu þin yrre   wraðe mode
of cynne on cynn   and on cneorisse;
gecyr us georne to ðe,   Crist ælmihtig,
and ðin folc on ðe   gefeo swiðe.

6   Æteow us milde mod,   mihtig Drihten,
and us þine hæle syle   her to genihte.

7   Syþþan ic gehyre,   hwæt me halig God
on minum mod-sefan   mælan wille;
sybbe he his folces   seceð geornast,
and swiðust to þam   þe hine seceað.

8   Hwæðere he is mid soðe   forswiðe neah
þam þe egsan his   elne healdað,
hæleð mid hyldo,   and him her syleð
ure eorðan   æðele wuldor.

Psalm 84

1   [2] Gracious God, you blessed an excellent land, and also removed that oppressive captivity from Jacob.

2   [3] You forgave all your people their iniquities, and speedily made right their transgressions.

3   [4] You withdrew all your anger at once; you certainly did not revenge our sins with terror.

4   [5] Savior Lord, turn us around quickly, and also avert your anger from us, [6] so that you will not continue to be angry with us.

5   Do not vent your anger with a hostile attitude from generation to generation and forever; [7] Christ almighty, turn us eagerly to you, and may your people rejoice greatly in you.

6   [8] Mighty Lord, show us a merciful disposition, and give us your salvation in abundance here on earth.

7   [9] Afterward I will hear what holy God wishes to say to me in the recesses of my mind; he tries most eagerly to obtain peace for his people, and especially for those who seek him.

8   [10] Nevertheless, he is in truth very close to those who strongly maintain their awe of him, loyal followers, and gives resplendent glory to them here on our earth.

9   Him gangað ongean   gleawe cræftas,
mild-heortnesse mod   and mihte soð,
and hine sybbe lufu   swylce clyppeð.

10   Up of eorðan cwom   æþelast soða,
beseah soðfæstnes   samod of heofenum.

11   Syleð us fremsum god   fægere Drihten,
þonne us eorðe syleð   æðele wæstmas.

12   Hine soðfæstnes   symble foregangeð
and on weg setteð   wise gangas.

Psalm 85

1   Ahyld me þin eare,   halig Drihten,
for ðon ic eom wædla,   þu me wel gehyr,
and ic sylfa eom   sorhfull þearfa.

2   Geheald mine sawle,   for ðon ic halig eom,
hæl þinne scealc,   for þon ic ðe hihte to.

3   Miltsa me Drihten,   þonne ic mægene to ðe
þurh ealne dæg   elne cleopade;
do þines scealces   sawle bliðe,
for ðon ic hi to ðe   hebbe genehhige.

4   For ðon þu eart wynsum,   Wealdend-Drihten;
is þin milde mod   mycel and genihtsum
eallum þam þe þe   elne cigeað.

9   ¹¹ Discerning virtues advance to meet him, a disposition to mercy and powerful truth, and love of peace also embraces him.

10   ¹² From out of the earth issued the noblest of truths, at the same time justice looked down from the heavens.

11   ¹³ The Lord will graciously bestow on us acts of kindness, while the earth yields excellent fruits for us.

12   ¹⁴ Justice will always go before him and will carefully lay down steps along the way.

Psalm 85

1   ¹ Holy God, incline your ear to me, because I am needy, listen to me carefully, seeing that I myself am an anxious, needy person.

2   ² Preserve my soul, for I am holy; save your servant because I hope in you.

3   ³ Lord, have mercy on me, seeing that I invoked you forcefully all through the day; ⁴ make your servant's soul glad, because I raise it up to you frequently.

4   ⁵ For you are kind, sovereign Lord; your gentle spirit is magnanimous and generous toward all those who boldly call on you.

5   Þu mid earum onfoh,   ece Drihten,
     min agen gebed,   and eac beheald,
     hu ic stefne to ðe   stundum cleopige.

6   Þonne me on dæge   deorc earfoðe
     carelice cnyssedan,   þonne ic cleopode to ðe
     for þon þu me gehyrdest   holde mode.

7   Nis þe goda ænig   on gum-rice
     ahwær efne gelic,   ece Drihten,
     ne ðe weorc magon   wyrcean anlic.

8   Ealle þu geworhtest   wera cneorissa,
     þa þe weorðiað,   wuldres Aldor,
     and naman Drihtnes   neode cigeað.

9   For ðan ðu eart se mycla   mihtiga Drihten,
     þe wundor miht   wyrcean ana.

10   Gelæd, Drihten, me   on þinne leofne weg,
     and ic on þinum soðe   syþþan gancge.

11   Heorte min ahlyhheð,   þonne ic ðinne halgan
                                    naman
     forhtige me on ferhðe;   forð andette
     mid ealre heortan hyge,   þæt þu eart, halig
                                    God,
     nemned Drihten,   and we naman þinne
     on ecnesse   a weorðien.

12   Ys þin mild-heortnes mycel   ofer me, Drihten,
     and þu mine sawle   swylce alysdest
     of helwarena   hinder-þeostrum.

13   God min se leofa,   gram-hydige me
     mid unrihte   oft onginnað,

332

5   6 Eternal Lord, give ear to my personal prayer, and observe also how I invoke you from time to time.

6   7 When, by day, dark troubles oppressed me with anxiety, I called to you because you listened to me graciously.

7   8 Eternal God, no god anywhere in the world is your equal, nor are they able to perform works like you do.

8   9 Prince of glory, you created all the generations, those who will worship you and eagerly call out the Lord's name.

9   10 For you are the great, mighty Lord, who alone is able to work wonders.

10   11 Lord, direct me in your cherished path, and I will afterward walk in your truth.

11   My heart will exult whenever in my soul I fear your holy name; 12 from now on, I will acknowledge with my heart's full purpose that you, holy God, are called the Lord, and let us honor your name always, and forever.

12   13 Lord, your mercy to me is great, and you also rescued my soul from the underground darkness of hell's inhabitants.

13   14 Beloved God of mine, hostile people frequently assail me unjustly, and assemblies of the very powerful have

and gesamnincge   swið-mihtigra
sohton mine sawle   swyþe geneahhe;
ne doð him for awiht   egsan Drihtnes.

14   Hwæt, þu eart, min Drihten God,   dædum
                              mild-heort,
   þenden geðyldig,   þearle soðfæst.

15   Beseoh nu on me,   and me syþþan weorð
   milde on mode,   mihtig Drihten;
   geteoh hrore meaht   hysse þinum,
   do þinre þeowan sunu,   Drihten, halne.

16   Do gedefe mid me,   Drihten, tacen,
   and þæt god ongitan,   þa me georne ær
   fæste feodan;   habban forð sceame.

17   For þon þu me wære fultum   fæste, Drihten,
   and me frefredest,   frea ælmihtig.

Psalm 86

1   Healdað his staðelas   halige beorgas;
   lufude Sione duru   symble Drihten
   ofer Iacobes wic   goode ealle.

2   Wærun wuldurlice wið þe   wel acweðene:
   þæt þu si cymast   ceastra Drihtnes;
   eac ic gemyndige   þa mæran Raab
   and Babilonis   begea gehwæðeres.

sought my soul very often; they set no store at all by fear of the Lord.

14   15 My Lord God, you are compassionate in deeds, patient in the meantime, exceedingly upright.

15   16 Mighty Lord, look at me now, and afterward become kindly disposed to me; assign robust power to your young man, save your handmaid's son, Lord.

16   17 Lord, convey a suitable message through me, and may they who had eagerly and consistently hated me, recognize that advantage; may they experience shame from here on.

17   For you were steadily a support for me, Lord, and you, almighty ruler, consoled me.

Psalm 86

1   1 His foundations uphold the holy mountains; 2 the Lord has always loved Zion's doors over all Jacob's excellent dwellings.

2   3 Glorious things were eloquently said about you: that you are the loveliest of the Lord's cities; 4 I will be reminded also of the famed Rahab and of Babylon, each of them.

3   Efne, fremde cynn   foran of Tyrum,
    folc Sigelwara   naman þær fæstne eard.

4   Modor Sion   "man" cwæð ærest,
    and hire mære gewearð   mann on innan,
    and he hi þa hehstan   her staðelade.

5   Drihten þæt on gewritum   dema sægde
    þam þe frum-sprecend   folces wæron,
    eallum swylce,   þe hire on wæron.

6   Swa ure ealra bliss   eard-hæbbendra
    on anum þe   ece standeð.

Psalm 87

1   Þu eart me, Drihten God,   dyre hælend;
    ic on dæge to ðe   dygle cleopode,
    and on niht fore þe   neode swylce.

2   Gange min in-gebed   on þin gleawe gesihð;
    ahyld eare þin   and gehyr min gebed,

3   for ðon is sawl min   sares and yfeles
    fæste gefylled;   is min feorh swylce
    to hell-dore   hylded geneahhe.

4   Wenað þæs sume,   þæt ic on wraðne seað
    mid fyren-wyrhtum   feallan sceolde;
    ic eom men gelic   mære geworden,
    þe mid deadum bið   betweox deaðe freo.

3   Indeed! Alien peoples journeyed from Tyre, the Ethiopians took up permanent residence in Zion.

4   [5] Mother of Zion first said "man," and man became glorious within her, and he established her as the most exalted one on earth.

5   [6] The divine judge declared that verdict in writing through those who were foretellers to the people, also through all who were living within Zion.

6   [7] So, the joy of all of us landowners resides eternally in you alone.

Psalm 87

1   [2] Lord God, you are for me a beloved savior; I called out to you secretly in the daytime, and also eagerly at night in your presence.

2   [3] Let my secret prayer enter into your discerning sight; incline your ear and listen to my appeal,

3   [4] because my soul is steadily filled with sorrow and evil; my life also is frequently verging toward hell's door.

4   [5] Certain people think that I am destined to fall into the horrible pit among the evildoers; I am become notorious, like one [6] who consorts with the dead, free in the midst of death.

5   Swa gewundade   wraðe slæpe
       syn þonne geworpene   on widne hlæw,
       þær hiora gymynde   men ne wænan,
       swa hi syn fram þinre handa   heane adrifene.

6   Hi me asetton   on seað hinder
       þær wæs deorc þeostru   and deaþes scua.

7   Þær me wæs yrre þin   on acyþed,
       and þu me oferhige on   ealle gelæddest.

8   Feor ðu me dydest   freondas cuþe;
       settan me symble,   þær me unswæsost wæs;
       eam ic swære geseald,   þær ic ut swican ne
                                 mæg.

9   Eagan me syndon   unhale nu
       geworden for wædle;   ic me to wuldres Gode
       þuruh ealne dæg   elne clypige
       and mine handa to þe   hebbe and ðenige.

10   Ne huru wundur   wyrceað deade,
       oþþe hi listum   læceas weccean,
       and hi andettan þe   ealle syþþan.

11   Cwist þu, oncnawað hi   wundru ðine
       on ðam dimmum   deorcan ðystrum,
       oððe ðine rihtwisnesse   recene gemeteð
       on ofergyttolnesse   manna ænig?

12   Ne on ðeostrum ne mæg   þances gehygdum
       ænig wislicu   wundur oncnawan,
       oððe þin soðfæstnes   si on þam lande
       þe ofergytnes   on eardige.

5   Just as those wounded by cruel death are then thrown into an open pit, where they are not expected to be remembered, so those other people are contemptuously driven out by your power.

6   [7] They placed me in a pit down where gloomy darkness and death's shadow reigned.

7   [8] In that place your anger was made clear to me, and you brought down on me all your pride.

8   [9] You removed intimate friends far from me; those others constantly put me where it was most unpleasant; I am sadly consigned to a place from which I cannot escape.

9   [10] My eyes have now become faint from want; all day long I call out vociferously to the God of glory and raise and stretch out my hands to you.

10   [11] Surely the dead will not work miracles, or physicians skillfully revive them, so that all of them acknowledge you afterward.

11   [12] Can it be said that in those dim shades they understand your mysterious wonders, or does any mortal in a state of oblivion instantly encounter your justice?

12   [13] Nor can any of your proven wonders be comprehended with obscure cogitations, or your truth be present in that land where oblivion lives.

13   Ic me to ðe,   ece Drihten,
mid mod-gehygde   mægene clypade,
and min gebed   morgena gehwylce
fore sylfne þe   soðfæst becume.

14   Forhwan ðu min gebed   æfre woldest,
soð God, wiðsacan,   oððe þinre gesihðe me
on þissum ealdre   æfre wyrnan?

15   Wædla ic eom on gewinne,   worhte swa on
geoguðe;
ahafen ic wæs and gehyned,   hwæðere næs
gescended.

16   Oft me þines yrres   egsa geðeowde,
and me broga þin   bitere gedrefde.

17   Hi me ealne dæg   utan ymbsealdan,
swa wæter-flodas   wæron ætsomne.

18   Þu me afyrdest   frynd þa nehstan
and mine cuðe eac   cwicu geyrmdest.

Psalm 88

1   Mild-heortnesse þine,   mihtig Drihten,
ic on ecnesse   awa singe;
fram cynne on cynn   and on cneorisse
ic þine soðfæstnesse   secge geneahhe
on minum muþe   manna cynne,

13   ¹⁴ I invoked you forcefully in my thoughts, eternal Lord, and may my prayer, in its sincerity, enter every morning into your very presence.

14   ¹⁴ Faithful God, why did you always wish to deny my prayer, or ever avert your face from me in this life?

15   ¹⁶ I am a needy person in difficulty, and so I labored in my youth; I was raised up and humbled, but not confounded.

16   ¹⁷ Often fear of your anger overpowered me, and terror of you greatly disturbed me.

17   ¹⁸ They have besieged me all day from without, like torrents of water piled up together.

18   ¹⁹ You have removed from me my closest friends, and you also afflicted those acquaintances of mine still alive.

Psalm 88

1   ² Mighty God, I will sing of your mercy forever, to eternity; from one generation to the next, I will frequently declare your truth to humankind in full voice,

2   for þon þa ðu cwæde   cuðe worde
þæt on ecnesse   awa wære
þin milde mod   micel getimbrad
heah on heofenum   hæleða bearnum,
and þin soðfestnes   symble gearwad.

3   Ic minum gecorenum   cuðe gesette,
hu min gewitnes   wolde gangan,
ic Dauide   dyrum esne
on að-sware   ær benemde
þæt ic his cynne   and cneow-magum
on ecnesse   a geworhte
ful sefte seld,   þæt hi sæton on.

4   Heofenas andettað,   halig Drihten,
hu wundor þin   wræclic standeð;
and þa halgan eac   hergeað on cyricean
þine soðfæstnesse,   secgeað geneahhige.

5   Nis under wolcnum,   weoroda Drihten,
ænig anlic,   ne ðe ænig byð
betweox Godes bearnum   gyt gelicra.

6   Þu bist gewuldrad God,   þær bið wisra geðeaht
and haligra   heah gemetincg;
micel and egeslic   ofer eall manna bearn,
ða ðe on ymb-hwyrfte   ahwær syndon.

7   Þu eart mægena God,   mihtig Drihten,
nis þe ealra gelic   ahwær on spedum;
is þin soðfæstnes   symble æghwær.

8   Þu wide sæs   wealdest mihtum;
þu his yþum miht   ana gesteoran,
ðonne hi on wæge   wind onhrereð.

2   3 because you then said with familiar words that your kind disposition was greatly established high in the heavens for humankind, for ever and ever, and your truth was always made ready.

3   4 I clearly arranged how my covenant would work for my chosen ones, having already declared in a solemn oath to David, my beloved servant, 5 that I would make for his family and posterity forever a truly untroubled throne, which they would occupy forever.

4   6 Holy Lord, the heavens will declare how your wonders endure as a marvel; and the holy ones in the assembly will also praise your truth, relate it frequently.

5   7 Lord of hosts, your equal is not to be found under the heavens, nor in future times will anyone remotely like you exist among God's children.

6   8 God, you are glorified wherever an assembly of the wise or an important meeting of saintly people is held; you are great and fearsome beyond all humankind's children living anywhere around us.

7   9 Mighty Lord, you are the God of hosts, there is no one like you anywhere in power; your truth is present everywhere.

8   10 You control the broad seas with might; only you can restrain its waves, when the wind whips it up into billows.

9   Þu miht oferhydige   eaðe mid wunde
heane gehnægean;   hafast ðu heah mægen
þines earmes sped   wið ealle fynd.

10   Heofonas þu wealdest,   hrusan swylce;
eorðan ymbehwyrft   eall þu gesettest.

11   Þu norð-dæl and sæ   niode gesceope,
Tabor et Hermon   on naman ðinum;
hi mid strencgðe eac   upp ahebbað
þinne swiþran earm   swylce, Drihten.

12   Wesan hea-mihte   handa þinre
ahafen ofer hæleðas,   halig seo swyðre;
is þines setles dom   soð gegearwod.

13   Mild-heortnes and soðfæstnes   mægene
                       forgangað
þinne andwlitan;   þæt bið eadig folc
þe can naman ðinne   neode herigean.

14   Þa on ðinum leohte   lifigeað and gangað
þe him ansyn þin   ær onlihte;
and on naman þinum   neode swylce
beoð ealne dæg   eac on blisse
and þine soðfæstnesse   symble æghwær,

15   for þon þu heora mægenes eart   mærost
                       wuldor,
and we þinum wel-dædum   wurdan ahafene.

16   Us an nimeð   ece Drihten
and Israhela cyning   eac se halga.

9   ¹¹ You can readily reduce the arrogant to abjection by wounding them; you possess lofty power, the force of your arm, against all enemies.

10   ¹² You control the heavens and earth also; you fully arranged earth's environment.

11   ¹³ You diligently created in your name the northern region and the sea, Tabor and Hermon; ¹⁴ and through their power they also elevate your right arm, Lord.

12   Let the lofty powers of your hand be exalted over men, that right hand is holy; ¹⁵ truth, the judgment of your throne, is made ready.

13   Mercy and truth will advance powerfully before your face; ¹⁶ the people that knows how to praise your name diligently is blessed.

14   They will live and proceed in the light which your face had illuminated for them; ¹⁷ and in your name, they likewise will also eagerly continue all day long in joy and in your truth, always and everywhere,

15   ¹⁸ because you are the most vaunted glory of their power, and we were exalted by your favors.

16   ¹⁹ The eternal Lord and Israel's king, the holy one, will possess us.

17   Þonne ðu ofer ealle   undearnunga
      þine bearn sprecest   and bealde cwyst:
      "Ic me on þyssum folce   fultum sette
      ofermihtigne,   þone ic me ær geceas.

18   Ic me deorne scealc   Dauid gemette,
      and hine halige ele   handum smyrede.

19   Heo him fultumeð   and min fæle earm,
      and hine mid mycle   mægene geswyðeð.

20   Ne mæg him ænig facen   feond æteglan,
      ne unrihtes bearn   ænig sceððan.

21   Of his ansyne   ealle ic aceorfe
      þa ðe him feondas   fæcne syndon,
      and his ehtendas   ealle geflyme.

22   Hine soðfæstnes min   samod ætgædere
      and mild-heortnes min   mægene healdeð,
      and on naman minum   neode swylce
      his horn bið ahafen,   heane on mihtum;

23   and ic his swiðran hand   settan þence
      þæt he sæ-streamum   syþþan wealde.

24   He me him to fælum   fæder gecygde:
      "Wæs me andfencge, God,   ecere hælu."

25   And ic þonne frum-bearn   forð asette
      ofer eorð-cyningas,   ealra heahstne.

26   Ic him to widan feore   wille gehealdan
      min milde mod   and him miht syllan,
      mine gewitnesse   weorðe and getreowe.

17 ²⁰ Then to all your children you will speak openly and boldly declare: "I will set myself up as a towering support for this people, whom I previously chose for my own.

18 ²¹ I found myself a beloved servant, David, and anointed him by my hand with consecrated oil.

19 ²² That hand, and my trusty arm, will help and strengthen him with great power.

20 ²³ No deceitful enemy will be able to harm him, nor any spawn of iniquity injure him.

21 ²⁴ I will completely cut off from his sight those who are treacherous enemies to him, and totally put his persecutors to flight.

22 ²⁵ My truth and mercy together will powerfully sustain David, and in my name his horn will also be raised up eagerly, that one exalted in power;

23 ²⁶ and I intend so to position his right hand that it will afterward rule the waters of the sea.

24 ²⁷ He invoked me as his trusty father: 'God, be for me the shield of eternal salvation.'

25 ²⁸ And then I will appoint him henceforth the firstborn over earth's kings, the most exalted of them all.

26 ²⁹ I intend to maintain my compassion for him forever and bestow power on him, my well-deserving and faithful witness.

27   Ic to widan feore   wyrce syððan
      þin heahsetl   hror and weorðlic,
      swa heofones dagas   her mid mannum.

28   Gif mine bearn nellað   mine bebodu efnan,
      ne mine domas   dædum healdan,

29   gif hi mine rihtwisnessa   fracoðe gewemmað,
      and hi mine bebodu   bliðe ne healdað,

30   þonne ic heora unriht gewrece   egsan gyrde,
      and hiora synne   swinglum forgylde.

31   Ne ic him mild-heortnesse   mine wille
      fægere afyrran;   ac him forð swa þeah
      mine soðfæstnesse   syllan þence.

32   Ic æne swor   að on halgum,
      þæt ic Dauide   dæda ne leoge,
      þæt on ecnesse   his agen cynn
      wunað on wicum;   bið him weorðlic setl
      on minre gesihðe   sunnan anlic,
      and swa mona   meahte on heofenum,
      þe is ece gewita   æhwær getreowe."

33   Þu þonne wiðsoce   soþum criste,
      and hine forhogodest;   hwile yldest
      and awendest fram him   gewitnesse
      esnes þines,   ealle gewemdest
      his halignesse   her on eorðan.

34   Ealle þu his weallas   wide todældest,
      towurpe fæsten his   for folc-egsan.

27   ³⁰ Afterward I will make your throne strong and distinguished for all time, like the days of heaven among humankind on earth.

28   ³¹ If my children are unwilling to carry out my commands, or observe my judgments with actions,

29   ³² if they shamefully profane my laws, and blithely disregard my commands,

30   ³³ then I will punish their iniquity with a rod of fear, and repay their crime with blows.

31   ³⁴ Nor will I justifiably remove my mercy from them; rather, in spite of everything, I intend to bestow forthwith my truth on them.

32   ³⁶ I once swore an oath among the holy ones that I would not play false with David in my actions, ³⁷ so that his own people will have permanent dwellings forever; ³⁸ he will have a worthy seat in my sight like the sun and like the moon with dominion in the heavens, which stands as an eternal witness, constant in every way."

33   ³⁹ You, however, rejected the one legitimately anointed, and spurned him; ⁴⁰ for a while you procrastinated and removed your servant's covenant from him, you totally profaned his consecrated status here on earth.

34   ⁴¹ You widely scattered all his walls, overthrew his strongholds to create general terror.

35   Hine þa towurpon   weg-ferende,
and he on edwit wearð   ymb-sittendum.

36   Handa þu ahofe   heah ehtendra,
gebrohtest his feondas   fæcne on blisse.

37   Fultum þu him afyrdest   fagan sweordes,
nafað æt gefeohte   fælne helpend.

38   Þu hine of clænnesse   clæne alysdest,
setl his gesettest   sorglic on eorðan.

39   Þu his dagena tid   deorce gescyrtest,
and mid sarlicre   sceame onmettest.

40   Wilt þu hu lange,   Wealdend-Drihten,
yrre þin acyðan   swa onæled fyr?

41   Gemune, mære God,   hwæt si min lytle sped;
ne huru ðu manna bearn   on middan-geard
to idelnesse   æfre geworhtest?

42   Hwylc is manna   þæt feores neote,
and hwæþere on ende   deað ne gesceawige;
oððe hwylc manna is   þæt his agene
fram helle locum   sawle generige?

43   Hwær is seo ealde nu,   ece Drihten,
micel mild-heortness,   þe þu man-cynne
and Dauide   deope aðe
þurh þines sylfes   soð benemdest?

44   Gemune þinra esna   edwit-spræce,
þa him fracuðlice   fremde þeode
utan ætywað,   oðre mægðe.

35   ⁴²Those passing by then tore his reputation to shreds, and he became a reproach to his neighbors.

36   ⁴³You raised up high the hands of the persecutors, induced a state of joy in his treacherous enemies.

37   ⁴⁴You removed from him the support of the gleaming sword, he does not have trusty help in battle.

38   ⁴⁵You have totally stripped him of his integrity, you dropped his sorry throne on the ground.

39   ⁴⁶You have sadly shortened the duration of his days, and painted him with painful confusion.

40   ⁴⁷How long, sovereign Lord, will you manifest your anger like a consuming fire?

41   ⁴⁸Remember, glorious God, what my meager substance consists of; surely you never placed humankind on earth without a purpose?

42   ⁴⁹Who is there among humankind who enjoys life, yet will not ultimately face death; or who of humankind can deliver his own soul from the shackles of hell?

43   ⁵⁰Eternal Lord, where now is that great mercy of old, which you declared to humankind and to David with a solemn oath affirmed by your very own truth?

44   ⁵¹Remember the insulting remarks about your servants, which alien peoples from outside, other tribes, basely spread about them.

45   Cweþað him þæt edwit,   ece Drihten,
feondas þine,   fæste ætwitað
and þæt þinum criste   becweþað swiðe.

46   A sy gebletsad   ece Drihten
to widan feore.   Wese swa, wese swa!

Psalm 89

1   Þu eart frið-stol us   fæste, Drihten,
of cynne on cynne   and on cneorisse.

2   Ær ðon munta gesceaft   ofer middan-geard
oððe ymb-hwyrft   eorðan wære,
oþþe world wære,   þu eart, wuldres God.

3   Ne ahwyrf þu fram mænn   heah eadmedu,
and þu cuðlice   cwæde sylfa:
"Ic manna bearnum   mod onwende."

4   For þinum eagum,   ece Drihten,
þusend wintra bið   þon anlicast,
swa geostran dæg   gegan wære.

5   And swa hi on niht hyrdnesse   neode begangað;
ne heora winter-rim   for wiht ne doð.

6   Morgen gewiteð   swa gemolsnad wyrt;
oðre morgene   eft gebloweð,
and geefneð swa,   oþ þæt æfen cymeð,
þonne forwisnað   weorðeð to duste.

45   52 Eternal Lord, your enemies heap scorn on them, consistently taunt them, and vehemently make the same reproach about your anointed one.

46   53 May the eternal Lord be blessed forever. So be it, so be it!

Psalm 89

1   1 Lord, you are truly a seat of refuge for us, from generation to generation and forever.

2   2 Before the creation of the mountains on the earth, or its surroundings existed, or the world came into being, you are present, God of glory.

3   3 Do not turn away sublime humility from humankind, since you yourself clearly stated: "I will effect a change of heart in them."

4   4 Eternal Lord, to your eyes a thousand years is just as if yesterday had passed,

5   or like those diligently keeping a night-watch; 5 nor does the reckoning of these years count for anything.

6   6 A morning will pass away like a withered plant; on the next morning it will bloom again, continuing so until evening comes, when it will dry up and turn to dust.

7 For þon we on þinum yrre ealle forwurdon,
  wæron on þinum hat-hige hearde gedrefde.

8 Þu ure unriht eall asettest,
  þær þu sylfa to eagum locadest;
  and ure worulde þu eac gestaðelodest
  on alihtincge andwlitan þines.

9 For þam ðe ure dagas ealle geteorudun,
  and we on þinum yrre synt swiðe gewæhte.

10 Wæran anlicast ure winter
  geonge-wifran þonne hio geornast bið
  þæt heo afære fleogan on nette;
  beoð ure gear-dagas gnorn-scendende,
  þeah þe heora hundred seo samod ætgædere.

11 Gif on mihtigum mannum geweorðeð,
  þæt hi hund-ehtatig ylda gebiden,
  ealle þe þær ofer beoð æfre getealde
  wintra on worulde, þa beoð gewinn and sar.

12 Us man-ðwærnes becwom micel ofer ealle,
  and we on þam gefean forhte gewurdan.

13 Hwa ðæs soð ne cann sæcgean ænig,
  hu þines yrres egsa standeð
  and seo micle miht? Nis þæt mann ænig
  þe þa ariman rihte cunne.

14 Do us þa þine swiðran hand, Drihten, cuðe,
  þam þe on snytrum syn swyðe getyde,
  and þa heora heortan healdað clæne.

15 Gehweorf us hwæt-hwiga, halig Drihten;
  wes þinum scealcum wel eað-bede.

7 ⁷ For we utterly perished from your anger, we were severely afflicted by your fury.

8 ⁸ You laid out for inspection all our iniquities, where you yourself scrutinized them; and you also established our world with the majesty of your appearance.

9 ⁹ For all our days are spent, and we are exceedingly weakened by your anger.

10 ¹⁰ Our years most resembled a spider whenever it becomes intensely eager to lure a fly into its web; the days of our years are hastening away in sadness, even though there may be a hundred of them altogether.

11 Should powerful men happen to live to see eighty years, all their years ever recorded here beyond that number constitute a struggle and an affliction.

12 An overpowering meekness came upon all of us, yet in that happiness we became fearful.

13 ¹¹ Who cannot say something of truth about how the terror of your anger endures, as well as that great power? There is no one who knows how ¹² to describe those things accurately.

14 Lord, make known that right hand of yours to us, to those who are exceedingly well instructed in wisdom, and they will keep their hearts pure.

15 ¹³ Holy Lord, return to us just a little; be very receptive to your servants' entreaty.

16   We synd gefyllede   fægere on mergenne
þinre mild-heortnesse;   þæs we on mode nu
habbað ealle dagas   æþele blisse.

17   We gefeoð swylce   for þon fægerum dagum
on þam þu us to eadmedum   ealle gebrohtest,
and for ðam gearum þe we gesawon   yfela feala.

18   Beseoh on þine scealcas   swæsum eagum
and on þin agen weorc,   ece Drihten,
and heora bearn gerece   bliðe mode.

19   Wese us beorhtnes ofer   bliðan Drihtnes,
ures þæs godan Godes   georne ofer ealle;
gerece ure hand-geweorc   heah ofer usic.

Psalm 90

1   Me eardað æt   æþele fultum
þæs hehstan   heofon-rices weard,
þe me æt wunað   awa to feore.

2   Ic to Drihtne cwæð: "Þu me dyre eart
fæle fultum" (hæbbe ic freond on him,
min se goda God), "and ic on ðe geare hycge,"

3   for ðon he me alysde   of laðum grine,
huntum unholdum,   hearmum worde.

4   He me mid his gesculdrum   sceade beþeahte;
for þon ic under fiðrum   fæle hihte.

16   ¹⁴ In the morning we are pleasantly filled with your mercy; afterward we now experience glorious happiness within ourselves all our days.

17   ¹⁵ We also rejoice therefore in the pleasant days when you fully humbled us, and for those years in which we witnessed many evils.

18   ¹⁶ Eternal Lord, look with kind eyes on your servants and your own works, and guide their children in a friendly spirit.

19   ¹⁷ May the brilliance of the gracious Lord, that God of ours, truly excellent beyond all others, be attentively present over us; may he direct our handiwork on high above us.

Psalm 90

1   ¹ With me resides the glorious support of the most High, the guardian of the heavenly kingdom, who dwells with me, forever to eternity.

2   ² I said to the Lord: "You are precious to me, a trusty support" (in him I have a friend, that virtuous God of mine), "and I will readily think of you,"

3   ³ because he released me from the evil snare, from hostile predators, from malicious words.

4   ⁴ With his shoulders he enveloped me in protection; and so I always felt confident under his wings.

5   Hwæt, me soðfæstnes min   scylde wið
                                  feondum;
    ne ðu þe niht-egsan   nede ondrædest,

6   ne forhtast þu ðe on dæge   flan on lyfte,
    þæt þe þuruhgangan   garas on ðeostrum,
    oððe on midne dæg   mære deoful.

7   Fealleð þe on þa wynstran   wergra þusend,
    and eac geteledra   tyn þusendo
    on þine þa swiðran,   and þe ne sceaðeð ænig.

8   Hwæðere þu ðæs eagan   eall sceawadest,
    gesege fyrenfulra   frecne wite.

9   Þu me eart se hehsta hyht,   halig Drihten;
    þu me frið-stol on ðe   fæstne settest.

10   Ne mæg þe ænig yfel   egle weorðan,
    ne heard sweopu   huse þinum
    on neaweste   nahwær sceþþan,

11   for þon he his englum bebead,   þæt hi mid
                                    earmum
    þe on heora handum   heoldan georne,
    þæt þu wil-wega   wealdan mostest.

12   And þe on folmum   feredan swylce,
    þe læs þu fræcne on stan   fote spurne.

13   Þu ofer aspide miht   eaðe gangan,
    and bealde nu   basiliscan tredan,
    and leon and dracan   liste gebygean.

14   For ðon he hyhte to me,   ic hine hraðe lyse;
    niode hine scylde,   nu he cuðe naman minne.

5   5 May my truth protect me against enemies; neither will you intensely dread terrors by night,

6   6 nor will you fear during the day the arrow in flight for you, or that spears may impale you in the dark, or the notorious noonday devil.

7   7 To your left a thousand reprobates will fall, and on your right also an estimated ten thousand, yet not one will harm you.

8   8 Nevertheless, you observed everything with your gaze, witnessed the terrible punishment of sinners.

9   9 For me, holy Lord, you are the loftiest hope; you arranged a secure refuge for me in you.

10   10 Not a single serious evil can befall you, nor any fierce affliction cause injury anywhere near your house,

11   11 because he gave orders to his angels that they should carefully support you with their embracing hands, so that you might be in control of pleasant ways.

12   12 And they carried you likewise in their arms, lest you should perilously strike a rock with your foot.

13   13 You have the ability to step lightly on an asp, and to tread boldly now on the basilisk, and to subdue with cunning the dragon and the lion.

14   14 Because he trusted in me, I will quickly free him; I will zealously protect him, seeing that he knew my name.

15   He cigde me,   and ic hine cuðlice
hold gehyrde,   and hine hraðe syþþan
of earfoþum   ut alysde.

16   Ic hine generige   and his naman swylce
gewuldrige   geond ealle wer-ðeoda,
and him lif-dagas   lange sylle;
swylce him mine hælu   holde ætywe.

Psalm 91

1   God is, þæt man Drihtne   geara andette,
and neodlice   his naman asinge,
þone heahestan   hæleða cynnes;

2   and þonne on morgene   mægene sæcge
hu he milde wearð   manna cynne,
and his soðe   sæcge nihtes.

3   Hwæt, ic on tyn strengum   getogen hæfde,
hu ic þe on *psalterio*   singan mihte,
oððe þe mid hearpan   hlyste cweman,
for ðon þu me on þinum weorcum   wisum
                                 lufadest;
hihte ic to þinra handa   halgum dædum.

4   Hu micle synt þine mægen-weorc,   mihtig
                               Drihten;
wærun þine geðancas   þearle deope.

15 ¹⁵ He called me, and I, always gracious, kindly heard him, and soon after freed him from troubles.

16 I will rescue him, and also glorify his name among all the races of humankind, ¹⁶ and will give him a long life; I will also graciously reveal my salvation to him.

Psalm 91

1 ² It is desirable to acknowledge the Lord wholeheart-edly, and to chant his name eagerly, the noblest of the line of heroes;

2 ³ and then in the morning to relate forcefully how he behaved gently toward humankind, and at night to announce his truths.

3 ⁴ I have plucked on the ten-stringed instrument, how-ever best I could sing to you on the psaltery, or please you with the sound of the harp, ⁵ because you have shown your love for me in your skillful works; I rejoice in the holy deeds of your hands.

4 ⁶ How great are your mighty works, powerful Lord; your intentions were truly profound.

5   Won-hydig wer   þæs wiht ne cann,
    ne þæs andgit hafað   ænig dysigra.

6   Þonne forð cumað   fyrenfulra ðreat,
    heap synnigra   hige onlic;
    ealle þær ætywað,   þa ðe unrihtes
    on weoruld-life   worhtan geornast,
    þæt hi forwordene   weorðen syþþan
    on worulda woruld   and to widan feore.

7   Þu on ecnesse   awa, Drihten,
    heahesta bist,   heofon-rices weard.

8   Þi nu ðine feond   fæcne, Drihten,
    on eorð-wege   ealle forweorþað,
    and weorðað towrecene   wide ealle,
    þa þe unrihtes   æror worhtan.

9   Þonne an-horna   ealra gelicost
    min horn weorðeð   ahafen swiðe,
    and mine yldo beoð   æghwær genihtsum.

10 And eage þin   eac sceawode,
    hwær fynd mine   fæcne wæran,
    and mine wergend   wraðe gehyrde
    efne þin agen   eare swylce.

11 Se soðfæsta   samed anlicast
    beorht on blædum   bloweð swa palma,
    and swa Libanes beorh   lideð and groweð.

12 Settað nu georne   on Godes huse,
    þæt ge on his wicum   wel geblowan.

5   [7] The careless man does not know a whit of that, nor do any of the foolish understand it.

6   [8] Then a band of the wicked, a company of sinners, will crop up like hay; all those who in this life most eagerly committed iniquity will make an appearance there, so that they will be ruined forever after and into eternity.

7   [9] Lord, guardian of the heavenly kingdom, you are the most high, always to eternity.

8   [10] Therefore, your treacherous enemies, Lord, will utterly perish now on earth, and all those who previously committed iniquity will be widely scattered.

9   [11] Then my horn, resembling most of all a unicorn, will be mightily raised up, and my old age will be in every way contented.

10   [12] And your eyes also observed where my malicious enemies were, and equally your own ears heard with anger my defamers also.

11   [13] The just one will blossom altogether like a palm, resplendent in foliage, and like Mount Lebanon he will spring up and grow.

12   [14] Plant eagerly now in God's house, so that you may truly flourish in his dwellings.

13 Nu gyt syndan manige manna swylce,
  þe hiom yldo gebidan ær to genihte,
  and þa mid geþylde þenden sægdan,

14 cwædon, þæt wære soðfæst sylfa Drihten
  and hine unrihtes awyht ne heolde.

Psalm 92

1 Drihten hine gegyrede gode strengðe,
  and hine þa mid micle mægene begyrde.

2 Drihten rixað, dema usser,
  and hine mid weorðlice wlite gegyrede;

3 and þa ymb-hwyrft eorþan getrymede,
  swa folde stod fæste syþþan.

4 Gearu is þin setl, and þu, ece God,
  ær worulde fruman, wunast butan ende.

5 Hofan heora stefne streamas, Drihten,
  hofan and hlynsadan hludan reorde
  fram wæter-stefnum widra manigra.

6 Wræclice syndon wægea gangas,
  þonne sæ-streamas swiðust flowað;
  swa is wundorlic wealdend usser
  halig Drihten on heanessum.

13   [15] There are still many people also, who had expected for themselves an old age in prosperity, and in the meantime they spoke with patience,

14   saying that the Lord himself was just and did not carry within him the slightest trace of evil.

Psalm 92

1   [1] The Lord girded himself with virtuous strength, and then encircled himself with great might.

2   The Lord, our judge, reigns, and has clothed himself with a distinguished appearance;

3   and he strengthened the earth's surroundings, so that the ground stood firmly thereafter.

4   [2] Your seat is ready, and before the world's beginning, you, eternal God, live without end.

5   [3] Lord, the rivers raised their clamor, they sounded and resounded with a loud roar [4] from the torrential noise of many broad waters.

6   Extraordinary are the surges of the waves when the ocean's waters run most violently; in the same way our ruler, the holy Lord, is awesome in the heavens.

7 Þin gewitnes is weorcum geleafsum,
and mid soðe is swiðe getreowed.

8 Huse þinum halig gedafenað,
Drihten usser, and dagas lange.

Psalm 93

1 Þu eart wracena God, and þu miht wrecan
swylce,
ana gefreogan æghwylcne mann.

2 Ahefe þe on ellen, eorþan dema,
gyld ofer-hydigum, swa hi ær grame worhton.

3 Hu lange fyren-wyrhtan foldan wealdað,
oþþe man-wyrhtan morðre gylpað?

4 Hi oftust sprecað, unnyt sæcgeað
and woh meldiað; wyrceað unriht.

5 Folc hi þin, Drihten, fæcne gehyndan,
and yrfe þin eall forcoman.

6 Ælðeodige men, earme wydewan,
steop-cilda feala stundum acwealdon.

7 Sægdan and cwædan, þæt ne gesawe
Drihten æfre, dyde swa he wolde,
ne þæt Iacobes God ongitan cuðe.

7   ⁵ Your testimony is made credible by works, and is fully confirmed with truth.

8   Our Lord, that which is holy befits your house, and length of days.

Psalm 93

1   ¹ You are the God of vengeance, and you alone also has the power to avenge and free every human.

2   ² Judge of the earth, vigorously rouse yourself, repay the arrogant in the measure that they acted cruelly before.

3   ³ How long will sinners dominate the world, or criminals boast of murder?

4   ⁴ They talk very often, saying evil things and proclaiming iniquity; they perpetrate injustice.

5   ⁵ Lord, they greatly humiliated your people, and thoroughly afflicted your inheritance.

6   ⁶ They savagely killed strangers, poor widows and many stepchildren.

7   ⁷ They stated repeatedly that the Lord never noticed— he did as he pleased—nor could Jacob's God understand it.

8   Onfindað þæt and ongeotan   þe on folce nu
unwiseste   ealra syndon,
dysige hwæt-hwygu   deope þæt oncnawan.

9   Se ðe ærest ealdum   earan worhte,
hu se ofer-hleoður   æfre wurde;
and him eagena gesyhð   eallum sealde
and he scearpe ne mæge   gesceawian?
And se þe ege healdeð   eallum þeodum,
and his þrea ne si   þær for awiht,
se þe men læreð   micelne wisdom?

10   God ealle cann   guman geðancas
eorð-buendra,   for ðon hi idle synt.

11   Þæt bið eadig mann,   þe þu hine, ece God,
on þinre soðre æ   sylfa getyhtest,
and hine þeodscipe   ðinne lærest,
and him yfele dagas   ealle gebeorgest,
oð þæt bið frecne seað   þam fyrenfullan
deop adolfen   deorc and ðystre.

12   Næfre wiðdrifeð   Drihten ure
his agen folc,   ne his yrfe þon ma
on ealdre wile   æfre forlætan.

13   Hwylc þonne gena   gehwyrfed byð,
þæt he on unriht   eft ne cyrre,
oððe hwylc nymeð me,   þæt ic man fleo
and mid riht-heortum   rædes þence?

14   Hwylc ariseð mid me,   þæt ic riht fremme
and wið awyrgedum   winne and stande,
þe unrihtes   ealle wyrceað?

8   8 Let those who are the most foolish of all among the people learn and recognize now, let the thoughtless understand a little more seriously what follows.

9   9 He who first created ears for our ancestors, how could he ever fail to hear; and he who gave sight to them all, can he not sharply observe? 10 And he who intimidates all peoples, teaching humankind much wisdom, does not his threat count for something in that case?

10   11 God knows all human thoughts, those of earth's inhabitants, because they are insignificant.

11   12 Happy the one whom you yourself, eternal Lord, will instruct in your law and teach your discipline, 13 and fully protect from evil days, until such time as a perilous pit, deep, dark, and gloomy, is dug for the sinner.

12   14 Our God will never drive away his own people, any more than he ever wishes to abandon his inheritance at any time.

13   15 Even so, who will be truly converted so as not to revert to injustice, or who will adopt me so that I may flee wickedness and contemplate wisdom among the upright of heart?

14   16 Who will rise up with me, so that I may perform what is right, and stand and fight against evildoers, who perpetrate iniquity to the full?

15   Nymðe me Drihten,   dema usser,
     gefultumede   fægere æt þearfe,
     wenincga min sawl   sohte helle.

16   Gif ic þæs sægde,   þæt min sylfes fot
     ful sarlice   asliden wære,
     þa me mild-heortnes   mihtigan Drihtnes
     gefultumede   þæt ic feorh ahte.

17   Æfter þære menigeo   minra sara,
     þe me ær on ferhðe   fæste gestodan,
     þa me þine frofre   fægere, Drihten,
     gesibbedan   sawle mine.

18   Ne ætfyligeð þe ahwær   facen ne unriht;
     ðu gefæstnast   facen sares.
     Hi soðfæste   sneome gehæftað,
     and heora sawle   ofslean þenceað,
     blod soðfæstra   bitere ageotan.

19   For ðon me is geworden   Wealdend-Drihten
     to frið-stole   fæst and gestaðelad;
     is me fultum his   fæst on Drihtne.

20   Þonne him gyldeð   God ælmihtig
     ealle þa unriht   ðe hi geearnedan,
     and on heora facne   fæste todrifeð
     Drihten eall-mihtig,   dema soðfæst.

15   [17] If the Lord, our judge, had not kindly helped me in need, my soul would perhaps have ventured to hell.

16   [18] If I declared later that my own foot had stumbled most grievously, then the mighty Lord's mercy would have helped me save my life.

17   [19] Lord, according to the multitude of my sorrows, which had weighted heavily on my mind, your consolations after that gently brought peace to my soul.

18   [20] Neither deceit nor injustice form any part of you; you firmly chain the evil of suffering. [21] They will quickly take captive the righteous, planning to destroy their souls, to spill cruelly the blood of the just.

19   [22] So the ruling Lord is become for me a place of refuge, established and immovable; his support for me continues constant in the Lord.

20   [22] Then God almighty will requite them for all the iniquities by which they have merited punishment, and the Lord almighty, the upright judge, will thoroughly scatter them for their deceit.

Psalm 94

1   Cumað nu togædere,   wutun cweman Gode,
wynnum Drihten   wealdend herigean,
urum hælende   hyldo gebeodan.

2   Wutun his ansyne   ærest secean,
þæt we andettan   ure fyrene
and we sealmas him   singan mid wynne,

3   for ðon is se micla God   mihtig Drihten
and se micla cynincg   ofer eall manna godu;

4   for ðon ne wiðdrifeð   Drihten usser
his agen folc   æfre æt þearfe.
He þas heah-beorgas   healdeð swylce;

5   eac he sæs wealdeð   and he sette þone;
worhte his folme eac   foldan drige.

6   Cumað him fore   and cneow bigeað
on ansyne   ures Drihtnes,
and him wepan fore   ðe us worhte ær,

7   for ðon he is Drihten God,   dema usser;
wærun we his fæle folc   and his fægere sceap,
þa he on his edisce   ær afedde.

8   Gif ge to dæge   Drihtnes stefne
holde gehyran,   næfre ge heortan geþanc
deorce forhyrden   Drihtnes willan,

9   swa on grimnesse   fyrn geara dydan
on þam wraðan dæge   and on westenne,

372

Psalm 94

1   ¹ Assemble now, and let us please God, joyfully praising the ruling Lord, offering homage to our savior.

2   ² Let us first seek his face, so that we may confess our sins and joyfully sing psalms to him,

3   ³ because the mighty Lord is the supreme God and the exalted king above all humankind's gods;

4   because our Lord will never repulse his own people in need. ⁴ He also controls those lofty mountains;

5   ⁵ likewise, he governs the sea and put it in place; his power also created the dry land.

6   ⁶ Enter into his presence and bend the knee in the sight of our Lord, and let us weep before him, who in an earlier time created us,

7   ⁷ because he is the Lord God, our judge; we were his loyal people and his gentle sheep, whom he previously fed in his enclosed pasture.

8   ⁸ If today you should hear the Lord's gracious voice, never perversely harden your heart's intent toward God's will,

9   ⁹ as those others did in provocation long ago in that day of anger in the desert, where your ancestors from this na-

þær min ðurh facen   fæderas eowre
þisse cneorisse   cunnedan georne;
þær hi cunnedan,   cuð ongeaton
and min sylfes weorc   gesawon mid eagum.

10   Nu ic feowertig   folce þyssum
wintra rimes   wunade neah,
aa and symble cwæð,   and eac swa oncneow,
þæt hi on heortan   hyge dysegedan.

11   Hi wegas mine   wihte ne oncneowan,
þæt ic ær on yrre   aðe benemde,
gif hi on mine reste   ricene eodon.

Psalm 95

1   Singað nu Drihtne   sangas neowe;
singe þeos eorðe eall   eceum Drihtne.

2   Singað nu Drihtne,   and his soðne naman
bealde bletsiað;   beornas sæcgeað
fram dæge to dæge   Drihtnes hælu.

3   Secgeað his wuldor   geond sige-þeode,
and on eallum folcum   his fægere wundor.

4   He is se mycla God,   for þon hine mæn sculon
elne herian;   he is egeslic God
ofer ealle godu   eorð-buendra.

tion severely tested me with their deceit; there they discovered, observed for a fact and witnessed with their eyes, my own works.

10 ¹⁰ I have now lived close to this people for forty years, always and ever declaring, and observing too, that in the disposition of their hearts they acted rashly.

11 ¹¹ They did not know my ways at all, what in my anger I had affirmed by oath, if they would quickly enter into my rest."

Psalm 95

1 ¹ Sing now new canticles to the Lord; let all this earth sing to the eternal Lord.

2 ² Sing now to the Lord, and boldly bless his upright name; let humankind declare from day to day the Lord's salvation.

3 ³ Announce his glory throughout the victorious peoples, and his beautiful wonders among all the peoples.

4 ⁴ Since he is the great God, humankind ought to praise him mightily; he is a God to be feared above all the gods of earth's inhabitants.

5   Syndon ealle hæþenu godu   hilde-deoful;
heofonas þænne worhte   halig Drihten.

6   Ys on þinre gesihðe   soð andetnes,
fæger halignes   fæste gebletsad,
and weorðlic wlite   wuldres þines.

7   Bringað nu Drihtne,   bu ætsomne,
wlite and are,   wuldor ðridde;
and þæt of hiora eðele don   ealle þeode,
þæt hi naman Drihtenes   neode herigean.

8   Genimað eow arlice lac   and in gangað
on his wic-tunas;   weorðiað Drihten
on his þære halgan   healle geneahhige;

9   for his ansyne sceal   eorðe beofian.
Secgað nu on cynnum   and on cneorissum,
þæt from treowe becwom   tirfæst rice
Drihten ure;   dome he syþþan
eorðan ymb-hwyrft   ealle gesette.

10   He ferhtlic riht   folcum demeð,
and on his yrre   ealle þeode.

11   Heofenas blissiað,   hrusan swylce
gefeoð fæstlice,   and floda þrym;
sealte sæ-streamas   sælðe habbað.

12   Habbað feldas eac   fægere blisse
and ealle þa þe on him   eard weardiað;
wærun wudu-bearuwas   on wyn-dagum

5   ⁵ All the heathen gods are demons; the holy Lord, however, created the heavens.

6   ⁶ True praise belongs in your presence, precious holiness constantly extolled and the worthy splendor of your glory.

7   ⁷ Bring now to the Lord splendor and honor, both together, ⁸ glory as a third; and let all the peoples from their homelands arrange to praise earnestly the Lord's name.

8   Take up offerings reverently and enter into his courts; ⁹ worship the Lord frequently in that holy hall of his;

9   before his face the earth shall tremble. ¹⁰ Declare now among the tribes and their generations that from a tree has issued a famous ruler, our Lord; he afterward fully fixed by decree the earth's environment.

10   He will render deliberative justice to the peoples, and in his anger judge all the gentiles.

11   ¹¹ The heavens will rejoice, the earth also, and the torrent of waters will exult unceasingly; the salty waters of the sea will enjoy prosperity.

12   ¹² The fields too, and all those who inhabit them, will experience exquisite joy; the forests continued in joyful days

for andwlitan   ecean Drihtnes,
for þon he cwom   on cyne-ðrymme,
þæt he þas eorðan   ealle demde.

13   Þonne he ymb-hwyrft   eorðan folca
soðe and rihte   syþþan demeð.

Psalm 96

1   Rixað nu mid rihte   rice Drihten;
is eorðe nu   eac on blisse,
and þæs fægerne   gefean habbað
ea-landa mænig   ut on garsæcge . . .

Psalm 97

8   . . . stundum onginnað
fægnian mid folmum   on gefean ælcne;
beorgas blissiað   (beacen oncnawað),
for ansyne   ecean Drihtnes,
for þon he eadig com   eorþan to demanne.

9   He ymb-hwyrft   eorþan demeð
soðe and rihte,   and his syndrig folc
on rihtnesse   ræde gebringeð.

13 before the eternal Lord's face, because he has come in royal majesty to judge all this earth.

13   Then he will afterward judge the full reach of the earth's people in truth and justice.

Psalm 96

1   1 The mighty Lord reigns justly; the earth also is happy now, and as a result many islands out on the ocean experience exquisite joy . . .

Psalm 97

8   8 . . . from time to time proceed to clap their hands with every expression of joy; the mountains are glad (they understand the signs) 9 in the presence of the eternal Lord, because he, the blessed one, has come to judge the earth.

9   He will judge the earth's expanse with truth and justice, and will lead his chosen people in the path of justice.

Psalm 98

1   Rixað Drihten,   and he reðe folc
healdeð on yrre   ungemete swiðe;
sitteð ofer cherubin,   se þe sona mæg
ana eorðware   ealle onstyrian.

2   Drihten is on Sion,   dema se mæsta,
heah and mære   ofer eall hæleða folc.

3   We andetað þinum   þam ecean naman,
þæt he mid mannum is   mycel and egeslic,
halig on helpe   hæleþa bearnum;
aare cyninges dom   æghwær lufade.

4   Þu gegearwadest   geara ærest,
þæt þu recene, God,   rihte beeodest:
þu on Iacobe   gode domas
æt fruman worlde   fægere settest.

5   Ahebbað haligne   heofena Drihten,
usserne God   ellen-cræfte,
and his fota sceamul   forð weorþiað,
for þon he halig is   hæleða bearnum.

6   Moyses et Aaron   mære gebroðor,
soðe sacerdas,   Samuhel ðridda;
þa gode his naman   neode cigdan.

7   Hi cymlice   cigdon Drihten,
and he hi gehyrde   holde mode,
spræc him wordum to   þurh wolcnes swyr.

Psalm 98

1   1 The Lord reigns, and he controls fierce peoples in their truly excessive anger; he sits above the cherubim, he who single-handedly can thoroughly disturb the inhabitants of the earth at once.

2   2 The Lord is present in Zion, that greatest of judges, lofty and eminent over all humankind.

3   3 We acknowledge your eternal name, that it is great and awesome among humankind, sanctified in its support for the human race; 4 the king's honor has loved justice in every way.

4   God, you prepared long ago what you quickly executed in accordance with justice: you expertly drew up at the beginning of the world sound laws for Jacob.

5   5 Exalt with courageous strength our God, the holy Lord of the heavens, and honor his footstool continually, because it is sacred to humankind.

6   6 Moses and Aaron, famous brothers, true priests, and Samuel, the third one; those virtuous men earnestly called out his name.

7   They invoked the Lord properly, and he heard them with a gracious disposition, 7 speaking to them in words through a column of cloud.

8   Hi þa gewitnesse   wel geheoldon
     and his bebodu   beorhte efnedan
     þa he him sealde   and sylfa bebead.

9   Þu gehyrdest hig,   halig Drihten,
     and him, meahtig God,   milde wurde,
     and heora æfþancan   ealle gewræce.

10   Hebbað urne God,   hælend Drihten,
     and hine on halgum   her weorðiað
     mærum beorge,   for ðon his meahte synt
     and halig is   heofon-rices weard.

Psalm 99

1   Nu ge mycle gefean   mihtigum Drihtne
     eall þeos eorðe   elne hyre,
     and blisse Gode   bealde þeowie.

2   Gangað on ansyne   ealle bliðe,
     witað wislice   þæt he is Wealdend-God;
     he us geworhte   and we his syndon.

3   We his folc syndan   and his fæle sceap,
     ða he on his edisce   ealle afedde;
     gað nu on his doru,   God andettað,
     and hine weorðiað   on wic-tunum
     mid lof-sangum   lustum myclum.

8 They adhered well to that covenant and carried out truly the commands which he transmitted to them and himself enjoined.

9 [8] Holy Lord, you heard them and were gentle toward them, yet you punished all their offenses, mighty God.

10 [9] Exalt our God, the savior Lord, and worship him here on that famous holy mountain, because all powers belong to him, and the guardian of the heavenly kingdom is holy.

Psalm 99

1 [2] Let all this earth boldly obey now the mighty Lord with great rejoicing, and serve God confidently with joy.

2 Enter into his presence most joyfully, [3] cautiously understanding that he is sovereign God; he created us and we belong to him.

3 We are his people and his trusty sheep, whom he amply fed in his pasture; [4] enter his doorway now, acknowledge God, and worship him in his courts with hymns of great joy.

4 Heriað naman Drihtnes, for þon he is niðum
swæs;
is þin milde mod ofer manna bearn.

Psalm 100

1 Mild-heortnesse and dom mihtigan Drihtnes
singe and secge, and soð ongyte
on unwemmum wege, hwænne þu me wylle to.

2 Ic mid unbealuwe ealre heortan
þurh ðin hus middan halig eode.

3 Ne sette ic me fore eagum yfele wisan;
ealle ic feode facnes wyrcend,
næs me wyn-gesið wiðerweard heorte.

4 Ic awyrgde fram me wende and cyrde;
nolde ic hiora andgit ænig habban,
þe tælnessa teonan geneahhige
wið heora þam nehstan nið ahofan;
þara ic ehte ealra mid niðe.

5 Ofer-hydegum eagum unsædre heortan
nolde ic mid þæm men minne mete ðicgean.

6 Ofer geleaffulle eorð-bugende
eagan mine georne sceawedun,
hwær ic tirfæste treowe funde,
þa me symble mid sæton and eodon;
he me holdlice her ðegnade.

4   Praise the name of the Lord [5] because he is gracious to humankind; your gentle disposition rests on the children of men.

Psalm 100

1   [1] I will sing and declare the mighty Lord's mercy and judgment, [2] will understand the truth with blameless conduct when you visit me.

2   With the innocence of a full heart, I passed sanctified through the middle of your house.

3   [3] I did not set before my sight anything evil; I passionately hated workers of iniquity, [4] the perverse heart was no fair friend of mine.

4   I turned and moved the accursed away from me; I refused to entertain any sympathy for those [5] who frequently stirred up hostility, the hurt of slander against their neighbors; all such people I aggressively pursued.

5   I had no desire to share my food with him of the overbearing eyes and insatiable heart.

6   [6] My eyes keenly scanned the earth's faithful inhabitants, to see where I might discover that famed loyalty, those who could sit and walk with me continually; such a one attended on me faithfully here on earth.

7 Ne eardað on midle   mines huses,
þe ofer-hygd   up ahebbe,
oþþe unriht cweþan   elne wille.

8 Ic on morgenne ofslea   manes wyrhtan,
ealle þe unriht   elne worhtan,
and fyrena fela   gefremed habbað;
ealle ic þa of Drihtnes   drife ceastre.

Psalm 101

1 Ðu min gebed,   mære Drihten,
gehyr, heofenes weard,   and gehlyde min
to ðe becume,   þeoda reccend.

2 Na þu andwlitan   æfre þinne
awend fram me,   wuldres Ealdor;
gif ic geswenced sy,   þu swæs to me
þin eare onhyld   and me ofestlice gehyr,
heofenes weard,   helpys benan.

3 For ðon dagas mine   gedroren syndan
smece gelice,   and forswyrcende synd
mine mearh-cofan   (þæs þe me þinceð),
swylce hi on cocer-pannan   cocas gehyrstan.

4 Ic eom hege gelic,   þam þe hraðe weornað,
ðonne hit byð amawyn   mannes folmum;
is min heorte eac   hearde geswenced,
for ðon ic ær forgeat,   þæt ic etan sceolde

386

7   7 He who exalts pride or longs to say wicked things will not dwell in the middle of my house.

8   8 In the morning I will slay the perpetrators of evil, all who boldly commit iniquities and have done many wrongs; then I will expel all of them from the Lord's city.

Psalm 101

1   2 Eminent Lord, guardian of heaven, hear my prayer, and may my cry reach you, ruler of peoples.

2   3 Never turn your face from me, Lord of glory; if I should be troubled, incline your kind ear to me, guardian of heaven, and speedily listen to me, a petitioner for help.

3   4 Because my days have vanished like smoke, and my bones are blackened (so it seems to me), as if cooks were to fry them in a pan.

4   5 I am like hay which quickly withers when it is mown by human hands; my heart is also sorely pressed because I had forgotten to eat my tasty bread; 6 as a result, grievous la-

minne swetne hlaf;   for ðon me is swære stefn
hefig gnorniende   heortan getenge,
ætfeolen eac min ban   flæsce minum.

5   Ic geworden eom   pellicane gelic,
se on westene wunað;   wat ic eac swiðe geare,
þæt ic genemned eam   niht-hrefne gelic,
þe on scræfe eardað,   and ic spearuwan swa
                                     some
gelice gewearð,   anlicum fugele.

6   Hwæt, me ealne dæg   edwit-spræce on
mine feondas   fæste brohtan,
and ða me heredan;   hi me hraþe æfter
full swyþe eft   swerigean ongunnon.

7   For ðon ic anlic ætt   æscean hlafe,
and ic minne drinc   mengde wið tearum,

8   for andwlitan   yrres þines;
feor þu me ahofe   and gehnæctest eft.

9   Dagas mine gedruran   swa se deorca scua,
and ic hege gelic,   swa hit hraðe weornað.

10   Þu on ecnysse wunast   awa, Drihten;
wunað þin gemynd,   þenden woruld standeð.

11   Aris nu, mihtig God,   miltsa Sione;
nu is hire helpe   heah-sæl cumen.

12   For þon þæs þancunga   þine scealcas
ambyht-mæcgas   ealle hæfdan,
for ðon þe þu stiðlice   stanum and eorðan
eallum ætgædere   ær miltsadest,

menting becomes my sad sound, burdensome to the heart, and my bones adhere to my flesh.

5   [7] I have become like the pelican which dwells in the desert; I also know very well that I am said to be like the night raven who lives in a cave, [8] and in the same way I am become like the sparrow, a similar type of bird.

6   [9] My enemies persistently taunted me all day, and then praised me; soon after they renewed very intensely their swearing against me.

7   [10] So, I ate ashes like bread, and mingled my drink with tears,

8   [11] on account of your angry countenance; you raised me up a long way, but afterward ruined me.

9   [12] My days have declined like a somber shadow, and I myself resemble hay as it quickly withers.

10   [13] Lord, you endure forever in eternity; the memory of you lasts while the world exists.

11   [14] Rise up now, mighty God, be merciful to Zion; now an opportune time is come to help her.

12   [15] So your servants and attendants were exceedingly grateful, because you had resolutely shown mercy to its stones and earth, all of them,

13   for þon neodlice   on naman ðinum
ealle eorð-buend   egsan habbað,
and þin wuldor ongitað   wise cyningas.

14   Eft timbrade   ece Drihten
and gesette Sion   þurh his sylfes miht;
ðær wæs gesyne   his seo soðe sped.

15   Oft he þearfendra bene   ðance gehyrde,
and he ne forhogode   heora hold gebed.

16   Ða wislice   awriten standað
and on cneoressum   cyðed syndan,
þæt he folc gesceop;   fægere Drihten
herað holdlice   hrore geþance,

17   for ðon he fæstlice   forð locade
of his þam hean   halgan setle;
Drihten geseah of heofenum   her on eorðan.

18   He þa gehyrde   heah-gnornunge
þæra ðe gebundene   bitere wæron,
and ða bealdlice   bearn alysde
þara ðe ofslegene   sliþe wæran.

19   Þonne byð on Sione sægd   soð nama Drihtnes,
and his lof swylce   leoda bearnum
on Hierusalem   gleawast and mærust.

20   Cumað folc syððan   feorran togædere,
and ricu eac,   þæt hraðe Drihtne
ful holdlice   hyran syþþan.

21   He him andwyrdeð   eallum sona
on wege worulde,   þær his gewis mægen

13   ¹⁶ for all earth's inhabitants earnestly fear your name, and wise kings perceive your glory."

14   ¹⁷ Using his own power, the eternal Lord rebuilt and re-established Zion; his true power was evident there.

15   ¹⁸ Many times he graciously heard the appeal of the needy, and he did not spurn their devout requests.

16   ¹⁹ Those facts endure, skillfully written, and are made known through the generations, namely, that he created the people; they will graciously and devoutly praise the Lord with busy gratitude,

17   ²⁰ because he gazed earnestly from that lofty, holy seat of his; the Lord looked from the heavens here on the earth.

18   ²¹ At that time he heard the loud groaning of those who were cruelly bound, and then boldly released the children of those who were savagely slain.

19   ²² Then the true name of the Lord will be proclaimed in Zion, and his praise likewise in Jerusalem to the children of the peoples, most clearly and most splendidly.

20   ²³ Afterward people will come together from afar, and kingdoms too, so that they may promptly and most faithfully follow the Lord thereafter.

21   ²⁴ He will respond immediately to all those on the journey of this life, where his manifest strength permanently en-

fæste standeð.   Ic þe feawe dagas
minra mættra   mode secge,
þæt þu me ne meaht on midle   minra dagena
sona gecigean,   gif þu sylfa wylt;
earon þines anes gear   awa to feore.

22   Æt fruman þu,   Drihten, geworhtest
eorþan frætwe   and upheofen;
þæt is heah-geweorc   handa þinra.

23   Sweotule þa forweorðað   and ðu sylf wunast;
eall forwisnað   wædum anlice,
and ðu hi onwendest,   swa man wrigels deð,
and hi beoð to worulde   wended syþþan.

24   Þu þonne byst se ilca   se þu ær wære;
ne beoð winter þin   wiht ðe sæmran.

25   Bearn þinra scealca   her bu namon,
and þær eardedan   ealle þrage;
and heora sylfra cynn   syððan to feore
on worulda woruld   well gerehtest.

Psalm 102

1   Bletsa mine sawle   bliðe, Drihten,
and eall min inneran   his þæne ecean naman.

2   Bletsige mine sawle   bealde, Dryhten;
ne wylt þu ofergeottul   æfre weorðan
ealra goda,   þe he þe ær dyde

dures. I will relate to you from the heart the short span of my miseries [25] so that you may not in the middle of my days summon me at once, provided you yourself agree; for only your years endure for ever and ever.

22 [26] Lord, at the beginning you created earth's adornments and those of the upper sky; that is your exalted handiwork.

23 [27] Clearly they will perish, but you yourself will endure; all will wear away like garments, and you will change them as one does one's cloak, and they will be altered forever afterward.

24 [28] You, however, will remain the same as you were before; your years will not deteriorate in the slightest.

25 [29] Your servants' children took up residence here, and lived in that place continually; and you will attentively care for their very own descendants afterward, for ever and ever.

Psalm 102

1   [1] Lord, joyfully bless my soul, and let all my being bless his eternal name.

2   [2] May the Lord confidently bless my soul; you will never forget all the good things which he previously did for you.

3   He þinum man-dædum   miltsade eallum
    and þine adle   ealle gehælde.

4   He alysde þin lif   leof of forwyrde,
    fylde þinne willan   fægere mid gode.

5   He þe gesigefæste   soðre miltse,
    and ðe mild-heorte   mode getrymede;
    eart þu edneowe   earne gelicast
    on geogoðe nu   gleawe geworden.

6   Hafast þu milde mod,   mihta strange,
    Drihten, domas   eallum þe deope her
    and ful treaflice   teonan þoliað.

7   He his wegas dyde   wise and cuðe
    Moyse þam mæran   on mænige tid,
    swylce his willan eac   werum Israhela.

8   Mild-heort þu eart and mihtig,   mode geþyldig
    ece Drihten,   swa þu a wære;
    is þin milde mod   mannum cyðed.

9   Nelle þu oð ende   yrre habban,
    ne on ecnesse   ðe awa belgan.

10 Na þu be gewyrhtum,   wealdend, urum
    wommum wyrhtum   woldest us don,
    ne æfter urum unryhte   ahwær gyldan,

11 for ðon þu æfter heah-weorce   heofenes þines
    mild-heortnysse,   mihtig Drihten,
    lustum cyðdest,   þam þe lufedan þe.

12 Swa þas foldan   fæðme bewindeð
    þes east-rodor   and æfter west,

3   ³ He forgave all your evil deeds and healed all your infirmities.

4   ⁴ He saved your precious life from destruction, ⁵ graciously satisfied your desire with good things.

5   He triumphantly decked you with true mercy, and strengthened you with a compassionate disposition; you are now well renewed in youth like an eagle.

6   ⁶ Lord, you maintain a meek disposition, powerful abilities, and just verdicts for all those on this earth who suffer injuries deeply and most painfully.

7   ⁷ He made his ways known and understood to the illustrious Moses on many occasions, in the same way also his wishes to the people of Israel.

8   ⁸ Eternal Lord, you are compassionate and mighty, patient in approach, as you always were; your gentle disposition is revealed to humankind.

9   ⁹ You are reluctant to harbor anger to the bitter end, or become angry for all time.

10   ¹⁰ Ruler, you have no desire to deal with us according to our deeds, our perverse actions, or to repay us in any way as our iniquity deserves,

11   ¹¹ for you gladly showed mercy to those who loved you, mighty Lord, in accord with the exalted creation of your heaven.

12   ¹² As the eastern part of the heavens, and beyond it the western, encompasses this earth in its expanse, so he, by the

he betweonan þam   teonan and unriht
us fram afyrde   æghwær symble.

13   Swa fæder ðenceð   fægere his bearnum
milde weorðan,   swa us mihtig God,
þam þe hine lufiað,   liðe weorðeð,
for ðan he ealle can   ure þearfe.

14   Gemune, mihtig God,   þæt we synt moldan
and dust;
beoð mannes dagas   mawenum hege
æghwær anlice,   eorðan blostman,
swa his lif-dagas   læne syndan.

15   Þonne he gast ofgifeð,   syþþan hine gærs-bedd
sceal
wunian wide-fyrh;   ne him man syððan wat
ahwær elles   ænige stowe.

16   Þin mild-heortnes   mihtig Drihten,
þurh ealra worulda woruld   wislic standeð;
deorust and gedefust   ofer ealle þa þe
ondrædað him.

17   Swa his soðfæstnyss   swylce standeð
ofer þara bearna bearn   þe his bebodu healdað
and þæs gemynde   mycle habbað
þæt heo his wisfæst word   wynnum efnan.

18   On heofen-hame   halig Drihten
his heah-setl   hror timbrade,
þanon he eorð-ricum   eallum wealdeð.

measure between them, continually distanced iniquity and injustice from us in every way.

13   [13] As a father benevolently desires to be kind to his children, so mighty God behaves graciously to us who love him, [14] because he fully knows what we need.

14   [14] Mighty God, remember that we are dust and dirt; [15] the days of man are in every way like mown hay, like earth's blossom, so that his appointed days are fleeting.

15   [16] When he gives up the ghost, a grave must then enclose him for all time; nor is any place elsewhere associated with him.

16   [17] Mighty Lord, your mercy remains assured through all ages; most precious and most fitting over all those who fear him.

17   In the same way his justice also endures over those children's children [18] who observe his precepts and conscientiously remember to carry out joyfully his wise words.

18   [19] The holy Lord has built his strong throne in his heavenly home, from where he governs all earthly kingdoms.

19   Ealle his englas   ecne Drihten
     bletsian bealde,   heora bliðne frean,
     mægyn and mihta,   þa his mære word
     habbað and healdað   and hyge fremmað.

20   Bletsian Drihten   eall his bearna mægen,
     and his ðegna ðreat   þe þæt þence nu
     þæt hi his willan   wyrcean georne.

21   Eall his agen geweorc   ecne Drihten
     on his agenum stede   eac bletsige,
     þær him his egsa,   anweald, standeð;
     bletsige min sawl   bliðe Drihten.

Psalm 103

1   Bletsa mine sawle   bliþe, Drihten;
     þu eart min Drihten, God,   dædum swyþe,
     meahtum mære   ofer manna bearn.

2   Þu þe weorðlice   wlite-andette
     gode gegyredest;   eart nu gleawlice
     swa lim-wædum   leohte gegyrwed.

3   Heofen þu aðenedest   hyde gelice,
     þone weardiað ufan   wætra ðryðe.

4   He wolcen eac   worhte and sette,
     þæt he mihte eaðe   upp astigan;
     se fotum tredeð   fiðru winda.

19 ²⁰ Let all his angels boldly bless the eternal Lord, their kind master, those Virtues and Powers, who maintain, observe, and purposefully fulfill his sublime commands.

20 ²¹ May all the forces of his children, and the troop of his servants who now eagerly intend to execute his will, bless the Lord.

21 ²² Let all his own creations also bless the eternal Lord in his proper place, where for them awe of him, and his domination resides; may my soul joyfully bless the Lord.

Psalm 103

1   ¹ Lord, joyfully bless my soul; God, you are my Lord, glorious in might, and especially in deeds, over humankind.

2   You clothed yourself worthily with a magnificent display of splendor; ² you are now skillfully covered with light as if with garments.

3   You stretched the heavens like a skin, ³ which the press of waters inhabits on high.

4   He also created and established the clouds, so that he could readily ascend; he treads with his feet the wings of the winds.

5   He his englas deð   æðele gastas
    and his frome ðegnas   fyr byrnende.

6   He gefæstnude   foldan staðelas,
    eorðan eardas;   ne seo æfre nu
    on worulda world   weorðeð ahylded.

7   He nywolnessa   neoðan swa swa ryfte
    him to gewæde   woruhte swylce;
    standað ofer mannum   muntas on wæterum.

8   Þa him þrea þine   þearle ondrædað,
    fleoð forhtlice   þunres brogan
    þinre stefne,   strangne egsan.

9   Beorgas and feldas   ba astigað
    on þæne stede   þe þu gestaðeludest him,
    and on ðære stowe   standað fæste;
    ne magon hi ofer gemære   mare gegangan,
    þæt hi ðysse eorþan   awyht habban.

10 Oft of denum yrnað   deope wyllan,
    and of midle   munta swylce
    wæter awealleð,   wide floweð

11 Of þam eorðan deor   ealle drincað,
    bidað assan   eac on þurste;
    ofer þan heofon-fugelas   healdað eardas,
    sendað of þam stanum   stefne mycle.

12 Beorgas onfoð   blædum and wæstmum,
    ufan eorð-wæstme   ealle growað;
    swylce of wæstmum   weorca þinra
    eall eorðan cið   ufan byð gefylled.

5   4 He makes noble spirits of his angels and a flaming fire of his brave servants.

6   5 He founded the earth's pillars, the regions of the world; nor will it ever be moved for all time.

7   6 He also created the depths below, like a garment; the mountains in the waters loom over humankind.

8   7 Then they will dread mightily your rebuke, they will fearfully flee the terror of your thunderous voice, that compelling fear of God.

9   8 Both mountains and plains will rise up in the place which you have established for them, and will remain fixed there; 9 they will have no power to advance further beyond their boundary to occupy any other part of this earth.

10   10 Deep springs frequently well up from the valleys, and likewise water will gush forth from out the middle of mountains, flowing widely.

11   11 All the wild animals will drink from that ground, asses in their thirst will also bide their time; 12 birds of the air will maintain their dwellings above the earth, emitting loud cries from the rocks.

12   13 The mountains will be endowed with leaves and fruits, the crops will grow abundantly in high places; likewise, all the buds in the ground will be replenished from above by the fruits of your creations.

13 Swylce þu of foldan fodder neatum
  lætest alædan, on þæm hi lif healdað;
  wyrta þu geworhtest to wraðe manna.

14 Eac þu him of eorþan ut alæddest
  hlaf to helpe, heortan manna
  must and win-drinc myclum blissað;

15 ele andwlitan eac gescyrpeð,
  and hlaf trymeð heortan mannes.

16 Swylce þu gefyllest fægrum blædum
  telgum treow-wæstme; tydrað ealle
  þa on Libanes lædað on beorge
  cwice ceder-beamas, þa ðu cuðlice
  sylfa gesettest; on þam swylce nu
  mid heora spedum spearwan nystlað.

17 Uphebbean hus hiora agen
  is latteow on lande; oft laðne beorh
  on hean muntum heortas wuniað,
  erinaces fleoð oft on stanas.

18 Monan he geworhte on þa mæran tid;
  sunne hire setl-gang sweotule healdeð.

19 Þystru ðu gesettest on þearle niht,
  on þære ealle wildeor wide toeornað;

20 and leon hwelpas lange swylce
  grymetigað gnorne, georne secað
  þæt him grædigum æt God gedeme.

21 Syþþan up cumeð æðele sunne,
  hi of siðum eft gesamniað,
  and hi on holum hydað hi georne.

13   14 You also cause fodder for animals to grow from the earth, by which they maintain life; you provided herbs as sustenance for humankind.

14   In addition you produced for them out of the earth bread as a staple, 15 must and wine to cheer greatly the human heart;

15   oil also enhances the face, and bread makes strong humankind's heart.

16   16 Likewise you will furnish the fruits of the trees with beautiful blossoms on their branches; all of those live cedars growing on Mount Lebanon, which you yourself skillfully planted, will propagate; 17 in them sparrows will nestle now with their substance.

17   The dwelling of the stork is their proper keeper on earth; 18 often harts inhabit the hostile peak in the high mountains, coneys duck into the rocks.

18   19 At that glorious time he created the moon, while the sun precisely maintains the time of its setting.

19   20 You established darkness in the somber night, during which all the wild animals roam widely;

20   21 and lion cubs also roar mournfully for long periods, eagerly seeking what God may assign to them in their hunger.

21   22 After the majestic sun rises, they congregate again from their forays, and they carefully conceal themselves in their dens.

22   Mægen-weorc on morgen   man onginneð,
and þæt geendað   on æfynne.

23   Mycel wærun þine weorc,   mihtig Drihten,
ealle þa þu mid snyteru   sylfa worhtest;
is þeos eorðe eac   eall gefylled
þinra gesceafta,   scyppend mære.

24   His is mycel sæ   and on gemærum wid,
þær is unrim   on ealra cwycra,
mycelra and mætra,   ofer ðæne mægene
oft scipu scriðende   scrinde fleotað.

25   Dracan þu þysne   dædum ðinum geheowadest,
hete syððan his bysmere   brade healdan.
Ealle to ðe,   ece Drihten,
ætes on eorðan   eac wilniað,

26   and him gesomnadum   swylce wylle
þine þa halgan   hand ontynan,
ealle hi gefyllan   fægere gode.

27   Gif þu þine ansyne fram him   æfre awendest,
þonne hi gedrefde   deope weorðað,
and him gast weorðeð   georne afyrred;
swylce teonlice   geteoriað,
on heora agen dust   æfter hweorfað.

28   Onsend þines sylfes gast,   sona weorþað
geedniwad,   and þu eac scyppest
eorðan ansyne   ealle swylce.

29   Wuldor si wide   weruda Drihtne,
and on worulda woruld   wunie syððan;
blissie on his weorcum   bealde Drihten.

22   ²³ People begin their great projects in the morning, and bring them to an end in the evening.

23   ²⁴ Mighty Lord, great were your works, all of which you yourself exquisitely executed; this earth also is totally filled with your creations, glorious creator.

24   ²⁵ His is the sea, vast and spacious in its boundaries, containing countless numbers of all living creatures, great and small, ²⁶ over which gliding ships frequently sail with power and speed.

25   By your actions you formed this dragon, then commanded it to govern far and wide for its sport. ²⁷ All of these earthly creatures also desire food from you, eternal Lord,

26   ²⁸ and also for them as a whole, that holy hand of yours will open, graciously providing all of them with excellent nourishment.

27   ²⁹ If you ever turn your face away from them, they will be severely troubled and the joy of life will be utterly taken from them; they will also seriously deteriorate, eventually reverting to their primal dust.

28   ³⁰ Send forth your own spirit, and they will at once be renewed, and you will also fully form the face of the earth.

29   ³¹ Glory be to the Lord of hosts far and near, and may it endure ever after; may the Lord confidently rejoice in his works.

30   He on ðas eorðan   ealle locað,
deð hi for his egsan   ealle beofian;
gif he mid his mihte   muntas hrineð,
hi ful ricene   reocað sona.

31   Ic on minum life   lustum Drihtne
singe soðlice   and secge eac,
þenden ic wunige   on woruld-dreamum.

32   Wese him herenes min   æt heortan weðe;
ic minne Drihten   deorne lufige.

33   And þa fyrenfullan   frecne forweorðaþ,
þa on ðysse eorðan synt,   ealle sniome,
þæt hio ne wunian   on world-life.
Bletsa mine sawle   bliðe, Drihten.

Psalm 104

1   Andetað Drihtne   and his ecne naman,
cegað cymlice   and cwyce secgeað
his wundor-weorc   ofer ealle wer-ðeode.

2   Singað him swylce   and salletað;
secgað his wundor eall   wide mæru.

3   Hergeað his naman   niode swylce;
heorte hyge-clæne   hlutre blissað
þam þe soðlice   secað Dryhten.

30 ³² He thoroughly inspects this earth, makes it absolutely tremble in fear of him; if he touches the mountains with his power, they will belch smoke immediately.

31 ³³ In my lifetime while I dwell in earthly joys, I will sing and speak to the Lord truthfully and with pleasure.

32 ³⁴ Let my praise be a joy to his heart; I will cherish my beloved Lord.

33 ³⁵ But sinners living on this earth will die horribly, quite quickly, and so will not remain in this world. Lord, joyfully bless my soul.

Psalm 104

1 ¹ Acknowledge the Lord and melodiously invoke his eternal name, and declare his marvelous works to be thriving among all the gentiles.

2 ² Likewise, sing and play on the harp to him; tell of all his marvels, celebrated far and wide.

3 ³ Likewise, earnestly praise his name; let the well-intentioned heart within those who genuinely seek the Lord sincerely rejoice.

4 Secað ge Drihten,   and ge syððan beoð
   teonan gehwylce   ful trume æghwær;
   secað his ansyne   symble georne.

5 Gemunað ge on mode   hu he mænig wundor
   worhte wræclice,   wundur unlytel,
   and his muþes eac   mære domas.

6 Hwæt, he Abrahames cynn,   þe his esne wæs,
   geweorðude   ofer wer-þeoda,
   and Iacobes bearn,   þone he geara geceas.

7 He is ure Drihten,   dædum spedig;
   earun his domas   deore and mære
   geond þisse eorðan   æghwylcne dæl.

8 He þæs on worulde   wearð gemyndig,
   þæt he worde gecwæð   on gewitnesse:
   þæt heo on þusende   þæt sceoldan healdan,
   þære cneorisse,   cwyc se þe lifde.

9 Þæt he mid aðsware   to Abrahame
   and to Isaace   eac gesohte,
   and gleawlice   Iacobe bead
   þæt awa to feore   Israheles cyn
   his gewitnesse   wel geheolde.

10 And him þa mid soðe   sægde cweðende:
   "Ic eowrum cynne   Khananea land
   on agene æht   yrfe gesylle."

11 Næs þæt mære cynn   mycel on rime,
   ac on þam folce   feawe wæran ænige,
   oð ðæt bigengum   beornas onwocan;

4   4 Seek the Lord, and afterward you will be fully fortified everywhere against every kind of injury; always seek his face eagerly.

5   5 Call to mind how wonderfully he created many marvelous things, numerous wonders, and also the famous judgments pronounced by him.

6   6 He has honored the descendants of Abraham, who was his servant, above the gentiles, and Jacob's progeny, whom he chose long ago.

7   7 He is our Lord, successful in deeds; his judgments are bold and renowned throughout every part of this earth.

8   8 He was forever mindful of what he solemnly declared in a covenant: that the Israelites should observe it for a thousand generations, whoever had life then.

9   9 He also exacted that promise from Abraham and Isaac with the swearing of an oath, 10 and prudently enjoined on Jacob that the people of Israel should diligently observe his covenant always.

10   11 And then he spoke to him truthfully, saying: "I will give to your people the land of Canaan, as an inheritance in your proper possession."

11   12 That famous stock was not large in number, on the contrary that people consisted of just a few, until children

cynn æfter cynne   cende wæran,
oð þæt hio oðer folc   egsan geðiwdan.

12   Ne let he him manna   mihte sceððan,
and he þearle for him   þrea geaf kyningum:

13   "Ne sceolon ge mine þa halgan   hrinan ne
                                      gretan,
ne on mine witigan   wergðe settan."

14   Cwom þa ofer eorðan   ermðu and hungor;
wurdon wide menn   wædlan hlafes.

15   He him snoterne beforan   sende æryst
ful wisne   wer to scealce,
and þa bebohtan   bearn Iacobes
Ioseph on geoguðe;   þær hine grame æryst
hæfdon to hæfte,   oþ þæt hine halig God
þurh his worda   wisdom ahof.

16   Sende him soð cyning   sweotule are,
alysde hine lungre,   and hine þam leodum þa
to ealdor-men   eallum sette.

17   He sette hine on his huse   to hlaf-wearde,
ealra him his æhta   anweald betæhte,

18   þæt he his ealdor-men   ealle lærde,
swa he his sylfes mod   geseted hæfde,
and þa yldestan   ealle lærde
þæt heo wisdomes   word oncneowan.

19   Þær Israhel becwom   on Egypta,
and se goda   Iacob syþþan
eft eardude   eorðan Khanaan.

were born to the settlers; ¹³ generation after generation was propagated until they oppressed other peoples with fear.

12   ¹⁴ He did not allow them to be harmed by human powers, and on their account he vigorously dispensed rebukes to kings:

13   ¹⁵ "You should not touch or lay hands on my consecrated ones, nor place a curse on my prophets."

14   ¹⁶ Then scarcity and hunger came upon the earth; humankind far and wide was deprived of bread.

15   ¹⁷ First he sent among them an intelligent and extremely prudent man, in the guise of a servant, and then the children of Jacob sold Joseph in his youth; ¹⁸ in that place they cruelly held him in bondage at first, ¹⁹ until holy God raised him up through the wisdom of his words.

16   ²⁰ A righteous king bestowed public favor on him, released him forthwith, and then established him as ruler over all the people.

17   ²¹ He confirmed him as steward of the royal house, entrusted to him control of all his possessions,

18   ²² so that he should thoroughly instruct his noblemen, just as he had informed his own mind, and fully teach the elders to grasp words of wisdom.

19   ²³ There Israel entered into Egypt, and afterward that excellent Jacob resided again in the land of Canaan.

20 He þæt eadige folc ehte swyðe,
and hio ofer heora feond fæste getrymede.

21 Hiora heortan he ongan hwyrfan æryst,
þæt heo his folc feodan swyðe
and his esnum eac inwit fremedan.

22 Þa he him þone mæran Moyses sende,
his sylfes scealc, samod ætgædere
and Aaron eac, þone he ær geceas.

23 He sette on hi sylfe soðne wisdom
worda and weorca wundor-tacna
and forebeacna, þæt hio fromlice
cyðdan cneo-magum cystum godum,
oðþæt heo geforan folc Khananea.

24 He hi mid þystrum ongan þrean æt frymþe,
for ðon hio word heora wel ne oncneowan.

25 And heora wæter swylce wende to blode
on ðam heora fisceas frecne forwurdan.

26 Sende on heora eorþan ealle swylce
toscean teonlice, þa teolum husum
on cyninga cofum cwyce eardedan.

27 He sylfa cwæð: sona cwoman
mysci manige, mid wæran gnættas;
fleoh-cynnes feala flugan on gemæru.

28 Sette him regnas reþe swylce,
hate of heofenum hagol byrnende;
se lige forgeaf land Egypta.

20 ²⁴ God greatly increased that blessed people, and steadily strengthened their hold over their enemies.

21 ²⁵ First he began to turn the hearts of the Egyptians, so that they intensely hated his people and also dealt deceit to his servants.

22 ²⁶ Then he sent to them the illustrious Moses, his very own servant, and together with him Aaron, whom he had chosen.

23 ²⁷ He established in them true wisdom in words and deeds, miracles and portents, which they vigorously made known to an elite of virtuous kinsmen, until they eventually overcame the people of Chanaan.

24 ²⁸ He began to threaten the Egyptians by means of darkness at first, because they did not properly understand the warnings of Moses and Aaron.

25 ²⁹ And he also changed their water into blood in which their fish cruelly perished.

26 ³⁰ He also sent to their entire land destructive frogs which, fully alive, occupied the finest houses, the king's chambers.

27 ³¹ He himself spoke: numerous flies came at once, accompanied by gnats; many species of flying insects swarmed the borders.

28 ³² He also ordained punishing rains for them, intense burning hail from the heavens; he surrendered the land of Egypt to fire.

29   Syððan forwurdan   heora win-geardas
     and fic-beamas;   furþor ne mihton
     blæda bringan   ne bearwa treow.

30   He þa syþþan cwæð: sona cwoman
     gangan gærs-hoppan   and grame ceaferas,
     ne mihte þa on moldan   man geriman,
     þe þær on foldan   fræton wæstmas.

31   Syþþan he æfter sloh   æghwylc frum-bearn
     þe on Egyptum wæs   ahwær acenned,
     and frum-cynnes   heora frean swylce.

32   And his þæt gode folc   golde and seolfre
     geweorþade,   and hi wislice
     leofe lædde;   næs þæra leoda ða
     ænig untrum,   yldra ne gingra.

33   Wurdon him Egyptas   æfter bliðe,
     syððan hi on fore   folc sceawedan,
     for ðon him þær egesa   angryslic stod.

34   He hi wolcne bewreah,   wraðum ahredde,
     het him neode   nihta gehwylce
     fyrenne beam   beforan wisian.

35   Flæsces hi bædon,   fuglas coman,
     of garsecge   ganetas fleogan;
     and hi heofon-hlafe   halige gefylde.

36   Het him of stane   streamas flowan,
     wæter on willan;   na him gewættan fot,
     þa hi on Iordane   gengdan æfter.

29 ³³ Afterward their vineyards and fig trees perished; moreover, these were unable to yield fruit or trees in the woods.

30 ³⁴ After that he spoke further: grasshoppers and troublesome beetles immediately began to emerge, countless in number, ³⁵ which consumed the fruits of the land there.

31 ³⁶ Afterward he proceeded to slay each firstborn child begotten anywhere in Egypt, as well as the lords of their highest lineage.

32 ³⁷ But he honored that noble people of his with gold and silver, and skillfully escorted his cherished ones; not one of them, young or old, was debilitated at that time.

33 ³⁸ The Egyptians coming behind them exulted when they spied the Israelites ahead, because terrible fear confronted that people there.

34 ³⁹ He covered them with a cloud, protected them from hardships, quickly summoned a fiery pillar to the front to escort them each night.

35 ⁴⁰ They begged for flesh, and birds arrived, gannets flying in from the sea; and he satisfied their hunger with holy manna.

36 ⁴¹ For them he ordered rivers to stream from a rock, waters welling up; these did not in the least wet their feet when later on they marched into the river Jordan.

37 Ac he wæs þæra worda   wel gemyndig,
halig heofenes weard,   þe he hleoðrade
to Abrahame,   his agenum hysse.

38 And his folc lædde   fægere on blisse
and his þone gecorenan heap   clæne on wynne.

39 Sealde þam leodum   landes anweald
on agene æht   oðre þeode,
and hi folca gewinn   fremdra gesæton.

40 Þær hi heoldan   halige domas,
and his soðfæst word   swylce georne,
and his æ-bebod,   awa to feore.

Psalm 105

1 Ic andette   ecum Drihtne,
georne ðam gleawan,   for ðan ic hine godne
                                    wat;
for þon he his mild-heortnysse   mannum
                                    cyðde,
on ðysse worulde   wis gestandeð.

2 Hwylc mæg æfre   mihta Drihtnes
asprecan and aspyrian,   oððe spedlice
eall his lof-mægen   leode gehyran
and his gehyrnesse   her oncnawan?

37 ⁴² But he, the holy guardian of heaven, clearly remembered those words which he proclaimed to Abraham, his chosen man.

38 ⁴³ And he graciously guided his people in joy and that chosen company of his in utter gladness.

39 ⁴⁴ He gave to those people control of the land, and alien peoples as their exclusive possession, and they appropriated the labors of foreign nations.

40 ⁴⁵ In that place they also diligently observed his sacred decrees, truthful words, and the rule of his law, always and forever.

Psalm 105

1 ¹ I acknowledge earnestly the eternal Lord, the wise one, because I know him to be good; because he revealed his compassion to humankind, he remains ever wise in this world.

2 ² Who can ever describe and explore the Lord's powers, or effectively listen to all the popular adulation of him, and understand its report throughout the world?

3   Eadige beoð æghwær,   þa ðe a wyllað
    soðe domas   sylfe efnan,
    on ealle tid   æghwæs healdan
    heora soðfæstnysse   symble mid dædum.

4   Gemune us, Drihten,   on mod-sefan
    forð hycgende   folces þines,
    and us mid hælo   her geneosa.

5   And us tidlice   teala sceawige,
    ceose mid gecorenum,   þenden we cwice lifgen,
    þæt we mid þinre ðeode   þær blissian,
    and þæt yrfe þin   æghwær herige.

6   We gefyrnedan   mid urum fæderum ær,
    and we unsoðfæste   ealle wæron,
    and unrihtes   æghwær worhtan.

7   Fæderas ure   fæste ne oncneowan
    ealle þa wundor,   þe ðu on Egyptum
    worhtest wræclice,   wundor unlytel;
    næron hi gemyndige   miltsa þinra,
    þa ðu him on ðære mægðe   manige cyðdest.

8   Hi bysmredan,   þa hi on brad wæter
    on þone readan sæ   randas bæron,
    þær ðu hi alysdest,   lifes Ealdor,
    and hi generedest   on naman þinum,
    þa ðu þine miht   mycle cyðdest.

9   Þær ðu readne sæ   ricene geðywdest,
    and þær wæron   þa wareðas drige;
    and hi betweonum wætera   weallas læddest,
    swa hi on westenne   wæron on drigum.

3   ³ They will be blessed everywhere, who are determined to fulfill forever those same true decrees, to uphold their justice in every way with action at all times.

4   ⁴ Lord, remember us, as you continually keep your people in mind, and visit us here with your salvation.

5   ⁵ And may you look in a timely and proper manner at us, selecting us for the company of the elect, as long as we are alive, so that we may rejoice there with your people, and praise your inheritance everywhere.

6   ⁶ We previously sinned with our fathers, and were utterly unjust, committing iniquity in every way.

7   ⁷ Our fathers did not properly understand all those wonders, a multitude, which you miraculously performed in Egypt; they did not remember your acts of mercy, which you showed them in that generation in great numbers.

8   They provoked you when they carried their shields into the broad waters of the Red Sea, ⁸ where you, Lord of life, saved and rescued them for your name's sake, when you bountifully revealed your power.

9   ⁹ In that place you quickly rebuked the Red Sea, and the seaweed dried up there; and you guided them between walls of waters, as if they were walking on dry land in a desert.

10 Swa hi alysde   lifes Ealdor
of heora feonda   fæcnum handum
and of feogendra   folmum swylce;
and heora feondas   flod adrencte
þæt þæra æfre ne com   an spell-boda.

11 Syððan hi his wordon   wel gelyfdan
and him lof-sangum   lustum cwemdan,
and þæs eft hraðe   ealle forgeaton
weorca wræclicra;   na hi wel syþþan
his geæhtunge   ahwær heoldan.

12 Hi on westenne   wraðe ongunnan
gitsunge began   and gramlice
heora Godes þær   geare costedan.

13 He him been sniome   brohte and sealde,
sende on heora muþas   mete to genihte.

14 Ongunnon hi on þam wicum   wraðe swylce
mærne Moyses   ma bysmrian,
and Aaron mid   eac þone halgan.

15 Þa eorðe togaan   and eall forswealh,
on deope forwyrd,   Dathanes weorod
and Abirones   eall ætgædere.

16 Þær fyr abarn   frecne swylce
on heora gemetinge,   and þær maan-sceaðan
þa synfullan   sniome forbærnde.

17 Hi on Choreb swylce   cealf ongunnan
him to god-gylde   georne wyrcean,
onwendan heora wuldor   on þæne wyrsan had
hæðen-styrces   hig-etendes.

10   ¹⁰ So the Lord of life rescued them from the deceitful hands of their enemies and those who hated them; ¹¹ and the surge of water drowned their enemies so that not a single one of them ever survived to tell the tale.

11   ¹² Subsequently, the people believed firmly in his words and pleased him with enthusiastic canticles, ¹³ but very soon after that they totally forgot his marvelous works; they did not afterward properly follow his counsel at all.

12   ¹⁴ In the desert they perversely began to indulge a craving, and there for sure severely tempted their God.

13   ¹⁵ He quickly brought and supplied their request, sending food in abundance for their mouths.

14   ¹⁶ In the camps they also began bitterly to provoke the illustrious Moses even more, and also the venerable Aaron with him.

15   ¹⁷ Then the ground opened up and entirely swallowed up, in complete annihilation, the followers of Dathan and Abiram all at once.

16   ¹⁸ There in their assembly, fire also burned fiercely, and in that place consumed those guilty sinners immediately.

17   ¹⁹ In Horeb they also diligently set about casting a calf as their idol, ²⁰ exchanging their glory for the more depraved form of a grass-eating heathen calf.

18   Godes hi forgeaton   þe hi of gramra ær
feonda folmum   frecne generede,
þe on Egyptum   æðele wundur,
and on Chananea   cymu worhte,
and recene wundur   on þam readan sæ.

19   Þa hi wolde toweorpan   wuldres Aldor,
þær heora Moyses   mægene ne hulpe;
he þæt folc forstod   feonda mægene,
for ðon he him his yrre   of acyrde,
þæt he hi ne towurpe   geond wer-þeoda.

20   Ne hi for awyht   eorþan, cyste,
þa selestan   geseon woldan,
ne his wordum eac   woldan gelyfan;
ac hi granedan   and grame spræcan,
noldan his wordum   wel gehyran.

21   He his handa ahof,   and hi hraðe wolde
on þam westenne   wide todrifan
and heora swæs cynn   sendan on wid-land.

22   Hi Belphegor   bædon are,
æton deadra lac—swa hit gedefe ne wæs.

23   And hi bysmredon   bealde Drihten
on heora gemetincge   mægene ealle,
and þær healicne   on hryre gefremedan.

24   Hi þæs feond-ætes   Finees awerede,
þa he on þam folce   feond-gyld gebræc;
he þæs hæl gehleat   and helpe fand
of cynna gehwam   and on cneorisse.

18 ²¹ They forgot the God who had boldly rescued them from the power of fierce enemies, who had performed magnificent marvels in Egypt, ²² glorious things in Canaan, and instant miracles in the Red Sea.

19 ²³ Then when Moses failed to relieve their want with a miracle, the Lord of glory wished to destroy them; Moses protected that people from the violence of enemies, for he turned away God's anger from them, so that he did not disperse the peoples.

20 ²⁴ Nor were they willing to regard that most excellent land, a prize, as anything of value, or to believe also in his words; ²⁵ on the contrary, they grumbled and spoke angrily, refusing to listen properly to his words.

21 ²⁶ He raised up his hand, intending at once to disperse them widely in the desert ²⁷ and drive their precious progeny into far-flung lands.

22 ²⁸ They entreated Baalpeor for favors, consumed offerings made to the dead—most inappropriate behavior.

23 ²⁹ And they brazenly provoked the Lord in their assembly with vehemence, and there worked toward profound ruin for themselves.

24 ³⁰ Phinehas protected them from eating food dedicated to false gods, when he shattered the idol among the people, ³¹ for which he won salvation and found support from each generation and for all time.

25   Eac hi gefremedan   oðer bysmer,
    þær hi wiðercwyde   wæteres hæfdon,
    þær Moyses wearð   mægene gebysgad
    for heora yfelum,   swa he oftor wæs;
    on his gaste gram,   ne mihte him Godes willan
    mid his welerum   wisne getæcean.

26   Noldan hi toworpan   wraðe þeode,
    swa him Drihten ær   dema sægde;
    ac hi wið manfullum   mengdan þeode
    and leornedan   lað weorc Gode,
    and sceucc-gyldum   swyþe guldan,
    him þæt eall gewearð   to æ-swyce.

27   Ongunnan heora bearn   blotan feondum,
    sceuccum onsæcgean   suna and dohter;
    agutan blod swylce   bearna feala,
    þa unscyldige   ealle wærun,
    syðþan hi gecuran   Chananea god.

28   Þanon eorþe wearð   eall mid blode
    mane gemenged,   misdædum fah.

29   Eall hi forheoldan   heah-weorc Godes,
    for ðan him yrre wearð   ece Drihten,
    and he his yrfe   eall forhogode.

30   He hi on hand-geweald   hæðenum sealde,
    and heora weoldan,   þa him wyrrest ær
    on feondscipe   fæste gestodon.

31   Heora costedan   cuþe feondas,
    and under handum   hynþe þoledan;
    hi alysde oft   lifes Ealdor.

25   ³² Moreover, they perpetrated another outrage, when they experienced the "contradiction of water," where Moses was mightily troubled, as he more than often was, by their wickedness; ³³ exasperated in spirit, he was unable to instruct them in God's wise will.

26   ³⁴ They refused to destroy hostile peoples as the Lord judge had commanded them; ³⁵ instead, they intermarried with depraved gentiles and learned practices hateful to God, ³⁶ and enthusiastically paid homage to idols, all of which became a stumbling block for them.

27   ³⁷ They began to sacrifice their children to demons, to offer sons and daughters as sacrifices to idols; ³⁸ likewise, after they selected a Canaanite god, they shed the blood of many entirely innocent children.

28   From then on, the ground was totally mired with blood from that outrage, ³⁹ stained by evil deeds.

29   They neglected all God's noble works, ⁴⁰ so that the eternal Lord was angry with them, and utterly despised his inheritance.

30   ⁴¹ He gave them over to the power of heathens, and these latter, who had consistently stood worst in enmity to them before, now tyrannized them.

31   ⁴² Familiar enemies persecuted them, and they suffered humiliation at their hands; ⁴³ the Lord of life frequently freed them.

32   Hi hine on geþeahte   oft abylgdan;
    wæron on unrihtum   oft gehynde.

33   Swa he furðum oncneow   þæt heora fynd
                               ehtan,
    he heora bene   bealde gehyrde.

34   Þonne he his word-gebeot   well gemunde;
    hreaw hine sona,   þonne hi hynþa drugan,
    æfter his miltsa   menigu godes.

35   Syððan he him sealde   sona miltse,
    þær hi on gesawon   ealle ætgædere,
    þe ehtend him   ær gestodan.

36   Do us hale nu,   halig Drihten,
    and us, se goda God,   georne gesamna
    of widwegum,   þær we wean dreogað,
    þæt we þinne naman   nede motan
    þone halgestan   her andettan,
    and we on lofe þinum   lungre weorðan
    ofer wer-ðeode   wuldre geherede.

37   Wese Israhela God   aa gebletsad,
    on worulda woruld,   Wealdend-Drihten;
    and þæt fægere becweðe   folca æghwylc,
    "Wese swa, wese swa,"   þurh eall wide ferhð.

32   They often provoked him in their deliberations; they were frequently debased by sin.

33   [44] As soon as he realized that enemies persecuted them, he heard their appeal without hesitation.

34   [45] Then he clearly recalled his solemn promise; whenever they suffered affliction, he immediately grieved, in accord with the abundance of the gift of his compassion.

35   [46] Afterward he soon showered mercy on them, when all those together who had previously been their persecutors, took notice.

36   [47] Holy Lord, save us now and, virtuous God, gather us diligently from the distant regions where we endure troubles, so that we can eagerly praise here that most holy name of yours, and may be promptly honored with your glory beyond other people.

37   [48] Blessed be the God of the Israelites, the sovereign Lord, for ever and ever; and may every people fittingly declare for all eternity, "So be it, so be it."

Psalm 106

1   Ic andette   ecne Drihten,
     þæne goodan God,   for ðan ic hine gleawne
                                         wat;
     is his mild-heortnes   mycel to worulde.

2   Secge þæt nu ða   þæt hi sylfa God alysde,
     lifes weard,   laðum of handa,
     and hi of sid-folcum   gesamnade.

3   Fram upp-gange   æryst sunnan
     oþ þæt heo gewiteð   on west-rodur,
     and fram sæ norðan   swycedan geond westen;
     ne meahton ceastre weg   cuðne mittan,
     þe hi eardunge   on genaman.

4   Hæfde hi hungor and þurst   heard gewyrded,
     þæt him frecne on   feorh aðolude.

5   And hi þa on þære costunge   cleopedan to
                                    Dryhtne,
     and he hi of þam earfeðum   eallum alysde.

6   Hi þa gelædde   lifes Ealdor
     þær hi on rihtne weg   ricene eodan
     oð þæt hi cuðlice   on becwoman
     to hiora cestre   eardung-stowe.

7   For ðon hi mild-heortnesse   mihtigan Drihtnes
     ealle andettað,   and eac sæcgeað
     mycel wundur hys   manna bearnum,

Psalm 106

1   [1] I acknowledge the eternal Lord, that virtuous God, because I know him to be wise; his mercy is great forever.

2   [2] I declare now that the same God, the guardian of life, has rescued them from hostile hands, gathering them together from far-flung nations.

3   [3] From where the sun is first sighted until it disappears in the western sky, and from the sea and the north, [4] they wandered in the desert; they were not able to find a familiar route to a city where they might take up residence.

4   [5] Hunger and thirst had severely crippled them, so that they suffered cruelly in spirit.

5   [6] And then in that trial they called out to the Lord, and he rescued them from all those tribulations.

6   [7] The Lord of life then directed them to where they could travel quickly on the right path until they entered with certainty into the dwelling place of their city.

7   [8] Therefore, they wholeheartedly acknowledge the mighty Lord's mercy and also declare his great miracles to humankind,

8   for ðon he gesedeð   sawle idle,
      and þa hungrian   her mid godum
      fæste gefylleð   to feore syþþan;

9   þa þe her on ðystrum   þrage sæton,
      and on deaðes scuan   deorcum lifdan,
      gebundene   bealuwe feterum,
      on wædle wrace   and on iserne.

10   For ðon hi dydan   Drihtnes spræce
      æghwæs ægype,   and his geðeaht swylce
      þæs heahstan him   hæfdan on bysmer,

11   hiora heorte wæs   hean on gewinnum,
      and untrume   ealle wæran;
      næfdan þa on foldan   fultum ænne.

12   Hi on costunge   cleopedan to Drihtne,
      and he hi of þam earfoðum   eallum alysde;

13   and he hi of þam þystrum   þanon alædde,
      and of deaðes scuan   deorcum generede,
      and heora bendas towearp   bitre sneome.

14   For ðan hi mild-heort mod   mihtigan Drihtnes
      ealle andettan   and eac cweþan
      mycel wundur his   ofer manna bearn,

15   for ðon he æren dor   eaðe gescæneð,
      and iserne steng   ana gebigeð.

16   He hi of unrihtum   ealle swylce
      þam wraðan wege   wis alædeð,
      þær hi wæron on woo ær   wraðe besmitene.

8   9 because he satisfies the empty soul, and constantly fills those who suffer hunger here with good things forever after;

9   10 those who resided on earth for a long time in darkness, living in death's gloomy shadow, bound by fetters of evil, in the misery of want, and in irons.

10   11 Because they treated the Lord's words as altogether worthless, and likewise held in contempt the advice of the most high to them,

11   12 their hearts were rendered abject with struggles, and they became totally enervated; they lacked then any source of help on earth.

12   13 In distress they called out to the Lord, and he rescued them from all those troubles;

13   14 and guided them from out of that darkness, and saved them from the gloom of death's shadow, and sharply snapped their chains at once.

14   15 Let them, therefore, fully acknowledge mighty God's merciful intent and also declare his great marvels throughout humankind,

15   16 because he shatters brass doors with ease, and single-handedly bends the iron bar.

16   17 The wise one also guides them away completely from iniquity, that evil path on which they had been horribly defiled in wickedness.

17   Hi onhysctan   æghwylcne mete
        mode mægen heora,   oð unmihte,
        þæt hy wið deaða duru   drencyde wæran.

18   Þa hi on costunge   cleopedan to Drihtne,
        and he hi of þam earfoþum   eallum alysde.

19   He him wisfæstlic   word onsende,
        þurh þæt hi hrædlice   hælde wæron
        and of heora forwyrde   wurdan generede.

20   For ðon hi nu andettan   ecum Drihtne,
        þæt he milde wearð   manna cynne;
        mycel ys his wundur   ofer manna bearn.

21   Hi him sculon laces lof   lustum bringan,
        and his weorc wynsum   wide sæcgean.

22   Þa þe sæ seceað,   mid scipe liðað,
        wyrceað weorc mænig   on wæter-ðryþum.

23   Hi Drihtnes weorc   digul gesawon
        and his wundra wearn   on wæter-grundum.

24   Gif he sylfa cwyð,   sona ætstandað
        ystige gastas   ofer ege-wylmum,
        beoð heora yþa   up astigene;

25   þa to heofenum up   heah astigað,
        nyþer gefeallað   under neowulne grund;
        oft þa on yfele   eft aþindað.

26   Gedrefede þa   deope syndan,
        hearde onhrerede   her anlicast,
        hu druncen hwylc   gedwæs spyrige;
        ealle heora snytru beoð   yfele forglendred.

17   ¹⁸ They abhorred in their mind every kind of food, their sustenance, to the point of debility, so that they were drawn near to death's door.

18   ¹⁹ Then in their difficulty they called out to the Lord, and he rescued them from all those tribulations.

19   ²⁰ He sent them his wise words, by means of which they were quickly cured and rescued from destruction.

20   ²¹ Therefore, let them now give praise to the eternal Lord for being merciful to humankind; great is his miraculous power over them.

21   ²² They should bring to him willingly the adoration of a sacrifice, and widely announce his joyful works.

22   ²³ Those who venture upon the sea, sail in ships, do many transactions in mighty waters.

23   ²⁴ They have perceived God's hidden works and a great deal of his marvels in the depths of the sea.

24   ²⁵ If he himself speaks, stormy spirits immediately rise up above the fearsome surges, their waves are lifted up;

25   ²⁶ they mount up on high to the heavens, they sink downward below the bottom of the ocean; often they become once more puffed up with evil.

26   ²⁷ The depths are troubled, severely tossed about, just like some foolish drunk making his way on land; all their wisdom is devoured by evil.

27   Hi on costunge   cleopedan to Drihtne,
        and he hi of earfeðum   eallum alysde.

28   He yste mæg   eaðe oncyrran,
        þæt him windes hweoðu   weorðeð smylte,
        and þa yðe   eft swygiað;
        bliþe weorðað,   þa þe brimu weþað.

29   And he hi on hælo   hyþe gelædde,
        swa he hira willan   wyste fyrmest,
        and he hig of earfoðum   eallum alysde.

30   Hi andettan   ealle Drihtne,
        hu he milde wearð   manna cynne;
        mære synd his wundur   ofer manna bearn.

31   For ðon hine on cyrcean   cristenes folces
        hean ahebbað;   and him hælu and lof
        on sotelum soðfæstra   secgean to worulde.

32   He on westenne   wynne streamas
        soðfæst sette,   þær he sarig folc
        geðewde þurste   þa blissade.

33   He ða weaxendan   wende eorðan
        on sealtne mersc   for synn-dædum
        þara eardendra,   þe hire on lifdan.

34   Westen he geworhte   on widne mere,
        and swylce eorðan   eac butan wætre
        on utgange   æþelast burnan.

35   Þær he hungrium   ham staðelude,
        and þær gesetton   swylce ceastre
        þær hi eard namon   awa syþþan.

27   28 In their tribulation they called out to the Lord, and he rescued them from all their difficulties.

28   29 He can readily transform a gale, so that the wind's breath becomes gentle for them, and the waves fall silent again; 30 they are happy because the sea's surges abate.

29   And he guided them into a haven of safety, for he perfectly understood their wish, and he freed them from all their troubles.

30   31 Let them all praise the Lord for being compassionate to humankind; great are his miraculous powers over them.

31   32 Therefore extol him in the exalted assembly of the Christian community; and let them declare health and praise to him in the seats of the righteous, forever.

32   33 The just God established rivers of joy in the desert, where he then gladdened sorrowful peoples oppressed by thirst.

33   34 He changed that flourishing land into a briny marsh in reaction to the sinful deeds of those who lived there.

34   35 He made the desert into a broad sea and likewise arid land into an outlet for the noblest river.

35   36 There he established a home for the hungry, and there also placed a city where they took up residence forever after.

36   Hi win-geardas   wyrcean ongunnon,
       sæde seowan;   syþþan growan
       lungre land heora   aloden wæstmum.

37   Þa he bletsade,   and hi brade þa
       weoxan weorðlice,   wide greowan;
       næs heora neata   nan geyfelad.

38   Oft hi fea wurdan   feondum geswencte
       fram þære costunge   þe him becwom æfter,
       sares and yfeles,   þe hi syþþan begeat,

39   syððan hi forhogedan   halige lare.
       Hiora ealdor-men   ealle wæron
       sare beswicene,   swicedan oftust,
       and on wegas werige,   wendan hwilum of.

40   Þær he þearfendra   þa miltsude,
       and hi of wædle   wean alysde,
       sette heora staðol   sceapum anlice.

41   Syþþan þæt soðfæste geseoð,   sniome æfter
       bliðe weorðað,   beot geþenceað,
       þæt unrihta gehwylc   eft oncyrreð,
       and his sylfes muð   symble nemneð.

42   Hwylc is wisra nu,   wel snotera,
       þe þas mid gehygde   healdan cunne,
       and milde mod   mihtigan Drihtnes
       full gleawlice   ongite syþþan?

36 37 They began to cultivate vineyards, to sow the land with seed; afterward their lands quickly flourished, springing up with crops.

37 38 He blessed them, and then they gloriously multiplied far and wide, thrived mightily; not one of their beasts was injured.

38 39 Few in number, they were often harassed by enemies in the ordeal of suffering and evil which afterward befell them, afflicting them,

39 40 when they spurned sacred doctrine. Their chiefs were all grievously led astray, they blasphemed very often and, exhausted on the road, they sometimes wandered from it.

40 41 There he took pity on the needy then, rescuing them from the misery of poverty, establishing for them a homestead, as one does for sheep.

41 42 When the just perceive that, they will immediately after become joyful, will remember his solemn promise that he will reverse every evil and will continually invoke his own mouth.

42 43 Which one is wiser now, truly more prudent, who knows on reflection how to maintain these things, and afterward understands very clearly the mighty Lord's kind disposition?

Psalm 107

1 Ys min heorte gearu,   halig Drihten,
gearu is min heorte   þæt ic Gode cweme,
sealmas singe   soþum Drihtne.

2 Aris nu, wuldur min,   þæt ic wynlice
on *psalterio* þe   singan mote,
and ic ðe on hleoðre   hearpan swylce
on ær-mergen   eac gecweme.

3 Ic þe andette,   ece Drihten,
on folca gehwam   fægrum wordum;
and ic þe on ðeodum   on þanc mote
sealmas singan   swyþe geneahhe.

4 Is þin mild-heort mod   mycel oð heofenas
ahafen healice   ofer hæleða bearn;
ys þin soðfæstnes   seted oþ wolcen.

5 Ahafen þu eart ofer heofenas,   halig Drihten;
is wuldur ðin   wide swylce
ofer þas eorðan   ealle mære,
and þine þa gecorenan wesan   clæne and alysde.

6 Do me þin swyðre hand   swylce halne,
and me gehyre,   hælynd Drihten,
þe on halgum spreceð   her on eorðan:
"And ic blissige,   bu gedæle,
þa sele-gesceotu,   þa on Sycimam nu
and on Metibor   mære standað.

Psalm 107

1 ² Holy Lord, my heart is ready, it is ready to please God, to sing psalms to that faithful Lord.

2 ³ Rise up now, glory of mine, so that I can sing to you joyfully on the psaltery, and also delight you in the early hours of the morning with the music of the harp.

3 ⁴ I will acknowledge you, eternal Lord, with pleasant words among every one of the peoples; and let me be allowed to sing psalms to you very frequently in gratitude among the nations.

4 ⁵ That great merciful spirit of yours is loftily exalted to the heavens above humankind; your truth is established up to the clouds.

5 ⁶ Holy Lord, you are raised up above the heavens; likewise your glory is illustrious far and wide over all this earth, ⁷ and may those chosen ones of yours be pure and set free.

6 Let your right hand also make me safe, and hear me, ⁸ savior Lord, who says to the holy ones here on earth: "And I will rejoice, will divide both the tents which now stand splendid in Shechem and in Metibor.

7   Min is Galaad,   gearwe Mannases;
is Effrem his   agen broður
efne heah strengðu   heafdes mines.

8   Ic me to cyninge   cenne Iudas,
syndan me Moabitingas   magas swylce;
ic Idumea   ealle cenne
and min gescy þyder   sendan þence;
syndan me fremde cynn   fæste underþeoded."

9   Hwylc gelædeð me   on lifes byrig
fæste getrymede,   þæt ic forð þanon
on Idumea wese   eft gelæded?

10   Hwæt, þu eart se sylfa God,   þe us synnige iu
adrife fram dome;   ne do þu æfre swa,
þæt þu of urum mægene   mod acyrre.

11   Syle us on earfoðum   æþelne fultum,
for þon hælu byð   her on eorðan
manna gehwylces   mægene idel.

12   Us sceal mægenes gemet   mihtig Drihten
soðfæst syllan,   and he sona mæg
ure feond gedon   fracuþe to nawihte.

Psalm 108

1   Nelle ic lofes þines,   lifigende God,
geswigian,   þeah þe me synfulra
inwitfulra muðas   on ganian.

7   [9] Gilead is mine, Manasseh as well; Ephraim, his own brother, is no less the lofty strength of my head.

8   I nominate Judah as my king, [10] the Moabites likewise are my kinsmen; I will fully endorse Edom, and I intend to project my sandals there; alien peoples are strictly subjugated to me."

9   [11] Who will lead me into the city of life, strongly fortified, so that from there I may be guided onward once more into Edom?

10   [12] You are the same God who in the past expelled us sinners from our state of glory; may you never shift your attention from our army.

11   [13] Grant us glorious help in tribulations, because here on earth any human help is void of strength.

12   [14] That mighty, trustworthy Lord is sure to grant us a proper measure of power, and he can at once reduce our enemies to nothing, ignominiously.

Psalm 108

1   [2] I will not keep silent about praising you, living God, even though the mouths of crafty sinners are wide open against me.

2   Hio þa innwit feala   ywdan on tungan,
and me wraðra wearn   worda spræcon,
fæcne firenlicu,   and afuhtan me
ealle earwunga   ungemete swyðe.

3   Hi me wið lufan   laþum dædum
torne telnysse   teodan mænige;
ic him a gebæd   ungemete georne.

4   Hi me yfel settan   a wið goode,
and feounge   for minre lufan.

5   Gesete him synnfulle   symble to ealdrum;
stande him on þa swyþeran hand   swylce
                                           deoful.

6   Gange of dome gehwam   deope gehyned,
and him his gebed   hweorfe to fyrenum.

7   Gewurðe him weste   eall his onwunung
and on hys eardung-stowe   næfre gewurþe
þæt þær on gewunige   awiht lifigendes.

8   Wesan him dagas deorce   and dimme and
                                          feawe,
and his bisceophad   brucan feondas.

9   Weorðan his agene bearn   ealle steop-cild,
and his wif wyrðe   wydewe hreowlic.

10   Syn his bearn swylce   toboren wide,
and he ut weorpe   earme þearfan,
þonne hi to his huse   hleowes wilnian.

2   ³ At that time they uttered many slanders and addressed me with many cruel words, treacherous and wicked words, and absolutely without cause assailed me most outrageously.

3   ⁴ With hateful deeds in return for affection, they cruelly contrived many slanders against me; yet I continuously prayed for them most earnestly.

4   ⁵ They constantly prepared evil for me in return for good, and hatred in place of my love.

5   ⁶ Appoint sinners as leaders over them always; let a demon also stand on their right hand.

6   ⁷ Let him emerge from every judgment severely condemned, and may his prayer turn to iniquities for him.

7   May his dwelling become an utter wasteland for him, and may it never happen that any living creature occupies his place.

8   ⁸ May his days be gloomy and dismal and few, and may enemies enjoy his position of authority.

9   ⁹ May all of his own children be orphans, and his wife a wretched widow.

10   ¹⁰ May his children also be dispersed far and wide, and when, as wretched paupers, they ask for shelter at his house, may he throw them out.

11   Ealle his æhta   unholde fynd
       rice reðe-mann   rycene gedæle,
       and his feoh onfon   fremde handa;

12   ne him ahwær wese   ænig fultum,
       ne his steop-cildum   stande to helpe.

13   Gangan ealle his bearn   on ece forwyrd,
       and on anum cneowe   eall gewyrðe
       his nama nyhsta   nede adilgad.

14   Eall þæt unriht   þe his ealdras ær
       manes gefremedan,   on gemynd cume
       and on ansyne   ures Drihtnes;
       ne adilgode wesan   deorce fyrene,
       þa his modur ær   mane fremede.

15   Wesan hi wið Drihtne   dædum swylce;
       and hine adilgie   dome ealne
       of ðysse eorðan   awa to feore.

16   Næs him milde gemynd   on mod-sefan,
       and he þearfendra   ðriste ehte,
       symble þæt on heortan   hogode geornust
       hu he mid searuwe   swylce acwealde.

17   He wolde wergðu   wyrcean georne,
       and hine seo ylce on   eft gesette;
       nolde he bletsunge   biddan ne tilian,
       for ðon hio him wæs afyrred   of ferhð-cofan.

18   He hine gegyrede   mid grame wyrgðu,
       swa he hine wædum   wræstum geteode;
       and sio his innað   yðde swylce

11 ¹¹ May some powerful moneylender quickly deal out all his goods to a malicious enemy, and alien hands take hold of his wealth;

12 ¹² nor may any help be available anywhere for him, or be on hand as a support for his orphans.

13 ¹³ May all his progeny enter into eternal damnation, and may his very recently acquired reputation be thoroughly wiped out in a single generation.

14 ¹⁴ Let all the criminal wrongs that his forefathers formerly perpetrated enter into our Lord's memory and sight; let not the sinister iniquities, which his mother had impiously committed, be blotted out.

15 ¹⁵ Likewise, let them be opposed in their actions to the Lord; and may he expel him perpetually by decree from this earth for ever and ever.

16 ¹⁶ There was no thought of compassion in his mind, ¹⁷ so he brazenly harassed needy people, constantly weighing up most attentively how to do away with such people by deceit.

17 ¹⁸ He desired eagerly to engage in cursing, but that same activity rebounded on him; he did not want to request or provide a blessing, because it was far removed from his thinking.

18 He girded himself with fierce cursing, as if decked out in the finest clothing; but his cursing also ravaged his intes-

wan wætere gelic   and wyn-ele,
se þe banes byrst   beteð and hæleð.

19   Wese he hrægle gelic   þe her hraðe ealdað,
and gyrdelse,   ðe hine man gelome gyrt.

20   Þis is weorc þara   þe oft wraðe me
trage tældan;   tyne hine Dryhten
þam þe sar sprece   sawle minre.

21   And þu, min Drihten God,   do me þine nu
mycle mild-heortnesse   for þinum þam mæran
naman,
swa ðu oft þin milde mod   manegum cyðdest.

22   Alys me, lifes weard,   for þan ic eom lama
þearfa;
is me heorte on   hearde gedrefed.

23   Ic eom scuan gelic   swyþe ahylded,
oðlæded godum   swa se gærs-hoppa.

24   Me synt cneowu swylce   cwicu unhale
for fæstenum;   is min flæsc swylce
for fægrum ele   frecne onwended;
eom ic to edwit-stæfe   eallum geworden.

25   Swa hi me gesawon,   sona hig wegdan
hrerdan heora heafod.   Help min, Drihten
God,
and me halne gedo,   hælynde Crist,
for þinre þære myclan   mild-heortnysse,

26   þæt hi soð witan,   þæt si þin sylfes hand,
and þu þas gedydest,   Drihten usser.

tines, making its way like water and the gladdening oil which cures and heals a broken bone.

19   19 May he be like an earthly garment which wears thin quickly, and like a girdle with which one often girds oneself.

20   20 This is the handiwork of those who spoke ill of me in anger; may the Lord close himself off from him who says hurtful things about my soul.

21   21 As for you, my Lord God, grant me now your great mercy for the sake of your renowned name, just as you frequently made known your compassionate spirit to many.

22   Guardian of life, free me, 22 because I am a feeble, needy person; my heart is sorely troubled.

23   23 Like a shadow, I have drastically declined, removed from good things like a grasshopper.

24   24 My knees also, while still working, are weak on account of fasting; my flesh too, because of fragrant oil, is dangerously altered; 25 I am become a reproach to all of them.

25   As soon as they saw me, they waggled and shook their heads. 26 Lord God, help me, and save me, redeeming Christ, in consideration of your great mercy,

26   27 so that they may truly recognize that it is the work of your own hand, and that you, our Lord, have accomplished those things.

27   Weorðan þa awyrgde,   wes þu gebletsad;
       and þa þe me mid unryhte   ænige styrian,
       and hi þær sceande   sylfe agon;
       wese þin esne on þe   ungemete bliðe.

28   Syn ða butan are   ealle gegyrede
       þe me tælnysse   teonan ætfæstan,
       and him si abrogden,   swa of brec-hrægle
       hiora sylfra sceamu   swyþust ealra.

29   Ic on minum muðe   mihta Drihtnes
       ealle andette,   and eac swylce
       hine on midle   manna herige.

30   He sylfa gestod   on ða swyðran hand,
       þær he þearfendra   þinga teolode;
       he mine sawle   swylce gehealde
       wið ehtendra   egsan griman.

Psalm 109

6   ... hefige gefylleð;
       heafod he gebreceð   hæleða mæniges,
       and swa geweorðeð   wide geond eorðan.

7   Þa þe on wege weorðað,   wætres æt hlimman
       deopes ondrincað;   beoð þy dæd-fromran,
       and for ðon hiora heafod   hebbað syþþan.

27   [28] Let them be cursed, may you be blessed; and may those who agitate me with any kind of harm suffer shame themselves in that matter; let your servant be exceedingly happy in you.

28   [29] Let all those who attach to me the pain of reproach be clothed with ignominy and, most of all, may their very own genitals be exposed on them, as if they had removed their trousers.

29   [30] I will declare with my mouth all the Lord's powers, and also praise him among humankind.

30   [31] He himself stood on the right hand, where he attended to the concerns of the needy; he likewise protected my soul from the dire danger of persecutors.

Psalm 109

6   . . . he will carry out severely; he will smash the heads of many men, and so it will happen throughout the earth widely.

7   [7] Those passing on the road will drink from a torrent of deep waters; they will be all the more vigorous in deeds and therefore will hold their heads high afterward.

Psalm 110

1   Ic andytte þe,   ece Drihten,
mid hyge ealle   heortan minre
for gesamnuncge   þæra soðfæstra
and on gemetingum;   mycel Drihtnes weorc.

2   Swylce ic his willan   wylle georne
swyþe secean,   samed andettan
hu his mægen-þrymnes   mycellic standeð,
and his soðfæstnyss wunað   symble ece.

3   He gemynd dyde   mærra wundra;
mild-heort he is and modig   mihtig Drihten,
syleð eallum mete   þam þe his ege habbað.

4   And he on worulde   wearð gemyndig
his gewitnesse,   þe he wel swylce
myhtum miclum   and mær-weorcum
fægrum gefylde,   and to his folce cwæð
þæt he him wolde yrfe   ellþeodigra
on agene æht   eall gesyllan.

5   Ys his hand-geweorc   hyge soðfæstra,
ryhte domas,   þa he ræran wyle;
wærun his bebodu   ealle treowfæste,
on ealra weorulda weoruld   wurdan soðfæste,
and on rihtnysse   ræda getrymede.

6   He alysinge   leofum folce
soðe onsende,   and him swylce bebead

Psalm 110

1   [1] Eternal Lord, with the most sincere intentions I will acknowledge you before the assembly and in the meetings of the just; [2] great are the works of the Lord.

2   I will also seek most eagerly to do his will, [3] acknowledging at the same time how his great majesty endures, and his justice constantly lives on forever.

3   [4] The mighty Lord has caused his famed miracles to be remembered; he is gentle and magnanimous, [5] giving food to all those who hold him in awe.

4   And he was mindful of his covenant in this world, [6] which he also faithfully carried out with mighty works and noble, notable deeds, declaring to his people [7] that he would give them the gentiles' inheritance in full as their proper possession.

5   The minds of the righteous are his handiwork, and the just judgments which he will establish; [8] all his commands were honorable, truthful for ever and ever, and confirmed in the fairness of his precepts.

6   [9] He truly sent redemption to his beloved people, com-

þæt hi on ecnysse   a syððan
his gewitnesse   well geheoldan
and his þone halgan naman   hæfdan mid egsan.

7   Þæt byð secga gehwam   snytru on frymðe
þæt he Godes egesan   gleawe healde;
and þæt byð andgit good   eallum swylce
þe hine wyllað well   wyrcean and healdan.

8   Herenes Drihtnes   her sceal wunian,
on worulda woruld   wynnum standan.

Psalm 111

1   Eadig byð se wer   se þe him ege Drihtnes
on ferhð-cleofan   fæste gestandeð,
and his bebod healdeð   bealde mid willan.

2   He on eorðan byð   eadig and spedig,
and his cneorisse byð   cyn gebletsad.

3   Him wuldur and wela   wunað æt huse,
byð his soþfæstnys   swylce mære,
þenden þysse worulde   wunaþ ænig dæl.

4   Leoht wæs on leodum   leofum acyðed,
þam þe on ðystrum   þrage lifdan
and hiora heortan   heoldan mid rihte;
milde is on mode   mihtig Dryhten,
and he ys soðfæst   symble æt þearfe.

manding them to observe his covenant faithfully and constantly hold his sacred name in awe, forever after.

7   ¹⁰ For each human being the essence of wisdom in the first instance is to carefully maintain a fear of the Lord; and that will become a sound basis of understanding also for all those willing to observe and practice it well.

8   Praise for the Lord is destined to live on in this world, to continue joyfully, for ever and ever.

Psalm III

1   ¹ Happy is the man who steadfastly maintains fear of the Lord in his heart, and confidently observes his commandments with good intentions.

2   ² He will be happy and successful on earth, and his offspring's descendants will be blessed.

3   ³ Glory and wealth will continue for him in his house, likewise his justice will be renowned while any part of this earth endures.

4   ⁴ A light was revealed to a favored people, to those who lived for a long time in darkness, yet maintained their hearts in integrity; the mighty Lord is gentle in disposition, and he is forever trustworthy in trouble.

5   Glæd man, gleaw-hydig,   god and mild-heort,
    seteð soðne dom   þurh his sylfes word,
    se on ecnysse   eadig standeð.

6   Byð on eceum gemynde   æghwylc þæra
    þe his soþ and riht   symble healdeð,
    ne him on hlyste   mycelum ondrædeð
    awiht on ealdre   yfeles syððan.

7   Byð his heorte gearo   hyhte to Drihtne
    getrymed and getyhted,   þæt him teonan ne
                                  mæg
    fæcne ætfæstan   feonda ænig;
    ac he ealle forsyhð   æghwær georne.

8   Se þe his æhta   ealle tostredeð
    and þearfendum   þa gedæleð,
    his soðfæstnyss wunað   symble oð ende;
    byð his horn wended   her on wuldur.

9   Swa þæt synfull gesyhð,   sona yrsað,
    toþum torn þolað,   teonum grimetað,
    þearle þindeð,   oþþæt þonne byð,
    þæt fyrenfulra lust   fæcne forweorðeð.

Psalm 112

1   Herigean nu cnihtas   hælynd Drihten,
    and naman Dryhtnes   neode herigan.

2   Wese nama Dryhtnes   neode gebletsad
    of ðyssan forð   awa to worulde.

5   ⁵ An agreeable man, wise of thought, moral and merciful, by his very words administers true judgment, ⁶ he will
remain content forever.

6   ⁷ Everyone who constantly observes God's truths and
laws, while never excessively fearing at all the report of evil
afterward, will be held in everlasting remembrance.

7   His heart, strengthened and instructed, is prepared to
hope in the Lord, ⁸ with the result that not a single enemy
can deceitfully fix blame on him; in fact, he will diligently
despise all of them everywhere.

8   ⁹ He who distributes all his possessions and gives them
to the needy will see his justice endure continually to the
end; his horn will be turned into glory in this world.

9   ¹⁰ As soon as the sinner sees that, he will immediately
become angry, suffer pain from gnashing his teeth, howl
with vexation, explode with fury, until finally it comes about
that the desire of the wicked utterly dies away.

Psalm 112

1   ¹ Children, praise now the redeeming Lord, and eagerly
praise his name.

2   ² Let it be diligently blessed from this point on, for ever
and ever.

3 Fram upgange æryst sunnan
oðþæt heo wende on west-rodur
ge sculon Dryhtnes naman dædum herigean.

4 He is ofer ealle in-geþeode
se heahsta hæleða cynnes;
is ofer heofenas eac ahafen his wuldur.

5 Hwylc ys anlic urum Dryhtne,
þam halgan Gode, þe on heofon-rice
eadig eardað, ofer ealle gesyhð,
þa eadmedu æghwær begangæð
on eorð-wege, up on heofenum?

6 He of eorðan mæg þone unagan
weccan to willan, and of woruf-torde
þone þearfendan þriste areccan;

7 and hine on ealdordom upp asettan
his folces fruman on fæger lif.

8 Se þe eard seteð unwæstmbærre
on modor hus manigra bearna;
hio ofer hire suna symblað and blissað.

Psalm 113

1 Þa ut eode Israheles cynn
and of Ægyptum ealle foran
Iacobes hus of gramum folce,
þa elreordige ealle wæron,

3   ³ From the earliest sighting of the sun until it turns toward the western sky, you should praise the Lord's name with deeds.

4   ⁴ He, the most high, is above all nations of humankind; his glory is also exalted above the heavens.

5   ⁵ Who is comparable to our Lord, the holy God who dwells in a blessed state in the heavenly kingdom, gazes upon all the lowly, ⁶ and from above in the heavens takes care of them everywhere on earth?

6   ⁷ He can at will raise up from the dirt the person without possessions, and boldly lift up the needy from the dung heap;

7   ⁸ and establish him in authority as prince of his people in a pleasant state of life.

8   ⁹ He who arranges a place for the sterile woman, a home for her as mother of many children; she will celebrate and rejoice in her sons.

Psalm 113

1   ¹ When the tribe of Israel departed, and the entire house of Jacob journeyed out of Egypt, away from a hostile people, all of them barbarians,

2 þa wæs geworden werude Iudea,
 þæt heo hæl gehlutan haliges syþþan;
 hæfdan ealdurdom ofer Israhelas,
 mihta mære and mycel rice.

3 Swa heo sæ geseah, he hio sniome fleah;
 for him Iordanen gengde on hinder.

4 Hæfdan þær beorgas bliðe sæle
 and rammum þa restan gelice;
 wæron geswyru swyðe on blisse,
 swa on sceapum beoð sceone lambru.

5 Hwæt wæs þe, sæ swiþa, forhwan fluge þu swa;
 oððe þu, Iordanen, for hwi gengdest on
              bæcling?

6 Beorgas wæron bliðe, gebærdon swa rammas;
 wurdan gesweoru on sele-dreame,
 swa on sceapum beoð sceone lambru.

7 For ansyne ecan Dryhtnes
 þeos eorþe sceal eall abifigan,
 and for Iacobes Gode geara forhtigean.

8 He wendeð stan on widne mere,
 and clifu cyrreð on cwicu swylce
 wæteres wellan mid his gewealdendre hand.

9 Nalæs us, nalæs us, nergend Dryhten,
 ac we naman þinum neode secgeað
 wuldur wide geond woruld-ricu,

10 for ðinre þære myclan mild-heortnysse
 and for þinre soðfæstnysse (samed ætgædere),

2 ² then it came about later for the tribe of Judah that it obtained the holy one's blessing; they had dominion over the Israelites, distinguished powers and great authority.

3 ³ As soon as the sea saw them, it fled immediately from them; the river Jordan retreated before them.

4 ⁴ The mountains there experienced a joyous time, and then rested like rams; the hills were exceedingly happy, like comely lambs among sheep.

5 ⁵ You mighty sea, what happened to you, why did you flee like this; and you, Jordan, why did you flow backward?

6 ⁶ The mountains were joyful, behaving like rams; the hills were in a festive mood, as comely lambs among sheep.

7 ⁷ Before the gaze of the eternal Lord, this earth must totally tremble and be thoroughly afraid, before the sight of Jacob's God.

8 ⁸ He changes rock into an expansive lake, and likewise transforms cliffs into active springs of water by means of his governing hand.

9 ⁹ Not to us, not to us at all, but rather to your name, redeeming Lord, we zealously attribute the glory for this throughout the kingdoms of earth, widely,

10 ¹⁰ on account of your great mercy and truth (joined to-

þy læs þæt æfre cweðan   oðre þeode:
"Hwær is heora agen God   ahwær nu ða?"

11   Ys ure se halga God   on heofon-dreame
uppe mid englum,   and he eall gedeð,
swa his willa byð,   on woruld-rice.

12   Þa wæron deoful-gild   deorce hæþenra
golde and seolfre,   þa her geara menn
worhtan wig-smiðas   wræste mid folmum.

13   Þa muð habbað,   and ne magon hwæþere
wiht hleoðrian   ne word sprecan;
beoð onforan eagan,   ne magon feor geseon.

14   Earan habbað swylce   and opene nose,
ne magon eþian,   awyht gehyran.

15   Handa hi habbað,   ne hio hwæðere magon
gegrapian   godes awiht;
and fet habbað,   ne magon feala gangan.

16   Ne cleopigað hi care,   þeah þe hi ceolan
habban,
ne him hluttur gast   on hracan eardað.

17   Ac heo wæron þam wyrcendum   wel gelice
and æghwylcum   þe him on treowað.

18   Israhela hus   ærest on Drihten
helpe gehogedan,   holdne begeaton
fælne fultum;   he hi wið feondum geheold.

19   Aarones hus   eac on Dryhten
leofne gelyfdan;   he him liðe wearð
and him fultum gestod   fæste æt þearfe.

gether), lest gentile peoples ever say: "Where is their very own God, does he exist now in any place?"

11   11 That holy God of ours exists above in heavenly joy with angels, and he fully acts as he pleases in this earthy kingdom.

12   12 Those sinister idols of the gentiles were made from gold and silver, which in times past people on earth, makers of idols, skillfully fashioned with their hands.

13   13 They have mouths, and yet cannot make the least sound or speak a word; they have eyes in front, yet cannot see very far.

14   14 They have ears too and open noses, yet they cannot hear anything or breathe.

15   15 They have hands, yet they are not able to take hold of anything material; and they have feet, yet cannot walk very much.

16   Though they have throats, they do not voice distress, nor does pure breath exist in their gullet.

17   16 But they were very like their makers and all those who trust in them.

18   17 In the beginning the houses of Israel looked for help from the Lord, obtaining kind, trusty assistance; he protected them from enemies.

19   18 The house of Aaron also believed in a beloved Lord; he was gracious to them and steadily remained their support in difficulty.

20   Þa ðe a wegen   egsan Dryhtnes
        hio hyht heora   habban on Drihten;
        he him fultum   fæste gestandeð
        and him scyldend byð   symble æt þearfe.

21   Weorð þu ure gemyndig,   mihtig Dryhten,
        and þine bletsunge   bring ofer us;
        þu gebletsudest   bearn Israheles,
        Aarones hus   eac gebletsadest;
        þu gebletsadest   bliðe mode
        ealle þa þe on ðe   egsan hæfdan,
        mycle and mæte   ofer middan-geard.

22   Gemænigfealdige þis   mihtig Dryhten
        ofer eow ealle   and ofer agene bearn.

23   Wesað ge fram Gode   geara gebletsade,
        þam þe heofon worhte   hrusan swylce;
        heofonas healdeð   halig Dryhten,
        sealde þas moldan   manna bearnum.

24   Næfre þe, Dryhten,   deade heriað,
        ne ealle þa þe heonan   helle seceað.

25   Ac we lifigende   leofne Dryhten
        balde bletsigað,   ne þæs blinnað
        nu of ðyssan forð   awa to worulde.

20 ¹⁹ May they who constantly carry the fear of the Lord maintain their hope in him; he steadily remains their support and will always be their protector in difficulty.

21 ²⁰ Mighty Lord, be mindful of us, and impart to us your blessing; you blessed the children of Israel and the house of Aaron also; ²¹ you blessed with a cheerful disposition all those who feared you, great and small, throughout the earth.

22 ²² May this mighty Lord be magnified over all of you, and over your own children.

23 ²³ May you be blessed promptly by God, who created heaven and earth as well; ²⁴ the holy Lord controls the heavens, gave this earth to humankind.

24 ²⁵ The dead will never praise you, Lord, nor all those who venture from here to hell.

25 ²⁶ But we, the living, confidently bless the beloved Lord, nor will we cease from doing so from now on, always and forever.

Psalm 114

1   Ic lufie þe,   leofa Drihten,
     for þan þu mines gebedes   bene gehyrdest,

2   and þu þin eare to me   eadmodlice
     hold ahyldest   and gehyrdest me,
     þa ic þe on dagum minum   dyrne cigde.

3   Sar me ymbsealde   swylde deaðes,
     and me frecne ætfealh   fyrhtu helle.

4   Me costung and sar   cnyssedan geneahhe,
     þonne ic naman Drihtnes   nyde cigde.

5   Eala, þu leofa God,   alys mine nu
     sawle on gesyntum;   ic to soþan wat,
     þæt þu wære mild-heort,   mihtig Dryhten,
     and ure God   æghwæs soðfæst;
     mihta us þine   milde weorðan.

6   Drihten gehealdeð   dome þa lytlan;
     ic hean gewearð,   he me hraðe lysde.

7   Gecyr mine sawle   clæne on þine
     rædæs reste,   rice Drihten;
     þu me wel dydest   on woruld-life,

8   for þon þu mine sawle   sylfa generedyst,
     and hig of deopum   deaþe gelæddest;
     eagan mine wið tearum   æghwær geheolde
     and fet mine   wið fær-slide.
     Ic gelicie   leofum Drihtne
     on lifigendra   lande nu ða.

Psalm 114

1   [1] I love you, dear Lord, because you heard my prayerful appeal,

2   [2] and, gracious as you are, you humbly inclined your ear to me and heard me, when I called to you inwardly during my days.

3   [3] Sorrow besieged me with the pangs of death, and fear of hell clung perilously to me.

4   Sorrow and trouble frequently oppressed me, [4] then I earnestly called out the Lord's name.

5   Beloved God, release my soul now into a secure state; [5] I know for a fact that you were kind, mighty Lord, and that our God was entirely just; may your powers be gentle with us.

6   [6] The Lord protects the little ones with discernment; when I was humiliated, he quickly freed me.

7   [7] Powerful Lord, turn my soul entirely to your advantageous rest; in worldly matters you have treated me well,

8   [8] for you yourself saved my soul and steered it from total death; you saved my eyes from crying in every situation, and my feet from a sudden fall. [9] I will now please the beloved Lord in the land of the living.

Psalm 115

1   Ic þæt gelyfde,   for þon ic lyt sprece;
ic eom eadmede   ungemete swiðe.

2   Swylce ic sylfa cwæð,   þa me swa ðuhte
on mod-seofan   minum geþancum,
þæt wæron ealle menn   ungemete lease.

3   Hwæt mæg ic to gode   gyldan Dryhtne
for eallum þam godum   þe he me ærur dyde?

4   Ic her hælu calic   hæbbe befangen
and naman Dryhtnes   neode cige.

5   Beorht ys and fæger   beacen Dryhtne
on his gesyhðe   swylt haligra.

6   Eala, ic eom þin agen   esne, Dryhten,
and þin swylce eom   scealc ombehte
and þinre þeowan sunu   on ðe acenned.

7   Þu me tobræce   bendas grimme,
þæt ic þe laces lof   lustum secge.

8   Ic min gehat   halgum Dryhtne
on his getynum   tidum gylde,
þe ymb Dryhtnes hus   deore syndan;
þær hit eagum folc   eall sceawiað,
and on Hierusalem   georne midre.

Psalm 115

1 ¹⁰ I believed that, so I will say little; I am exceedingly humbled.

2 ¹¹ I myself spoke in the same vein, when it seemed to me from my innermost reflections that all humankind was exceedingly mendacious.

3 ¹² What material return can I make to the Lord for all the good things which he earlier did for me?

4 ¹³ I have accepted the chalice of salvation here on earth and will earnestly call out the name of the Lord.

5 ¹⁵ The death of the holy ones is a bright and beautiful symbol in the Lord's sight.

6 ¹⁶ O Lord, I am your very own servant, your subject in service, and your handmaiden's son born through you.

7 You have broken apart for me harsh bonds ¹⁷ so that I may eagerly deliver sacrificial praise to you.

8 ¹⁸ I will fulfill my vows to the holy Lord at proper times in the courts elegantly surrounding his house; ¹⁹ there, in the center of Jerusalem, all the peoples will eagerly observe it with their own eyes.

Psalm 116

1 Ealle þeode   ecne Drihten
   mid hyge-cræfte   herigan wordum,
   and hine eall folc on efn   æðelne herigan,

2 for þon his mild-heortnyss   is mycel ofer us
   torhtlice getrymed,   til man-cynne;
   and soðfæstnys   swylce Dryhtnes
   wunað ece   awa to feore.

Psalm 117

1 Ic andette   ecum Dryhtne
   þam godan Gode;   ic hine gleawne wat;
   ys his mild-heortnys   mycel to worulde.

2 Þæt Israela cwæðan   ealle nu ða,
   þe he is se goda God,   and gearu standeð
   his mild-heortnys   mære to worulde.

3 Cweðe Aarones hus   eac þæt sylfe:
   he ys se goda God,   and gearu standeð
   his mild-heortnys   mære to worulde;

4 cweðan ealle þæt   unforcuðe,
   þe him on standeð   egsa Dryhtnes,
   for ðon he ys se goda God,   and gearu standeð
   his mild-heortnys   mære on worulde.

Psalm 116

1   ¹ Let all the nations render praise to the eternal Lord with mental vigor, and all the peoples together praise that noble one,

2   ² because in us is clearly confirmed his great mercy, a kindness to humankind; and the Lord's truth also endures eternally, always and forever.

Psalm 117

1   ¹ I will acknowledge the eternal Lord, the virtuous God, for I know him to be wise; his mercy is great forever.

2   ² Let all the Israelites declare that now, for he is the virtuous God, and his famed mercy stands ready forever.

3   ³ Let the house of Aaron also declare the same: he is the virtuous God, and his famed mercy stands ready forever;

4   ⁴ let all reputable people, in whom fear of the Lord resides, declare the same, for he is the virtuous God, and his famed mercy stands ready forever.

5   Ic on costunge   cigde to Dryhtne,
      and he me gehyrde   on heare brædu.

6   Nu me fultum is   fæle Dryhten,
      nis me ege mannes   for ahwæðer.

7   Nu me fultum ys   fæle Dryhten,
      ic fracuþe forseo   feondas mine.

8   God ys on Dryhten   georne to þenceanne
      þonne on mannan wese   mod to treowianne.

9   God ys on Dryhten   georne to hyhtanne
      þonne on ealdor-men   ahwær to treowianne.

10   Ealle me ymbsealdon   side þeode,
      and ic wæs on Dryhtnes naman   deorum
                                  gehæled.

11   Me ymbstodan   strange manige,
      and me Godes nama on him   georne gehælde,

12   þa hi me ymbsealdon   samod anlice,
      swa beon bitere,   oððe þu bærne eac
      þornas þyre   þicce fyre,
      þær me nama Dryhtnes   neode scylde.

13   Ic wæs hearde cnyssed,   and ic me helpe fand,
      þæt ic fæste ne feoll,   ac ic me frofre begeat,
      þa me Dryhten onfeng,   swa hit gedefe wæs.

14   Me wæs strengðu strang   stiþ on Dryhtne
      and herenes heah,   and he me eac ys
      a to worulde   worden on hælu.

15   A byð blisse stefn   beorht gehyred
      on soðfæstra   swæsum muðe.

5   ⁵ I called out to the Lord in my tribulation, and he heard me in a lofty, spacious place.

6   ⁶ Since that faithful Lord is my help, I have no fear of anyone on any score.

7   ⁷ Since that faithful Lord is my help, I will despise my enemies with ignominy.

8   ⁸ It is good to meditate eagerly on the Lord rather than to be trusting in the human heart.

9   ⁹ It is good to hope earnestly in the Lord rather than to trust in a prince in every situation.

10   ¹⁰ All the peoples surrounded me widely, and I was saved by the Lord's formidable name.

11   ¹¹ Many powerful ones surrounded me, but God's name greatly protected me against them,

12   ¹² when they surrounded me entirely, like stinging bees, or like dry thorns set ablaze by dense fire, in that situation the Lord's name carefully protected me.

13   ¹³ I was severely tossed about, but I found help for myself, so that I was not overcome entirely, for I obtained support when the Lord accepted me, as was fitting.

14   ¹⁴ In the Lord was my firm, resolute strength and highest praise, and he has also become my salvation, for ever and ever.

15   ¹⁵ Always the clear sound of joy will be heard in the sweet mouths of the just.

16   Dyde gedefe mægen   Dryhtnes swyðre,
      and me seo swyðre   swylce Drihtnes
      ahof hrædlice   æt heah-þearfe.

17   Ne swelte ic mid sare,   ac ic gesund lifige
      and weorc Godes   wide secge.

18   Me clænsude,   se þe him clæne wæs,
      Dryhten ælmihtig,   nolde to deaðe me
      on ecnysse   æfre gesyllan.

19   Undoð me sniome duru   soðfæstra eac,
      þær ic gange inn,   Gode andette;
      soðfæste on þa duru   seceað inn-gang.

20   Ic þe andette,   ece Dryhten,
      for ðon þu me gehyrdest   æt heah-þearfe
      and me þa gewurde   wis on hælu.

21   Þone sylfan stan   þe hine swyðe ær
      wyrhtan awurpan,   nu se geworden is
      hwommona heagost;   halig Dryhten
      to wealles wraðe   wis teofrade;
      þæt is urum eagum   eall wundorlic.

22   Þis ys se dæg   þe hine Drihten us
      wisfæst geworhte   wera cneorissum,
      eallum eorð-tudrum   eadgum to blisse.

23   Eala, þu Dryhten God,   do me halne;
      Eala, þu Dryhten min,   do us gesunde.

24   Gebletsad is, se þe com   ofer bearna gehwylc
      on Dryhtnes naman   dædum mærum;
      we eow æt Godes huse   gearwe bletsiað,
      nu us Drihten God   deore onlyhte.

16   ¹⁶ The right hand of the Lord manifested appropriate power, and it also raised me up promptly in dire necessity.

17   ¹⁷ I will not die from affliction, but will live secure, declaring far and wide the works of God.

18   ¹⁸ He chastised me, the almighty Lord, who in himself was exempt from sin, he did not ever wish to surrender me to death for eternity.

19   ¹⁹ Open to me at once the gates of the upright, where I will enter in, acknowledging the Lord; ²⁰ the upright will seek entry through them.

20   ²¹ Eternal Lord, I will give glory to you, because you heard me in my great need, and became for me then the one experienced in the ways of salvation.

21   ²² That same stone which the masons had rejected outright is now become the most important of the corners; ²³ the holy Lord, with his expertise, has decorated it as the wall's support; that is absolutely marvelous in our eyes.

22   ²⁴ This is the day which the wise Lord made for us, for the generations of humankind and all the blessed human race, as an occasion for rejoicing.

23   ²⁵ O Lord God, save me; O Lord of mine, make us prosperous.

24   ²⁶ He is blessed who came with illustrious deeds in the Lord's name to each person; we eagerly bless you at God's house, ²⁷ seeing that the Lord God had lovingly enlightened us.

25 Wutan us to symbel-dæge settan georne,
and ðone gelome lustum healdan
oð wig-bedes wræste hornas.

26 Þu eart min Dryhten God, and ic dædum þe
ecne andette;
þu eart min hælend God, and ic herige ðe.

27 Ic ðe andette ecne Dryhten,
for ðon þu me gehyrdest æt heah-þearfe,
and þa wurde me wis to hælu.

28 Eac ic andette eceum Dryhtne,
for ðon he ys se goda God, and ic ful geare wat,
þæt þin mild-heortnyss ys mycel to worulde.

Psalm 118

1 Eadige beoð on wege, þa þe unwemme
on hiora Dryhtnes æ deore gangað.

2 Eadige beoð swylce, þa þe a wyllað
his gewitnesse wise smeagan,
and hine mid ealle innancundum
heortan hord-cofan helpe biddað.

3 Ne magon man-wyrhtan mægene feran
on his mærne weg, mihtigan Drihtnes.

4 Þu þine bebodu bealde hete
ealle eorð-buend elne haldan.

25   Let us eagerly establish a day of celebration for ourselves and frequently observe it with pleasure right up to the firm finials of the altar.

26   [28] You are my Lord God and I will acknowledge you, the eternal one, with my actions; you are my savior God, and I will praise you.

27   I will acknowledge you, the eternal Lord, because you heard me in dire necessity, and became for me then the one experienced in the ways of salvation.

28   [29] I will also acknowledge the eternal Lord because he is a virtuous God, and I truly know that your mercy is great, forever.

Psalm 118

1   [1] Blessed on the way are the undefiled, who lovingly walk in their Lord's law.

2   [2] Blessed also are those who constantly desire to contemplate his revelation with discernment, asking him for assistance with all the heart's deepest thoughts.

3   [3] Those who practice evil are incapable of walking virtuously on the mighty Lord's exalted way.

4   [4] You boldly commanded all earth's inhabitants to observe your precepts with diligence.

5   Ic þæs, la, wisce,   þæt wegas mine
on ðinum willan   weorþan gereahte,
þæt ic þin agen bebod   elne healde.

6   Ne beo ic þonne on ealdre   æfre gescynded,
gif ic on ealle þine bebodu   elne locie.

7   Ic þe andette,   ece Dryhten,
mid minre heortan   holde geþance
on þan þe ic geleornode   and gelæstan mæg,
þæt ic þine domas   dædum healde.

8   And ic þine soðfæstnysse   swylce mote
on hyge healdan,   þæt þu huru me
on ðyssum ealdre   ænne ne forlæte.

9   On hwan mæg se iunga   on godne weg,
rihtran þe rædran,   ræd gemittan,
þonne he þine wisan   word gehealde?

10   Ic þe mid ealre   innancundre
heortan sece;   ne þu huru me
fram þinum bebodum   feor adrife.

11   For ðon ic on minre heortan   hydde georne
þæt ic þinre spræce   sped gehealde,
þy læs ðe ic gefremme   fyrene ænige.

12   Þu eart gebletsud,   bliþe Dryhten;
lær me mid lufan,   hu ic læste well
and ic þine soðfæstnysse   sweotule cunne.

13   Ic on minum welerum   wordum secge
ealles þines muðes   meahte domas.

5 ⁵ O! I wish my ways to be directed to your will, so that I may zealously observe your very own precepts.

6 ⁶ Then I will never be shamed in my lifetime, if I diligently look into all your precepts.

7 ⁷ I will acknowledge you, eternal Lord, with my heart, will devoutly thank you in so far as I have learned, and am able, to practice your precepts with actions.

8 ⁸ And may I be allowed also to keep your truth in mind, so that at least you do not leave me by myself in this life.

9 ⁹ By what other means can a young man on the right path find more correct guidance, as it becomes more available, than by observing your wise words?

10 ¹⁰ I will seek you with a totally earnest heart; do not, at least, drive me far away from your precepts.

11 ¹¹ And so I carefully concealed within myself that I have hoarded the abundance of your speech, lest I commit any sin against you.

12 ¹² You are blessed, gracious Lord; lovingly teach me how I may best be of service and clearly come to know your truth.

13 ¹³ With the words on my lips I will declare in full the powerful pronouncements issuing from your mouth.

14 And ic on wege swylce   wynnum gange,
    þær ic ðine gewitnesse   wat ful clæne,
    swa ic ealra welena   willum bruce.

15 Swa ic on þine soðfæstnysse   soðe getreowe,
    þæt ic ne weorðe   worda þinra
    ealra ofergittul   awa to feore.

16 Ic on þinre soðfæstnysse   symble meteode,
    þæt ic þine wislicu   word geheolde.

17 Gild þinum esne   gode dæde;
    ic on lif-dagum   lustum healde
    þinra worda waru   mid wisdome.

18 Onwreoh þu mine eagan,   þæt ic wel mæge
    on þinre æ   eall sceawian,
    wundur wræclicu   þa þu worhtyst ær.

19 Ic eom on eorðan   earm bigenga;
    ne do þu me dyrne   þine þa deoran bebodu.

20 Þæt sawul min   symble wilnað,
    þæt ic þin soðfæst word   gesund mote
    on ealle tid   elne healdan.

21 Þu ofer-hydige   ealle þreadest,
    þa þu awyrgde   wistest gearuwe
    and þine bebodu   efnan noldan.

22 Afyr þu fram me   facen and edwit,
    oððe ic ofer-hydige   awiht wylle,
    for ðan ic þine gewitnesse   wylle secan.

23 Ac nu ealdor-menn   ealle ætgædere
    sæton on seldum,   swyþe spræcon,

14   ¹⁴ And I will also joyfully walk the path on which I understand your revelation very clearly, just as I pleasurably enjoy the use of all materials things.

15   ¹⁵ So I will truly trust in your justice, so that I will not forget the sum of your words for ever and ever.

16   ¹⁶ I continually meditated on your truth, in order that I might observe your wise words.

17   ¹⁷ Repay your servant with a favorable action; in my lifetime I will gladly maintain the observance of your words with wisdom.

18   ¹⁸ Open my eyes so that I can readily scrutinize your law in full, the extraordinary wonders which you created in a former time.

19   ¹⁹ I am a wretched inhabitant of this earth; do not conceal from me those precious precepts of yours.

20   ²⁰ What my soul constantly desires is that I may be allowed, safe and sound, to observe earnestly your truthful words at all times.

21   ²¹ You thoroughly reproved the arrogant, whom you knew for certain were cursed, and who were unwilling to follow your precepts.

22   ²² Remove far from me treachery and contempt, and then I will remove the arrogant by all means, because I desire to search out your revelation.

23   ²³ Now princes have sat all together on thrones, talked volubly, and leveled charges with hostile words against me;

and wið me wraðum   wordum scirdan;
hwæþere þin esne   elnes teolode,
þæt he þine soðe word   snotur beeode.

24   Me wæs þin gewitnys   wyrð and getreowe,
and ic hi on mode   metegie georne;
and me to frofre wat   þæt ic forð heonun
his soðfæstnysse   sece georne.

25   Ætfealh min sawul   flore geneahhige;
do me æfter þinum wordum   wel gecwician.

26   Ic þe wegas mine   wise secge,
and þu me gehyrdest   holde mode;
lær me on life,   hu ic lengest mæge
þine soðfæstnysse   selest gehealdan.

27   Þu me soðfæstnysse weg   swylce getacna,
þæt ic on þinum wundrum   me wel begange.

28   Min sawl aslep,   þa me sorh begeat
for langunga;   læt me nu þa
on þinum wordum   weorðan trumne.

29   Afyr fram me   unryhte wegas,
and me on þinre æ geweorþ   ealles milde.

30   Ic me wise geceas   wegas soðfæste;
ne weorðe ic þinra doma   gedweled æfre.

31   Swa ic fæste ætfealh,   þæt ic forð heonun
þine gewitnysse   wel geheolde;
ne wylt þu me on ealdre   æfre gescyndan.

however, your servant, now wise, strove for the courage to devote himself to your true words.

24   24 Your revelation was precious and trustworthy to me, and I ponder it carefully in my mind; and I feel as a consolation that from now on I will seek his truth earnestly.

25   25 My soul frequently stuck to the ground; please revive me fully according to your words.

26   26 I declare my ways to you discreetly, and you heard me with a favorable disposition; teach me, while still alive, how I can best observe your truth for the longest time.

27   27 Likewise, make known to me the way of truth, so that I may fully occupy myself with your wonders.

28   28 My soul fell asleep when anxiety provoked by weariness took hold of me; through your words, cause me to become strong now.

29   29 Remove far from me wicked ways, and in the exercise of your law be altogether gentle with me.

30   30 I prudently chose for myself truthful ways; I will never be led astray from your judgments.

31   31 So, I firmly applied myself, and as a result I properly adhered to your revelation ever since; you will never at any time put me to shame.

32   Nu ic on wisne weg   worda þinra
reðne rinne;   and þu rice nu
mine heortan geheald   on hyge brade.

33   Æ þu me sete,   ece Dryhten,
þæt ic on soðfæste wegas   symble gange
and ic þa secan   symble mote.

34   Syle me andgit eac,   þæt ic æ þine
smeage mid soðe,   swylce healde
on ealre minre heortan   holde mode.

35   Gelæd me on stige,   þær ic stæpe mine
on þinum bebodum   bryce hæbbe,
for ðan ic hy mid soðe   symble wolde.

36   Ahyld mine heortan,   þæt ic halige nu
on þine gewitnysse   wise gecyrre;
nalæs me gitsung   forniman mote.

37   Gewend þu mine eagan,   þy læs ic weorc idel
gese þurh synne;   ac me on soðne weg
þinne þone leofan   læde cwiculice.

38   Sete ðinum esne   oðer swylce,
þæt he þinre spræce   sped leornige
and þa on ege þinum   ealle healde.

39   Þu me scealt edwitt min   of awyrpan,
þæt me to incan   ahwær gangeð;
for þon ic eom on þinum domum   gedefe glæd.

40   Efne, ic þine bebodu   bealde wolde
wis wylle gegan;   wene ic swylce,
þæt þu me on rihtes   ræd gecwycige.

32   [32] Now I run on the wise and just way of your words; at the same time, mighty one, maintain now in my heart an expansive mood.

33   [33] Eternal Lord, lay down a law for me, so that I may constantly walk in truthful ways, and be allowed to seek them always.

34   [34] Give me understanding too, so that I may contemplate your law sincerely, and also observe it in the fullness of my heart with devout purpose.

35   [35] Lead me on the path where, with my steps, I will gain advantage from your precepts, because I have always truly desired it.

36   [36] Bend my heart so that I may wisely turn now to your holy revelation; by no means let greed be allowed to consume me.

37   [37] Avert my eyes for fear that I should witness useless actions because of sin; instead, invigorate me on that cherished truthful path of yours.

38   [38] Ordain for your servant another such mandate, that he may learn the power of your declaration, and, awed by you, fully hold to it.

39   [39] You should remove from me my disgrace, which at any time turns into a source of doubt for me; as a result, I will be suitably happy with your judgments.

40   [40] Truly! Wise in my wishes, I confidently desired to observe your precepts; I also expect that you will renew me on the path of justice.

41 And me ofer cume, ece Dryhten,
   þæt milde mod, mære hælu,
   æfter þinre spræce spowendlice.

42 And ic andwyrde, þam þe me edwit-stafas
   wordum wrað cweþað, þæt ic gewene on ðe
   and on þinum wordum wære hæbbe.

43 Ne afyr þu me æfre fæle spræce,
   þa ic me on muðe mægene hæbbe,
   and ic soðfæst word on sylfan healde,
   þæt ic on ðinra doma dæde getreowige.

44 And ic æ þine efne and healde;
   and to worulde on ðære wunian mote
   and on ecnysse efnan and healdan.

45 And ic on bealde brædu gange,
   for ðan ic þine gewitnysse wel getrymede.

46 And ic þæt fore cyningum cyðan mote,
   þær hig eagum on locian,
   hu me þin gewitnyss ys weorð and getreowe,
   and on ðam ne beon æfre gescynded.

47 And ic on þinum bebodum bealde mote
   gemetegian swyþe mærne ræd,
   for þan ic hi on lufan minre lange hæfde.

48 And ic mine handa hof gelome,
   þær ic þine bebodu bryce lufade,
   þa ic mid ðysse þeode þearle begange,
   and on ðine soð-cwydas symble ic getreowige.

41 [41] And may that gentle spirit, glorious salvation, prosperously descend upon me, eternal Lord, according to your word.

42 [42] And to those who taunt me with hostile comments, I will reply that I hope in you, and find protection in your words.

43 [43] Do not ever take away from me that trusty eloquence which I powerfully possess in my mouth, and in that same eloquence I will hold to truthful words, so that I will trust in the efficacy of your decrees.

44 [44] And I will fulfill and observe your law; may I be allowed to remain in it forever, fulfilling and observing it for all time.

45 [45] And I will walk boldly in a spacious place, because I have truly confirmed your revelation.

46 [46] And may I make known before kings, when they are paying full attention, that your revelation is honorable and trustworthy to me, and that they will never be put to shame in observing it.

47 [47] And may I be allowed to consider confidently the very excellent counsel inherent in your precepts, because I have long made them the object of my love.

48 [48] And I frequently raised my hands, whenever I passionately loved your precepts, those which I faithfully follow among this people, while always trusting in your infallible pronouncements.

49 Gemun nu, Dryhten, þines wordes,
on þam þu me þinum þeowe hyht gesealdest.

50 Þas ic me on frofre fæste hæbbe
on minum eaðmedum ungemete swyðe,
for ðon me þin spræc spedum cwycade.

51 Oftust ofer-modige unriht fremmað,
oþ þæt hi on eorðan ealle forweorðað;
ic þinre æ a folgode.

52 Ic wæs gemyndig mærra doma
þinra geþancol, ðeoden Dryhten,
þæt ic on worulde æt ðe wurde afrefred.

53 Me wearð gemolten mod on hreðre
for fyrenfulra facen-dædum,
þa hi æ þine anforleton.

54 Ac me to sange symble hæfde
hu ic þine soðfæstnysse selest heolde,
þær ic on elelande ahte stowe.

55 Nede ic þæt gemunde nihta gehwylcre,
þæt ic naman þinne nemde, Dryhten,
and ic æ þine elne heolde.

56 Þas me andweardum ealle gewurdan,
for þon ic þine soðfæstnysse sohte georne.

57 Me ys on dæle, Dryhten user,
cwide cynlice, þæt ic cwic wylle
þine æ healdan elne mycle.

49   49 Remember now, Lord, your promise with which you imparted hope to me, your servant.

50   50 This statement of yours I resolutely retain as my comfort in very great humiliations, because it quickly revived me.

51   51 Very frequently the proud commit sins until they entirely perish on this earth; I followed your law always.

52   52 I remembered your excellent judgments, was mindful of them so that I might forever be consoled by you, Lord and ruler.

53   53 My mind failed inwardly at the sight of the wicked perpetrating iniquity, when they disregarded your law.

54   54 But the constant subject of my song was that I maintained your truth most thoroughly, wherever I possessed property in a foreign land.

55   55 In my difficulty I remembered every night to invoke your name, Lord, and to observe your law resolutely.

56   56 Those things happened entirely in my presence, because I eagerly sought your truth.

57   57 My lot in life is the fitting command that I will observe your law, our Lord, with great courage, while I am alive.

58 Ic bidde þinre ansyne   ungemete georne
mid ealre gehygde   heortan minre,
þæt þu me on mode   milde weorðe
æfter þinre spræce   spowendlice.

59 Swa ic wegas þine   wise þence
to ferenne   fotum minum,
þæt ic on þinre gewitnysse   wel gefere.

60 Gearo ic eom symble,   nalæs grames modes,
þæt ic betst cunne   þine bebodu healdan.

61 Me fyrenfulra   fæcne rapas
ungemet geneahhie   oft beclyptan;
næs ic ofergittul,   þæt ic æ þine
mid hyge-cræfte   heolde and læste.

62 Ic æt midre niht   mæla gehwylce
ricene arise,   and hraðe gange
þær ic ðe andette   eall ætgædere,
secge þine domas   dædum rihte.

63 Ic eom dæl-neomend   þe heom ondrædað þe,
and þine halige bebodu   healdað georne.

64 Þeos eorðe is   eall gefylled
þinre mild-heortnesse,   mihtig Drihten,
þine soðfæstnesse   þu me swylce lær.

65 Þu ymb þinne esne   æghwær dydest
wel weorðlice;   wene ic, Drihten,
þæt þu þin word wylle   wis gehealdan.

58   ⁵⁸ With my heart's full intent I most earnestly entreat you to be abundantly compassionate to me according to your promise.

59   ⁵⁹ So I prudently intend to travel your ways with my feet, so that I may proceed prosperously in your revelation.

60   ⁶⁰ I am always ready, not at all distressed in mind, to understand best how to observe your precepts.

61   ⁶¹ The treacherous ropes of the wicked often encompassed me extremely often; yet I did not forget to observe and follow your law with purpose.

62   ⁶² I will arise instantly at midnight, in whatever season, and quickly proceed to the place where I will acknowledge you fully at once, recite your judgments, just in practice.

63   ⁶³ I belong with those who fear you and zealously observe your holy decrees.

64   ⁶⁴ This earth is totally filled with your mercy, mighty Lord, teach me your truth also.

65   ⁶⁵ In every respect you have behaved very honorably toward your servant; I expect, Lord, that you intend to keep your well-considered promise.

66 Þu me þeodscipe lær   þinne tilne
and wisdomes   word to genihte,
for ðon ic þin bebod   þriste gelyfde.

67 Ær þon ic gehened   hean gewurde,
ic agylte   ungemetum swiðe;
hwæðere ic þinre spræce geheold   sped on
                                        mode.

68 God þu eart, Drihten,   and me god swylce
on þinum tile gelær,   þæt ic teala cunne
þin soðfæst weorc   symble healdan.

69 Ys nu mænigfeald ofer me   man and unriht
ofer-hydigra;   ic nu mid ealre
minre heortan hige   hycge swiðe,
þæt ic þin bebod   beorht atredde.

70 Ys heora heorte nu   her anlicast
swa meoluc wese   mægene gerunnen;
ic æ þine   ungemete georne
on mod-sefan   minum healde.

71 Selre me wæs and seftre,   þæt þu sylfa me
heane gehnægdest,   and ic hraðe syþþan
þin soðfæst weorc   wel leornade.

72 Me is micle betere,   þæt ic bebodu healde,
ðines muðes gemet,   þonne mon me geofe
geara ðusende   goldes and seolfres.

73 Handa me ðine   holde geworhton
and gehiwedan   mid hige-cræfte;
syle me nu andgyt,   þæt ic eall mæge
þine bliðe bebodu   beorhte leornian.

66 ⁶⁶ Teach me your good discipline, as well as words of wisdom in abundance, because I have confidently believed your commands.

67 ⁶⁷ Before I was made abject, I sinned inordinately; despite that, I held the eloquence of your speech in my mind.

68 ⁶⁸ Lord, you are virtuous, and in your goodness teach me virtue also, so that I may fittingly know how to observe your truthful works always.

69 ⁶⁹ The iniquity and wickedness of the arrogant is multiplied against me; I truly resolve now with my heart's full intent that I will investigate your clear precepts.

70 ⁷⁰ Their hearts now most resemble milk on this earth that is massively coagulated; I will keep your law most eagerly in my mind.

71 ⁷¹ It was better for me, and easier, that you yourself abjectly humbled me, so that soon afterward I properly learned your righteous works.

72 ⁷² It is much better for me to observe precepts, your spoken law, than to be immediately given thousands in gold and silver.

73 ⁷³ Your hands graciously created and fashioned me with purposeful skill; grant me now the understanding to learn fully your joyous precepts with discernment.

74 Þa ðe on feore forhtigað, þa me on fægere
               geseoð
 and blissiað, þu geðenceað,
 þæt ic þinum wordum wel getreowde.

75 Ic þæt, Dryhten, ongeat, domas þine
 reðe rihtwise, and ðu ricene me
 on ðinre soðfæstnesse dydest samed
                eadmedne.

76 Wese þin milde mod mihtum geswiðed,
 and me to frofre fæste gestande,
 swa ðu on þinre spræce sped gehete.
 þinum agenum esne æt þearfe.

77 Cumen me ðine miltsa mihtum geswyþede,
 and ic lange on þam lifian mote,
 for ðon me is metegung on modsefan,
 hu ic æ þine efnast healde.

78 Beon þa ofer-hydegan ealle gescende,
 þe me unrihte ahwær gretan;
 ic þine bebodu bealde gegange.

79 Gehweorfen to me, þa þe hyldu to ðe
 egsan ahtan, and ealle þa
 ðe þine gewitnesse wise cuðan.

80 Wese heorte min on hige clæne
 and ic on þin soðfæst word symble getreowige,
 þæt ic on ealdre ne wese æfre gescended.

81 Min saul gewearð swancur on mode,
 þær ic on þinre hælu hogode, and sohte
 hu ic on þinum wordum wel getrywade.

74   74 Both those who fear you intensely and those who look at me favorably and rejoice, will conclude that I truly trusted in your words.

75   75 Lord, I perceived that your judgments were strictly fair, and in your justice you instantly humbled me as well.

76   76 May your gentle spirit be fortified with power, and become securely a source of consolation to me, just as you promised in your eloquent speech to your very own servant in distress.

77   77 May your mercies, strengthened with power, come to me, and may I be allowed to live long by them, because I am considering in my mind how to observe your law most consistently.

78   78 May the proud, who treat me unjustly in every way, be utterly confounded; I will boldly practice your precepts.

79   79 Let those who entertained for you the loyalty born of fear, and all those who wisely understood your revelation, turn to me.

80   80 May my heart be pure of thought, and I will trust always in your truthful words, so that I will never for all time be confounded.

81   81 My soul became slack of purpose, when I thought on your salvation and sought how I might truly trust in your words.

82   Eagan me swylce   eac teoredon,
    þær on þinre spræce   spede eodan;
    cwædon cynlice: "Hwa cwicenne me
    on ðysum ealdre   eft frefrade?"

83   Ic eom nu geworden   werum anlicast,
    swa þu on hrime setest   hlance cylle;
    ne eom ic ofergyttol,   þæt ic ealle nu
    þine soðfæste weorc   smicere healde.

84   Hwæt synt þinum esne   ealra dagena,
    þe þu mine ehtend for me   ealle gedeme?

85   Me man-wyrhtan   manige on spellum
    sægdon soðlice;   na ic hit swa oncneow,
    swa hit þin æ hafað,   ece Dryhten.

86   Wærun þine ealle gebann   æðele and soðfæst;
    min ehtan oft   unriht-wyrhtan,
    gefultuma me   fægere, Drihten.

87   Hio me lytle læs   laþe woldan
    ðisses eorð-weges   ende gescrifan;
    ic þin gebod   þa ne wolde
    on þysum ealdre   anforlætan.

88   Æfter ðinre þære myclan   mild-heortnesse
    weorð me, mihtig God,   milde and bliðe,
    and ic gewitnesse   wel gehealde
    muþes þines,   þe þu men lærdest.

89   On ecnesse   awa, Drihten,
    þin word wunað   weorð on heofenum.

90   And on worulda woruld   wunað ece forð
    þin soðfæstnes   swylce, Dryhten.

82 ⁸² Likewise, my eyes also became tired, when they ventured into the eloquence of your speech; quite rightly, they said: "Who consoled me once more while still living in this world?"

83 ⁸³ I am now become very like other mortals, as fragile as a slender leather bottle exposed to hoar frost; I will not forget that I should now carefully uphold all your righteous works.

84 ⁸⁴ How many days in all remain for your servant, during which you may thoroughly judge my persecutors for me?

85 ⁸⁵ Many evildoers spoke to me truly in fables; I did not recognize in that telling what your law contains, eternal Lord.

86 ⁸⁶ All of your decrees were noble and true; since agents of evil have often persecuted me, kindly help me, Lord.

87 ⁸⁷ In their hate they would almost have decreed the end of my earthly journey; I had no desire at that time to abandon your mandate in this life.

88 ⁸⁸ Mighty God, be mild and gentle to me according to your great mercy, and I will properly observe the revelation from your mouth, which you have taught humankind.

89 ⁸⁹ Lord, your word will endure, honored in heaven, always and forever,

90 ⁹⁰ And your truth likewise will endure eternally from here on, Lord.

91   Ðu þas eorðan   ealle worhtest,
    swa heo nu to worulde   wunian ðenceað;
    þurh þinra dæda sped   dagas her gewuniað,
    for ðon ðu ealles   anweald hafast.

92   Þær me þin æ   an ne hulpe,
    ðe ic on mode   minum hæfde,
    þonne ic wende   on woruld-life,
    þæt ic on minum eadmedum   eall forwurde.

93   Ne mæg ic þæs æfre forgytan   on ecnesse,
    nymðe ic soð word   symble gehealde;
    for þon ic cuðlice on ðæm   her nu cwicu lifige.

94   Ic eom þin hold scealc;   do ðu halne me,
    for ðon ic þin soð weorc   sece geneahhe.

95   Me fyrenfulle   fæcne seceað,
    wyllað me laðe   lifes asecean;
    ic ðine gewitnesse   wat and sohte.

96   Ic soð geseah   and swylce wat,
    ealre þysse worulde   wurðeð ende;
    brad is þin gebann   and beorht swyðe.

97   Hu ic æ þine,   ece Drihten,
    lustum lufode;   ic þæt lange dyde,
    þæt ic þa on mode   metegade georne.

98   Þu me snoterne gedydest   swylce ofer mine
    feondas on foldan   fæcne ealle,
    for ðon ic beorhtlice   þine bebodu læste.

99   Ofer ealle þa   þe me ær lærdon,
    ic þæs hæfde andgyt   æghwær gleawast
    þæt ic þine gewitnesse   wise sohte.

91   You so perfectly created this earth, that they now think it will endure forever; [91] through the efficacy of your actions the days continue here, because you control everything.

92   [92] If your law alone, which I retained in my mind, did not help me, I imagine that I would utterly perish in the abject state of my earthly existence.

93   [93] I cannot ever banish that prospect from my mind, unless I constantly observe your true words; therefore, while still alive on this earth, I will now certainly live by them.

94   [94] I am your loyal servant; save me, because I earnestly seek your true works.

95   [95] The wicked treacherously pursue me, desiring in their hostility to claim my life; I searched for and understand your revelation.

96   [96] I have observed, and also understand, the certainty that all this world will come to an end; your decree is broad and exceedingly clear.

97   [97] Eternal Lord, how I have passionately loved your law; for a long time I made myself ponder it eagerly in my mind.

98   [98] You also made me prudent beyond all my treacherous enemies on earth, because I truly observed your precepts.

99   [99] Ahead of all those who previously taught me, I grasped very clearly in every way that I should wisely seek your revelation.

100   Ic þæt ofer yldran oncneow   and þæt a geheold,
          þæt ic þine bebodu   bliðe geheolde.

101   Ic minum fotum   fæcne siðas
          þa wraþan wegas   werede georne,
          þæt ic þine word mihte   wel gehealdan.

102   Na ic fram þinum domum   dædum swicade,
          for ðon þu me æ-bebod   ærest settest.

103   Me is on gomum   god and swete
          þin agen word,   ece Drihten;
          hit is halwende,   hunige mycle
          and beo-breade   betere and swetre.

104   On bebodum ðinum   ic me betst oncneow,
          þæt ic unrihte wegas   ealle feode,
          for ðon þu me æ þine   ær gesettest.

105   Þæt is fæle blacern   fotum minum,
          þæt ic þin word, Drihten,   wel gehealde,
          and þæt ys þæt strange leoht   stige minre.

106   Ic aðas swor   and eac hycge,
          þæt ic soðne dom   symble healde.

107   And ic eadmedu   ungemetum georne
          efnan þence;   forgif me, ece God,
          þæt ic æfter ðinum wordum   weorðe bliðe.

108   Mines muðes me   modes willa
          on heah-sælum   hraðe gebringe;
          and me þine domas alær,   Drihten, swylce.

100 ¹⁰⁰ More than my elders I understood and constantly kept in mind to observe your precepts gladly.

101 ¹⁰¹ I have earnestly restrained my feet from deceitful ways and those evil paths, so as to be fittingly faithful to your words.

102 ¹⁰² I certainly did not stray from your judgments with my actions, because you first established a rule of law for me.

103 ¹⁰³ Eternal Lord, your very own speech is pleasant and sweet to my palate; it is salvific, much better and sweeter than honey and bee bread.

104 ¹⁰⁴ From your precepts I best understood that I should detest all wicked ways, because you already established your law for me.

105 ¹⁰⁵ Lord, fully observing your word is a trusty lamp for my feet and a powerful light for my path.

106 ¹⁰⁶ I swore oaths and intend, moreover, to maintain your true judgments always.

107 ¹⁰⁷ And I mean to endure abasement most willingly; eternal God, forgive me, so that I may become joyful in accordance with your words.

108 ¹⁰⁸ May the desire of my mind and mouth quickly lift me into transports of joy; Lord, teach me your judgments also.

109   Is sawl min   symble on ðinum
holdum handum,   ne ic þine þa halgan æ
on ðysum ealdre forgitan   æfre þence.

110   Me firenfulle   fæcne gyrene
awriþan wraðe,   and ne wolde ic
fram þinum bebodum   feor geswican.

111   Ic me eowde begeat,   æðele hæbbe
þine gewitnesse   wel getreowe
on ecnesse   awa to feore;
þæt byð heah-bliss   heortan minre.

112   Ahylde ic mine heortan   holde mode,
þæt ic þin soðfæst weorc   symble worhte;
for ðon ic ðæs ece   edlean hæbbe.

113   And ic synfulle   symble feode,
and ic æ þine   elne lufade.

114   Þu me fultumian scealt,   fæle gestandan
and andfenga   æghwær æt ðearfe;
and ic on þin word   wel getreowe.

115   Gewitað fram me,   þe awyrgede synt,
þenden ic Godes bebodu   georne smeage.

116   Onfoh me freondlice,   fæle Drihten,
æfter þam þe þu sylfa   sægdest and cwæde,
þæt ic sceolde lifigan   lange ðrage;
ne gescend me on siðe,   nu ic þin swa onbad.

117   Gefultuma me fæste;   ðonne beo ic fægere hal,
and ic þine soðfæstnysse   symble þence.

109 ¹⁰⁹ My soul resides continually in your trusty hands, nor do I ever intend, while alive, to forget your sacred law.

110 ¹¹⁰ The wicked in their anger prepared cunning snares for me, but I had no intention of wandering far from your precepts.

111 ¹¹¹ I have obtained an inheritance for myself, I have your exalted revelation, truly trustworthy, forever into eternity; it is the supreme joy of my heart.

112 ¹¹² Devoutly I inclined my heart to fulfill your just works always; so I will possess an eternal reward for that.

113 ¹¹³ I have both perpetually hated sinners and zealously loved your law.

114 ¹¹⁴ You must help me, by remaining faithful to me and being my defender in every difficult situation; and I will sincerely trust in your word.

115 ¹¹⁵ Let those who are accursed leave me alone, as long as I eagerly meditate on God's precepts.

116 ¹¹⁶ Trusty Lord, receive me kindly, in accord with your own statement and declaration that I would live for a long time; do not cause me dismay on the way, seeing that I so ardently expected you.

117 ¹¹⁷ Assist me constantly; then I will be perfectly safe, and will continually meditate on your truth.

118   Ealle ðu forhogodest,   ða ðe unrihtes
       wæran wyrhtan;   wat ic gearewe,
       þæt heo on unriht   ealle þohtan.

119   Ic ofer-hylmend   ealle getealde,
       þa on eorðan her   yfele wæron,
       for ðon ic þine gewitnesse   wyrðe lufade.

120   Gefæstna þinne egsan   flæsce minum,
       þæt ic me ondræde   domas ðine.

121   Ic soðne dom   symble worhte;
       ne syle þu me ehtendum   æfre minum.

122   Onfoh þu þinum esne   fægere mid gode,
       þæt me ofer-hydige   æfre ne motan
       hearm-cwyddian;   hyldo ne gymað.

123   Hwæt, me eagan mine   atule gewurdan,
       þær ic on ðinre hælo   hyldo sohte
       and on þinre spræce   sped soðfæste.

124   Do þinum agenum   esne swylce
       mycel milde mod,   and me mægene eac
       þin soðfæst word   sylfa lære.

125   Ic eom esne þin;   syle andgit, þæt ic
       þine gewitnesse   wel leornige.

126   Þis is wynne tid,   þæt man eac wel do,
       Drihten ure;   ne læt ðu dole æfre
       þin æ-bebod   ahwær toweorpan.

127   For ðon ic þin bebod   beorhte lufode,
       ða me georne synd   golde deorran,
       topazion þæra   teala gimma,

118   118 You despised all those engaged in iniquity; I know for certain that they have fully contemplated evil.

119   119 All those who lived wickedly here on earth I reckoned to be transgressors, which is why I loved your revelation dearly.

120   120 Firmly imprint on my flesh the fear of you, so that I may be afraid of your judgments.

121   121 I have always imposed a just sentence; do not ever hand me over to my persecutors.

122   122 Receive your servant graciously, to his advantage, so that the arrogant may never be allowed to calumniate me; they care not for acts of kindness.

123   123 My eyes deteriorated on me when I sought favor in your salvation and true power in your speech.

124   124 Adopt an exceedingly gentle approach toward your own servant also, and ably teach me your very own truthful words also.

125   125 I am your servant; grant me understanding, so that I may thoroughly learn your revelation.

126   126 Our Lord, this is a good time for people to behave well also; never allow the foolish to undo your commands anywhere.

127   127 Because I dearly loved your precepts, which are infinitely more precious to me than gold, or a topaz from the finest gems,

128   for ðon ic eall þin bebod   elne healde,
and ic unrihte wegas   ealle feoge.

129   Wundorlic is ðin gewitnes,   Wealdend-
                        Dryhten;
for ðon heo min sawl smeað   and seceð georne.

130   Worda me þinra   wise onleohteð,
beorhtnesse blæc-ern;   and þu bealde sylest
andgit eallum   eorð-buendum.

131   Muð ic ontynde   minne wide,
þæt me min oroð   ut afæmde,
þær ic ðin bebod   efnede mid willan.

132   Beseoh þu on me,   and me syððan hraðe
mære gemiltsa,   swa ðu manegum dydest,
þe naman þinne   nyde lufedon.

133   Gerece ðu me swylce,   þæt ic on rihtne weg
æfter þinre spræce   spedum gange,
þy læs min ænig unriht   ahwær wealde.

134   Ahrede me hearm-cwidum   heanra manna,
þæt ic ðine bebodu   bealde healde.

135   Do þine ansyne   esne þinum
leohte and leofe;   lær me syþþan,
hu ic ðin soðfæst word   selest gehealde.

136   Eagan mine gesawon,   hu yða gelaac,
wid gang wætera,   wundrum gangeð;
swa ðam ilcum byð,   þe ær nellað
þinre æ-bebod   elne healdan.

128 ^{128} I will vigorously observe all of them, and detest all wicked ways.

129 ^{129} Ruling Lord, your revelation is wonderful; my soul, therefore, eagerly meditates and seeks it.

130 ^{130} The instruction of your words, a lamp of illumination, enlightens me; and you confidently give understanding to all earth's inhabitants.

131 ^{131} Whenever I willingly fulfilled your command, I opened my mouth wide, so that I gasped for breath.

132 ^{132} Regard me and take pity on me without delay, illustrious one, as you did for many who earnestly loved your name.

133 ^{133} Show me also how to proceed successfully on the right way in accordance with your words, so that not a single vice controls me in any way.

134 ^{134} Rescue me from the calumnies of depraved people, so that I may confidently observe your precepts.

135 ^{135} Make your face luminous and lovely to your servant; then teach me how best to observe your truthful words.

136 ^{136} My eyes have seen how a tumult of waves, a vast expanse of waters, advances astonishingly; so it will turn out for those same people who already refuse to observe courageously your rule of law.

137 Drihten is soðfæst; synd his domas eac
reðe mid ræde   rihte gecyðde.

138 Hwæt, ðu soðfæst weorc   symble hete
on þinre gewitnesse   wel gehealdan.

139 Me heard ehtnes   huses þines
on bearme me   gebrohte oft;
ealles forgeaton,   þa me grame wæron,
worda þinra   and me wa dydan,
ða þin word noldan   wel gehealdan,
þa me feondas ær   fæste wæron.

140 Is þin agen spræc   innan fyren,
sylf swiþe hat,   and symble ða
þin esne her   ealle lufade.

141 Ic wæs on geoguðe,   grame me forhogedon;
næs ic ofergittol   æfre hwæðere
þæt ic þin soð weorc   symble heolde.

142 Is þin soðfæstnes   symble, Drihten,
seo soðfæste,   and seo symble bið
on ecnesse   awa to feore;
is þin swylce æðelnes   and æ soðfæst.

143 Me costunga   cnysdan geneahhe,
and nearonessa   naman gelome,
ac ic þine bebodu   efnde and læste;
eac on minum mode   hi metegade georne.

144 Ys me þin gewitnes   weorðast and rihtast,
and ða me on ece   andgyt hæbbe;
syle me ða to soðe,   and ic syþþan lifige.

137 ¹³⁷ The Lord is just; his judgments, moreover, are severe, promulgated with fair decrees.

138 ¹³⁸ In your revelation you always decreed that just works be properly practiced.

139 ¹³⁹ Severe harassment of me often led me into the intimacy of your house; those hostile to me totally forgot your words and caused me misery, the same people who refused to hold to your words faithfully, who were decidedly my enemies already.

140 ¹⁴⁰ Your own speech is fiery within, itself exceedingly hot, and always your servant here on earth unconditionally loved it.

141 ¹⁴¹ I was then in my youth, enemies despised me; despite that, I never forgot to uphold your true works constantly.

142 ¹⁴² Lord, your justice endures perpetually, it is just and will remain so for ever and ever; likewise, your majesty and law are just.

143 ¹⁴³ Troubles severely oppressed me, and anxieties frequently overpowered me, yet I fulfilled and carried out your precepts; moreover, I seriously weighed them in my mind.

144 ¹⁴⁴ For me your revelation is most honorable and just, and may it then have meaning for me, forever; grant me that revelation in truth, and I will afterward live.

145 Ic mid ealle ongann   inn-gehygde
heortan minre   hige to Drihtne
ceare cleopian;   he me cynlice
hraðe gehyrde,   hyldo cuðe,
þæt ic his soðfæstnesse   sohte geneahhe.

146 Ic cleopode to ðe: "Do me cuðlice
halne, heah-cyning,   heofona wealdend,
hælende Crist;   ic þæt hicge nu,
þæt ic ðine bebodu   bliðe gehealde."

147 And ic ðe on ripe forecom,   and hraðe swylce
ceare cleopode;   þu me cynlice
wel onfencge,   wistest gearwe,
þæt ic on ðinum wordum   wel getruwade.

148 Þe eagan mine   eac forecoman;
on ær-mergen   ic elne ongann
þine spræce   spyrian georne.

149 Gehyr mine stefne,   halig Drihten,
æfter ðinre þære myclan   mild-heortnesse,
and æfter þinum domum   do me halne.

150 Me syndon eahtend   ungemete neah aa
and ða synfullan;   syndan ealle hi
fram æ þinre   unneah gewiten.

151 Wes me swiðe neah,   wuldres Drihten;
synt ealle þine wegas   wise and cuðe.

152 Ic gewitnesse   wise þine
ongeat gleawlice,   þæt þu geara hi
on ecnesse   ær staþelodest.

145 ¹⁴⁵ With a full heart, I began inwardly to express sorrow to the Lord; he quickly and fittingly heard me, recognized my loyalty, in that I earnestly sought his truth.

146 ¹⁴⁶ I cried to you: "Kindly save me, high king, ruler of the heavens, savior Christ; I now resolve to observe your precepts gladly."

147 ¹⁴⁷ So in my maturity I came before you, and soon called out also in sorrow; you received me warmly, most properly, readily understood that I truly trusted in your words.

148 ¹⁴⁸ My eyes also anticipated you; I began boldly in the early morning to investigate your speech eagerly.

149 ¹⁴⁹ Holy Lord, hear my voice in your great mercy, and save me by your judgments.

150 ¹⁵⁰ Persecutors and sinners constantly linger much too close to me; they have all strayed far from your law.

151 ¹⁵¹ May the glory of the Lord remain very close to me; all your ways are wise and certain.

152 ¹⁵² I clearly recognized your profound revelation and also that you had established it in former times for all eternity.

153 Ac min eaðmedu geseoh   eall ful georne,
     genere niode,   nu me ned belæg,
     for þon ic wolde æ þine   elne healdan.

154 Dem minne dom   and me deore alys,
     for þinre spræce,   do me spedlice
     and cuðlice   cwicne nu ða.

155 Wærun fyrenfulle feor   fælre hælu,
     for ðon hi þine soðfæstnesse   secean noldan.

156 Miltsa synt þine,   mihtig Drihten;
     æfter þinum domum   do me cwicne.

157 Ic manige geseah,   þe min ehton;
     nolde ic cwic æfre   swaþeah hwæðere
     þine gewitnesse   wræste forlætan.

158 Ic manige geseah   men þa þe noldan
     heora friðo-wære   fæste healdan,
     and ic þand wið þan   þe hi teala noldan
     þinre spræce   sped gehealdan.

159 Swylce ic sylf geseah,   þæt ic þin soð bebod
     lustum lufige,   leofa Drihten;
     on þinre mild-heortnesse   me scealt acwician.

160 Þæt is weorðlic fruma   worda þinra,
     þæt þær byð soð   symble meted,
     and on ecnesse   awa to feore
     ealle þine domas synt   dædum geseðde.

161 Min earwunga   ehtan ongunnon
     ealdur-manna gehwylc   ungemete swiðe;
     wearð me heorte forht,   þær ic þin halig word
     on þinum egesan ærest   æðelu tredde.

153 ^{153} But regard with full diligence my humiliation, rescue me promptly, seeing that necessity has encompassed me, because I was willing to observe your law with courage.

154 ^{154} Render a verdict on my behalf, and lovingly release me, for the sake of your words, promptly and kindly bring me back to life right now.

155 ^{155} Sinners remained far from true salvation, because they were not willing to seek your justice.

156 ^{156} Mighty Lord, to you belong acts of mercy; give me life in accord with your verdicts.

157 ^{157} I have seen many who persecuted me; in spite of that, I never had any wish, while alive, to forsake your sublime revelation.

158 ^{158} I saw many people who refused to honor strictly their peace pledge and I was furious, because they were very unwilling to respect the power of your words.

159 ^{159} I myself also perceived that I love your true precepts eagerly, beloved Lord; in your mercy you must restore me to life.

160 ^{160} The fitting starting point of your words is that truth is always found in them, and that all your judgments are affirmed by actions, forever into eternity.

161 ^{161} The elders individually began harassing me too much, without good reason; my heart became fearful when in awe of you I first investigated your holy, noble words.

162   Ic blissige   bealde mode
        ofer ðinre spræce   spede þa myclan,
        swa se bið bliðe,   se þe beorna reaf
        manige meteð,   þær hit mannum losað.

163   And ic unrihta gehwylc   elne feode
        and onhyscte   æghwær georne;
        wolde ic æ þine   elne lufian.

164   Swa ic þe seofon siþum   symble wolde
        leofum lustlice   lof-sang cweðan
        daga æghwylce,   for þon ic þine domas wat
        on soð fæste   smicere gefylde.

165   Þam bið sib mycel   þe him þenceð,
        þæt hi naman þinne   neode lufien;
        ne bið him æ-swic on þon   æfre to feore.

166   Ic þinre hælu bad,   halig Drihten,
        and þine bebodu   bealde lufode.

167   Hafað sawl min   soð gehealden
        þinre gewitnesse,   worda æghwylc,
        and ic þa lustum   lufade swiðe.

168   Heold ic þine bebodu   holde mode
        and þine gewitnesse   wordum trymede,
        for ðon ealle mine wegas   wise syndan
        on þinre gesihðe   soðe, Drihten.

169   Nu genealæceð   neode minum
        gebedum bealde,   þæt ic bidde nu
        on þinre gesihðe   symble, Drihten;
        æfter þinre spræce   syle me spedlice
        þæt þu me generige   niða gehwylces.

162 ¹⁶² I will rejoice with confidence in the great eloquence of your speech, like the lucky person who stumbles on a hoard of military booty, in a place where it is lost to all.

163 ¹⁶³ And I fervently hated and zealously detested in every way each single act of iniquity; I wanted to love your law with courage.

164 ¹⁶⁴ So, I would constantly recite a hymn of praise seven times every day devoutly to you, beloved one, because I know that your judgments are finely and firmly executed in justice.

165 ¹⁶⁵ They who recognize the need to cherish your name zealously will enjoy great peace; in doing that they will never encounter a stumbling block at any time.

166 ¹⁶⁶ Holy Lord, I waited for your salvation, and confidently loved your precepts.

167 ¹⁶⁷ My soul held on to the truths of your revelation, each of its words, and I loved them most joyfully.

168 ¹⁶⁸ I observed your precepts faithfully and corroborated your revelation with words, because all my ways are known for sure in your sight, Lord.

169 ¹⁶⁹ Lord, that which I request constantly in your sight now comes close to my entreaties boldly and eagerly; according to your speech, successfully grant me your protection from every kind of evil.

170   Ingange min ben,   ece Drihten,
on þinre gesihðe   symble æt þearfe;
æfter þinre spræce   do spedlice
ðæt ðu me generige   niða gehwylces.

171   Nu mine weleras ðe   wordum belcettað
ymnas elne,   gif þu me ærest wylt
þine soðfæstnesse   sylfa læran.

172   Hwæt, tunge min   teala foresægde,
hu þinre spræce   spede eodan;
wærun eall þin bebodu   æghwær rihtwis.

173   Syn me þine handa   on hælu nu,
and þæt domlice   gedon weorðe,
for ðon ic þine bebodu geceas   bealde æt
þearfe.

174   Ic þinre hælu   her wilnade,
Drihten ælmihtig;   do me symble,
þæt ic æ þine   elne metige.

175   Leofað sawl min   and þe lustum hereð,
and me þine domas   dædum fultumiað.

176   Ic gedwelede   swa þæt dysige scep,
þætte forweorðan   wolde huru;
la, sece þinne esne   elne, Drihten,
for ðon ic þinra beboda ne forgeat   beorhtra
æfre.

170 ¹⁷⁰ Eternal Lord, let my request in my need enter into your sight always; by your speech successfully effect my protection from every kind of evil.

171 ¹⁷¹ My lips will now sing hymns to you in full voice, provided you yourself are willing first to teach me your truths.

172 ¹⁷² My tongue rightly proclaimed that your truths sprang from the eloquence of your speech; all your commands were in every way just.

173 ¹⁷³ May your hand be my salvation now, and may it be done solemnly, because in my difficulty I confidently accepted your precepts.

174 ¹⁷⁴ Almighty Lord, I desired your salvation here on earth; make me always meditate on your law with vigor.

175 ¹⁷⁵ My soul will live and gladly praise you, and your judgments will help me in my actions.

176 ¹⁷⁶ I went astray like that foolish sheep, which even wanted to die; O Lord, boldly seek out your servant, because I have never forgotten your sublime precepts.

Psalm 119

1   Ic me to Drihtne   deorum cleopode,
þonne me costunga   cnysdon geneahhe,
and he me gehyrde   holde mode.

2   Alys mine sawle,   lifes Drihten,
of þam welerum   þe wom cweðen,
and from þære tungan   þe teosu wylle.

3   Hwæt bið þe ealles seald   oþþe eced swa
from þære inwitfullan   yflan tungan?

4   Strele beoð scearpe,   strange and mihtige,
syððan of gledon wesað   gearwe ahyrde.

5   Wa me þære wyrde,   þæt min wynn alæg
and min bigengea gewat   bryce on feor-weg;
sceal ic eard niman,   swa me eðe nis,
mid Cedaringum;   nis min cyð þær,
þe mine sawle   swiðe beeode.

6   Mid þam þe hi sibbe   swyþost feodan,
ic sibbe mid him   soðe hæfde;
þonne ic him spedlice to   spræce and hi lærde,
ðonne me earwunga   ealle onfuhtan.

Psalm 120

1   Hof ic mine eagan   to þam hean beorge,
þær ic fultum fand   fælne æt þearfe.

Psalm 119

1   ¹ Whenever trials frequently oppressed me, I called to my beloved Lord, and he graciously heard me.

2   ² Lord of life, deliver my soul from lips that speak falsely, and from the tongue eager to inflict harm.

3   ³ For what will be really conferred on you or enhanced by that crafty evil tongue?

4   ⁴ Arrows are sharp, strong and powerful, after they are thoroughly hardened by live coals.

5   ⁵ Alas, it was my bad fortune that my happiness came to an end, and my productive farmer departed far away; I am obliged to take up residence, such as is not pleasant for me, among the inhabitants of Kedar; ⁶ my kinsfolk who truly cared for my soul are not living there.

6   ⁷ When they most hated peace, I sincerely maintained peace with them; whenever I succeeded in speaking to them and admonished them, they clashed with me entirely without cause.

Psalm 120

1   ¹ I raised my eyes to that lofty mountain, where I found reliable help in my need.

2   Is min fultum eac   fæger æt Drihtne,
se ðe heofon worhte,   hrusan swylce.

3   Ne sylle he þinne fot   on feondes geweald,
ne hycge to slæpe   se ðe healdeð þe.

4   Efne, se on hygde   huru ne slæpeð
ne swefeð swyðe,   se þe sceal healdan nu
Israela folc   utan wið feondum.

5   Gehealde þe   halig Drihten,
and þin mund-bora   mihti weorðe
ofer þa swiðran hand   symble æt þearfe.

6   Ne þe sunne on dæge   sol ne gebærne
ne þe mona on niht   minne geweorðe;
ac þe gehealde   halig Drihten
wyð yfela gehwam   æghwær georne,
and ðine sawle   swylce gehealde.

7   Ut-gang þinne and in-gang   ece Drihten,
sawla soð-cynincg,   symble gehealde
of þisson forð   awa to worulde.

Psalm 121

1   Ic on ðyssum eom   eallum bliðe,
þæt me cuðlice to   acweden syndon,
and on Godes hus   gange syððan.

2   Wæron fæststealle   fotas mine
on þinum cafer-tunum,   þær ure cyðð wæs,
on Hierusalem   geara ærest.

2   [2] Pleasing is my help from the Lord, who created heaven, and earth as well.

3   [3] May he who protects you neither surrender your foot to the enemy's power, nor think of sleep.

4   [4] Indeed! He will not even slumber, or sleep deeply, the one who must now guard the people of Israel against enemies from without.

5   [5] May the holy Lord guard you, and your mighty protector yield power continually over that right hand in need.

6   [6] Let neither the sun burn you by day nor the moon cause you harm by night; [7] but may the holy Lord diligently guard you everywhere against every kind of evil, and protect your soul likewise.

7   [8] May the eternal Lord, true king of souls, continually guard your going out and coming in from now on, for ever and ever.

Psalm 121

1   [1] I am delighted at all these things which are kindly said to me, and after that I will enter into God's house.

2   [2] My feet were standing firmly in your courtyards, where our home in Jerusalem was located in the beginning.

3   Hierusalem,   geara ðu wære
      swa swa cymlic   ceaster getimbred,
      þær syndon dælas   on sylfre hire.

4   Þær cneorisse   cende wæron
      cynn æfter cynne;   cuðan þa Drihten
      and on þære gewitnesse   wæran Israelas,
      þe his naman   neode sceoldon
      him andetnes   æghwær habban.

5   Oft hi þær on seldon   sæton æt domum;
      þu eart ðonne dema,   Dauides hus,
      þæt on heofenum siteþ   heah gestaðelod.

6   Biddað eow bealde   beorhtere sibbe,
      ða ðe on Hierusalem   gode syndan;
      and geniht agun,   þa þe neode þe
      on heora lufun   lustum healdað.

7   Si þe on þinum mægene sib,   mæst and fyrmest,
      and on þinum torrum wese   tidum genihtsum.

8   For mine broðru   ic bidde nu—
      and mine þa neahstan   nemne swylce—
      þæt we sibbe on ðe   symble habbon.

9   And ic for mines Godes huse   georne þingie,
      and to minum Drihtne   deorum sece,
      þæt ic god æt him   begitan mote.

3   ³ In former times, Jerusalem, you were built like a beautiful city with its constituent districts.

4   ⁴ Tribes were propagated there, generation after generation; the Israelites were then intimate with the Lord and a party to that covenant, which obligated them to treat his name earnestly on every occasion as an acknowledgment to him.

5   ⁵ Often they sat there on thrones in judgment; yet you, house of David, are the judge that sits in the heavens, established on high.

6   ⁶ You people in Jerusalem who are virtuous, boldly ask for a more glorious peace; and may they who cheerfully love you enjoy prosperity.

7   ⁷ Peace be to you in your strength, to the greatest and fullest extent, and let there be abundance in your towers continually.

8   ⁸ For the sake of my brothers—and I mention those neighbors of mine also—I ask now that we may continually experience peace living within you.

9   ⁹ And I eagerly plead for the house of my God, and seek from my beloved Lord that I obtain good things from it.

Psalm 122

1   To þe ic mine eagan hof,   ece Drihten,
þu þe heofon-hamas   healdest and wealdest.

2   Efne, mine eagan synt   ealra gelicast
þonne esne bið,   þonne ondrysnum
his hlaforde   hereð and cwemeð.

3   And swa eagan gað   earmre þeowenan,
þonne heo on hire hlæfdigean   handa locað,
swa us synt eagan to ðe,   ece Drihten,
urum þam godan Gode;   geare lociað,
oþþæt us miltsige   mihta wealdend.

4   Miltsa us nu ða,   mihtig Drihten,
miltsa us swylce   for þon we manegum synt
forhogednessum   hearde gefylde,

5   and we manegum synd   manna wordum
ure sawle   swiðe gefylled
mid edwite,   oft and geneahhe,
and us ofer-hydige forseoð   oft and gelome.

Psalm 123

1   Nymþe us on wese   ece Drihten,
cweþað Israhelas   ealle nu ða,
nymþe us eardige on   awa Drihten,

Psalm 122

1   1 Eternal Lord, to you I raised up my eyes, you who maintain and govern the heavenly dwellings.

2   2 Truly! My eyes are most like those a servant shows, when he praises and pleases his lord respectfully.

3   And as the eyes of the lowly maidservant turn when she gazes at the hands of her lady, so are our eyes toward you, eternal Lord, excellent God of ours; they gaze eagerly until the ruler of the angelic Powers takes pity on us.

4   3 Mighty Lord, have mercy on us now, take pity on us also because we are painfully oppressed by many expressions of contempt,

5   4 and we, our souls, are utterly permeated with shame all too frequently by the numerous comments of the people, and the arrogant despise us all too often.

Psalm 123

1   1 Unless the eternal Lord be with us, so all the Israelites now declare, 2 unless the Lord dwells continually in us,

2   þonne us manfulle   menn onginnað;
wen is, þæt hi us lifigende   lungre wyllen
sniome forsweolgan,   gif hi swa magon.

3   Þonne us ðara manna   mod yrsade,
and us wiðerwearde   wæron geneahhe;
wen is, þæt hi us woldan   wætre gelice
sona gesupan,   gif hit swa wolde.

4   Oft ure sawl   swyþe frecne
hlimman gedegde   hludes wæteres;
wene ic for þon,   þæt heo wel mæge
þæt swyðre mægen,   sawel usser,
wæteres wenan   ðæs wel gedegean.

5   Drihten si gebletsad,   þe þæt ne dyde æfre,
þæt us on hearde   hæft-nyd sealde,
þam þe us mid toðum   toteon woldan.

6   Wærun ure sawla   samod anlice
niþa generede,   swa swa neod-spearuwa
of grames huntan   gryne losige.

7   Grin bið on sadan   grame torænded,
and we synd alysde   lifes wyrðe;
we us naman Drihtnes   neode habbað
on fultume   fæstne and strangne,
þæs þe heofon worhte,   hrusan swylce.

2   then the wicked will assail us; [3] perhaps they wish to swallow us up alive suddenly at once, if they can do so.

3   Then those people's feelings became inflamed against us, and they were seriously hostile toward us; [4] perhaps they wished to swallow us up at once like water, if it was so ordained.

4   [5] Often in great danger our soul passed safely through a torrent of noisy water; so I surmise that, after that experience it can well escape successfully that more powerful force, the prospect of that water.

5   [6] Blessed be the Lord, because he never acted so as to surrender us to harsh captivity, to those wishing to tear us to pieces with their teeth.

6   [7] Our souls were rescued from dangers, just like a sparrow in difficulty who escapes the cruel hunter's snare.

7   [8] The noose in the snare is forcefully severed, and we are freed, made fit for living; [8] we truly consider the Lord's name to be constant and strong in assisting us, he who created heaven, and also the earth.

Psalm 124

1   Þa þe on Drihten heora   dædum getreowað,
hi beoð on Sion-beorge   swyþe gelice;
ne mæg hine on ealdre   ænig onhreran
þe eardfæst byð   on Hierusalem.

2   Hi synd mund-beorgas   micle ymbutan;
haldeð heora ymb-hwyrft   ece Drihten
of ðisson nu   awa to worulde.

3   Næfre forlæteð   lifes Drihten
firenfulra tan   furðor gangan,
þonne he soðfæstra   settan wylle.

4   Ne he soðfæste   swylce læteð,
þæt hi to unrihte   ahwær willen
handum ræcean,   ac he him hraþe gyldeð;
do þu, Drihten, wel   þam þe gedefe her
hiora heortan riht   healdað mid gode.

5   Þa ðe gearwe beoð   to gramum bendum,
eft hi gelædeð   ece Drihten
mid þæm þe unriht   æghwær wyrceað.
Sibb si Israhelum   symble ofer ealle.

Psalm 124

1   ¹ Those who in their actions trust in the Lord are very like Mount Zion; no one can disturb for all time the one settled ² in Jerusalem.

2   Great protecting hills encircle her; the eternal Lord perpetually guards their perimeter from now on, and forever.

3   ³ The Lord of life will never allow the apportioned land of sinners to extend further than he will fix that of the just.

4   Nor, by the same token, will he permit that the just will reach out to iniquity in any way, but he will promptly punish them if they do; ⁴ Lord, treat well those who properly maintain here the principles of their conscience with virtuous conduct.

5   ⁵ The eternal Lord will afterward lead out, in the company of evildoers everywhere, those who are receptive to cruel bonds. Peace be to Israel always beyond all others.

Psalm 125

1   Þonne Drihten wyle   gedon æfter,
   þæt he of Sione   swære ahweorfe
   hæft-ned hefige,   syððan we hraðe weorðað
   afrefrede   fægere ealle.

2   Sona beoð gefylde   mid gefean syþþan
   muðas ure,   and we ma sprecað,
   beoð ure tungan   teala wynsume.

3   Þonne hi geond þeode   cweðað þriste;
   æghwær hi gemiclade   mihtig Drihten,
   þa he him wundur mid   worhte seldlic;
   gemicla ðe swylce,   mihtig Drihten,
   þæt þu wundur mid us   wyrce mære,
   and we bealde on þam   bliðe weorðan.

4   Gehweorf ure hæft-ned,   halig Drihten,
   swa suð-healde   swiþe hlimman.

5   Þa her on tornlicum   tearum sawað,
   hi eft fægerum   gefean sniðað;
   gangende and ferende   georne wepað
   and heora sylfra sæd   sniðað æfter.

6   Cumað þonne mid cumendum   cuðe mid blisse
   and on heora sceafas berað,   swa hi
                               gesamnedon.

Psalm 125

1   ¹ When the Lord decides later to turn away an oppressive, burdensome captivity from Zion, then we will be quickly and altogether pleasantly consoled.

2   ² Our mouths will be filled with rejoicing immediately afterward, and we will become more voluble, our tongues will be very happy.

3   ³ They will speak then with assurance among the foreign peoples; in every place they magnified the mighty Lord when he worked remarkable wonders among them; mighty Lord, magnify yourself also, because you execute marvelous things among us and, emboldened by these, we become joyful.

4   ⁴ Holy Lord, turn around our captivity, like a torrent inclining strongly to the south.

5   ⁵ Those who sow here with grievous tears will reap afterward in harmonious rejoicing; ⁶ exiting and departing, they will weep bitterly, but will reap the fruit of their own seed afterward.

6   ⁷ With advances, they will finally arrive, plainly with joy, and in their sheaves will carry as they have gathered.

Psalm 126

1   Nymþe hus timbrige   halig Drihten,
on idel gylp   oðre winnað
þe þæs huses   hrof staðeliað.

2   Nymðe gehealde eac   halig Drihten
ceastre mid cynnum,   ne mæg hi cynlice
wæccende   weard gehealdan.

3   For hwan ge mid idelnesse   ealle arisað,
ær ðon leoht cume   leoda bearnum?
Arisað nu ricene,   and hraðe sittað,
þa ðe sares hlaf   swiðe æton.

4   Þonne he slæp syleð   swiðe leofum,
þæt is yrfe eac   ecean Drihtnes
and herde bearn,   þa her mannum beoð
of innaðe   ærest cende.

5   Swa seo stræle byð   strangum and mihtigum
hrorum on handa   heard ascyrped,
swa lyðra bearn   lungre gewitað.

6   Þæt bið eadig wer,   se ðe a þenceð,
þæt he his lust on ðon   leofne gefylle;
ne bið he on ealdre ealre   æfre gescended,
þonne he on gaton greteð   his grame feondas.

Psalm 126

1 ¹ Unless the holy Lord builds a house, those others, who raise its roof, labor in idle boasting.

2 Unless the holy Lord protects the town with tribes as well, watchful guards cannot properly do it.

3 ² Why do you all rise futilely before dawn with the rest of humankind? Rise now at once and sit down quickly, you who have bitterly eaten the bread of sorrow.

4 Then he will give sleep abundantly to his favorites, ³ those are the eternal Lord's inheritance and familial children, those on earth first brought forth from the womb as mortals.

5 ⁴ As the arrow is severely filed down by a deft hand, strong and powerful, so the children of the wicked will soon disappear.

6 ⁵ Happy is the man who continually plans to fulfill his cherished desire in that; he will never be confounded at any time when he deals with his fierce enemies at the gates.

Psalm 127

1 Eadige syndon ealle   þe him ecne God
   Drihten ondrædað,   and his gedefne weg
   on hyra lifes tid   lustum gangað.

2 Þonne þu þines gewinnes   wæstme byrgest,
   etest oretes;   and þu eadig leofast,
   and þe wel weorðeð   on wyn-burgum.

3 Beoð þines wifes   welan gelice,
   swa on win-gearde   weaxen berigean
   and on þines huses   hwommum genihtsum.

4 Synd þine bearn swylce   samed anlicast,
   swa ele-beamas   æþele weaxen,
   ymb þinne beod utan   blæda standen.

5 Efne, swa bið gebletsad   beorna æghwylc
   mann on moldan,   þe him metodes ege
   on his dædum   Drihten forhtað.

6 Þe of Sion-beorge   swylce Drihten
   bealde bletsige,   and þu bruce eac
   on Hierusalem   goda gehwylces
   ealle lange dagas   lifes þines.

7 And þu þinra bearna   bearn sceawige,
   geseo samed gangan   sibb ofer Israhel.

Psalm 127

1   ¹ Blessed are all those who fear the Lord, the eternal God, and during the course of their lives walk willingly on his proper path.

2   ² You will then enjoy the fruits of your endeavor, receive the reward of the struggle; and you will live blessed, and you will thrive in pleasant towns.

3   ³ Your wife's possessions will be like vines flourishing in a vineyard and abundant in the corners of your house.

4   Likewise your children will be just like olive trees grown vigorous, standing firm around your table.

5   ⁴ Truly! Every person, mortal on earth, who with awe of the creator, in his actions fears the Lord, will be so blessed.

6   ⁵ May the Lord boldly bless you also from Mount Zion, and may you enjoy every good thing in Jerusalem, all the extended days of your life.

7   ⁶ And may you see your children's children, and witness peace advancing at the same time over Israel.

Psalm 128

1   Oft me fuhtan to   fynd on geoguðe;
    cweðan Israhelas nu   eac þæt sylfe:
    oft me fuhtan to   fynd on geoguþe,
    ne mihton hi awiht æt me   æfre gewyrcean.

2   Ofer minum bæce   bitere ongunnon
    þa firenfullan   facen timbrian,
    and heora unriht   eft gelengdon.

3   Drihten is soðfæst,   and gedeð sniome,
    þæt he firenfullra   fæcne geðancas
    wis toweorpeð;   weorðað gescende
    and hiora scamiað   swiþust ealles,
    þa to Sione hete   swiðost hæfdon.

4   Wesen hi hige   her gelicast
    þam þe on huses þæce   heah aweaxeð,
    þæt bið forwisnad   wraðe sona,
    ær hit afohten   foldan losige.

5   Of þam he ne gefylleð   folme æfre,
    þeah þe he hit mawe   micle elne;
    ne mid his sceafe ne mæg   sceat afyllan,
    þeah þe he samnige   swiðe georne.

6   And þæt ne cweðan,   þa his cwide weoldan
    on ofergeate   æghwær hæbben:
    "Us gebletsige   bealde Drihten
    and ofer eow wese   eac his bletsung;
    we eow neodlice   on naman Drihtnes
    swylce bletsiað   bliðe mode."

Psalm 128

1   [1] Often enemies fought against me in my youth; let the Israelites repeat that same statement now: [2] often enemies fought against me in my youth, yet they failed to achieve anything against me, ever.

2   [3] The wicked began to build up evil cruelly on my back, and subsequently prolonged their iniquities.

3   [4] The Lord is just, and in his wisdom acts quickly to overturn treacherous plans of the wicked; [5] they who most passionately harbored hatred toward Zion will be confounded and shamed most intensely of all.

4   [6] Let them most resemble earth's grass flourishing high in the house's thatch, which soon becomes harshly desiccated, uprooted before it is lost to the soil.

5   [7] He will never fill his hand with that grass, even though he mows it with great vigor; nor can he fill his lap with a proper sheaf of it, though he gathers very busily.

6   [8] And may those who would have entirely consigned his saying to oblivion, not say: "May the Lord boldly bless us and may his blessing be upon you also; we likewise bless you mightily with a joyful spirit in the Lord's name."

Psalm 129

1   Ic of grundum to þe   geomur cleopode,
    Drihten; Drihten,   do þu nu ða
    þæt þu mines gebedes   bene gehyre.

2   Wesan þine earan   eac gehyrende
    and beheldende   mid hige swylce
    on eall gebedd   esnes þines.

3   Gif þu ure unriht wilt   eall behealdan,
    Drihten, Drihten,   hwa gedeð æfre,
    þæt he þæt geefne   eall mid rihte?

4   Ys seo mild-heortnes mid þe,   mihta wealdend,
    and ic for ðinre æ,   ece Drihten,
    þas oþer eall   eaðe aræfnige.

5   Hwæt, þæt sawl min   symble aræfnede,
    þæt ic on þinum wordum   me wel getreowde;
    for ðon min sawl on þe   symble getreoweð.

6   Fram þære mæran   mergen-tide
    oð þæt æfen cume   ylda bearnum,
    Israhelas on Drihten   a getreowen,

7   for ðon is mild-heortnesse   miht on Drihtne
    and he alyseð   lustum ealle,
    þa ðe hiht on hine   habbað fæste.

8   He Israhelas   ealle alyseð
    of unrihte   æghwær symble.

Psalm 129

1   [1] Lord, in my depression I called to you from the depths; [2] Lord, be sure to hear the appeal of my prayer at this time.

2   [2] Be all ears also and purposefully alert to all your servant's prayers.

3   [3] Lord, if you decide to examine all our iniquities, who will ever manage to endure all that with equanimity?

4   [4] Mighty ruler, compassion belongs to you, and because of your law, eternal Lord, I may easily endure all those other things.

5   My soul has constantly adverted to the fact that I truly trust in your words; [5] therefore, it trusts in you always.

6   [6] From glorious morning until evening comes for humankind, may the Israelites always trust in the Lord,

7   [7] because in the Lord rests the power of compassion, and he will willingly redeem all those who steadily maintain their hope in him.

8   [8] He will free all the Israelites from iniquity, always and everywhere.

Psalm 130

1   Nis min heorte wið þe   ahafen, Drihten,
ne mine eagan wið þe   on ofer-hygde;

2   ne ic on mægene   miclum gange,
ne wundur ofer me   wuniað ænig.

3   Ac ic mid eaðmedum   eall geþafige;
is min sawl on ðon   swyþe gefeonde.

4   Swa man æt meder   bið miclum feded,
swa þu minre sawle   symble gyldest.

5   Israhelas on Drihten   a getreowigen
of ðyssum nu   awa to worulde.

Psalm 131

1   Gemune þu, Drihten,   mærne Dauid
and ealle his mann-þwærnesse   micle and
goode.

2   "Swa ic æt frymðe geswor   ferhðe wið Drihten
and gehat gehet"   (he geheold teala
wið Iacobes   God þone mæran),

3   "þeah þe ic on mines huses   hyld gegange
oþþe sele-gesceot   (þænne swæs wese)
oððe on min rest-bedd   ricene gestige,

Psalm 130

1   ¹ Lord, my heart is not raised up against you, nor are my eyes haughty toward you;

2   neither do I strut about in majesty, nor do any marvels hover above me.

3   ² But I endure all things with humility; my soul continues to rejoice exceedingly in that.

4   As one is abundantly fed at a mother's breast, so you constantly reward my soul.

5   ³ Let the Israelites always trust in the Lord from now on and forever.

Psalm 131

1   ¹ Lord, remember illustrious David and all his meekness, great and good.

2   ² "So in the beginning I swore in my soul to the Lord and made a vow" (David behaved well toward the illustrious God of Jacob)

3   ³ although I should enter into the protection of my house or into my tent (whenever I pleased), or quickly ascend to my bed of rest,

4 gif ic minum eagum unne slæpes,
oþþe minum breawum beode hnappunga,
oþþe ic on þun-wange þriste gereste,

5 oþ þæt ic gemete mære stowe,
Drihtne gecorene, dyre sele-gesceot,
Iacobes Gode georne gecweme."

6 Efne, we þas eall on Eufraten
sæcgean gehyrdon, syððan gemitton
forwel manegu on wudu-feldum.

7 We on his sele-gesceot swylce gangað,
and þære stowe stede ariað
þær his fotas ær fæste gestodan.

8 Aris on þinre reste recene, Drihten;
þu earce eart eall-haligra.

9 Synd þine sacerdas on soðfæstnesse
gode gegierede, and gleawe nu
þine þa halgan her blissiað.

10 For þinum agenum esne swylce,
deorum Dauide, þu ne do æfre,
þæt þu andwlitan ut oncyrre
þines þæs halgan her on eorðan.

11 Þæs deopne að Drihten aswor,
and þone mid soðe swylce getrymede,
þæt he hine for hole ær ne aswore;
gehet Dauide, swa he him dyde syþþan,

12 þæt he weorðlicne wæstm gesette
þe of his innaðe agenum cwome,

4 ⁴ if I should grant sleep to my eyes, or offer slumber to my eyelids, ⁵ or rashly give repose to my temples,

5 until I found an excellent place, the choicest for the Lord, a precious tent, thoroughly acceptable to the God of Jacob."

6 ⁶ Truly! We heard all those words spoken in Ephratah, afterward we encountered very many of them in the fields of the forest.

7 ⁷ We will also enter into his tabernacle and pay our respects at the site where his feet had firmly stood.

8 ⁸ Lord, ascend quickly to your resting place; you are the ark of all sanctified things.

9 ⁹ Your priests are clothed virtuously with truth, and those holy ones of yours now fully rejoice on earth.

10 ¹⁰ For the sake also of your own servant, noble David, do not turn away the face of your sanctified one on earth.

11 ¹¹ Afterward the Lord swore a solemn oath, while also confirming it with a guarantee that he had not earlier sworn to him in vain; to David he made a promise, which he subsequently fulfilled,

12 that he would set upon your high throne a distinguished lineage springing from his own body. ¹² "If your own

ofer þin heahsetl.   "Gif nu healdað well
þines sylfes bearn   soðe treowa
and þa gewitnesse,   þa ic hig wel lære,

13   þonne hiora suna   swylce motan
a þysse worulde   wynnum brucan
and on þinum setle   sittan geneahhe."

14   For ðon him Sione geceas   sylfa Drihten,
and him to earde geceas   ærest æt frymðe.

15   "Þis is min rest,   þe ic recene nu
on worulda woruld   wunian þence,
þær ic eard nime,   for ðon ic hi ær geceas.

16   His wuduan ic   wordum bletsige
and gesegnade,   sylle geneahhe
heora hungrium   hlaf to fylle.

17   Ic his sacerdas   swylce mid hælu
georne gegyrwe;   and gode eac
his þa halgan her   habbað blisse.

18   Þær ic Dauides horn   deorne bringe,
forð gelæde,   fægre gearuwe
byrnende blacern,   bere for minum
criste gecorenum,   þe ic hine cuðne wat.

19   Ic his feondas eac   facne gegyrwe
mid scame swiðust;   ofer hine scir cymeð
minra segnunga   soðfæst blostma."

children will now dutifully keep true faith and the covenant which I will carefully teach them,

13 then their sons likewise will be allowed to partake of this world's pleasures perpetually, and often to occupy your throne."

14 [13] For the Lord himself chose Zion for himself, and made it his dwelling place in the very beginning.

15 [14] "This is my resting place which I now plan to occupy at once, for ever and ever, where I will take up residence because I chose it already.

16 [15] I will bless and consecrate its widows with words, supplying bread abundantly to satisfy their hungry ones.

17 [16] Likewise I will gladly clothe its priests with security; and its virtuous people also will enjoy great happiness on earth.

18 [17] There I will bring David's precious horn, leading it forth, a flaming lamp elegantly prepared, I will carry for my chosen anointed one, whom I know to be illustrious.

19 [18] His enemies, however, I will harshly clothe especially with shame; but on him will descend the shining honest crown of my blessings."

Psalm 132

1 Efne, hu glædlic bið and god swylce,
þætte broður on an begen hicgen
þær hig ænne sculan eard weardian,

2 swa *unguentum* mæg, æðele wyrt-cynn,
heafde healdan hrore stence,
mid þy Aaron his beard oftast smyrede.

3 Seo niðer astah on his reafæs fnæd,
swa æþele deaw on Hermone,
se ofer Sion-beorge sneome astigeð.

4 For þon her bebead halig Drihten
lifes bletsunga lange to feore
of þisson nu awa to worulde.

Psalm 133

1 Efne, bletsien nu bliðe Drihten
ealle his agene onbyht-scealcas,

2 ge þe on Godes huse gearwe standað,
and on cafer-tunum Cristes huses
ures þæs halgan Godes held begangað.

3 Hebbað neodlice nihta gehwylcere
eowre handa on halig lof,
and bletsiað balde Drihten.

Psalm 132

1 ¹ Truly! How agreeable it is, and good also, that two brothers plan in unison where they should share a single dwelling place,

2 ² just as the ointment, an excellent herb, with which Aaron most often anointed his beard, has the power to overwhelm the head with its fragrant scent.

3 It flowed downward into the hem of his garment, ³ like the pleasant dew on Hermon, which quickly descends on Mount Zion.

4 For here on Mount Zion the holy Lord promulgated life's blessings from now on, for evermore.

Psalm 133

1 ¹ Truly! Let all his very own servants now joyfully bless the Lord,

2 you who stand prepared in God's house, and keep watch in the courtyards of Christ's house, our holy God.

3 ² Every night raise up your hands eagerly in reverent praise, and confidently bless the Lord.

4   Þe bletsige   bliðe Drihten
of Sion-beorge   symble æt þearfe,
se þe heofon worhte,   hrusan swylce.

Psalm 134

1   Heriað naman Drihtenes;   neode swylce
herigen hine his scealcas   swiðe ealle.

2   Ge þe on Godes huse   gleawe standað
and on cafer-tunum   Cristes huses
þæs godan Godes   gearwe syndan,

3   lofiað ge Drihten,   for þon he lungre is
fæstræd and fremsum   fira æghwam;
weorðiað his naman,   for þon he wyrðe is.

4   For ðon him godne geceas   Iacob Drihten,
and on agene æht   Israeles cynn.

5   Ic þæt gearwe ongeat,   þæt is god and mycel
Drihten ure;   for þon him dom standeð
ofer ealle godu   eorð-buendra.

6   Ealle þa þe wolde,   worhte Drihten
on heofon-rice   and her on eorðan,
on sidum sæ   swylce on eallum,
þær he dyrne wat   deorce grundas.

7   And he fram þysse eorðan   ende lædeð
wolcen wræclicu,   wind and liget,
and þa to regne   recene wyrceð,

4   3 May the Lord happily bless you always from Mount Zion in your need, he who created heaven and the earth also.

Psalm 134

1   1 Praise the name of the Lord; may all his servants also zealously praise him altogether.

2   2 You who stand attentively in God's house, and are ready in the courtyards of the house of Christ, that excellent God,

3   3 praise the Lord, because he is actively constant and gracious to every person; honor his name because he is esteemed.

4   4 For God chose the virtuous Jacob for himself, and the people of Israel as his personal possession.

5   5 I fully perceived that our Lord is great and good; so, his dominion presides over all the gods of earth's inhabitants.

6   6 The Lord created all that he wished in heaven and here on earth, likewise in all of the spacious sea, where he knows the dark, obscure abysses.

7   7 And he conducts from the end of this earth curiously wrought clouds, wind, and lightning, and speedily converts them into rain,

8   þe forð lædeð   fægere windas
    of his gold-hordum   godra manegum;
    se Ægipta sloh   æðele frum-bearn,
    æghwylc ealra   oð þa nytenu.

9   He sige-tacen   sende manegum,
    fore-beacn fæle,   folce Ægipta,
    and þa Pharaones   folce gecyðde
    and his scealcum   samed ætgædere.

10 Se sloh þeode folc   þearle manige,
    and eac acwealde   cyningas strange.

11 Wæs Seon efne   sum þara kynincga,
    and Og kyning,   se þe æror wæs
    on Basane   breme and mære.

12 Sealde heora eard-land   eall Israhelum
    and heora yrfe   eac his folce.

13 Ys þin nama, Drihten,   nemned ece,
    and þin gemynd,   mihtig Drihten,
    on ealra worulda woruld   wynnum standeð.

14 For þon his folc demeð   fægere Drihten,
    and he bið on his esnum   agenum frefriend.

15 Beoð deofol-gyld   dysigra þeoda
    gold and seolfur,   þe her geotað menn,
    and mid heora folmum   fægere wyrceað.

16 Þa muð habbað,   and ne meldiað wiht,
    fægere eagan,   ne magon feor geseon.

8   which produces pleasant winds from his many treasuries of good things; ⁸ he struck down the noble firstborn of the Egyptians, each one of them, as far even as the animals.

9   ⁹ He sent out signals of victory, reliable portents, to many of Egypt's people, and made them known to the people of Pharaoh and his servants altogether.

10   ¹⁰ He struck down exceedingly many allied people, and also killed strong kings.

11   ¹¹ Sihon indeed was one of those kings, and King Og, who previously had been famous and illustrious in Bashan.

12   ¹² He gave all their homeland to the Israelites, and their inheritance also to his people.

13   ¹³ Lord, your name is spoken of as eternal and your memorial, mighty Lord, stands joyfully for all ages.

14   ¹⁴ For the Lord will judge his people fairly, and will be a comforter to his own servants.

15   ¹⁵ The idols of the foolish gentiles are gold and silver, which people here on earth cast, and finely craft with their hands.

16   ¹⁶ They have a mouth, but say nothing, beautiful eyes, but cannot see far.

17   Earan habbað,   ne hi awiht magon
       holdes gehyran,   þeah ðe him hleoðrige;
       and nose habbað,   nawiht gestincað.

18   Handa hi habbað,   ne hi hwæðere magon
       gegrapian   godes awiht;
       habbað fet swylce,   ne magon feala gangan.

19   Ne hi on hracan awiht   hlude ne cleopiað,
       ne him gast warað   gomum on muðe.

20   Synt anlice þæm   þe hi ær worhtan,
       and ealle þa ðe on hi   æfre getreowað.

21   Hus Israela   holdne Drihten
       bletsien bealde;   biddan swylce
       þæt Aarones hus   ecne Drihten
       bliðe bletsien;   beornas ealle,
       þa on Lefes hus   leof eardiað,
       bletsien Drihten   bliðe mode.

22   Þa þe him ondræden   Drihtnes egsan,
       bletsien Drihten   beornas ealle;
       se Drihten is   deore gebletsad
       of Sion sniome,   þe soðfæst ær
       on Hierusalem   God eardode.

Psalm 135

1   Ic andette   ecum Drihtne,
       for ðon he god is,   and ic ful gearwe wat,
       þæt he to worulde byð   wis and mild-heort.

17   ¹⁷ They have ears, yet they cannot hear anything melodious, even if it should cry aloud to them; and they have noses, yet smell nothing.

18   They have hands, yet in spite of that they cannot grasp anything of substance; likewise, they have feet, yet they cannot walk much.

19   Nor do they emit any sound out loud from their throats, nor does breath reside inside their mouths.

20   ¹⁸ They resemble those people who earlier constructed them, and all those who ever trust in them.

21   ¹⁹ May the houses of Israel confidently bless that faithful Lord; likewise, may they require the house of Aaron to boldly bless the eternal Lord; ²⁰ may all the people who dwell in the beloved house of Levi bless the Lord cheerfully.

22   Let all humankind, who fear his terror, bless the Lord; ²¹ that Lord, who previously dwelt in Jerusalem as a just God, is lovingly and readily blessed from Zion.

Psalm 135

1   ¹ I acknowledge the eternal Lord, because he is good, and I know full well that he will be wise and merciful forever.

2   Eac ic andette   þam þe ece is
       ealra godena God,   for ðon ic hine godne wat.

3   Andette ic swylce   þam þe ealra is
       drihtna Drihten   dædum spedigast,
       for ðon he god is,   and ic gearwe wat,
       þæt his mild-heortnes is   mycel to worulde.

4   He wundur dyde   weorþlic ana,

5   se heofon worhte,   hæleða andgit.

6   He eorðan æfter wæter   ærest sette.

7   He leoht-fatu   leodum ana
       micel geworhte   manna bearnum,

8   sette on miht dæges   mære sunnan,

9   on miht nihte   monan and steorran.

10   He Ægyptas sloh   and eall heora frum-bearn;

11   and he Israhelas   ealle oðlædde
       of Ægyptum   ealle gesunde,

12   on mihtigre   mære handa,
       and on eall-mihte   earmes swylce.

13   He readne sæ   recene todælde,

14   lædde Israhelas   ealle þurh midne.

15   Þær Pharaon gefeol,   and his fæge werud
       on þam readan sæ   recene forwurdan.

16   He gewealdendlice   þuruh westen eft
       his þæt leofe folc   lædde swylce.

2　²I acknowledge also that one who is eternal, God of all gods, because I know him to be good.

3　³I acknowledge likewise him who is the Lord of all lords, most powerful in deeds, because he is good, and I know well that his mercy is great forever.

4　⁴By himself he performed splendid wonders,

5　⁵who created heaven and human understanding.

6　⁶He first set the earth upon the waters.

7　⁷He singlehandedly made great lamps for the people, for the children of men,

8　⁸established the resplendent sun to rule over day,

9　⁹the moon and stars to rule over night.

10　¹⁰He struck down the Egyptians and all their firstborn;

11　¹¹and he led all the Israelites out of Egypt, totally unharmed,

12　¹²with a mighty, glorious hand, and also in the full power of his arm.

13　¹³He parted the Red Sea in an instant,

14　¹⁴leading all the Israelites through the middle.

15　¹⁵There Pharaoh fell, and his doomed army quickly perished in the Red Sea.

16　¹⁶Afterward, he also led that beloved people of his masterfully through the desert.

17   He of stan-clife   stearce burnan
      leodum lædde   on leofne þanc.

18   Swylce he acwealde   cyningas mycle,

19   and he eac ofsloh   æðele cyningas,
      weras wræclice,   þa þe weoruld heoldan.

20   Þær Seon cyning   swylt dreorig fornam,
      þe Amorrea   anweald hæfde,

21   and Og swylce,   þe æror wæs
      swyþe breme cyning   on Basane.

22   Sealde heora eorþan   on yrfe-land,

23   and þæt yrfe   on Israele,
      þe his esnas   agene wæron,

24   for þon ure eaðmedu   ece Drihten
      gemyndgade,   and us mycel sealde.

25   And he us aferede   feondum of handa,
      þa ðe wraðe   wæron ealle.

26   He eac afedeð   flæscea æghwylc.

27   Andetað nu ealle   þam ecean Gode,
      þe on heofonum is   heah eardiende,

28   and ge ealra godena Gode   geara andettað,
      for þan his mild-heortnes is   mycel to worulde.

17   ¹⁷ He produced from an unyielding rock streams of water for the peoples to their grateful satisfaction.

18   He killed great kings likewise,

19   ¹⁸ and slew eminent kings as well, extraordinary men, who ruled the world.

20   ¹⁹ There cruel death carried off King Sihon who ruled the Amorites,

21   ²⁰ and Og likewise, who formerly was a very famous king in Bashan.

22   ²¹ He delivered their territories as an inheritance,

23   ²² and that legacy to the Israelites, who were his very own servants,

24   ²³ because the eternal Lord was mindful of our abject state, and granted us great things.

25   ²⁴ And he removed us from the hands of enemies, those who were entirely evil.

26   ²⁵ Moreover, he feeds every living animal.

27   ²⁶ Let all acknowledge that eternal God, who is living above in the heavens,

28   and may you eagerly acknowledge the God of all good things, because his mercy is great forever.

Psalm 136

1   Ofer Babilone   bradum streame,
þær we sittað   and sare wepað,
þonne we Sion gemunan   swiðe georne.

2   On salig we sarige   swiðe gelome
ure organan   up ahengan,

3   for þon us þær frunon   fæcnum wordum,
woh meldedan,   ða us on weg læddan:

4   "Singað us *ymnum*   ealdra sanga
þe ge on Sione   sungan geneahhige."
Hu magon we singan   sangas Drihtne
on þære foldan   þe us fremde is?

5   Gif ic þin, Hierusalem,   forgyten hæbbe,
forgyte min seo swyðre   symble æt þearfe;
ætfeole min tunge   fæste gomum,
gif ic ofergittol þin   æfre weorðe,

6   gif ic ne forsette þe   symble æt frymðe;
ac ic on Hierusalem   georne blissie.

7   Gemune þu, Drihten,   manigra bearna,
þe on Edom synt   eal lifigende,
þonne þu Hierusalem   gegodie;
þa nu oft cweðað: "Wutun hi idle gedon,
oð þæt hi heora   eard geceosan."

8   Hwæt, þu eart Babilone   bitere ætfæsted
ænge and yfele,   hire earm dohter;

Psalm 136

1   ¹ Above the broad river of Babylon, there we sit and sorrowfully weep, whenever we most vividly recall Zion.

2   ² Grieving very often, we hung up our musical instruments on a willow tree,

3   ³ because in that place our abductors asked of us with cunning words, speaking maliciously:

4   "Sing to us a hymn of the ancient songs, which you frequently sang on Zion." ⁴ How can we sing songs to the Lord in that land which is alien to us?

5   ⁵ If I have forgotten you, Jerusalem, may my right hand perpetually forget me in need; ⁶ may my tongue stick firmly to my jaws, if I ever forget you,

6   or fail to rank you always as preeminent; still, I will eagerly rejoice in Jerusalem.

7   ⁷ Lord, when you improve the lot of Jerusalem, bear in mind the many people who live wholly in Edom; at present they often say: "Let us make them destitute until they select their dwelling place."

8   ⁸ You are tied to Babylon, painfully, anxiously, and wrongly, as her wretched daughter; he will be blessed, how-

eadig byð hwæðere   se þe eft gyldeð
þa þu him on ealdre   ær forgeafe,
and us eallum   eac gesealdest.

9   Eadig byð se þe nimeð   and eac seteð
his agen bearn   on þone æþelan stan.

Psalm 137

1   Ic þe andette,   ecne Drihten,
on minre gehygde   heortan ealre,
for ðon þu ealle mine word   earum gehyrdest,
þa ic mid muðe   and mid mode cweðe;
and on þinra engla   ealra gesihðe
ic þe singe   swiðe geneahhige.

2   Eac ic þin tempel   tidum weorðige,
þæt halige hus,   holde mode,
and þær þinne naman   on neod secge.

3   Ofer þine þa miclan   mild-heortnesse
and soðfæstnesse,   samed ætgædere,
þu þinne þone halgan naman   neode gedydest,
ofer us ealle   æghwær micelne.

4   Swa hwylce daga   ic þe deorne cige,
gehyr me hwætlice,   and me hraðe gedo
micle mine sawle   on þines mægenes sped.

ever, who will repay what you earlier dispensed to him continually, and gave also to all of us.

9   9 He will be blessed, who takes and also places his own children on that eminent rock.

Psalm 137

1   1 I will praise you, eternal Lord, in my most sincere deliberations, because you heard with your ears all the words that I voiced with mouth and purpose; and I will sing to you very earnestly in the sight of all your angels.

2   2 I will also regularly pay reverence, with devout intent, to your temple, that holy house, and there zealously pronounce your name.

3   Beyond your great mercy and truth, both together, you eagerly magnified that holy name of yours over all of us everywhere.

4   3 On whatsoever day I will call upon you, my darling, hear me promptly, and with the power of your might quickly enlarge in me my soul.

5   Ealle þe andettan   eorðan kyningas,
for ðon þe hi gehyrdon   hlude reorde
þines muðes   þa mæran word;
þa on sangum   singan Drihtne,

6   for þon þin wuldur is   wide geond eorðan
micel and mære   ofer middan-eard.
Eart þu healice   ahafen, Drihten,
þu eadmodra   ealra locast
on heofon-hame   her on eorðan.

7   Þeah þe ic on midle   manes gange,
þær me costunga   cnysdan geneahhe,
a þu me weredest   wraþum feondum
þe me woldan yrre   on acyðan;
þu me geræhtest   recene mid handa,
and me þin swyðre   sneome hælde.

8   Drihten for me   dome gylde,
is his mild-heortnes   mycel on worulde;
ne forseoh æfre,   þæt þu sylfa ær
mid þinum handum   her geworhtest.

Psalm 138

1   Þu min costadest   cynnum, Drihten,
and me ongeate   gleawe mode;
þu min setl   swylce oncneowe,
and minne ærist   æfter gecyðdest.

5   ⁴ Let all the kings of the earth acknowledge you, because they have heard in a sonorous voice the sublime words of your mouth; ⁵ let them sing then to the Lord in canticles,

6   because your glory is widespread throughout the world, ⁶ great and famous on this earth. Lord, you are highly exalted, as you regard from your heavenly home all the lowly here on earth.

7   ⁷ Though I should walk in the very heart of wickedness, where tribulations severely oppressed me, you always protected me from malicious enemies who desired to show their anger toward me; you quickly reached out to me with your hand, and your right hand swiftly saved me.

8   ⁸ May the Lord retaliate on my behalf with a verdict, his mercy is great, forever; do not ever despise what you yourself formerly created with your hands on this earth.

Psalm 138

1   ² Lord, you have rightly tested me, and with your penetrating mind understood who I am; you took note also of my sitting down, and revealed my subsequent rising up.

2   And mine geðohtas eac   þriste oncneowe,
feorran ongeate   fore mine,
and mine gangas   gearwe atreddest,
and ealle mine wegas   wel foresawe,
for þan me inwit næs   ahwær on tungan.

3   Efne, þu, Drihten,   eall oncneowe
þa ærestan,   eac þa nehstan;
þu me gehiwadest   handa þinre,
me ofer heafod   holde gesettest.

4   Wundorlic is geworden   þin wisdom eall,
se is beutan me   eac gestrangod;
ne mæg ic him on neode   a neah cuman.

5   Hwider mæg ic fram þinum gaste   gangan
                                       ahwær,
oþþe þinne andwlitan befleon   eorðan dæles?

6   Gif ic on heofenas up   hea astige,
þu me þær on efn   andweard sittest;
gif ic on helle gedo   hwyrft ænigne,
þu me æt byst   efne rihte.

7   Gif ic mine fiðeru gefo,   fleoge ær leohte,
oþ þæt ic beutan wese   eallum sæwum,

8   hwæt, me þin hand þyder   ofer holma begang
lædeð lustum,   and me lungre eft
þin seo swiðre   þær gehendeð.

9   Ic on mode cwæð   minum swylce:
"Wen is, þæt me þystru   ðearle forgripen
and me on nihte   neode onlihte,
þæt ic minum bleom   bregde neahhige."

2 ³ And you also knew my thoughts with confidence, recognized my course from afar, thoroughly investigated my excursions, ⁴ and clearly foresaw all my ways, because there was no deceit at all on my tongue.

3 ⁵ Truly! Lord, you knew all things, the furthest back and the most recent; you created me with your hand, placing it graciously on my head.

4 ⁶ All your knowledge has become a matter of wonder, and it has also become powerful outside me; yet with all my endeavor I am never able to get close to it.

5 ⁷ Where in any direction can I go from your spirit, or flee from your face to some part of the earth?

6 ⁸ If I ascend high into the heavens, you are sitting there physically present alongside me; if I make any detour to hell, you are right beside me.

7 ⁹ If I take wing, flying before dawn, until I am beyond all the seas,

8 ¹⁰ your hand will willingly lead me over the course of the waves to that place, and your right hand soon after will seize me there.

9 ¹¹ I said to myself as follows: "Perhaps darkness may overwhelm me with its might, and actively give me light at night such that I may frequently change my appearance."

10   Ne beoð þeostru deorc   butan þinre miht,
      þurh þa onlihtest niht   þæt heo byð dæge gelic.

11   Swa þragum gæð   þeostru wið leohte,
      for þon þu hi settest   swylce, Drihten,
      canst mine ædre   ealle gearuwe,
      onfenge me fægere,   swa ic furðum wæs
      of modur hrife   minre acenned.

12   Ic þe andette,   ece Drihten,
      for þon þu mid egesan eart   eall gewuldrad,
      and þine weorc wæron   wræclice swyþe,
      þa min saul oncneow   sona georne.

13   Nis min ban wið þe   deope behyded,
      þæt þu wislice   worhtest on diglum,
      þeh min lic-hama   lytle ðrage
      on niðer-dælum   eorðan wunige.

14   Eagan þine gesawon   þæt ic ealles wæs
      unfrom on ferhþe;   eall þæt forð heonan
      on þinum wisbocum   awriten standeð.

15   Dagas syndon trymede,   swa hi Drihten
                                            gesceop,
      ne mæg ænig on þam   awa lifigean;
      me synd arwyrðe   ealle swiðe,
      þe þine frynd wærun   fæste, Drihten,
      is heora ealdordom   ungemete swiðe
      on cneorissum   cuð gestrangod.

16   Gif ic hi recene nu   riman onginne,
      hi beoð ofer sand-corn   sniome manige;
      syþþan ic arise   and recene nu gyt

10   ¹² But darkness is not dark without the exercise of your power, by means of which you illuminate the night so that it resembles day.

11   Thus, darkness sometimes coexists with light, because you arranged them so, Lord, ¹³ you know me inside out, embraced me kindly, as soon as I was extracted from my mother's womb.

12   ¹⁴ I will acknowledge you, eternal Lord, because you are fully glorified in reverential awe, and your creations were exceedingly wonderful, which my soul recognized right away.

13   ¹⁵ My bones, which you expertly created in secret, are not really hidden from you, even though my body, after a short period, will dwell in the lower regions of the earth.

14   ¹⁶ Your eyes perceived that I was completely inert in spirit; all of that will stand recorded in your books of wisdom from here on.

15   The days are fixed just as the Lord arranged them, and nobody can live them forever; ¹⁷ those who were your steadfast friends, Lord, are exceptionally worthy of my respect, their rule is recognized as immensely strengthened through the generations.

16   ¹⁸ If I begin to enumerate them right now, they will quickly multiply beyond grains of sand; later I will rise up

mid þe sylfum eom,   gif þu syþþan wylt
þa firenfullan   fyllan mid deaðe.

17   Blod-hreowe weras,   ge bebugað me,
þe þæt on geþohtum   þenceað cweðende,
"Wutun þurh idel searu   ealle tiligean
þæt we heora burh   tobrecan moton."

18   Ealle þa þe feodan   þurh facen God,
ic hi feode nu   fæste mid niðe,
and ofer þine feondas beo   facne gebolgen.

19   Swa ic hi mid rihte   recene feoge,
for þon hi me feondas   fæcne wurdan.

20   Costa min, God,   swa hit cyn wese,
and minre heortan gehygd   her gesceawa,
þone fælan geþanc;   frine me syþþan
and mine stige ongit   gestaðelode.

21   And þu sylfa geseoh,   gif ic on swiculne weg
oþþe on unrihte   ahwær eode;
gelæd me þonne,   lifes Ealdor,
þæt ic on ecne weg   æghwær gange.

Psalm 139

1   Genere me wið niþe   on naman þinum
fram yfelum menn,   ece Drihten,
and fram þam were,   þe wom fremme.

and will still remain with you, [19] if you afterward desire to fell the wicked mortally.

17   Move away from me, you bloodthirsty men, [20] because in your thoughts you plot, saying, "Let us labor mightily for the power to destroy their city with a frivolous plot."

18   [21] I firmly hated at once with venom all those who hated God with spite, and 1 will vehemently vent my rage upon your enemies.

19   [22] So I promptly hate them with good reason, because they have become treacherous enemies to me.

20   [23] Test me, God, as may be appropriate, and scrutinize the thoughts of my heart and its good intentions here on earth; afterward interrogate me, and know my established paths.

21   [24] And see for yourself, if I have in any situation ventured on a false or unjust path; Lord of life, lead me then, so that I may walk entirely on the everlasting way.

Psalm 139

1   [2] In your name, eternal Lord, rescue me from enmity, from the evil person, and from the man who commits sins.

2   Þa ealne dæg   inwit and facen
hycgeað on heortan   þurh hearme geþoht;
hi þæt to gefeohte georne   gefremed habbað.

3   And heora tungan   torn-cwidum
neode serwað,   swa oft nædran doð,
and him aspidas   (ætrene wyrmas)
under welerum is   gewunad fæste.

4   Geheald þu me, Drihten,   wið hete-niðas
and wið firenfulles   folmum swylce;
and fram þam mannum   þe man fremmen,
alys þu me lungre,   lifes Ealdur.

5   Þa on hyge þohtan,   þæt hi ahyltan me
and minne gang   georne swylce;
forhyddan ofer-hygde me   inwit-gyrene,
wraðan wealsadan   wundnum rapum,
woldan mine fotas   gefæstnian,
settan me swyce,   þær ic siþade.

6   Ic þa to Drihtne cwæð: "Þu me eart dyre God;
gehyr min gebed,   halig Drihten,
nu ic stefne to þe   styrme hlude."

7   Drihten, Drihten,   þu eart gedefe mægen
hælo minre,   and þu min heafod scealt
on gefeoht-dæge   feondum awergean.

8   Ne alyf þu me æfre   ofer lust minne
on fyrenfulra   fæcne geðancas,
þa wiðerwearde me   wraðe hycgeað;
ne forlæt þu me   on lif-dagum,
þy læs hi ahafene ofer me   hwile weorðen.

2   ³ All through the day they ponder deceit and sin in hearts driven by malignant thoughts; they have enthusiastically done that by picking fights.

3   ⁴ And with offensive speech their tongues eagerly dissimulated, as serpents often do, and they are firmly habituated to asps (poisonous reptiles) lurking under their lips.

4   ⁵ Protect me, Lord, from hostilities and from the hands of the sinner also; and from those people who commit crimes, free me quickly, Lord of life.

5   ⁶ They eagerly decided in their minds to make me and also my steps stumble; those arrogant people concealed a treacherous snare for me, fastened nooses with twisted ropes, desiring to bind my feet, to set a snare for me wherever I went.

6   ⁷ Then I said to the Lord: "You are my beloved God; holy Lord, hear my prayer, now that I invoke you with a full voice."

7   ⁸ Lord, Lord, you are the proper power to save me, and you will protect my head from enemies in the day of battle.

8   ⁹ Never surrender me, against my wishes, to the treacherous designs of the wicked, who cruelly conspire against me; do not abandon me in my lifetime, lest they become exalted above me for a time.

9   Him ymb heafod   hefegast gewinna,
þæt hi mid welerum   geworht habbað,
him þæt ilce sceal   on gesittan.

10   Eac hi feallað   on fyres glede,
and þu hi mid fyre   facnes gehnegest,
þæt hi þam yrmðum   a ne wiðstanden.

11   Se getynga wer   on teosu-spræce,
ne bið se ofer eorþan   gereaht ahwær;
unsoðfæstne wer   yfel gecnysseð,
oþþe he on eorðan   eall forweorðeð.

12   Ic þæt gearuwe ongeat,   þæt gode deð
Drihten domas,   þe on dagum þyssum
wædlum weorðað,   wreceð þearfendra.

13   Soð is hwæðere,   soðfæste nu
þinne naman willað   þuruh neod herigean;
scylan eard niman   on þinre ansyne,
þa mid ræde her   rihte lifigeað.

Psalm 140

1   Ic þe, Drihten, to   dyrum clypige;
gehyr me hrædlice   holdre stefne,
þonne ic bene to þe   bidde ceare full.

2   Sy on þinre gesihþe   mines sylfes gebed
ful recene gereht,   swa ricels byð,
þonne hit gifre   gleda bærnað,

9   10 The most complicated plots circling in their heads, which they have articulated with their lips, are destined to haunt them.

10   11 Moreover, fiery coals will fall on them, and you will vanquish them with the flame of treachery, so that they may not withstand those miseries ever.

11   12 The man facile with hurtful speech will not be controlled anywhere on earth; evil will overwhelm the unjust man, until he totally perishes on earth.

12   13 I readily perceive that the Lord renders fair judgments, he who in these days will reward the needy and avenge the poor.

13   14 It is true, nevertheless, that the just in their distress will now be earnest in praising your name; those who live uprightly with good sense on earth are destined to take up residence in your sight.

Psalm 140

1   1 Lord, my beloved, I invoke you; hear me promptly with a gracious voice whenever, weighted down with worry, I make a request to you.

2   2 Let my own prayer be very speedily directed into your presence as incense, when greedy coals consume it,

3   swylce is ahafenes   handa minra,
    þonne ic þe æfen-lac   estum secge.

4   Sete swæse geheald   swylce, Drihten,
    muðe minum,   ne læt man sprecan,
    and æþele dor   ymb-standende,
    þæt on welerum   wisdom healde.

5   Ne hyld þu mine heortan,   þæt ic hearme word
    þuruh inwit-stæf   ut forlæte,
    and ic lædend wese   laðra firena.

6   Ne ic æfre mid mannum   man-fremmendum
    gemænnesse   micle hæbbe,
    ne on heora gecorenesse   becume æfre.

7   Ac me soðfæst   symble gerecce
    and mild-heorte   mode þreage;
    ele synfulra   æfre ne mote
    heafde minum   hrinan ahwær,

8   for þon min gebed nu gyt   becnum standeð,
    þæt him on wisum is   wel lycendlice.
    Syndon hi æt strangum   stane forswolgene;
    noldan heora deman   mine gedefe word
    earan gehyran,   eft ne mihton.

9   Swa unefne is   eorþe þicce
    (syndon þas moras   myclum asprotene),
    swa ure ban syndon   bitere toworpene
    be helwarena   hæfte-neodum.

10   For þon ic, Drihten, on þe   dædum minum,
    eagum and mode,   æghwær gelyfe,
    ne ascuf þu fram me   sawle mine.

3   and as the raising up of my hands, whenever I devoutly recite to you the evening service.

4   [3] Lord, set a benevolent watch on my mouth also, to prevent it from speaking evil, and also a well-made door circumventing it, to guard wisdom on my lips.

5   [4] Do not dispose my heart to release harmful words out of malice, so that I become an apologist for loathsome sins.

6   Nor may I ever share significant fellowship with people who commit crimes, or ever fall in with their chosen company.

7   [5] But may the just person direct me always, and chastise me in a gentle way; may the oil of sinners never be allowed to touch my head in any way,

8   because as yet my prayer is maintained with outward appearances so as to be very gratifying to them in conduct. [6] They are swallowed up beside a powerful rock; their judges did not want to listen to my righteous words, afterward they were not able to.

9   [7] Just as the earth's surface is unevenly dense (these raised bogs are thrown up abundantly), so our bones are cruelly strewn close to the prison of hell's inhabitants.

10   [8] Lord, since I believe entirely in you with my actions, eyes, and mind, do not banish my soul from me.

11   Geheald me wið þare gryne   þe me grame
                                               setton,
     þæt me ne beswice   syn-wyrcende,
     þa þe unrihtes   æghwær þenceað.

12   Feallað firenfulle   on heora feng-nettum;
     ic me syndrig eom,   oþ þæt ic swa fere.

Psalm 141

1   Min stefn to þe   styrmeð, Drihten,
     and ic mid strangere   stefne swylce
     eam biddende   bealde Drihten.

2   Ic mine bene   bealde swylce
     on his gesihðe   symble ageote,
     and mine earfeþu   ealle full georne
     fore him sylfum   sæcge geneahhe,

3   gif mine grame þenceað   gast teorian;
     and þu mine stige   strange ongeate.

4   On þyssum grenan wege,   þe ic gange on,
     me oferhydige   æghwær setton
     gearwe grine;   geara ic sceawade,
     geseah on þa swyðran,   ne me sylfne þær
     ænig mid gode   ongitan wolde.

5   Ða me eac frecne fram   fleam gedydan,
     næs þa þe mine sawle   secean wolde;

11 9 Protect me from the snare which they have cruelly set for me, so that the evildoers may not deceive me, those who plot evil everywhere.

12 10 The wicked will fall into their own net; I stand apart by myself, and so I pass on.

Psalm 141

1 2 My cry assaults you, Lord, while I am also boldly be-seeching the Lord with a powerful voice.

2 3 I will confidently pour out my petition in his sight constantly, and state frequently all my troubles most ear-nestly in his very presence,

3 4 even if my enemies plan to exhaust my soul; and you assuredly understood my path.

4 On this grassy road which I travel, the proud set traps everywhere in readiness for me; 5 I examined carefully, checked on the right hand, nor would anyone there ac-knowledge me with a kindness.

5 Moreover, they cruelly removed from me any means of escape, not one then would come looking for my soul; 6 then

þa ic to þe, Drihten,   digle cleopode
and sona cwæð: "Þu eart min se soða hiht,
eart þu on lifigendra   lande swylce
se gedefa dæl,   Drihten, æghwær."

6   Beheald mine sawle,   hæleþa wealdend,
for þon ic geeadmeded eom   ungemete swiðe;

7   alys me fram laþum,   hi me lungre synt
ealle ofer me   ungemete strange.

8   Alæd me of carcernes   cluse swylce
mine sawle,   þæt ic syþþan forð
þinne naman mote   neode sæcgean.

9   Min soðfæste   snotere bidað,
oþ þæt þu me edlean   eft forgylde.

Psalm 142

1   Drihten, min gebed   deore gehyre,
and mid earum onfoh   ungemetum georne
mine halsunge;   heald me syððan
on þinre soðfæstnesse   and me on soðe gehyr.

2   Ne ga þu mid þinum esne   in to dome,
for þon on þinre gesihðe ne bið   soðfæst ænig
þe on ðisse foldan   feorh-lif bereð.

3   For þon mine sawle   swiðe feondas
ealle ehtan   ungemete strange;

I secretly called out to you, Lord, and at once said: "Lord, you are my true hope, you are also my just portion everywhere in the land of the living."

6   [7] Ruler of men, attend to my soul, because I am humiliated beyond measure;

7   free me from hateful people, all of whom have suddenly become too strong for me.

8   [8] Release me and my soul also from the prison cell, so that from now on I can earnestly declare your name.

9   The just in their wisdom wait for me, until you once more reward me.

Psalm 142

1   [1] Lord, lovingly hear my prayer, and give ear most earnestly to my pleading; afterward maintain me in your truth, and hear me in your justice.

2   Do not enter into judgment with your servant, because in your sight no one living on this earth is justified.

3   [3] For all my enemies very strenuously persecuted my

habbað me gehnæged   heanne to eorðan
and min lif swylce   gelytlad is.

4   Hi me on digle   deorce stowe
settan sarlice   samed anlice,
swa þu woruld-deade   wrige mid foldan;
is me ænge gast   innan hreðres,
and me is heorte on   hearde gedrefed.

5   Þonne ic on mode   gemyndgade,
hu me ærran dagas   oft alumpan,
metegade on mode   ealle þine mæran weorc
and ymbe þine hand-geweorc   hogode georne.

6   Þonne ic mine handa to þe   holde þenede
and mine sawle   sette mid mode,
swa eorðan bið   ansyn wæteres;
gehyr me hrædlice,   hæl me syþþan.

7   Nu me deope is,   Drihten leofa,
min sylfes gast   swær geworden,
ne awend fram me,   wuldres Ealdur,
þine ansyne,   wese ic earmum gelic
þe on sweartne grund   syþþan astigað.

8   Gedo þæt ic gehyre   holde on morgene
þine mild-heortnesse,   mihtig Drihten,
for þon ic hycge to ðe,   helpe gelyfe.

9   Do me wegas wise,   þæt ic wite gearwe
on hwylcne ic gange   gleawe mode;
nu ic to Drihtnes   dome wille
mine sawle   settan geornast.

soul; they have abased me to the ground, and my life likewise is diminished.

4   At the same time they spitefully placed me in an obscure dark place, just as you might cover the dead of this world with earth; my spirit is afflicted within me, and my heart is severely troubled.

5   [5] Then I recalled in my mind how former times had often played out for me, meditated inwardly on all your famous works, and actively pondered on the works of your hand.

6   [6] Then I devoutly extended my hands to you and purposefully surrendered my soul, like earth parched for water; [7] speedily hear me, afterward save me.

7   Beloved Lord, now that my own soul has become profoundly sad on me, do not turn away your face from me, Lord of glory, or I may become like those wretches who later descend to the bottom of hell's dark pit.

8   [8] Mighty Lord, make me devoutly heed your mercy in the morning, because I hope in you, trusting in your help.

9   Make known to me the ways, so that I may readily perceive on which one I may proceed with a clear purpose; now I desire most earnestly to assign my soul to God's judgment.

10   Afyrr me, frea Drihten,   feondum minum,
    nu ic helpe to þe   holde gelyfe;
    lær me, hu ic þinne willan   wyrce and fremme,
    for þon þu min God eart,   þu me god dydest.

11   Me þin se goda gast   gleawe lædde,
    þæt ic on rihtne weg   reðne ferde;
    for naman þines   neod-weorðunge,
    Drihten usser,   do me halne,
    þæt ic on ðinum rihte   rædfæst lifige.

12   And þu of costunge   clæne alæddest
    sawle mine,   þær heo syððan forð
    on þinre mild-heortnesse   mote wunian;
    and þu mine feondas   fæcne todrife,
    and eac forleose   laðra gehwylcne
    þe mine sawle   synne ætfæsten,
    for þon ic þin esne eom   agen symble.

Psalm 143

1   Drihten is gebletsad,   min se deora God,
    þe mine handa   to hilde teah
    and mine fingras   to gefeohtanne.

2   He is mild-heortnes   min æt þearfe,
    frið and fultum,   fæst andfengea
    and alysend is   lifes mines.

10   ⁹ Lord God, remove me from my enemies, seeing that I faithfully believe in your help; ¹⁰ teach me how to do and accomplish your will, because you are my God, you have done good things for me.

11   That generous spirit of yours expertly led me, so that I journeyed on the right and just path; ¹¹ our Lord, on account of your fervent worshipping, save me, so that I may live my life wise in your justice.

12   And you led my soul out of trouble completely, to where it may dwell from then on ¹² in your mercy; and may you thoroughly dispel my enemies, and also destroy every hateful person who afflicts my soul with sin, because I am your very own servant always.

Psalm 143

1   ¹ The Lord is blessed, that beloved God of mine, who trained my hands to battle and my fingers to fight.

2   ² For me in need, he is my mercy, security, and help, the loyal defender and savior of my life.

3   Min þu mære eart   mihtig scyldend;
     ic hiht on ðe   hæbbe fæste,
     þæt þu me folc mænig   fægere underþeoddest.

4   Hwæt is se manna,   mihtig Drihten,
     þe þu him cuðlice   cyþan woldest,
     oððe mannes sunu,   þæt hit gemet wære,
     þæt þu him aht wið   æfre hæfdest?

5   Man byð merwe gesceaft,   mihtum idel;
     beoð his dagas swylce   demde gelice,
     swa þu on scimiendre   sceade locige.

6   Ahyld þine heofenas,   halig Drihten,
     onhrin þissum muntum,   and hi hraðe reocað.

7   Þine ligetta   leohtað and beorhtað,
     and þu hi toweorpest   wide æfter;
     synd þine strele   strange swylce,
     and ðu hi gedrefed hafast   deope syþþan.

8   Onsend þine handa   of heanessum,
     alys me and genere   wið lagu-streamum
     manegum wæterum   and wið man-folmum
     fremdra bearna   and frecenra,

9   þara muðas sprecað   man-idel word;
     bið hyra seo swiðre   symble abysgod,
     þæt hi unrihtes   elne tiligeað.

10   Ic niwlice   niwne cantic
     þam godan Gode   gleawne singe
     on *psalterio*   þe him swynsað oft
     mid tyn strengum   getogen hearpe,
     on þære þe ic þe singe   swiþe geneahhe.

3   You, the illustrious one, are my mighty protector; I steadfastly trust that you will successfully subjugate many peoples to me.

4   ³ Mighty Lord, what human being is there, such that you were willing to be made known familiarly to him, or a child of humankind, such that would justify your ever having anything to do with him?

5   ⁴ A human being is a frail construct, devoid of strength; its days likewise are judged to be like glancing at a shimmering shadow.

6   ⁵ Holy Lord, bend low your heavens, touch these mountains, and they will quickly vent smoke.

7   ⁶ Your flashes of lightning will illuminate and shine, and you will later dispel them widely; your arrows also are powerful, and you profoundly disturbed them afterward.

8   ⁷ Extend your hands from the heights, free and save me from the torrents of many waters and from the heinous hands of alien and dangerous people,

9   ⁸ whose mouths speak perjury; their right hand is always occupied with seeking boldly after iniquity.

10   ⁹ I will once more sing a new and wise canticle to that excellent God on the psaltery that often makes melody for him, a harp strung with ten strings, on which I will sing to you very devoutly.

11   Þu healdest and sylest   hælu cyningum;
þu alysdest eac   leofne Dauid,
þinne agenne   ombiht-mæcg,
of þam awyrgedan   wraðan sweorde.

12   Alys me and oðlæd   laþum wætrum,
manegum mere-streamum,   mærum handum,
þa me fremde bearn   fæcne syndan,

13   þara muðas sprecað   man-idel word;
byð hyra seo swiðre   symble abysgad,
þæt hi unrihtes   awa tiligean.

14   Þara bearn swylce   begað æþelum
settum beamum   samed anlice;
standað on staðule   stiðe wið geoguðe.

15   Wærun heora dohtru   deore gesette
and ymb frætwum   utan gegyrede,
efne anlicast   æþelum temple.

16   Heora frum-wæstme   fulle syndon,
þæt hi rumlice   roccettað swiðe,
of þissan on þæt   þonne wendað.

17   Heora sceap wærun   swylce tydred
and on siðfatum   swiþe genihtsum;
heora oxan eac   ungemete fætte.

18   Ne hreosað hi to hrusan   hearde gebiged,
ne þær fernes is   folca mænegum,
ne care micle   cleopiað on worðum.

11   ¹⁰ You give and maintain salvation for kings; you also rescued beloved David, your very own man servant, from the cursed, malignant sword.

12   ¹¹ Snatch and rescue me from hostile waters, that multitude of seawaters, from those notorious hands, when alien people behave very deceitfully toward me,

13   whose mouths speak perjury; their right hand is constantly occupied with seeking after iniquity.

14   ¹² Their children also incline quite like noble, planted trees; they are firmly upheld in stability from youth.

15   Their daughters were lovingly adorned and decked on the outside with ornaments, very like a noble temple.

16   ¹³ Their storehouses are full, so that they spill out very expansively, shifting then from this one to that.

17   Their sheep, likewise, were prolific, making many migrations to their pastures; ¹⁴ their oxen, moreover, were immeasurably fat.

18   They do not fall to the ground cruelly humiliated, nor do many of the people there experience passage, nor do they cry out with grievous sorrow in the streets.

19   Eadig bið þæt folc   (oðre hatað),
þe him swa on foldan   fægre limpeð;
eadig bið þæt folc   þe ælmihtig wile
Drihten God   dema weorðan.

Psalm 144

1   Ic me heahne God   hæbbe to kyninge,
and ic naman þinne   neode herige
on ecnesse   awa to worulde.

2   Þuruh syndrige dagas   symble ic ðe bletsige,
and naman þinne   neode herige
on ecnesse   awa to worulde.

3   Mycel is Drihten,   hine man mægene sceal
holde mode   herian swiðe;
nis his micel-modes   mægenes ende.

4   Cneorissa kynn   cwidum symble
þin weorc herigen   wordum georne,
and þine mihte eac   micle sæcgeon.

5   Mycel mod and strang   þines mægen-ðrymmes
and þine halignesse   holdes modes
wise wordum sprecað,   weredum secggeað
eall þin wundur   wide mære.

6   And hi mægen swylce   mære and egeslic
þinra wundra   wislic sæcgen
and þine mægen-strengðu   mærsien wide.

19   ¹⁵ That people is blessed (others call them so) for whom things work out comfortably on earth; blessed is that people for whom the Lord God, the almighty, will be judge.

Psalm 144

1   ¹ I will keep the illustrious God as my king, and I will zealously praise your name to eternity, always and forever.

2   ² Every day I will bless you continually, and will zealously praise your name, forever to eternity.

3   ³ Great is the Lord, he should be praised mightily with a devout disposition; there is no end to the potential of his magnanimity.

4   ⁴ Let generation after generation constantly praise your works enthusiastically in speech and words, and declare your great power also.

5   ⁵ They will describe wisely in words the intense and resolute temper of your majesty and the holiness of your gracious disposition, will declare far and wide to the multitudes all your celebrated wonders.

6   ⁶ And may they declare also the famed, terrifying, and wise power of your wonders, and make famous your great might far and wide.

7   Gemune þines modes   þa miclan geniht,
þinre weðnesse   wise sæcgenum
roccette   and ræd sprece,
and þine soðfæstnesse   sæcge geneahhe.

8   Mild-heort is Drihten   and mann-þwære
and geþyldig eac,   þearle mild-heort.

9   Swylce eallum is   ure Drihten
manna cynne   milde and bliðe;
syndan his miltsa   ofer us mære weorc
eall yldum cuð   awa to feore.

10   Andetten þe, Drihten,   ealle þine weorc
and þe þine þa halgan   her bletsien;

11   and hi þine mihte   manna bearnum
cyþan mid cynnum   and mid cneorissum,
þines mægen-þrymmes   mære wuldur,
riht and reðe,   rices þines.

12   Þæt þu cuð gedydest   ofer cneorisse,
þær synd manna bearn   manig ætsomne,
and þæt þin miht is   ofer middan-eard
and þines rices   rædfæst wuldur.

13   Rice is þin, Drihten,   ræde gefæstnod,
and þu woruld-ricum   wealdest eallum;
is þin anweald eac   ofer eorðware
of cynne on cynn   and on cneorissum.

14   Drihten is on wordum   dædum getreowe,
and on eallum his weorcum   wis and halig.

15   Ahefeð halig God   þa ðe hreosað ær,
and he ealle areceð   earme gebrocene.

7   7 Let him remember the great largesse of your mind, pour forth to those who can speak well the great generosity of your sweetness, and convey good counsel, and frequently declare your truth.

8   8 The Lord is compassionate, kind, long-suffering, and extremely merciful as well.

9   9 Our Lord is also gentle and agreeable to all human-kind; the excellent workings of his mercies for us are fully known to peoples, forever to eternity.

10   10 Lord, may all your works acknowledge you, and your holy ones bless you on earth;

11   11 and may they announce your might to humankind among the nations and their descendants, the sublime glory, fair and just, of your majesty and kingdom.

12   12 You made known to the people, wherever they huddle, both the ever-wise glory of your kingdom and that your power is present over the earth.

13   13 Lord, your kingdom is anchored by good counsel, and you govern all earthly kingdoms; your control also operates over earth's inhabitants from generation to generation, forever.

14   The Lord is faithful in words and actions, wise and holy in all his works.

15   14 Holy God lifts up those who fell just now, and raises up all the wretched who are shattered.

16   Eagan on þe   ealra, Drihten,
wisra gewenað   wiste to genihte,
and þu him mete sylest   mæla gehwylce,
and þæs tidlice   tid gemearcast.

17   Onhlidest ðu þine handa   and hi hraðe fyllest,
ealra wihta gehwam   wis bletsunga.

18   Soðfæst is Drihten   on his sylfes wegum
eallum on eorðan,   and he æfter þan
on his weorcum is   wis and halig.

19   Neah is Drihten   niþum eallum
þe hine mid soðe hige   seceað and ciegað,
and his willan her   wyrceað georne,
and his ege swylce   elne ræfnað;
he heora bene   bealde gehyreð
and hi hrædlice gedeð   hale sona.

20   Ealle gehealdeð   halig Drihten
þe lufan wið hine   lustum healdeð,
and he synfulle   swylce todrifeð
geond wid-wegas   wearnum ealle.

21   Sceal lof Drihtnes   on lust sprecan
min muð mannum   mæla gehwylce,
and flæsca gehwylc   þurh fæle word
his þone haligan naman   her bletsian
on ecnesse   awa to feore.

16   ¹⁵ Lord, the eyes of all the wise expect from you nourishment in abundance, and you give them food for every occasion, measuring its season opportunely.

17   ¹⁶ You open your hands and, ever wise, you quickly furnish them with blessings for each one of all living creatures.

18   ¹⁷ The Lord is just in all his very own ways on earth, and wise and holy in his works afterward.

19   ¹⁸ The Lord is close to all people who seek and call on him with genuine feelings, ¹⁹ earnestly do his will on earth, and also courageously maintain their fear of him; he will boldly listen to their prayer and soon speedily save them.

20   ²⁰ The holy Lord will protect all who gladly maintain their love for him, but he will also scatter in droves all sinners throughout the distant regions.

21   ²¹ My mouth shall declare with satisfaction the Lord's praise to people at every opportunity, and may all creatures bless in faithful words that holy name of his on earth, forever to eternity.

Psalm 145

1   Herige min sawl   hælend Drihten,
and ic on minum life   lustum Drihten
herige haligne   and holdum Gode
sealmas singe,   þenden ic sylf lifige.

2   Nelle ge on ealdur-menn   ane getreowian,
ne on manna bearn;   nis þær mycel hælu.

3   Heora gast gangeð,   gearwe onwendeð
on þa eorðan   þe hi of comon;
of þam sylfan dæge   syðþan forweorðað
ealle þa geþohtas   þe hi þohtan ær.

4   Þonne bið eadig   þe him æror wæs
Iacobes God   geara fultumiend,
and ær his hiht on God   hæfde fæste,

5   se þe heofon worhte,   hrusan swylce
and sidne sæ   samed ætgædere,
and ealle þa þe him on   ahwær syndon.

6   He his soðfæst word   swylce gehealdeð,
and on worulde his   wise domas
deð gedefe   þe her deorce ær
teonan manige   torne geþoledan;
syleð mete swylce   þe her murcne ær
hungur heaðu-grimne   heardne geþoledan.

7   Wreceð to ræde   rice Drihten
þara manna bearn   þe ær man gebræc;

Psalm 145

1 ² My soul, praise the savior Lord, while I, in my lifetime, will gladly praise the holy Lord and sing psalms to that gracious God, while I myself live.

2 May you refuse to trust only in a prince, ³ or in people; not much salvation lies in that direction.

3 ⁴ Their soul will depart, will certainly return to the earth from which they came; from that very day forward all the thoughts which they had previously entertained will perish.

4 ⁵ Then he will be blessed, to whom Jacob's God previously was a helper in days past, and who had firmly maintained his trust in God,

5 ⁶ who created heaven and earth also, the broad sea entirely, and all those things that exist anywhere in them.

6 ⁷ He also keeps his truthful word, and forever renders his wise judgments, favorable to those who had suffered many sad wrongs on earth; he gives food also to those who had endured on earth the misery of hunger, fierce and harsh.

7 The mighty Lord will avenge, to their advantage, the children of those who were earlier oppressed; likewise, the

swylce þa gefetredan   fægre Drihten
lungre alyseð   and him lif geofeð,
and blinde eac   bealde Drihten
on heora eagum   eft onleohteð;
soðfæste Drihten   swylce lufade.

8   Þa elðeodigan   ealle Drihten
lustum healdeð,   and lif geofeð
weodewum wencelum,   he hiom wel onfehð;
fyrenfulra weg   frecne toweorpeð.

9   Rixað mid ræde   rice Drihten
on ecnesse   awa to feore,
and þin, Sione, God   symble to worulde.

Psalm 146

1   Heriað Drihten,   he is heah and good;
singað him sealmas   swiðe geneahhe,
and hine wlitegum   wordum herigeað.

2   Eft Hierusalem   georne Drihten
timbreð tidum,   and to somnað
þa þe ut gewitan   of Israhelum.

3   Se hæleð eac   heortan geðræste,
and heora unrotnesse   ealle gewriðeð.

4   He recene mæg   riman steorran
and þa neodlice   be naman sona
full cuðlice   cigean ealle.

Lord will fittingly free the captives quickly and give them life, 8 and he will confidently restore sight to the blind besides; the Lord also cherished the just.

8   9 The Lord will gladly guard all strangers, and will bestow life on widows and children, embracing them warmly; but the way of sinners he will fiercely destroy.

9   10 That powerful Lord will rule with good judgment, forever to eternity, and your God, Zion, for all time.

Psalm 146

1   1 Praise the Lord, for he is supreme and good; sing psalms to him frequently, and praise him with eloquent words.

2   2 The Lord diligently rebuilds Jerusalem time and again, and gathers to her those exiled from Israel.

3   3 That hero has also afflicted hearts, but he will completely bind up their sorrow.

4   4 He is able to count the stars at a glance and very expertly call out all their names methodically at once.

5   Micel is ure   mihtig Drihten,
and his mægen is micel   and mihtum strang;
ne his snytru mæg   secgean ænig
on þyssum ealdre   æfre ariman.

6   Milde mode   and man-þwære
he onfehð fægere,   and fyrenfulle
wið eorðan niþer   ealle gehnegeð.

7   Onginnað ge Drihtne   geare andettan,
singað Gode urum   gleawe be hearpan,

8   se þe heofen þeceð   hadrum wolcnum,
and regn þanon   recene sendeð
þe þeos eorðe fram   æfter groweð.

9   He of beorgum ut   blæde lædeð,
hig to helpe   hæleða bearnum.

10   Se þe mete syleð   manegum neatum,
hrefnes briddum,   þonne heo hropende
him cigeað to   cuðes æses.

11   Nafast ðu to manna   mægene willan,
ne þe on þinum sele-gescotum   swiðe licað,
þeah þe weras wyrcean   wræst on eorðan;

12   ac wel licað   wuldres Drihtne,
þa þe hine him ondrædað   dædum and
                            wordum,
and on his milde mod   mægene gewenað.

5   5 Great is our mighty God, and great is his power, and exceptionally strong; nor can anyone describe his wisdom or ever quantify it in this world.

6   6 He graciously accepts those who are mild and gentle of disposition, but sinners he brings down to the ground entirely.

7   7 Begin to acknowledge the Lord promptly, sing well on the harp to our God,

8   8 who covers the heavens with bright clouds, and from there swiftly sends rain by which this earth flourishes afterward.

9   He produces grass from the mountains, hay as a support to humankind.

10   9 He who gives food to many kinds of cattle, to the raven's nestlings, when they call to him, screaming for familiar carrion.

11   10 You will have no desire for human power, nor do you enjoy very much to be in your tents, even though men on earth fashion elegant things;

12   11 rather, the Lord of glory is well pleased with those who fear him in words and deeds, and vigorously hope in his kind spirit.

Psalm 147

1   Herige Hierusalem   georne Drihten;
      here þu, Sion, swylce   þinne soðne God,

2   for þon he getrymede   wið teon-hete,
      þæt þu þine doru mihtest   bedon fæste,
      and gebletsade   bearna æghwylc
      þe on innan þe   ahwær wæren.

3   He þine gemæru   gemiclade,
      þu on ut-landum   ahtest sibbe;
      and þe gesadade   mid þy selestan
      hwæte-cynnes   holde lynde.

4   He his spræce hider   spowendlice
      on þas eorðan   ærest sendeð,
      and his word yrneð   wundrum sniome.

5   He snaw sendeð   samed anlice
      swa þu wulle flys   wolcnum bringe,
      and þone toweorpeð   wide swa æscean.

6   He his *cristallum*   cynnum sendeð,
      swylc swa hlaf-gebrece,   of heofon-wolcnum;
      for andwlitan celes   þær ænig ne mæg
      him standan   stiðe mode.

7   He his word sendeð   þuruh windes gast,
      blaweð beorhtlice,   burnan floweð,
      and to wætere   weorðeð sniome.

Psalm 147

1   [12] Jerusalem, eagerly praise the Lord; and you, Zion, also praise your true God,

2   [13] because he fortified you against the malice of hate, so that you were able to shut your doors firmly, and he blessed each of the children present anywhere within you.

3   [14] He expanded your frontiers, you gained peace in the borderlands; and he graciously satiated you with the finest fat of wheat.

4   [15] He first sends his speech successfully to this earth, and his word runs wonderfully fast.

5   [16] He sends snow, just as one might carry wooly fleece in balls, and scatters it widely like ashes.

6   [17] He fittingly sends his ice crystals from the clouds in heaven, like morsels of bread; in the face of that cold, no one there can withstand it with any determination.

7   [18] He sends his word in a gust of wind, which blows intensely, flows as a stream, and is quickly changed to water.

8   He his word eac   ær mid wisdome
    godum Iacobe   geara foresægde,
    and Israhele   eac his domas.

9   Ne dyde he ahwær swa   eldran cynne
    þæt he him his domas   digle gecydde.

Psalm 148

1   Heriað ge on heofenum   hælend Drihten,
    heriað hlude   on heanessum.

2   Heriað hine ealle   engla ðreatas,
    lofige hine swylce   eall his leod-mægen.

3   Herigen hine swylce   sunna and mona,
    æghwylc steorra   and þæt æðele leoht.

4   Heofenas hine heofena   herian georne,
    and þa wæter swylce   ðe ofer wolcnum synt
    on heofen-hame,   herigen Drihten.

5   For ðon he sylfa cwæð,   sona wærun
    wræclice geworht   wætera ðryþe,
    and gesceapene wærun,   þa he sylfa het.

6   Þa he on ecnesse   eall staðelade
    and on worulda woruld   wolde healdan;
    he sette bebod,   syþþan heo þæt heoldon.

7   Herigen dracan swylce   Drihten of eorðan,
    and ealle neowelnessa   herian naman Drihtnes,

8   [19] He had, moreover, proclaimed his word judiciously in olden days to virtuous Jacob, and his judgments also to Israel.

9   [20] He did not ever behave so toward people of an earlier time by revealing his judgments to them secretly.

Psalm 148

1   [1] Praise the savior Lord in the heavens, loudly praise him in the heights.

2   [2] Praise him, all the companies of angels, let all his angelic host likewise praise him.

3   [3] Let the sun and moon also praise him, each one of the stars and the brilliant light.

4   [4] Let the heavens' heavens enthusiastically praise him, and likewise those waters situated above the clouds in the celestial home, [5] let them praise the Lord.

5   Because he himself spoke, the forces of the waters were wondrously formed at once, and those things which he commanded took shape.

6   [6] He established fully those things forever and wished them to be maintained for all time; he imposed nature's decree, which they subsequently observed.

7   [7] Let dragons likewise praise the Lord from the earth, and may all the depths praise the name of the Lord,

8   fyr, forst, hægel   and gefeallen snaw,
is and yste,   ealra gastas
þe his word willað   wyrcean georne,

9   muntas and geswyru,   micle beamas,
þa þe mæst and wæstm   mannum bringað,
and on eallum cedrum   ciið alæded.

10   Deor and neat,   do þæt sniome,
nifle nædran cynn   be naman ealle,
and fugla cynn   fiðerum gescyrped;

11   eorð-cyningas eac,   ealle swylce
þe folcum her   fore wisien,
and ealdor-men   ahwær syndan,
and ealle þe þas eorþan   ahwær demeð.

12   Beon ge, hæge-stealdas   and glade fæmnan,
ealde and geonge,   ealle ætsamne
herian naman Drihtnes   mid neod-lofe,

13   for þon his anes nama   ofer ealle is
ahafen healice   hæleða ealra;
is upp ahafen   his andetness
heah ofer myclum   heofone and eorðan.

14   He horn hefeð   holdes folces,
he lofe leohteð   leofe þa halgan;
wese awa frið   on Israhela
fælum folce,   and hi forð heonan
on his neaweste   neode wunian.

8   ⁸ fire, frost, hail, and fallen snow, ice and storms, the life forces of all elements which eagerly desire to fulfill his word,

9   ⁹ mountains and hills, great trees, those which supply mast and fruit for humankind, and the bud produced in all the cedars.

10   ¹⁰ Let beasts and cattle praise him promptly, all the named species of the prone serpent, and fowl equipped with wings;

11   ¹¹ the kings of the earth, too, and also all who direct in the front rank the peoples on earth, and princes wherever they live, and all those who ever render judgments on this earth.

12   ¹² Young men and cheerful maidens, old and young, be as one in praising the Lord's name with enthusiastic worship,

13   ¹³ because his name alone is nobly exalted beyond that of all humankind; ¹⁴ the praise of him is raised high above the great firmament and the earth.

14   He raises the horn of the faithful people, he lights up with a song of praise those holy beloved ones; may peace always reign in Israel for a faithful people, and from now on may they eagerly dwell very close to him.

Psalm 149

1   Singað sam-heorte   sangas Drihtne,
      and him neowne sang   nu ða singað;
      wese his herenes   on haligra
      clænre cyricean   cyðed geneahhe.

2   Israhelas on hine   eac blissien,
      and Sione bearn   symble hihtan
      swiðust ealra ...

3   Herigen his naman   neode on ðreatum,
      on *timpano*   tidum heriað
      and on *psalterio*   singað georne,

4   for ðon on his folce is   fægere Drihtne
      wel licendlic,   and he wynlice
      þam man-þwærum syleð   mære hælu.

5   Þonne on wuldre gefeoð   wel þa halgan,
      beoð on heora husum   bliðe gedreme.

6   Him on gomum bið   Godes oft gemynd;
      heo þæs wislice   wynnum brucað,
      and sweord habbaþ   swylce on folmum,

7   mid þy hi wrecan þenceað   wraðum cynnum
      and ðrea þearle   þeodum eawan.

8   And hio bindan   balde þenceað
      cyningas on campum,   and cuðlice
      heora æðelingas don   on isene bendas,

Psalm 149

1   ¹ Sing songs to the Lord with one accord, and sing a new song to him at this time; may his praise be frequently reported in the hallowed assembly of the holy ones.

2   ² Let the Israelites also rejoice in him, and the sons of Zion exult always most of all . . .

3   ³ Let them zealously praise his name in choirs, render praise with the timbrel regularly, sing eagerly on the harp,

4   ⁴ because that noble Lord is truly pleased with his people, and he will joyfully bestow sublime salvation on the meek.

5   ⁵ Then the holy ones will fully rejoice in glory, will be blissfully happy in their houses.

6   ⁶ The memory of God will often be in their mouths; they will certainly relish that with joy, and they will also have a sword in their hands,

7   ⁷ with which they plan to take revenge on hostile peoples and with harshness chastise the peoples.

8   ⁸ And they boldly plan to bind kings in battles, and fetter their nobles publicly in iron chains,

9   þæt hio dom on him   deopne gecyðan,
    and þæt mid wuldre   awriten stande;
    þis is haligra wuldor   her on eorðan.

Psalm 150

1   Heriað on þam halgum   his holdne Drihten,
    heriað hine on his mægenes   mære hælu.

2   Heriað hine swylce   on his heah-mihtum,
    heriað hine æfter mode   his mægen-þrymmes.

3   Heriað hine on hleoðre   holdre beman . . .

9   [9] so that they may execute extreme judgment on them, a verdict which endures, inscribed triumphantly; this is the glory of the holy ones here on earth.

Psalm 150

1   [1] Praise the gracious Lord in his holy ones, praise him in the sublime security of his power.

2   [2] Praise him, likewise, in his lofty powers, praise him according to the temper of his majesty.

3   [3] Praise him in the sound of his trusty trumpet . . .

Abbreviations

Bright-Ramsay = James W. Bright and Robert L. Ramsay, eds., *Liber Psalmorum: The West-Saxon Psalms, Being the Prose Portion, or the "First Fifty," of the so-called Paris Psalter* (Boston, 1907)

B-T = Joseph Bosworth and T. Northcote Toller, eds., *An Anglo-Saxon Dictionary* (Oxford, 1882–1898)

BTS = T. Northcote Toller, ed., *An Anglo-Saxon Dictionary . . . Supplement* (Oxford, 1908–1972)

DOE = *Dictionary of Old English: A–G,* ed. Angus Cameron, Ashley Crandell Amos, and Antonette diPaolo Healey (Toronto, 2007).

Ga = the Gallican Psalter, ed. Robert Weber, *Biblia Sacra iuxta Vulgatam Versionem,* 2 vols., 2nd improved ed. (Stuttgart, 1975)

Grein = Christian W. M. Grein, ed., *Bibliothek der angelsächsischen Poesie,* vol. 2 (Göttingen, 1858). (The Paris Psalter, 147–276)

He = the Hebrew Psalter, ed. Robert Weber, *Biblia Sacra iuxta Vulgatam Versionem,* 2 vols., 2nd improved ed. (Stuttgart, 1975)

MS = manuscript

Pa = Paris Psalter (Paris, Bibliothèque nationale de France, Fonds latin MS 8824)

Ro = the Roman Psalter, ed. Robert Weber, *Le Psautier romain et les autres anciens psautiers latins,* Collectanea Biblica Latina 10 (Vatican City, 1953)

Vi = Vitellius Psalter (London, British Library, MS Cotton Vitellius E. xviii)

Note on the Texts

The text of the first fifty psalms, or the Prose Psalms, is based on the edition of O'Neill, *Prose Translation,* with significant changes to the punctuation to make the Old English harmonize as far as possible with the facing modern English translation. To supply the missing Old English text for the Introductions preceding the verses of Psalms 21 and 26, recourse is had to the text of the Vitellius Psalter, which also contains significant variant readings that are given in the Notes to the Texts.

For Psalms 51 to 150, the Metrical Psalms, the present edition broadly reproduces the text of Krapp, with some emendations and some rearrangements of the verses. The punctuation of the present edition differs from that of Krapp in two signficant respects. First, it emphasizes (by the use of the semicolon) the bipartite syntactical structure of many verses in the Latin of the Roman Psalter. Second, it allows more scope for run-ons between verses, where the meaning justifies it, while preserving their structural integrity as units of meaning (indicated by the spacing). The aim is to facilitate the flow of the Old English translation in a process evidently envisaged by its author.

In the two Old English texts of the present edition, the verses within each psalm are delimited and numbered to reflect their division in the Paris Psalter manuscript, in which each new verse is marked by means of a decorated initial. This system of numbering is the one conventionally employed by scholars of Old English when referring to these two works; for example, "Psalm 77.16" means the sixteenth verse (in the numbering of the Paris Psalter) of Psalm 77. However, the more pervasive system, used in modern editions of medieval Latin psalters (and commentaries), follows that of the Latin Vulgate Bible, so that "77.16" of the Old English has the corresponding Vulgate numbering "77:14" (with colon instead of period separating psalm and verse number). To help readers correlate the vernacular and Latin texts, the present edition provides both numbering systems in the facing translation, where the Vulgate (and Roman) numbering is entered as superscript numerals placed directly before the first word of their particular verse. The Vulgate text is available through the Dumbarton Oaks Medieval Library series in *The Vulgate Bible, Volume III: The Poetical Books* (for the full reference see the Bibliography). One should also note that the Vulgate numbering differs at several critical points from that found in the Authorized and Revised Versions of the Bible.

Notes to the Texts

Psalm 1

Intro: lacking in Pa and Vi
1 wol-bærendum: *Bright-Ramsay emends to* wolberendum   2 ac: *initial capital blotted*   4 þæt: *initial capital blotted*   7 hwylcne: hwylce

Psalm 2

Intro: he is: *erased in Pa but faintly visible (see the Notes to the Translations)*   hys: he ys *with punctum delens under* e

Psalm 3

Intro: manna: *omitted in Vi*   5 min: mid

Psalm 4

1 Þonne: *decorated initial missing*   8 and ealra: and ealra and ealra

Psalm 5

Intro: sylfes: sylfe
6 þu: *followed by erasure of six to seven letters at the end of the first column, probably* forsyhst   11 ne mægen: nægen

Psalm 6

Intro: lacking in Vi
3 to me: to to me

Psalm 7

Intro: þæ: *a blot on the upper part of the vertical stroke of* a *makes this reading uncertain*   teonode and wyrde: and *supplied;* od *underscored as if for deletion (see the Notes to the Translations)*   Geminis: Geniminis
6 on: of   ræs: sær

Psalm 8

Intro: lost in Vi   He cwæð: *entered by scribe as first words of verse 1*
8 fleogende: *decorated initial missing*

Psalm 9

Intro: on þa ylcan gerad: on ðæt ylce gerad *Vi, the reading adopted by Bright-Ramsay*
6 byrig: *supplied (see the Notes to the Translations)*   15 cuð: *supplied, following Bright-Ramsay, though after rather than before* Drihten; *Sisam* oncnawen   26 And: c *partially erased after* A, *perhaps originally intended for* Ac   29 sætað: settað *(as suggested by BT under* sætian *for the following verse)*   32 oð: on *(see the Notes to the Translations)*

Psalm 10

Intro: þer: þes   swa þer spearuwa: <. . .>wa deð hine *Vi, reconstructed by Bright-Ramsay as* <swa þes spearu>wa deð hine <sylfne>   þa *(3rd): Vi has* <. . .>oð *preceding, perhaps* doð
1 ge: *supplied, following Grattan*

Psalm 11

Intro: þa *(1st):* omitted in *Vi*   seofode: *Bright-Ramsay reads* geo<mro>de *in Vi, though only* de *is now visible*
1 tidum: didum   soðfæstnes: foðfæstnes   6 and *(1st):* Ac

Psalm 12

5 Þy: *decorated initial missing*   strengra: strenga

Psalm 13

Intro: seofað: <. . .>fað to *Vi*
10 min *(1st):* mine, *Bright-Ramsay emends to* mines   yrmingæs: e *of ligature* æ *added later, Bright-Ramsay emends to* yrminges   11 hæft-nyd: hæftAnyd, *decorator mistakenly inserted a colored initial* A *before* nyd, *the opening syllable of a new line and consequently did not supply an initial capital* B *before* lissie *of the next line (v. 12)*

Psalm 14

Intro: ecre: ec, *Bright-Ramsay emends to* ece
5 weorþað: þeowað, *with initial* þ *altered to* w, *medial* w *altered to* þ, *and* r *added above the line*

Psalm 15

1 þu me: hine   4 ic *(2nd):* cic *with punctum delens under first* c   5 yrfes: yr *added after* mines

Psalm 16

2 þone: þoñ   dom: dō,   3 to me: tome, *with* t *altered from* c; *misread by Bright-Ramsay as* come   9 ymbhringdon: *preceded by* be *underscored for deletion*   12 minra: mina   13 tostence: tostencte   15 æteawed: æeawed

Psalm 17

Intro: oþþe hine: *Bright-Ramsay conjectures that these words were omitted in Vi*
þonne *(2nd):* þa *Vi*
11 þystru: *supplied*   betwuh: betwū, *Bright-Ramsay* betwux   nære: *supplied, Bright-Ramsay supplies* wæs *(see the Notes to the Translations)*   12 wolcnu: *supplied*   ligetu: litegu   14 strælas: stræ   15 gehroren: gehropen
18 from: for   20 æfter *(1st):* æften   26 ofer-modena: ofermodenena
39 nan: *supplied*   40 swa swa *(1st):* ⁊ swa swa   48 ðe: ða

Psalm 18

3 gehyre: gyre, *Bright-Ramsay emends to* gyrre   4 ofer *(2nd):* fer, o *omitted, probably because the scribe mistakenly thought it should be an initial capital*   6 .i. ent: *written above* gigant *in same hand, but much smaller*

Psalm 19

Intro: gebæde: <...>bæd *Vi*   apostolas: *in Caroline script*
6 swyðran: swyðan

Psalm 20

Intro: hine singð *(2nd): apparently omitted in Vi*
3 on: *supplied*   4 þe: *omitted by Bright-Ramsay*   5 *folio 20v ends with* wul *(and parallel Ro* gloria), *see the Notes to the Translations*

Psalm 21

Intro: missing in Pa; Vi's reconstruction by Bright-Ramsay supplied in the edition (see the Notes to the Translations)
1 me *(2nd):* m *altered from* n, *and a blank space for about six letters between* m *and* e   5 leahtrunge: leahtungre   þer: þes   6 forsyhð: forforsyhð
11 þe: he   12 þær: *Bright-Ramsay emends to* þæt   13 nd min mægen ys *initially entered below the final line of verse 12, erased and partially rewritten on next line to bring it into alignment with the parallel Latin of verse 13*   15 gerimdon: gerimde

Psalm 22

Intro: alysnesse: <. . .> ysednesse *Vi, Bright-Ramsay,* <a>lysednesse

Psalm 23

1 gefyld: gefylð   3 þæs: þær   he: *supplied*   4 He: Ne

Psalm 24

Intro: of: on *Vi*   swa: <. . .>a þæt *Vi*   æfter *(2nd):* be *Pa,* æfter *Vi*
7 For þinre godnesse . . . rihtwis: *misplaced in the MS after* For þam . . . his
wegas *(the parallel Latin is in proper sequence)*   11 Swa: Hwa   13 cræft:
cræftig   16 And: *initial* A *supplied*   me gefriðie: mæge friðie

Psalm 25

9 *folio 26 ends with* unrihtwisnesse, *the folio following, containing the rest of
the psalm (vv. 11 and 12), is now lost*

Psalm 26

Intro: missing in Pa; Vi's reconstruction by Bright-Ramsay supplied in the edition
5 *paraphrase of the first two-thirds of this verse is missing*   7 min: miti   þin:
þi   offrunga: *a defining genitive possibly missing (see the Notes to the Translations)*

Psalm 27

Intro: singð: sing
7 ne: *supplied*   8 fultumend: scyltumend

Psalm 28

Intro: hi gelæston heora gehat: be <. . .> hyra geat *Vi*   sealdon, for, he *(1st),*
he *(2nd),* æt *(2nd): omitted Vi*
3 healle: ealle   5 ceder-treowu *(1st):* cecedertreowu

Psalm 29

Intro: he *(1st):* þe *Vi*
11 gehwyrfdest: *letter(s) erased after* ge   wite-hrægl: wlitehrægl *(Bright-Ramsay emends to* hwite hrægl)   begyrdst: bebyrgdst

Psalm 30

Intro: þe: þa, *Vi* þe   wurðan: geweorðan *Vi*
8 clemdes: *misread by Bright-Ramsay as* demdes *and emended to* demdest   15 for: or   20 leahtrunga: leahtungra   22 hi: *supplied*

Psalm 31

Intro: swa ylce he: *Bright-Ramsay reads* <. . .> æt ylce *in Vi*
5 helede: hedlede *with punctum delens under first* d *and vertical stroke (perhaps beginning of* l) *above it*   6 andettan: ꝥdettan   7 wæterena: *Bright-Ramsay emends to* wætera   toweardan: weardan   10 nan: *Bright-Ramsay omits*

Psalm 32

15 Þi: *Bright-Ramsay emends to* He

Psalm 33

10 welegan: *altered by scribe from* wædledon

Psalm 34

Intro: yrmða . . . ungelimp: *Vi has a fuller text, of which only* <. . .>ða ꝥ þ <. . .> fæ <. . .> geli <. . .> *is now visible, which Bright-Ramsay reconstructs as* yrmða and þæt ylce he eft *(?)* fægnode and tealde his *(?)* ungelimp   and eac *(2nd):* and *supplied*
1 Dem me: deme   4 þa *(2nd):* a *altered from* o, *Bright-Ramsay emends to* þe
9 Gefon: Gefo   13 wite-hrægl: hwitehrægl   17 angan: *Bright-Ramsay emends to* agnan   21 ealneh heora: ealne heora   26 smeað, sm- *written over ink blot*

618

Psalm 35

Intro: þysne *(1st): supplied from Vi*   þe *(3rd):* þa *Vi*   dydon: *Bright-Ramsay emends to* dyde

5 Drihten: rihten   mild-heortnes: mildheort   rihtwisnes: rihtwis   10 Læt: Læc   þæ: *originally* þa *with head and tongue of* e *added to back of* a *(Bright-Ramsay emends to* þe)   12 *Paraphrase ends abruptly at end of folio 40v with* ma, *which Bright-Ramsay expands as* magon standan

Psalm 36

Intro: þæt *(1st):* þæ

15 Betere: *initial* B *supplied*   26 Gecyr: *initial* G *supplied*   27 ecnesse: eenesse   29 Þa: *initial* Þ *supplied*   32 hawaþ: hopaþ   33 gesyhst: gesyht   36 læfð: lærð   38 Ac: Yc

Psalm 37

Intro: þæra: <. . .>re *Vi*   þæt ilce: þæt he ilce, *with* he *underscored and partially erased and* i *altered from* s   don: don on his ea <. . .> ðu <. . .> *Vi, read by Bright-Ramsay as* don on his earfoðum

6 unrot: ⁊ unrot   13 ne *(1st):* ne ne   15 ungemetlico: gemetlico   18 me: *supplied*   19 tælað: lætað

Psalm 38

Intro: þysan: þys

After the Introduction, the remainder of folio 45v, equivalent to nine lines, is left blank; a folio between folios 45 and 46, now missing, presumably contained the opening verses of Psalm 38 (Ro 2–6a) and the parallel Old English text   6 hit: hid   9 þære: þær

Psalm 39

Intro: alysnesse: <. . .> sednesse *Vi (Bright-Ramsay reads* alysednesse)

2 swiðe: stiðe   6 oflatan: oflata   13 þæra: þær   15 me arige: gearige

Psalm 40

2 Drihten: Drihtne *(editorial error in O'Neill, Prose Psalms)*   handa and andweald: hanweald *(see Notes to the Translations)*

Psalm 41

Intro: þara þe geswenced wære: þara þe geswence <. . .> wære *Vi*, þara geswenced *Pa,*
3 mine fynd cweþan: mine cweþan, *Bright-Ramsay emends to* to me cweþan
4 gemunde ic: gemunde   6 Hopa: *decorated initial missing*

Psalm 42

3 me *(1st):* þe

Psalm 43

Intro: he *(1st): omitted in Vi*
3 Þæt: *decorated initial missing*   fore-gengan: foregengena   swenctest: stenctest   7 beþurscon: bþurscon   21 Gif: *decorated initial missing*   23 For: *decorated initial missing*

Psalm 44

Intro: oferdrenct: oferdren, <. . .> dru <. . .> *Vi (Bright-Ramsay conjectures* oferdruncen)
3 weleras: weras   4 þe: he   17 apostolas: Aplas

Psalm 45

Intro: hatte: *supplied, Bright-Ramsay supplies* beoð   heregunge: herunge, <. . .>regu <. . .> *Vi*   Facces: Sacces
3 up ahafenan: upahafenas   þær: þer *with* e-*caudata, Bright-Ramsay emends to* þa

Psalm 46

Intro: lærde: he <. . .>e *Vi*

Psalm 47

Intro: wære: *supplied; Bright-Ramsay supplies* byð, *but after* gefriðod
7 he *(2nd):* hi

Psalm 48

18 man: *supplied*   19 þær: þæs

Psalm 49

Intro: sealme: *followed by erasure with space for ten letters*
13 ymb-hwyrft: ymbhyrft   21 broðor: *supplied*

Psalm 50

Intro: wæs *(1st):* he wæs *Vi*   Sancte Paule þam apostole: Scē PAULE þam
Apłe
6 min: mi   7 mænega: mægena   9 blissian: *marks the end of verse 9 at
the bottom of folio 63v; the remaining eleven verses of Psalm 50 (which ends at
50:21) are missing due to the loss of the two following folios*

METRICAL PSALMS

Psalm 51

*The two folios missing between 63 and 64 presumably contained the opening verses
of Psalm 51 in the metrical version, which now begins on folio 64r in the middle of
a verse corresponding to Ro 51:9. The numbering of the surviving Old English
verses (6–8) is conjectural, based on that of other English Ro Psalters.*

Psalm 52

1 gewordene: gewordenne 4 soð nan: socne 6 liste: lisne gehyrwede: gehyrnede

Psalm 53

6 niode: mode

Psalm 54

7 bete: bote modes: *supplied* 9 Þunie: Þume 10 man-sceat: ma scyte me: min *with* mi *altered to* me *and the minims of* n *used for first part of following* m (*of* min) 17 A: Þ 18 Þæt: *decorated initial missing* 19 adælde: todælde *with* t *marked for deletion and* o *altered to* a 22 soðe: seaðe *with first* e *partially erased and a hook above second* e 23 Se blodhreowa: Neblodheora ne: he

Psalm 55

5 on: ⁊ (= and)

Psalm 56

13 swylce: swylc

Psalm 57

8 Ær: *decorated initial missing*

Psalm 58

3 ofþryhtun: ofþryhtum 17 æghwær: æghær

Psalm 59

2 Eorðan: Forðan *(see the Notes to the Translations)*   ahrered: ahreded
3 Feala: Eeala   5 Do me: Þonne   on *(2nd)*: omitted

Psalm 60

5 he: *supplied*

Psalm 61

6 hælend: hældend   7 hælu: hæle   9 ilcan: *supplied*   11 wearnum:
wearmum   12 earnungum: earnung

Psalm 62

2 Min: *initial capital missing*   10 drihtne: driht   blisse: sibbe *with* be
altered to li, si *underlined for deletion and* sse *added*

Psalm 63

1 costunge: costunce   5 eft: oft   6 hælend: en *altered from* ig *and* d
added superscript

Psalm 64

4 hefeð: hafað *(see the Notes to the Translations)*   7 beoð: bið   11 cynnes:
cynne   13 geswiru: gespiru

Psalm 65

7 asecgean: asecgeað *with* ð *erased and* n *added after it*   8 ne: næ   læteð:
lætað   15 oþþe: oþ þa   16 Wealdend: wealden   17 strange: srange

Psalm 67

2 Rece: Sece   8 oððe: oðða   17 mænigfeald: mænigfeald mænigfeald
18 wæs: *supplied*   25 niode: mode   28 ðeoda: *remaining text lost with
missing folio (see the Notes to the Translations)*

Psalm 68

7 bidað: biddað   12 sæton: sæto   15 sæ-grundes: sęgrunges   19 ar
scame: *see the Notes to the Translations*   20 ænig: ænige   21 mengdan:
mengde   26 ecton: *supplied (see the Notes to the Translations)*   34 Herige:
decorated initial missing

Psalm 69

5 þine: þinæ   7 Þu: *decorated initial missing*

Psalm 70

2 þær: *emended to* þæt *by Krapp (see the Notes to the Translations)*   12 gedrecte: gedrette *(retained by Krapp; see the Notes to the Translations)*

Psalm 71

9 Hine: Þine   14 alysde: alysdon   16 up: us   17 eall: ealle
19 niode: mode *(retained by Krapp, but see Psalm 88:11)*

Psalm 72

4 beswungene: beswungenne   9 Hu: hu hu   11 me *(1st): supplied by
Krapp*   ænne: ænigne *with* ig *underscored for deletion*   ne: *supplied by
Krapp*   14 wendan: wendar

Psalm 73

6 gewemdan: gewemdað   7 gemot: *supplied by Grein*   9 ende: ęnde
14 adrigdest: adigdest   16 gesceafta: gesceafte   17 syle: syþe   18 nu
(2nd): hu   æghwær: æhwær

Psalm 74

2 fæstlicast: fæstlicas   8 forþam: fþam   9 þa: þo

Psalm 75

4 swæfun: sylfū   7 symbel-dæg: symbledæg *(see the Notes to the Translations)*

Psalm 76

3 gemyndgade: gemyndgadest   4 min: minę   9 þas: þeos   12 wiðferedes: wiðfæderas   14 wolcnas: wolcnes   15 Þonne: Þonni

Psalm 77

3 ealle: *decorated initial missing*   4 heora: heo   8 Gif: Fif   20 ne: *supplied by Grein*   25 manna *(1st)*: mannum   27 gefiðrade: gefriðade
31 In: *initial capital missing*   32 dædun: dædum   33 he: *supplied*
39 geon-cer: geomær *(see the Notes to the Translations)*   44 wæter: þær *(see
the Notes to the Translations)*   47 fornam: fornamon   49 æbyligðe: æb-
yligde   58 Swa hi his yrre oft: *written twice, the first time at the end of the
previous verse and with* wa *for* Swa   59 geðyde: gedyde   60 Selome: gelome *(see the Notes to the Translations)*   68 an-hornan: onhornan   71 hi
forð: *supplied by Krapp (see the Notes to the Translations)*

Psalm 78

1 ealh: heah   2 in: hi   5 Hu: *decorated initial missing*   10 þeoda:
þeodæ

Psalm 79

11 hi to: hit *(see the Notes to the Translations)*

Psalm 81

4 ge: He

Psalm 82

3 facen geswipere: facengeswipere, *Krapp (see the Notes to the Translations)*
6 Sele-gesceotu: Telege sceotu   Ismæhelita: isræhelita   swylce: *supplied by Grein*   8 wurdan: wurðan

Psalm 83

1 weorðe: leofe *with* l *altered to* w, f *to* r, *and* e *to* ð, *and final* e *added*   5 dene: dẹne   cnyssað: cnysseð   9 is: ic

Psalm 84

5 þin: þine   8 þam: aa *(see the Notes to the Translations)*   12 Hine: Þine

Psalm 85

15 geteoh: geseoh

Psalm 86

1 Healdað: Healdeð

Psalm 87

4 men: man   deadum: dædū   5 geworpene: geworpenne   11 Cwist þu . . . manna ænig: *on the relocation and renumbering of this verse, see the Notes to the Translations*   13 to: þo

Psalm 88

1 cynn: y *altered from* e   2 gearwad: gearwað   4 andettað: ꝺdettað   secgeað: seccgeað   11 niode: mode   12 þinre: þine *with superscript* r *inserted above* n   is: *located at end of second line by Krapp (see the Notes to the Translations)*   14 æghwær: æghær   17 ofermihtigne: ofermihtine   18 ele: *supplied (see the Notes to the Translations)*   22 bið: *supplied (see the Notes to the Translations)*   26 Ic: Ac   33 þonne: þonn   gewitnesse: ꝺgewitnesse

Psalm 89

3 bearnum: bearn   13 soð ne: *emended to* soð me *by Krapp (see the Notes to the Translations)*   15 hwæt-hwiga: hwæhwiga *with* a *altered from* u *(?)*   eað-bede: b *altered from* m *and a punctum under* d *(see the Notes to the Translations)*   17 þe we gesawon: þe we on gesawon, *Krapp*

Psalm 90

4 sceade: *superscript* scuan *(see the Notes to the Translations)*   14 niode: mode   16 geond: geon

Psalm 91

5 Won-hydig: Donhydig   7 heahesta: heahehsta   8 forweorþað: foweorþað   9 æghwær: æghær

Psalm 92

8 Huse: *decorated initial missing*

Psalm 93

8 ongeotan: *emended to* ongeotað *by Krapp*   16 wære: nære

Psalm 94

7 he *(2nd)*: þe

Psalm 95

3 fægere: fæger   11 Heofenas: *decorated initial missing*   13 Þonne: *decorated initial missing*

Psalm 98

3 æghwær: æghær   5 ellen-cræfte: ellencræfta   his: hit *with* s *altered from* t   6 Aaron: aarom

Psalm 99

3 andettað: ꝧdettað

Psalm 100

2 Ic: Ac   3 wyn-gesið: *followed by* fac *(of* facnes*) underlined for deletion*

Psalm 101

1 mære: mere   3 forswyrcende: forspyrcende *(see the Notes to the Translations)*   4 flæsce: flæcse   6 edwit-spræce on: edwit spræcon   12 þine: þina   þe: e *altered from* u   13 wise cyningas: wises cyninges   17 his: s *altered from* c   18 gebundene: gebundenne   21 his: is   gewis: s *altered from* t   standeð: standað   me ne meaht: me meaht *(see the Notes to the Translations)*

Psalm 102

6 eallum: ealle   þoliað: þoliaðn *with punctum delens under* ð *(see the Notes to the Translations)*   12 Swa: Hwa   æghwær: æghær   16 þa þe: þa þe þe   17 his: hit   healdað: healdeð

Psalm 103

2 wlite-andette: wlite ⁊dette   7 him: he him   swylce: swylce *followed by* swylc *underlined for deletion*   9 ba: bo   him: hi   11 ofer: of   16 lædað: lædeð   26 and him: Aan him *with superscript* d *inserted between the two words*

Psalm 104

1 cwyce: w *superscript above* c   3 blissað: blissiað   11 Næs: Wæs   31 æghwylc: æghylc   33 him *(1st)*: hi   40 heoldan: sceoldan

Psalm 105

3 æghwær: æghær *with superscript* w *above* h   4 Gemune: Gemunes *with* s *underlined for deletion*   11 him: hi   18 wundur: wundar   20 Ne: He   28 misdædum: middædum   36 geherede: generede

Psalm 106

1 mycel: myce   3 west-rodur: wes rodur   5 Dryhtne: dryhte   7 hi: he   9 gebundene: gebundenne   14 andettan: ⁊dettan   his: is   24 ætstandað: ætstandeð   26 forglendred: forgledred   28 him: hi   39 halige: haligne *with* n *underlined for deletion*   41 oncyrreð: oncyrrað   nemneð: *emended to* hemneð *by Krapp (see the Notes to the Translations)*

Psalm 107

6 standað: standeð   12 Us: Is

Psalm 108

3 teodan: teonan   16 geornust: geornus   18 yðde: ydwe, *emended to* ywde *by Krapp (see the Notes to the Translations)*   19 ðe: se ðe   24 Me synt cneowu: Me synt cneowu e synt cneowu

Psalm 110

2 mægen-þrymnes: mægenþrymmes   4 miclum: *supplied by Grein*
5 Ys: Y *altered from* U *by the decorator*

Psalm 111

3 Him: *decorated initial missing*

Psalm 113

6 gesweoru: gesweoru swa *with* swa *underlined for deletion*   15 hio: hio
hio   23 moldan: old *altered from* an

Psalm 114

3 Sar: Þar *(see the Notes to the Translations)*   ætfealh: ætfeah *(see the Notes to the Translations)*

Psalm 115

4 hæbbe: hebbe

Psalm 116

2 ece: *supplied*

Psalm 117

3 mild-heortnys: mildheortnys is   4 mild-heortnys: mildheortnys ys
5 heare: hearr   11 me *(2nd)*: *supplied*   nama: naman   18 Me: Se *(see the Notes to the Translations)*   24 mærum: mæreim   25 us: ut

Psalm 118

2 innancundum: innandundum   heortan: an *altered from* um   7 Ic: *decorated initial missing*   9 rihtran þe: rihtan ne   15 on: *supplied*   23 soðe:

þęode *with* þ *altered to* s *and* d *to* ð   26 soðfæstnysse: soðfæsnysse
37 læs: læc   38 þinre: þine   41 dryhten: dryhtnes   45 bealde: bealdu
55 nihta: mihta   67 gewurde: gewurðe   þinre: þine   68 eart: eard
71 seftre: seftra   102 Na: Þa   104 feode: ofeode *(see the Notes to the
Translations)*   114 and andfenga: ꝸandfenga   122 Onfoh: *decorated initial missing*   136 æ-bebod: æ bebod, *Krapp*   139 ealles forgeaton . . . me
wa dydon: *on the relocation of these two lines, see the Notes to the Translations*   142 æðelnes: æðeles   150 unneah: ungeneah *with* ge *underlined
for deletion*   gewiten: gewitan   153 geseoh: geseah   161 earwunga:
eawunga   164 lustlice: lustice   167 gewitnesse: gewitness þinre *with*
þinre *underlined for deletion*   lufade: lufa

Psalm 119

5 þe: he   6 spræce: spræc, *not noted by Krapp*

Psalm 120

6 minne: min ne *(see the Notes to the Translations)*   gehealde: gealde

Psalm 121

4 sceoldon: sealdon   6 geniht: gege niht

Psalm 122

5 sawle: sawl *(see the Notes to the Translations)*

Psalm 124

4 healdað: healdeð

Psalm 126

1 winnað: wuniað   2 wæccende: wæccend

Psalm 127

1 Eadige syndon: Eadige beoð syndon

Psalm 129

7 is: his   8 æghwær: æghwæ

Psalm 131

12 þines: þine   þa *(1st)*: we   þa *(2nd)*: *emended to* þe *by Krapp*   17 Ic: Ec
(see the Notes to the Translations)   19 minra: minre

Psalm 133

2 begangað: begangeð   4 Þe: Ge *(see the Notes to the Translations)*

Psalm 134

9 fæle: fala   18 feala: fea   21 Lefes: lifes *(retained by Krapp)*

Psalm 135

7 He: *decorated initial missing*   9 on: *decorated initial missing*   miht nihte:
mihte niht   10 He . . . and: *preceded by a line of erased text, possibly a misplaced version of itself*   11 and: *decorated initial missing*   19 and: *decorated
initial missing*   23 and: Oþ   26 flæscea: flæcsea

Psalm 136

3 woh: *supplied, as in Krapp*   9 seteð: seceð

Psalm 137

5 kyningas: kyniningas   6 þin: *supplied*   wuldur: wundur   8 gylde, is:
h *superscript inserted between the two words and then erased*   his: *superscript
(see previous note)*

Psalm 138

3 me *(1st)*: *supplied*   4 wisdom: wis *altered from* wor   11 of modur hrife minre: of minre modur hrife   12 andette: andetne   ece: ece ece 14 Eagan: eagon

Psalm 139

2 heortan: heortað   georne gefremed: ge *(2nd) superscript between the two words*   5 wundnum: wundrum   rapum: rawum   swyce: swyþe 7 heafod: *supplied*   11 gecnysseð: gecnyssed

Psalm 140

3 is: ic   4 Sete: Gete   ymb-standende: ymstandende   5 þæt: þær 7 Ac: Ic   9 hæfte-neodum: hæfteneodun

Psalm 142

4 ænge: ænige   5 on mode ealle: on mode hu ealle   11 Me: *decorated initial missing*

Psalm 143

2 He: Me   5 Man: Þan   7 leohtað: leohteð   beorhtað: beorhteð   9 unrihtes elne: rihtes un elne   11 ombiht-mæcg: ombihtmæcgum   14 standað: standan   18 mænegum: m *(1st) superscript*   worðum: wordum   19 Drihten: drih

Psalm 144

6 mægen-strengðu: mæge strengðu   9 syndan: syndas   17 Onhlidest: On þhlidest   19 ege: hyge

Psalm 145

6 teonan: teonam   mete swylce: te *superscript, inserted between* me *and* swylce

Psalm 146

5 Micel: Rice *(see the Notes to the Translations)*   6 and man-þwære he on-fehð: ⁊ he manþwære onfehð   9 hig: hio   11 Nafast: Hafast

Psalm 147

2 æghwylc: æghylc   5 þone: þonne   6 ænig: æni

Psalm 148

5 wræclice: wlæclice   9 ciið: cuð   alæded: alædeð   11 eorð-cyningas: Forðcyningas *with* F *altered to* E *by addition of lower horizontal stroke*

Psalm 149

1 cyðed: cyðe   8 on *(2nd): supplied*   9 wuldor: *supplied*

Notes to the Translations

PROSE PSALMS

Psalm 1

Although lacking an Introduction with its interpretative guidelines, the paraphrase shows a strong bias toward a moral interpretation of this psalm, no doubt influenced by its contents. In keeping with this approach, Latin perfects are rendered by Old English present tense verbs (*gæð, stent, byð,* vv. 1 and 2), which serve to make the actions of the psalm applicable to contemporary readers.

Psalm 2

Interpretation is historical, in accordance with the first clause of the Introduction; note the literal translation of *christum* as "him whom he chose and anointed as ruler" (*þam þe he to hlaforde geceas and gesmyrede,* v. 2), where *hlaford* denotes a secular lord. This historical (Davidic) approach is remarkable for a psalm that was almost universally interpreted as Messianic by medieval commentators. The words *he is* in the Introduction, although erased in the Paris manuscript (Pa), are restored here because they provide a required subject and verb for *gecweden,* and are also attested in the Vitellius copy of the Introductions.

Psalm 3

Interpretation is historical, in accordance with the first clause of the Introduction, as suggested by the rubric, which presents David as the speaker of the paraphrase, as well as by the absence in the latter of allegorical interpretations.

5   Sisam, "Notes," 474–75, suggests emending *ymbþringen* (throng about) to *ymbhringen* (surround), since the latter normally translates Ro *circumdantis,* but the manuscript reading makes good contextual sense.

Psalm 4

Interpretation is historical, but not as directed in the first clause of the Introduction; instead, the psalm is read as David's reproach to his people for their refusal to acknowledge God's gifts to them. The words of the biblical *titulus, psalmus cantici Dauid,* are taken by the paraphrast to mean that David sang this psalm aloud with the choir.

3   *wið gode* could mean "to good" or "to God "— or both.
4   The rendering of Ro *sanctum* by *his ðone gehalgodan* (his consecrated one) points to David as king.
5   The treatment of Ro *conpungimini* (be sorry) as involving a twofold process of abandoning (*forlætað*) and repenting of (*hreowsiað*) sin has a close parallel in Alfred's translation of Pope Gregory's *Pastoral Care;* see O'Neill, *Prose Translation,* 87.
8   "wheat . . . in abundance": *geniht hwætes* is closer to Ga *a fructu frumenti* than to Ro *a tempore frumenti.*

Psalm 5

A moral interpretation, the struggle of the just against the wicked, yet paraphrased so as to be equally applicable to all four personae and interpretations of the Introduction.

Psalm 6

The paraphrase is couched in such general terms as to be applicable to any of the four interpretations given in the Introduction, whose first (Davidic) clause is itself a summation of the other three interpretations.

Psalm 7

Historical interpretation for verses 1–6, in accordance with first clause of the Introduction (see 2 Samuel 15–16), and moral for verses 7–17, in accordance with the second clause of the Introduction. The emendation of the manuscript reading *teonode wyrde* to *teonode and wyr(g)de,* "abused and cursed" (first suggested by B-T under *teonian*) accords well with both *maledicens* of the biblical account (2 Samuel 16:13) and the paraphrast's predilection for verbal collocations.

6   *Aris . . . on þinum yrre, and ræs* (in your anger arise and launch an attack): *of* emended to *on* (as suggested by Sisam, "Notes," 475); and *sær* to *ræs* (rush upon, attack). B-T *sær* suggests *rær* (raise up) as a possibility, which, although it harmonizes with Ro *exaltare,* is never employed in the present work to translate that verb

       on minre feonda mearce (on the borders of my enemies): evidently based on Ga *in finibus inimicorum meorum* (Ro *in finibus inimicorum tuorum*).

13   The manuscript at this point in the text (folio 6r) has an ink drawing of the devil releasing two arrows at an amorous couple embracing inside a bower, no doubt a reference to "those on earth who are consumed by licentiousness and vices" of the paraphrase.

Psalm 8

Davidic, in accordance with the interpretation of the first clause of the Introduction; note the elaboration of Ro *uisitas* by *oftrædlice neosast* (you frequently visit, v. 5), which seems to rule out God's unique visit to humankind at the Incarnation (as proposed in the second interpretation).

Psalm 9

A historical interpretation (as enunciated in the first clause) for verses 1–17, and moral (as in the second clause) for verses 18–38; see verse 14, with its mention of evil contemplated, but not effected, which reflects the first clause.

6   The suggested emendation of MS *geteorode* (failed) to *geleorode*
     (passed away), although suitable in meaning, is quite unneces-
     sary; see B-T headword *geleoran,* where *geleorode* is incorrectly
     given as the manuscript reading.

     heora byrig (their cities): on the evidence of Ro *civitates eorum,* it
     appears that some noun corresponding to *civitates* is needed
     after *heora;* Bright-Ramsay supplies *ceastra,* which, although
     suitable in grammar and meaning, does not match the para-
     phrast's word choice for this concept; consequently, *byrig* is
     supplied.

30   *gefangen hafað* (has caught) seems closer to Ga *adtrahit* than Ro
     abstrahit.

32   *oð ende* (to the end): the emendation of *on* to *oð* accords with
     other translations in the paraphrase of Ro *in finem,* and besides
     matches the context of the poor man who needs help that is
     prolonged up to (rather than at) the time of his death.

Psalm 10

A historical interpretation in accordance with the first clause of the Introduction.

1   *Hwy lære ge* (Why do you advise): the addition of *ge,* suggested
     by Grattan, "Text," 187, not only supplies a direct subject but
     also explains the reduced ending on present plural *lære.*

Psalm 11

Moral interpretation, as proposed in the first clause of the Introduction,
with David commenting on the immorality of his times. Note the pervasive change of Ro perfect to Old English present tense verbs (e.g., vv. 2, 4,
and 9) and the addition "in these times" (v. 1).

3   *þa oferspræcan and þa yfel-spræcan tungan* (those boastful and those
     malicious tongues) evidently conflates Ga *linguam magniloquam*
     and Ro *linguam maliloquam,* respectively.

6   *and hi sette* (and nestle them): *ac* (probably a dittography)

emended to *and,* provides a smoother (and more logical) link
with *arise* of the preceding verse.

Psalm 12

A literal rendering that could reflect any of the four interpretations.

5   the emendation of *strenga* to comparative *strengra* (stronger) is
supported by the following *ponne* (than), as well as Ro *praevalui
adversus eum,* which implies a comparison.

Psalm 13

Historical interpretation, applied to Hezekiah, as proposed in the final
clause of the Introduction; note the elaboration of Ro *ubi non erat timor* by
ponne hi læst wenað, ege and ungelimp (terror and misfortune . . . when they
least expect it, v. 9), where *ungelimp* probably refers to the sudden catastro-
phe that struck the Assyrian army (4 Kings 19:35).

1   Sisam, "Notes," 475, proposed emending *unrihtwisa* (the wicked
one) to *unwisa* (the foolish one), no doubt on the evidence of
Ro *insipiens,* but since the subject's statement implies willful insouciance about God's existence, the manuscript reading can
stand.

       on heora won willan: Campbell in *Enlarged Addenda and Corri-
genda to BTS,* under *wanwilla,* would read *on heora wonwillan* (in
their willfulness), but the first element of the putative compound is privative, thus "lacking in will." Read *won* as accu-
sative/dative singular of *woh,* qualifying *willan,* hence "in their
perverse desire."

5   The syntax of *peah hi fægere sprecon* (though they speak pleasantly), which caused problems for previous editors (see O'Neill,
Prose Translation, 188), can readily be resolved by treating it as a
koinon to the clause preceding and following, in an *apo koinou*
construction.

10   *Hwi gedrefe ge* (why do you trouble) parallels in its plural form Ga
confudistis (Ro *confudisti*).

639

mine is emended to *min*, genitive singular of the personal pronoun in apposition to *yrmingæs*, both dependent genitives of *geþeaht* (that counsel of mine, one of no account). Bright-Ramsay's *mines*, qualifying *yrmingæs*, would make the latter someone other than the speaker and thus contradict the final clause of the sentence, which identifies *geþeaht* as the counsel of the psalmist himself.

Psalm 14

Moral interpretation in accordance with the third clause of the Introduction, as suggested by the change of Ro perfect into Old English present verbs (e.g., *deð*, v. 4; *hæfð*, v. 5; *syleð*, v. 6) to reflect the unchanging code of conduct proposed by the psalmist.

Psalm 15

The interpretation follows the Davidic theme of the first clause; note the renderings of Ro *hereditatem meam* by *min rice* (my kingdom, v. 5) and Ro *sanctum tuum* by *þinne gehalgodan* (the one consecrated to you, v. 10*)*, both clear references to David as anointed king.

11   *beforan þinre ansyne* (in your presence): compare He *ante vultum*
        tuum (Ro *cum vultu suo*).

Psalm 16

Interpretation follows the first clause of the Introduction, as evident from explicit references to the huge army (*heora menigo*, their multitude, v. 13) of David's enemies led by Saul (*þam unrihtan wisan*, that wicked leader, v. 12); see 1 Samuel 23–24.

12   *(æt þam) unrihtan wisan* (from that wicked leader): although
        the emendation proposed by Sisam ("Notes," 475), *unrihtwisan*
        (the wicked one), seems plausible and also accords with Ro

impio, the manuscript reading *wisan* (leader), referring to Saul, accords with historical Antiochene commentary; see O'Neill, *Prose Translation,* 195.

Psalm 17

Historical interpretation, in accordance with the first clause of the Introduction, reinforced by additional references to David's enemies (vv. 4, 7, 11, 28, 38, and 45), Saul specifically (see note on v. 38, below). At the same time the first clause presents David as reminiscing about past favors from God, hence the rendering of Ro present and future verbs as Old English preterites in verses 36, 40, 45, and 46.

11 *þystru* (darkness, Ro *tenebras*) supplied, as suggested by Bright-Ramsay, but in place of their addition of *wæs* (was) before *næfre gesewen* (was never visible), I have preferred subjunctive *nære,* on grounds both of syntax and likely scribal confusion with *næfre;* see O'Neill, *Prose Translation,* 197.

12 supplying *wolcnu* (clouds, Ro *nubes*), as suggested by Sisam, "Notes," 475.

14 *strælas* (arrows): the missing final syllable in the manuscript was presumably lost as the copyist moved from one line to the next.

15 the emendation of *gehropen* to *gehroren* (caved in) was suggested by Bright and Ramsay, "Notes," 473.

18 the emendation of *for* to *from* (from) suggested by Sisam, "Notes," 475.

29 *ælces þara þe him to hopað* (of everyone who trusts in him) is closer to Ga *sperantium in eum* than Ro *sp. in se.*

38 *þu ... me hine gesealdest* (you ... gave him over to me): an addition that probably refers to the occasion when David stole into Saul's camp while he was sleeping (1 Kings 26:7).

39 the editorial addition of *nan* (not one) accords with the partitive gen *þara* that follows and is consistent with the paraphrast's use of the same collocation at Psalms 24.2 and 39.5.

Psalm 18

Moral interpretation, in accordance with the single interpretative clause proposed in the Introduction and spoken by David.

3   *gehyre,* (hear, Ro *audientur*), the emendation of *gyre* proposed by Grattan, "Text," 187.

6   *on hyre weg/on his weg* (on its course/on his way) accords better with Ga *viam suam* (Ro *viam*).

     .i. ent was read by Bright-Ramsay as an alternative spelling of the second syllable of *gig-ant,* above which it is located in smaller script, though by the same scribe. More likely it is the independent noun *ent* (giant) glossing *gigant,* as suggested by its introductory *id est.*

     oð (þæs heofenes heanesse), "as far as," suggests the influence of the Old Latin reading *ad* rather than Ro *a (summo caelo).*

Psalm 19

Historical interpretation, but couched in such general terms as to make it difficult to determine whether it was shaped by the first or the second historical clause of the Introduction. The latter seems more likely given the directive of the Introduction's source to follow that interpretation, as well as the reference to the enemy's boasting of its military strength in verse 7, which recalls the huge Assyrian army that besieged Hezekiah (4 Kings 18–19). The psalm seems to be spoken by the Jewish people about their king (David or Hezekiah), as directed by the Introduction.

Psalm 20

Historical interpretation, in line with the second clause, as suggested by references to events of Hezekiah's reign, notably God's swift revenge on his enemies (v. 3) and the king's desire for a long life (v. 4). As in Psalm 19, the speaker of the paraphrase seems to be the Jewish people.

4   *he þe bæd* (he asked you) accords better with Ga *petiit a te* than Ro *petiit.*

5   the incomplete *his wul* is probably part of *his wuldor,* "his glory"
(Ro *gloria eius*).

Psalm 21

Although the Introduction is missing in the main manuscript (Pa), its framework survives in Vi, from which Bright-Ramsay reconstructed the text of the Introduction supplied in the present edition. For an accurate edition of Vi's fragments, see Pulsiano, "Old English Introductions," 20.

The interpretation is historical, in general accord with the first clause of the Introduction, though with a particular focus on David's struggle against Absalom. Note the translation of Ro *ipsi* (v. 15) by *mine getrywan frynd* (my "trustworthy" friends), probably referring to those who abandoned David for Absalom and who are described at verse 10 as *niwe fynd* (recent enemies). Remarkably, the paraphrase shows no evidence of the conventional medieval interpretation of this psalm as referring to Christ's passion and crucifixion; David is the protagonist, as suggested by the speaker's reference to his sins, *mine scylda* (v. 2).

15   Grattan's, "Text," 187, emendation of *gerimde* to *gerimdon* (they
           counted) is supported by the plural agent of the verse as well as
           by Ro *dinumeraverunt;* his alternative suggestion, *synt gerimde,* is
           less plausible on contextual grounds.

27   *cumað* (will enter) has a close parallel in Old Latin *procedunt* (Ro
           procident).

Psalm 22

The interpretation is historical (but not Davidic), as directed in the first clause of the Introduction, which relates the psalm to the Babylonian Captivity.

7   *þin folc* (your people) is usually explained as a misreading of Ro
           poculum as *populum,* but more likely it is a deliberate authorial
           modification to bring the verse into conformity with the sub-
           ject of the psalm (and the Introduction), the Jewish people in
           exile.

Psalm 23

The interpretation of verses 1–6 is moral, following the first clause of the Introduction, while that of verses 7–10 is historical (Davidic), in accordance with the final (third) clause of the Introduction.

8   The use of *hlaford* to translate Ro *Dominus* indicates that the paraphrast had in mind a secular lord (David) rather than the deity, which would have been rendered by *Drihten*.

Psalm 24

No clear interpretative line is evident, though verbal echoes of the first (historical) clause of the Introduction are found in verses 12, *his sawl hi gerest softe* (his soul will dwell without disturbance), and 20, *wilnode* (desired).

7   The scribe mistakenly entered this verse after the present verse 8, no doubt misled by the parallel Latin text in which the two successive verses begin with Ro *propter.*

11   Although MS *hwa* (retained by earlier editors) might seem to be a more accurate translation of Ro *quis,* the emendation *swa* is indicated by its correlative relationship with the *swa* following, as suggested by Sisam, "Notes," 475.

13   Other examples of the collocation *mægen and cræft,* "strength and power" (at Psalms 17.3, 17.37, and 37.9), lend support to the emendation of MS *cræftig* to *cræft,* first suggested by Sisam, "Notes," 475.

16   *tobræd and gemanigfealdod* (enlarged and multiplied) is probably a conflation of Ro *dilatatae* and the corresponding Ga *multiplicatae.*

Psalm 25

Follows a historical, probably Davidic, interpretation as enunciated in the first clause of the Introduction; note the verbal agreement between the latter and the first half of verse 1.

1   *þas mine fynd* (these enemies of mine), with its marked deictic
     probably refers to David's son and the false counselors men-
     tioned in the Introduction, in contradistinction to David's
     regular enemies.

Psalm 26

The Introduction, which is lacking in Pa, has been partially reconstructed
from the surviving fragment in Vi by Bright-Ramsay, whose text is supplied in the present edition. Though the first clause is no longer recover-
able, it was probably Davidic; certainly the paraphrast seems to favor a
historical interpretation, as suggested by literal translations of Ro *castra* by
getruman and scyld-ridan (troops and phalanxes, v. 4) and Ro *terra* by *lande,*
(denoting Israel, v. 15), as well as by additions in which the speaker mentions in verse 4 the threat of current enemies (*nu gyt,* "still") and his former
deliverance from enemies by "the God who previously freed me."

4   *ongean me* (against me) parallels Ga *adversus me* (Ro *in me*).
5   The Paris text lacks a translation of the first half of this verse,
     corresponding to Ro *unam petii a Domino hanc requiram ut inhab-
     item in domo Domini omnibus diebus vitae meae* (one thing I have
     asked from the Lord, this I will seek, that I may dwell in the
     house of the Lord all the days of my life), perhaps caused by
     scribal confusion of Ro *ut inhabitem* with *ut videam* (in the sec-
     ond half of the verse).
7   Bright-Ramsay's emendation of *miti* to *min (heafod)* is supported
     by Ro *caput meum.*
     After *þa offrunga* (those sacrifices), Sisam, "Notes," 475, sug-
     gested adding a defining genitive, to translate Ro *(hostiam) iubi-
     lationis* and proposed "some such word as *lofes,*" but *lof* nor-
     mally translates *laus* in the Prose Psalms, not *iubilatio,* and in
     any case would involve two uses of the same word in a single
     verse, a practice that the translator studiously avoids.
11   *Þu eart* (you are) parallels Old Latin *es tu* (Ro *esto*).

Psalm 27

Interpretation is historical, as suggested by the literal translation of Ro *christi* (v. 9) by *his gesmyredan* (his anointed one) and the historical rendering in verse 10 of Ro *hereditatem* by *þin yrfe-land* (the land which you have given them as an inheritance), a reference to the Promised Land. Although in theory the interpretation could apply to either the first or the second clause of the Introduction, the former seems more likely, given the general predominance throughout the Prose Psalms of the Davidic interpretation.

7   The addition of *ne* before *getimbrast* (You . . . will not resuscitate), first suggested by Schlutter (see Bright and Ramsay, "Notes," 473), is supported by both Ro *nec* and Ga *non*. Sisam's suggestion of *na* is less likely, since that particle normally occurs in the Prose Version in collocation with another negative particle.

Psalm 28

Interpretation is historical, as suggested by the speaker's rubric, *he cwæð* (David said), the addition of plural personal pronouns, "we, our, us" (referring to the Jewish people, v. 8), and the rendering of Ro future and present verbs with preterites in verses 6–7, all referring to favors already rendered by God. The reference to God's benevolence in allowing the speaker and the Jews "to live on after that people" (v. 8) suggests a reprieve after the Assyrian invasion, as outlined in the second clause of the Introduction.

3   *halgan healle* (holy palace), MS *ealle* emended to *healle* on the basis of Ro *aula sancta;* Thorpe, *Libri Psalmorum,* 441, treats *ealle* as an adjective and supplies *healle* after *halgan.*

8   on the evidence of Ro *Dominus diluuium inhabitat,* Bright and Ramsay, "Notes," 473, emended *folce* (people) to *flode* (flood). However, in the context of the historical interpretation proposed in the Introduction, *folce* referring to the Assyrians makes good sense; see O'Neill, *Prose Translation,* 219.

Psalm 29

Interpretation is historical, probably in accordance with the second clause, which applies the psalm to Hezekiah; note the translation of Ro *in mea abundantia* by *on minum wlencum and on minre orsorhnesse* (In my pride and insouciance, v. 6), evidently a reference to that king's boastful demonstration of his wealth and his failure to acknowledge God's role in his success, as narrated in 2 Chronicles 32:24–31.

2   *of neolnessum and of helle* (from the lower regions and from hell) is
        probably a conflation of Ro *ab inferis* and Ga *ab inferno.*

11   *wite-hrægl* (sackcloth) for MS *wlitehrægl,* first suggested by Grattan, "Text," 187, accords with Ro *saccum,* and suits well the context of mourning turned to joy, unlike Bright-Ramsay's *hwite hrægl* (white/shining garment).

        þu me begyrdst (you gird me) for *þu me bebyrgdst* of the manuscript, is the emendation suggested by Grattan, "Text," 188, which, unlike Bright-Ramsay's retention of *bebyrgdst* (you taste?), accords with Ro *praecinxisti.*

Psalm 30

Interpretation is historical, as suggested by the renderings of Ro *loco* in verse 9 by *swyðe brad land* (an exceedingly spacious land; namely, the Promised Land) and Ro *in civitate circumstantiae* (Ga *in civitate munita*) in verse 24 by *on þære fæstan byrig* (in that fortified city), a reference to Jerusalem. The use throughout of a first person singular speaker harmonizes with David's persona in the first clause rather than the Jewish people (OE *hi*) of the second clause.

8   *þu . . . ne clemdes* (you . . . did not enclose, Ro nec *conclusisti*): although otherwise unattested in Old English (and ignored in the DOE), the simplex *clemman* (to enclose, envelop) is present in Old English *beclemman* (to enclose, restrain) and well attested in later English; see *Oxford English Dictionary,* under *clem, clam.* The initial "cl" of the reading, *clemdes,* was misread as

"d" by previous editors, hence their incorrect reading *demdes* (you judge).

22   *þu hi gehydst* (you will hide them): the addition of *hi* by previous editors is justified by Ro *eos,* the plural inflected adjectives *hale* and *orsorge,* and the verbs *gehydst* and *gehyldst,* which both require an object.

27   *God lufiað* (God loves): the plural-looking form (for *lufað*) could be the result of contamination from the occurrence of *lufiað* (plural) earlier in the same verse, or possibly a late spelling; see Mitchell, *Syntax,* §20, and Hogg and Fulk, *Grammar of Old English,* II, 6.111.

Psalm 31

Interpretation is Davidic, closely agreeing in theme and contents with the directives of the first and third clause (itself based on vv. 3–5). The final clause of the Introduction, "and he prophesied also about Christ, that he likewise would praise such people," although purportedly Christological, actually refers to contemporary Christians who do what David failed to do in the preceding clause.

2   *mode* (inwardly): explained as a copyist's error for *muðe* (Ro *in ore eius*) in *Facsimile,* 16, but dependence on *Ga in spiritu eius* is more likely.

7   Following Bright and Ramsay, "Notes," 474, I emend *weardan* to *toweardan* (future) on the evidence of the same collocation, *andweardan . . . toweardan* at Psalm 48.12.

Psalm 32

Interpretation is moral (gratitude for God's favors), in accordance with the second clause of the Introduction; note the additions *gifum* (gifts, v. 1) and, in verse 11, *swylc god* (such a god, as has been described in the Introduction), which emphasize the agent of generosity, as well as *symle* (always, v. 16), which establishes the enduring character of God's benevolence.

Psalm 33

Interpretation is moral, probably in accord with the second clause, which has contemporary Christians as its interpretative focus. Thus the additions, *swa he me dyde* (as he did [rescue] me, v. 7) and *gehyre hwæt ic secge* (listen to what I say, v. 12), seem to be the words of David prophetically addressing and instructing contemporary Christians.

Psalm 34

Interpretation is probably Davidic, as formulated in the first clause of the Introduction; note that *ungelimp* (misfortune) of this clause is repeated as an addition in verses 15 and 23. The final, participial clause, *Ma witgiende . . . wilniende* (More in prophecy than condemning or wishing) applies to David (not Christ) in his role as author of the psalm, the harshness of which it serves to mitigate. The phrase, "David sang," has been added here for clarity.

13   *wite-hrægl:* see note on Psalm 29.11.

14   *hy me gedydon swa unrotne and swa wependne swa se byð þone þe he lufað* (they made me as dejected and sad as one is after a loved one): Sisam, "Notes," 475, suggests supplying *ne* before *lufað* to give the meaning "as he is whom He does not love," but in the present context the ones who withdraw their love are the psalmist's enemies, not the deity; see further O'Neill, *Prose Translation,* 230–31.

19   *þæt mine fynd ne blissien æfter me* (so that my enemies may not gloat over me) is closer to Ga *supergaudeant mihi* and He *laetentur super me* than Ro *ut non insultent in me.*

24   *þa ofer-sprecan þe me yfel cweðað* (those excessive talkers, who say evil things to me) seems to be a conflation of Ro *qui magna loquuntur* and the variant reading *maligna* (for *magna*) found in certain Ro and Ga Psalters.

Psalm 35

Interpretation is moral, in accordance with the second clause of the Introduction, as suggested not only by the absence of any reference to the historical context outlined in the first clause but also by modifications of verbal tense and mood, such as the rendering of all the Latin perfect verbs of verses 1–6 by present (e.g., v. 4, Ro *adstetit: he stent,* Ro *odivit: hatað*) and of Ro *ceciderunt* by optative subjunctive *gefeallen* (v. 12).

12   The remaining few words of the verse (and psalm) are missing, but probably consisted of *ma<gon standan>* (are not able to stand), as supplied by Thorpe and Bright-Ramsay.

Psalm 36

Interpretation is probably moral (in accordance with the first clause of the Introduction), as suggested by close verbal correspondences between the latter and verses 1–2; by changes of Latin perfect and subjunctive verbs to present (in vv. 15, 16, and 39); and by the addition of temporal adverbs, such as *(n)æfre* (never, vv. 20, 24, 27) and *symle* (constantly/always, vv. 32, 36–38), which impart a timeless character to the events described.

13   *besyrian* (ensnare) corresponds to Ga *decipiant* (Ro *deiciant*).

21   *beoð eorðan yrfe-weardas* (will be the earth's inheritors) is closer to Ga *hereditabunt* (Ro *possidebunt*).

23   *gebrysed . . . tobrocen* (bruised . . . broken) may be a conflation of Ga *conlidetur* and Ro *conturbabitur.*

32   *hawaþ* (watches): Bright-Ramsay retains the MS reading *hopaþ* (hopes); Sisam (as reported by Bright and Ramsay, "Notes," 474) suggests *hogað* (considers), which corresponds well to Ro *considerat* and suits the context but does not explain the genitive object, *þæs rihtwisan;* Schlutter's *hawaþ* (see Bright and Ramsay, "Notes," 474) meets all three requirements.

34   *swa swa sum ceder-treow* (just like some cedar tree) matches Ga *sicut cedros* (Ro *super cedros*).

36   *læfð* (leaves): Thorpe's emendation of *lærð* accords well with Ro *reliquiae.*

Psalm 37

Interpretation is Davidic and historical, referring to David's remorse for his adultery with Bathsheba, as outlined in the first clause of the Introduction. Note the correspondence between that clause's references to David's *ungelimp* and *earfeðum* (misfortune, tribulations) and the interpretative addition, *þa earfoðu þe ic nu þolie* (those . . . tribulations which I now endure, v. 2). Likewise, the Introduction's reference to David's *scylde* (sin) parallels *min unriht* (my crime) in verse 4, both equally specific in their singular form (referring to the Bathsheba affair), where Ro has plural *iniquitates*.

5   *fuledon* (festered) J. M. Bately, "Lexical Evidence for the Authorship of the Prose Psalms in the Paris Psalter," *Anglo-Saxon England* 10 (1982): 83, sees this rendering as a deliberate variation to avoid repeating the preceding *rotedon* (putrified), but compare also Ga *corruptae sunt* (Ro *deterioraverunt*).

13   *riht-andswaru*, a word evidently otherwise unattested, is defined by B-T as "an answer that corrects, a reproof, a rebuke," but the context and the corresponding Ga *redargutiones* (Ro *increpationes*), as well as commentary, suggest the meaning "retort, rejoinder."

19   *me tælað* (slander me), the emendation of MS *lætað* suggested by Grattan, "Notes," 188, is supported by use of the same verb to translate Ro *detrahere* at Psalm 49.21.

Psalm 38

Interpretation is primarily moral, in accordance with the second clause of the Introduction; note the shared parallels of ideas between this clause and verses 7 and 11, as well as the translation of Ro *homo* by the generalized *ælc (. . .) man* (each [. . .] person, vv. 6 and 10), a formula used in the Introductions for the subject of the moral clause. A Davidic theme, in accord with the final clause of the Introduction, is also evident, although subordinate, in references to the psalmist's sufferings in verses 9 and 13, the latter verse sharing with the Introduction the unusual compound *rot-hwil* (a period of ease). In the third interpretative clause, the phrase *þæt ylce don sceolde* (destined to do the same) refers back to the action of the first, not the second, clause.

6   After the Introduction, the remainder of folio 45v remains blank; the folio following, now missing, between folios 45 and 46, presumably contained the Ro text of Psalm 38:2–6a and the parallel Old English.

7   *mid þe is eall min æht* (all my possessions are with you) reflects Ga *substantia mea apud te est* rather than Ro *substantia mea tamquam nihil ante te est.*

12   MS *nifara* was emended by Grattan, "Text," 188, to *nydfara* (one who travels under compulsion), but *nifara* (a newcomer, stranger) accords well with Ga *advena* (Ro *incola*); see Tinkler, *Vocabulary and Syntax,* 60–61.

Psalm 39

Interpretation is Davidic, as suggested by close verbal similarities between the first clause of the Introduction and verse 1, as well as by the interpretative rendering of Ro *supra petram* by *on swyðe heah setl and on swyðe fæstne anweald* (on a very high seat and with very secure control, v. 2), which suggests royal dominion at Jerusalem.

7   *þa þa ic hy næfde* (when I did not possess them), where *hy* refers back to *ælmesan* (alms). The idea behind this addition is that one is not obligated to dispense alms when one does not have the means to do so. The same point is made in Psalm 40.1, and it also occurs in the Old English *Boethius,* all probably going back to Augustine's *Enchiridion* (Bk 19, 72–73), M. Evans, ed., *Enchiridion ad Laurentium de Fide et Spe et Caritate,* Corpus Scriptorum Ecclesiasticorum Latinorum 46 (1969): 48-114, at 88–89; see O'Neill, *Prose Translation,* 246.

13   Although *þær* of the manuscript would make sense as "there," emendation to *þæra* is supported by Ro *quorum (non est numerus).*

15   *ne lata þu* (do not delay) accords with Old Latin *intende* (Ro *respice*).

16–17   *ondræden . . . unnon* (Let them be afraid . . . who wish): corresponds to Ga *revereantur* (Ro *erubescant*) and *volunt* (Ro *cogitant*), respectively.

21   The collocation *friðiend . . . gescyldend* (defender . . . protector) is evidently a conflation of Ro *liberator* and Ga *protector;* also, in the same verse, *Drihten, min God* may combine Ro *Domine* and Ga *Deus meus.*

Psalm 40

Interpretation is Davidic, as stated in the latter part of the first interpretation of the Introduction. Note the mention there of David's discovery of true friends and enemies, which is expanded in verse 9, while the Introduction's reference to the speaker's *ungelimpe* (misfortune) parallels the addition *ungelimpes* of verse 11. An innovation of the paraphrast, evidently without the benefit of commentary, is the vivid narrative of verses 5–9, embellished with sarcastic first-person statements directed at David by his enemies.

2   With *gedeð hine gesæligne on eorðan* (will . . . make him happy on earth), compare Ga *beatum faciat eum in terra* (Ro *beatum faciat eum et emundet in terra animam eius*).

        I follow Bright and Ramsay, "Notes," 474, in emending MS *hanweald* to *handa and anweald,* a collocation attested at Psalm 44.6.

8   The clause *and spræcon me yfeles* (and spoke evil of me) is awkward in context, since it has no counterpart in Ro and duplicates the clause following; perhaps it is a dittography.

10   *to þam þæt ic him mæge forgyldan þæs lean* (so that I can recompense them for that): the introductory purpose conjunction has a parallel in Old Latin *ut* (Ro *et*), though it could well be a contextual modification of the paraphrast. The collocation *þæs lean* (demonstrative *þæs* is incorrectly read as a by-form of deictic *þes* by O'Neill, *Prose Translation,* 247–48) is surely ironic: the psalmist will take revenge for the cruel treatment meted out to

him by both enemies and so-called friends. Exactly the same words occur in *Beowulf* 1584[b], with reference to the hero's beheading of Grendel's corpse; R. D. Fulk, Robert E. Bjork, and John D. Niles, eds., *Klaeber's Beowulf and the Fight at Finnsburg*, 4th ed. (Toronto, 2008), 54.

Psalm 41

Interpretation is historical, and probably Davidic, to judge by the consistent first person singular voice throughout; the additional references to the speaker's sufferings in *werig* (weary, v. 1), *witu* (punishments, v. 8), and *yrmðum* (miseries, v. 9); and implied references in verse 4 that the speaker is far from his homeland, as in *ic sceolde cuman . . . to* (I would come . . . to, Ro *ingrediar*) and *þyder ic sceal cuman* (I shall come there).

3   Supplying *fynd* (enemies) after *mine,* suggested by Sisam, "Notes," 475, is implied by the context, and supported by verses 11–12, where the very same question is posed by *mine fynd* (my enemies).

7   *Wið me sylfne* (against myself) accords with Ga *ad me ipsum* (Ro *a me ipso*).

9   *singan his sang* (sing his song) accords with Ga *declaravit canticum eius* (Ro *declaravit*).

Psalm 42

Interpretation is probably Davidic, in accordance with the first clause, as suggested by verbal agreements between it and verse 1.

3   *þa me geo-geara læddon* (which formerly led me): I follow Thorpe, and Grattan, "Text," 188, in reading *me* for MS *þe,* though Grattan treats *þa* as an independent rather than a relative pronoun on the strength of Ro *ipsa me deduxerunt.*

6   *ic hine gyt andette* (I will continue to praise him) is closer to Ga *adhuc confitebor illi* than Ro *confitebor illi.*

Psalm 43

Interpretation is Davidic, in accordance with the second clause of the Introduction, which contrasts God's providential care of David's ancestors with his apparent disregard for the psalmist's generation. Not only is this theme explicitly included in verse 6 as an aside, *swa ylce swa þu heora wære* (just as you were theirs), but temporal adverbs such as *þa* (at that time, thereafter, vv. 5 and 10) and *geo* (formerly, v. 11) are added to emphasize that God's prompt favors belong to the past. In the same regretful vein, the additions *geþafodest* (you allowed, vv. 13 and 20) and *woldest* (you wished, v. 20) imply divine complacency. Yet for all these modifications, the paraphrase could equally well reflect the directives of the third clause, which applies the psalm to the Maccabees. Note that in the second clause, *he* refers to God, not David.

3   *þu swenctest* (you harassed) for MS *þu stenctest,* as suggested by Thorpe, provides an accurate translation of Ro *adflixisti.*

5   *hy þe þa licodon, and þe licode mid him to beonne* (they [the people] at that time pleased you, and you enjoyed dwelling among them) may be a combination of Ro *conplacuit tibi in eis* and Ga *conplacuisti in eis.*

14   *nan folc mid us ne gehwyrfdest* (you did not exchange any people for us) is closer to Ga *in commutationibus nostris* than Ro *in commutationibus eorum.*

17   *beforan me and ongean me* (before and in front of me) matches the combination of Old Latin *ante me* and Ro *contra me.*

21–22   As suggested by *gif* (if) with subjunctive *wræce,* these verses are hypothetical, implying that the Jews were not guilty of the offenses mentioned; consequently, they did not deserve the punishments described in verses 11–20.

23   Translating *snædincg-sceapum* (Ro *oves occisionis*) as "sheep for slaughter," following Hall, *Concise Anglo-Saxon Dictionary,* 312 (compare Henry Sweet, *The Student's Dictionary of Anglo-Saxon* [New York, 1897], 157, "sheep to be killed"), whereas B-T translates, "sheep for eating."

Psalm 44

Interpretation is mystical, as expounded in the first sentence of the Introduction, a celebration of the marriage between Christ the King and his bride, the Queen (allegorically, the Church), from which union comes a progeny of just souls. Structurally, the paraphrase falls into four sections: (1) God the Father announcing the Incarnation of his Son (vv. 1–2); (2) David describing the Son (vv. 3–11); (3) David (assuming the persona of God the Father) addressing the Christian Church, invoked as "my daughter" (vv. 12–15); and (4) David addressing Christ (invoked as "king") as head of the Church (vv. 16–19).

4   *þe gebletsode God* (God has blessed you): the emendation of MS *he* to *þe* is supported by Ro *benedixit te Deus.*

       ofer þin þeoh (on your thigh) is closer to Ga *super femur tuum* than Ro *circa femur.*

7   Here the double meaning of *gefeallað* (Ro *cadent*) is exploited, first with *an andetnesse* (they will . . . apply themselves to acknowledging), second with *on helle* (they will fall into hell); this trope of antanaclasis is also employed by the translator of the Metrical Psalms.

10   *of þinum elpan-bænenum husum* (from . . . your ivory houses) reflects Ga *a domibus eburneis* (Ro *a gradibus eburneis*).

11   *mid golde getuncode* (arrayed in a brocaded dress; Ro *in vestitu deaurato*), following the emendation of *getucode* proposed by F. Holthausen, "Wortdeutungen," *Indogermanische Forschungen* 48 (1930): 263. BTS defines *getucode* as "worked with metal," which hardly suits a description of the queen, and in any case is otherwise unattested with this meaning.

16   *æfter þam* (following them) could also be read in a temporal sense, "after that"; Ro *postea* could signify either.

       The unusual interpretation of the queen's entourage as comprising virgins, committed penitents, and those enduring punishment for their sins probably derives from early Irish eschatology; see O'Neill, *Prose Translation,* 258.

Psalm 45

Interpretation is historical, as suggested by the substitution in verse 3 of *Ure fynd* (Our enemies) and *þa up ahafenan kynincgas* (those exalted kings) as the new subject in place of natural forces. In verse 5 the description of these enemies as *þa elðeodgan folc* (the foreign peoples), a reference to the Syrian kings (compare 4 Kings 16:5), points to dependence on the second interpretative clause rather than the first.

3   *afærde fram Gode:* DOE under *afæran* explains it as "to stand in fear of God," but context and commentary suggest the more vivid meaning "they were struck by God with terror"; see O'Neill, *Prose Translation,* 260.

4   The curious reference to a rainstorm that cleansed Jerusalem (Ro *fluminis impetus* refers to a river) probably goes back to Abbot Adomnán of Iona's *De locis sanctis;* see O'Neill, *Prose Translation,* 260.

Psalm 46

Interpretation is historical, as is evident from adaptations and additions that lend focus to the Jewish people's struggles against *orlega þeoda* (hostile nations), on the one hand, and *ure folc* (our own peoples) who sided with the enemy, on the other. This combination and their juxtaposition in verse 3 (see note) suggests the historical circumstances of the Maccabees, as outlined in the second clause.

3   The crucial addition of *ure* before *folc* shifts the focus from the expected meaning of "foreign peoples" (Ro *populos*) to "our own people," probably a reference to those Hellenistic Jews who apostasized under King Antiochus (1 Maccabees 1:12–16).

9   *swa þas godas* (like these gods) probably refers to the "other gods" mentioned in verse 2; alternatively, *þas* could be a scribal error or substitution for *þær,* thus, *swa þær godas* (like gods).

Psalm 47

Interpretation is historical, although in this instance it seems that the Introduction derived its primary interpretation (the first clause) from the contents of the psalm—an inversion of their normal relationship. Although the reference to *eorð-kyningas* (earthly kings) echoes the sentiment of Psalm 46.9, the description of their sudden reversal at Jerusalem (vv. 5–6) recalls the defeat of Sennacherib and the Assyrians in the reign of Hezekiah (4 Kings 18:13–19:36).

> *þe geswære wære and ofercumen, and eft gefriðod* (who was oppressed and subjugated and afterward liberated): cognizant of the need for a verbal complement to *geswære* and two past participles, Bright-Ramsay supplied *byð* after *geswære,* but subjunctive *wære* would suit better, and is likely to have been omitted through haplography.

2   *He tobrædde . . . is aset* (He spread . . . is founded) combines Ro *dilatans* and the corresponding Ga *fundatur.*

3   *on þære byrig* (in the city): Ga *in domibus eius* (Ro *in gradibus eius*).

7   *þe he gestaþelode* (which he established): the emendation of MS *hi* to *he* is supported by Ro *deus fundauit eam.*

11   *dælað hire weorðias* (portion out its dwellings) probably reflects Ga *distribuite domus eius* (Ro *distribuite gradus eius*).

Psalm 48

Interpretation is moral, in close agreement with David's exhortation to beware of wealth, as stated in the first clause of the Introduction. Note parallels between the latter and verses 6 and 17, as well as the frequent addition of adverbs that juxtapose this life and the eternal, for example, *her* (vv. 7, 18) and *þyder* (vv. 15, 17). Structurally, the paraphrase opens with a prologue (vv. 1–5) inviting humankind to consider the fundamental questions about to be posed; it admonishes the rich and powerful (vv. 6–13), consoles the poor (vv. 16–19), and ends with the pessimistic conclusion that its exhortation will be lost on those for whom it is most intended.

7   *hu he on ecnesse swincan mæge* (the means whereby he can perpetually toil at work): although *on ecnesse* might seem to suggest that

swincan has associations with eternal punishment, the more likely meaning is that people seek out hard work as a necessary way to amass wealth during their lifetime; see O'Neill, *Prose Translation*, 265–66.

9   *Þeah hy gesibbe . . . ne doð* (Although they may have relatives . . . for them): in effect the blood relatives who inherit their property will be like strangers *(fremde)*, because they have no interest in performing good deeds for the souls of the deceased.

10   Although the personal pronouns *hi, hiora,* and *heora* are potentially ambiguous, the meaning seems to be that the inheritors *(hi)* will rename the lands and towns of the deceased *(hiora land)* after themselves *(be heora naman),* thus confirming the alienation described in verse 9.

12   *tiliað to cwemanne* (they try to please) agrees with Ga *conplacebunt* (Ro *benedicent*).

14   *heora wealdað* (they will dominate them) agrees with Ga *dominabuntur* (Ro *obtinebunt*).

15   *of helle handa* (from the power of hell) matches Ro variant *inferni* (Ro *inferi*).

Psalm 49

Interpretation is moral, in line with the guidelines of the Introduction, which castigates those who rely on offerings of sacrificial animals to placate God. However, whereas the Introduction advocates the offering of oneself to God, the paraphrase recommends praise of the deity and seems to depend on the contents of the psalm itself rather than commentary. Also, whereas the Introduction speaks of Christ's first coming (his time on earth), the paraphrase focuses on his second coming at Judgment; thus verses 1–6 are a hypotyposis of that event, contextualized with the addition of temporal adverbs *eft* (again, vv. 1 and 3) and *þonne* (then, v. 3), as well as eschatological images in verse 5 of the sky folding like a book, and the separation of the just and the wicked, with the former placed on God's right hand.

3   *openlice* (openly) agrees with Ga *manifeste* (Ro *manifestus*).

5   *hæt hine þæt he hine fealde swa swa boc* (commanding it to fold it-

self like a book) is an addition suggested by Apocalypse 6:14, "and the heavens departed as a book folded up."

6   *on þa swyðran hand* (on the right hand) comes from the Judgment scene in Matthew 25:32–33.

11   *wildeor* (wild animals) is treated in the present edition as the simplex *wildor,* contaminated by the compound *wilddeor* through late Old English folk etymologizing; see Hogg and Fulk, *Grammar of Old English,* 2.100 and note 4. The word also occurs at Psalms 67.27 and 103.19.

21   *ongean þinne broðor* (in opposition to your brother): the addition of *broðor,* adopted by Thorpe and Bright-Ramsay, is justified by Ro *adversus fratrem tuum.*

22   *Eall þis yfel* (all this evil) suggests the influence of Old Latin *haec omnia* (Ro *haec*).

     swiðe unryhte (very unjustly) accords with Ga *inique* (Ro *iniquitatem*).

Psalm 50

Interpretation conforms most closely to the first clause of the Introduction, though the paraphrase is so loosely worded as to be applicable to any of the other three proposed interpretations. The addition in verse 3, *þonne ic ær ðysse scylde wæs* (than I was before this sin), almost certainly refers specifically to David's adultery with Bathsheba.

5   the paraphrast shifts the focus of Ro *ut iustificeris in sermonibus tuis* (that you may be justified in your words) from concern about God's dignity to the penitent's purpose of amendment, *wið þe ænne ic sceal þæt betan* (to you alone I must make amends for that).

9   *þæt ic gehyre . . . þæt þæt ic nolde* (so that I may hear what I desire, and also others may hear about me what I desire, just as they previously heard what I did not desire): according to this elaboration of Ro *auditui meo dabis gaudium* (you will impart joy to my hearing), what David desires to hear is news of God's will-

ingness to forgive him; what he formerly did not want to hear was God's condemnation (through Nathan) of his sin.

þæt þonne mæge unrote mod blissian (so that my troubled heart can then rejoice) corresponds to Ro *et exultabunt ossa humiliata* and marks the end of its verse. The paraphrase of the remaining verses (Ro 11–21) was presumably entered on the first of the two missing folios lost between 63 and 64.

Metrical Psalms

Unlike the Prose Psalms, these do not have formal Introductions to each psalm, nor do they reveal much evidence of influence from Latin commentary on the psalms, nor does it appear that their composer followed a particular line of interpretation. On his approach to translation, see the Introduction, xvii–xxi.

Psalm 51

The opening verses corresponding to verses 3–8 in the Ro are lacking because of the loss of two folios between 63 and 64. Consequently, the numbering of the remaining Old English verses is conjectural.

Psalm 52

5   *Ac ge . . . ne þurfon:* H. Bartlett, *The Metrical Division of the Paris Psalter* (Baltimore, 1896), 38, notes that this is the only occasion where an indirect question in the Latin (Ro *nonne cognoscent . . .*) is changed into a statement.

Psalm 53

1   This verse is cited in the so-called *Junius* Office; see C. Jones, *Old English Shorter Poems, Volume 1: Religious and Didactic,* Dumbarton Oaks Medieval Library 15 (Cambridge, Mass., 2012), Appendix B, 298 (3.4).

Psalm 54

7   On the proposed meaning of Old English *mindom* as "lack of mental courage"/"pusillanimity of mind," see Tinkler, *Vocabulary and Syntax,* 18.

19   Ro *extendit manum suam in retribuendo illis* has not been translated, probably because its mention of divine vengeance did not fit well at this point with the overall theme of the wicked behavior of the psalmist's enemies.

    ne hi sylfe wel geseon æfre (nor are they themselves ever regarded positively), Ro *divisi sunt ab ira vultus eius:* taking *geseon* as originally past participle of *geseon* (from Anglian *gesegen*) in collocation with *synt* of the previous line.

22   *þæt him . . . hreðre* (Ro *fluctuationem iusto*): the syntax is awkward; I take *þæt* as qualifying *ypende mod* (that wavering disposition).

Psalm 55

9   *min word:* the translator took Ro *verbum* to refer to the psalmist's word rather than God's, as pointed out by Bartlett, *Metrical Division,* 28.

Psalm 56

5   Following the translation of *wæpen-strælas* as "arms and arrows," suggested by Tinkler, *Vocabulary and Syntax,* 20.

Psalm 57

7   *swa heo feallað on þæt* (so they will fall into that fire), Ro *super eos cecidit ignis:* as noted by Bartlett, *Metrical Division,* 28, the translator gives the reverse of the Latin.

9   *þonne he sið ongan* (whenever he sees ahead): I adopt Grein's reading of *sið* as equivalent to *sihð* (he sees) and *ongan* as adverb *ongean* (toward/ahead); compare Ro *cum uiderit vindictam impiorum;* see Krapp, *Paris Psalter,* 209.

Psalm 58

1–2   These verses occur in the *Junius* Office; see Jones, *Shorter Poems,* 306–8 (3.30–31).

4   *Gif ic on unriht bearn* (If I was involved in evil): the translator evidently depended on the variant reading *si iniquitatem cucurri* (Ro *sine iniquitate cucurri*), of which Bartlett, *Metrical Division,* 28, was evidently unaware.

Psalm 59

2   The emendation of *Forðan* to *Eorðan* is supported by Ro *terram;* likewise that of *ahreded* to *ahrered* by Ro *mota est.*

3   *ðu . . . hi hraþe . . . wine drenctest* (you inebriated them with wine that induces merriment) is odd as a rendering of Ro *potasti nos vino conpunctionis;* perhaps the translator invariably associated wine with celebration. Bartlett, *Metrical Division,* 28, argued that the translator did not understand the Latin.

4   *leofe þine* (your beloved ones) evidently translates Ga *dilecti tui* (a reading found in some Ro Psalters) rather than Ro *electi tui.*

5   *Sicimam et Convallem . . . on Metiboris* (Shechem and Convallem . . . in Metiboris): while the first is a genuine place-name, the second is a misreading of Ro *convallem* (a glen) as a place-name, and the third, likewise of a Latin verb *metibor* (I will measure). The latter error is repeated at Psalm 107.6.

7   *Allophilas:* the versifier misread Ro *allophili* (foreign peoples) as a proper noun.

Psalm 60

6   *Swa ic . . . gedefe wese* (So I . . . should be) occurs as a versicle in the *Junius* Office; see Jones, *Shorter Poems,* 308 (3.32). On this use of *swa . . . þæt* to introduce an intended result, see Mitchell, *Syntax,* §2846.

Psalm 62

3   *on wege* (on the road): as noted by Bartlett, *Metrical Division*, 28, a mistranslation of Ro *in invio* (in an impassable place).

5   *þwea* (I will purify): the translator evidently misread Ro *leuabo* as *lauabo*, as first noted by Bartlett, *Metrical Division*, 28.

Psalm 63

5   *þær hi mamriað man and unriht* (when they devise crime and injustice): I follow Tinkler, *Vocabulary and Syntax*, 32, who argues that the *hapax* verb, *mamrian*, is formed from Old English *mamor* (Latin *sopor*). B-T (under *mamorian*) tentatively suggests the meaning "to be in deep thought about anything," which would give the clause the sense "when they devise crime and injustice."

Psalm 64

4   I emend MS *hafað* to *hefeð* (he will raise up) on the evidence of Ro *adsumpsisti*.

5   *awa to feore* (for ever and ever) is perhaps a misreading of Ro *in equitate* as *in eternitate*.

6   This verse occurs in the *Junius* Office; see Jones, *Shorter Poems*, 308 (3.33), and Krapp, *Paris Psalter*, 211.

7   *þæt beoð . . . yþa hlude* (so that the waves are excessively loud): MS *byð* seems to be an error for plural *beoð*, as suggested to me by Professor R. Fulk.

9   *Drihten healdeð* (the Lord will control) is an odd translation of Ro *delectaberis* (Ga *delectabis*); perhaps the translator took it to be *delegabis*, from *delegare* (to delegate authority), and expanded accordingly.

11   *blowað and growað* (they will . . . grow and flourish) seems to reflect Ga *germinans* (Ro *dum exorietur*).

14   I take *eowde sceapum* to mean "from the sheep of the flock,"

with *sceapum* as dative/instrumental plural (dependent on *godre wulle*) and *eowde* as genitive singular feminine of *eowd* (see DOE under *eowd(e),* 1); Krapp, *Paris Psalter,* reads it as a compound, *eowdesceapum.*

Psalm 65

5 The final clause, Ro *ibi laetabimur in idipsum* (there we will rejoice in him), is not translated, presumably because it would have distracted attention from the enumeration of God's *cyme weorc* (glorious works, v. 4).

18 Treating *þe* as a causal conjunction rather than a relative pronoun, though Ro has *qui;* see Mitchell, *Syntax,* §3131.

Psalm 67

5 *steop-cildum* (to orphans): contrary to Bartlett, *Metrical Division,* 28, this is not an incorrect rendering of Ro *orfanorum.*

8 I take *oððe* here to mean "and (furthermore)," rather than "until" (as at Psalm 139.11), since the clause it introduces parallels the previous *þonne*-clause, both translating Ro *dum;* see Mitchell, *Syntax,* §1751.

10 *sundor-yrfe* (Ro *hereditati*): the additional element *sundor* (apart, special) probably refers to the Promised Land, an inheritance like none other.

13 Ro *inter medios cleros* (Old Latin *inter medio clero*) caused problems for the translator, who rendered it with the hybrid *on clero,* where *clērus* (an allotment of land) may have been misunderstood as a form of *clerus* (the clergy). The scribe Wulfwinus inserted a prominent stroke over each word, perhaps to highlight their oddity.

14 Despite Ro *eam* (Ga *eum*), *hi* in this verse is apparently plural, presumably referring to *fiðeru* (wings) of the preceding verse.

24 *on ciricean Crist . . . bearn Israela* (may Christ, the Lord God, boldly bless the children of Israel in their assembly): a rare in-

stance where the translator adds an expressly Christological perspective, equating Ro *Dominum Deum* with Christ and making him the subject (rather than the object) of Ro *benedicite*. See also Psalm 106.31.

25   *of Iudan (þe . . . leoda)* (from Judah, which continued to be the head of the tribes): this addition, reflects the medieval Christian view that the dominance of the kingdom of Judah over that of Israel was appropriate, since Christ was descended from the House of Judah through David. See also note to Psalm 113.2, below.

27   *under folcum* (among the people's cows) is a compound (dative plural) of *folc+cu,* a loan translation of Ro *vaccas populorum;* see Tinkler, *Vocabulary and Syntax,* 17.

28   *Toweorp þu þa ðeoda* (Scatter those peoples . . .): the folio missing between 79 and 80 probably contained the rest of this sentence (Ro *quae bella volunt,* who desire war), followed by the text and translation of the remaining verses of the psalm (32–36 in the numbering of Ro and perhaps 29–33 in the Old English).

Psalm 68

2   The meaning of Old English *hopig* (translated here by "surging") is unclear; see Tinkler, *Vocabulary and Syntax,* 60.

3   *æt þam earon* (from those waves): the mention of waves, not in Ro, was presumably prompted by the previous verse.

12   *spræcon me wraðe þa þe win druncon* (those who drank wine addressed me aggressively): the translator seems to have missed the spiteful import of Ro *in me psallebant,* "they made me their toast while singing."

19   This verse would have originally translated verses 20–21 of the Ro, though what survives in the manuscript is a translation of Ro verse 21, preceded by the letters *arsca me* only, which may contain the lexeme *scame* (shame) in an oblique case, translating *verecundiam* of Ro verse 20. For further discussion, see Krapp, *Paris Psalter,* 212–13.

26 The addition *ecton* (they increased), first proposed by Grein, "Zur Textkritik," 425, matches Ro *addiderunt.*

32 I take *geseoð* and *gefeoð* (observe, rejoice) as imperatives rather than indicatives; compare Ro *videant . . . laetentur.*

Psalm 69

1 This verse is cited as a versicle in the *Junius* Office; see Jones, *Shorter Poems,* 294–96, 304 and 314 (3.2, 3.24, and 4.3); and Krapp, *Paris Psalter,* 213.

4 *Weg la, weg la!* (Alas, alas!): although this translation runs counter to Ro *euge, euge* (fine, fine!), both serve to convey the feigned concern of the psalmist's enemies.

Psalm 70

2 *Iustum* is read as an adverbial modifier of *alys* (gladly free me), though it could be nominal, "(from) unlawful desires"; compare Cassiodorus, *Explanatio,* 629, 60, *Libera ab imminentibus periculis dicit; eripe a potestate diaboli.*

  þær þu me teala hæle (where you may justifiably save me): Krapp's emendation of MS *þær* to *þæt* accords with Ro *ut saluum me facias* (a purpose clause), but the original reading has been kept since it makes good sense as introducing an adjective clause of place; see B. Mitchell, "Pronouns in Old English Poetry: Some Syntactical Notes," *Review of English Studies* 15 (1964): 141.

12 Taking *gedrette* of the manuscript as a copyist's error for *gedrecte* (past participle plural of *gedreccan,* "to destroy"); Ro *deficient.*

13 I follow Tinkler, *Vocabulary and Syntax,* 31, in reading *hihte* as a variant spelling of *ihte* (I have added), preterite of *iecan,* which accords with Ro *adiciam.*

19 *on costunge cuðra manna* (Through the testing of well-known people): this expansion of Ro *tribulationes multas,* probably a reference in the first instance to Job, again shows the transla-

tor attempting to relate the psalms to other parts of the Old Testament.

Psalm 71

9   *seceað* (they will seek) is closer in meaning to the variant reading *precedent* (they will go ahead) rather than Ro *procident* (they will fall down).

14   The emendation of *alysdon* to *alysde* (he freed) proposed by Krapp, is supported by Ro *liberavit*.

16   *his yþa* (his waves): according to the common view, the translator misread Ro *fructus* (fruit) as *fluctus* (wave), thus Tinkler, *Vocabulary and Syntax,* 30–31; but more likely he had before him the reading *fluctus,* a well-attested variant of *fructus* in Ro manuscripts. Tinkler suggests that dependence on the reading *fluctus* necessitated a corresponding modification of Ro *superextolletur* in translation, hence *licgeað* (will flow). Moreover, since *beoþ blostmum fægere* (Ro *florebunt*) of the line following has no declared subject—*yþa* (waves) would hardly suit—it may be that the translator had in mind the alternative reading *fructus* (fruits), the subject of *florebunt* in the Ro.

Psalm 72

5   *wearð . . . untyned* (was revealed): as first noted by Bartlett, *The Metrical Division,* 28, Ro *operti* (covered) was misread as *aperti* (opened).

11   *leaw-finger* (finger of accusation) as a compound seems to conflate Ro *index meus* (my index finger) and the corresponding Ga reading, *castigatio mea* (my chastisement).

12   *þa ylcan ic ær foreteode* (for whom I have already predestined the same fate): the corresponding Ro *quibus disposui* suggests that the clause is relative and that some relative particle should be silently supplied; see further Mitchell, *Syntax,* §2310–12. With the translator's interpretation of *disposui,* compare Cassiodorus, *Expositio,* 665, 249–51, *praedicationes priores, quas Israelitis ante praedixerat.*

13 *þis gewinn* (this struggle): presumably, the human condition, and in particular why the wicked (and their progeny) seem to prosper while the just not only suffer but also feel guilt. The translator seems to have taken Ro *hoc* and *labor* as a collocation, against all the rules of Latin grammar.

17 *Ys minre . . . and clæne* (The thought of my heart is pure and clean): an unusual interpretation, since most allegorical commentators interpret Ro *delectatum est cor meum* as referring to the corrupting of the psalmist by worldly pleasures; compare Augustine, *Enarrationes,* 1000, 27, 4–7, *Potest et sic intellegi . . . libidines meae mutatae sunt, et castus totus factus sum.* Bartlett, *Metrical Division,* 28, suggests that Ro *delectatum* has been confused with *delicatum* but does not indicate whether the latter should be identified with *delicatus* (self-indulgent) or *delicatus* (from *delicare,* "to make clear").

Psalm 73

20 *hu . . . unwise* (that the ignorant) seems closer to the variant reading *quia insipientes* (Ro *qui ab insipienti*).

21 *fyll þa oferhydigan . . . ealle stigað* (kill the arrogant who hate you, and afterward all will ascend to you): Bartlett, *Metrical Version,* 35, notes that *fyll* (kill) has been added and *superbia* made its object; but more significant is the way in which *superbia eorum . . . ascendat semper ad te* has been broken into two discrete clauses, the first of which calls for the decisive destruction of proud people, while the second, which is distanced from the first by temporal *eft* (afterward) and the introduction of a new subject, *ealle,* envisages all the surviving virtuous people rising up to God. The purpose of these latter changes seems to be to avoid the impression that the proud will somehow be part of that company.

Psalm 74

2 *eac soð:* this occurrence is given by DOE under *eac* as an example of a collocation meaning "moreover, indeed"; however, *soð* here

seems to be substantive (just judgments), translating Ro *iusti-tiam.*

6   *eastan ne cymeð gumena ænig, ne of west-wegum wera cneorissa* (no-body will come from the east, nor any peoples from the west), Ro *neque ab Oriente neque ab Occidente:* for the translator's provision of a subject, compare Cassiodorus, *Expositio,* 688, 147–48, *Ergo cum omnibus generibus hominum Deus praesens.*

Psalm 75

4   Grein's emendation of *sylfum* to *swæfun* (they slept) matches Ro *dormierunt.*

7   *symbel-dæg* (a day of celebration), as emended in Krapp's edition, *Paris Psalter,* 37, accords well with Ro *diem festum.*

Psalm 76

9   *nu ic sona ongann . . . wenan ærest* (Now I have begun first of all to consider), Ro *nunc coepi:* with the addition of *wenan* as dependent infinitive of *coepi,* compare *Cassiodorus, Expositio,* 703, 218–19, *nunc coepi, quasi sapere, quasi intellegere.*

Psalm 77

4   *Noldan hi . . . heora synna dyrnan* (They certainly did not wish much to conceal their sins): as pointed out by Bartlett, *Metrical Division,* 33, the true subject of Ro *non sunt occultata* are the marvels done by God for Israel, for which the translator has substituted the "sins" of Israel.

10   *nis to wenanne . . . gyman awiht* (it is not to be expected that God would . . . maintain their souls . . .), Ro *non est creditus cum Deo spiritus eius:* as noted by Bartlett, *Metrical Division,* 29, Ro *Deo,* instead of *spiritus,* has been treated as subject, thereby inverting the meaning of the verse.

14   *on Campotanea:* a misreading of Ro *in campo Taneos* (on the plain

of Tanis) as a compound place-name, perhaps on the model of similar formations in Old English.

20   *we þæs ne wenað* (we do not expect that): Grein's addition of *ne* is supported by Ro *numquid (poterit).*

23   *his yrre barn* (his anger burned): Tinkler, *Vocabulary and Syntax,* 29, would explain *barn* as the result of misreading Ro *ascendit* as *accendit,* but the influence of Ro *ignis accensus* in the previous clause is just as likely.

24   *forhogedon* (they despised) may have arisen from misreading Ro *speraverunt* as *spreverunt.*

26   *Auster . . . Affricum:* respectively, the south and southwest winds.

30   See Exodus 32:1–34.

32   Krapp's emendation of *dædum* to *dædun* (they passed) is supported by Ro *defecerunt.*

39   Grein's emendation of *geomær* to *geon-cer* (return, second encounter)—normalized as *geancyr* by Krapp—agrees with Ro *rediens;* see DOE under *geancyrr.*

40   *eft gebrohtan* (they again put): *eft* may be a scribal error for *oft,* though the appearance of the latter word in the next line would adequately address Ro *quotiens.*

44   *ne meahte wæter drincan* (was able to drink that water): although the manuscript reading *þær* (2nd) before *drincan* could make sense, Krapp's suggestion (*Paris Psalter,* 215) to treat it as a dittography and replace it with *wæter* accords with Ro *aquas.*

46   *Sealde erucan yfelan wyrme* (He sent *eruca,* by means of a vile insect), Ro *dedit erugini:* Bartlett, *Metrical Division,* 29, believed that the translator did not understand the word *erugini* and substituted *eruca* for it. Certainly, *eruca* (a caterpillar), from which the Old English word derives, was commonly confused with *aerugo* (verdigris) and thus associated with plant disease; see Tinkler, *Vocabulary and Syntax,* 36. Krapp, *Paris Psalter,* 215, and DOE "?*eruca,* ? *eruce*" treat the locution *yfelan wyrme* as appositive (accusative) to *erucan,* but it makes better grammatical and contextual sense to take it as instrumental.

47   In the interests of grammatical concord, emendation of the manuscript reading *Heora win-geardas wraþe hægle nede fornamon* is required, either by making *hægle* plural or *fornamon* singular

The latter appears to be the better choice since it offers semantic and grammatical agreement with Ro *occidit* (with God as subject), while *wraþe hægle* can be read as instrumental, a reasonably accurate rendering of Ro *in grandine.* Thus, for *for-namon,* read *fornam,* and translate, "He utterly destroyed their vineyards with vicious hailstones."

57   *Hi . . . on wiðermede wendan* (they . . . turned to depravity): the translator omits the metaphor of Ro *conversi sunt in arcum perversum.*

60   For the emendation of *gelome* to *Selome,* see P. O'Neill, "The Lost Tabernacle of Selom: A Proposed Emendation in the Paris Psalter 77:60," *Notes and Queries* 31 (1984): 296–97.

64   As pointed out by Bartlett, *Metrical Division,* 33, Ro *viduae eorum* is incorrectly translated here to mean widows of the priests rather than widows of the slain mentioned in the previous verses.

66   The translator seems to have deliberately omitted a translation of the first clause, Ro *percussit inimicos suos in posteriora,* perhaps deeming it unsuitable since it probably referred to hemorrhoids.

71   Krapp's addition of *hi forð* before *lædeð* (he will lead them forth) provides a complete half-line, which accords with Ro *deduxit eos.*

Psalm 78

1   Krapp's emendation of *heah* to *ealh* (a temple) is paleographically plausible and agrees with Ro *templum.*

Psalm 79

5   *Tyhstð us and fedest* (you will feed and instruct us) as a translation of Ro *cibabis* parallels Cassiodorus, *Expositio,* 742, 101–2, *cibamur . . . erudimur.*

11   *hi to flodas forð aweaxað* (they will grow steadily toward the rivers): *hi to,* Krapp's emendation of *hit,* makes good sense, though it involves the rare usage of *to* taking an accusative.

18   Only the first three words of this verse have survived, as a result of a missing folio between 97 and 98; however, the remainder of the verse (and the psalm) can be plausibly restored from the translation of two earlier occurrences of the same verse in this psalm, at verses 4 and 7, "God of hosts, turn us around, and reveal to us your gentle face; we will all be saved." The same verse also occurs in the *Junius* Office; see Jones, *Shorter Poems*, 312 (3.49), and Krapp, *Paris Psalter*, 216.

Psalm 80

8   The preceding verses of the psalm (vv. 2–8 and part of v. 9 in Ro numbering) were lost with the folio missing between 97 and 98, a circumstance that makes the numbering of the Old English verses uncertain.

14   With *hiora yfele tid* (their time of misery) as a rendering of Ro *tempus eorum,* compare Cassiodorus, *Expositio,* 755, 292–93, . . . *tempus eorum, scilicet punitionis.*

Psalm 81

6   *ealle uphea and æðele bearn* (all of you elevated and noble offspring): as noted by Bartlett, *Metrical Division,* 29, Ro *(filii) Excelsi* has been read as nominative plural rather than as genitive singular dependent on *filii.*

Psalm 82

2   *þine feond . . . forwurdan* (your enemies . . . have utterly perished): an odd translation of Ro *sonaverunt* (they made a loud noise); Bartlett, *Metrical Division,* 29, suggests that *sonaverunt* was confused with Latin *solverunt.*

3   *geswipere* (cunningly), taken as an adverbial use of *geswipor,* accurately renders Ro *astute,* though it has also been read as a compound with the preceding *facen,* to mean "treachery"; see Tinkler, *Vocabulary and Syntax,* 49.

6   *onsægd* (come down), perhaps past participle of *onsægan,* as sug-

gested by B-T, though the meaning is doubtful; unfortunately, the corresponding Ro verse has no verb.

7   *on leod-stefnum* (in companionable clamor), Ro *in susceptionem:* compare Psalm 83.9, *on þeod-stefnum* (in the clamor of the people). E. A. Kock, "Interpretations and Emendations of Early English Texts: XI," *Anglia* 47 (1923): 270, translates *on leod-stefnum* with "in meetings," taking the second element as a borrowing from Old Norse, *stefna* (meeting), in apposition to *on wegum,* while Tinkler, *Vocabulary and Syntax,* 41, suggests "in general discussion."

8   *Ændor wylle* (the spring of Endor), Ro *in Endor:* as noted by Bartlett, *Metrical Division,* 29, the translator mistakenly identified Endor as a spring.

13   *þonne hi naman þinne neode seceað* (whenever they eagerly seek your name): it is unclear whether this verbatim repetition of the final line of the previous verse is a scribal dittography or a loose rendering of Ro *et cognoscant quoniam nomen tibi Domine.*

Psalm 84

1   Treating *fæle* (excellent) as an adjective; DOE favors an adverb, "constantly, well."

4   This verse occurs in the *Junius* Office; see Jones, *Shorter Poems,* 310 (3.40), and Krapp, *Paris Psalter,* 217.

5   *gecyr us . . . gefeo swiðe:* the appeal to *Crist ælmihtig* (Christ almighty) rather than God (Ro *Deus*), and the rendering of Ro *laetabitur* (future) with an optative present subjunctive, are modifications probably influenced by the frequent use of this verse as an intercessionary versicle in the Divine Office.

8   Grein's emendation of *áá* to *þam (þam þe egsan . . . healdað)* is supported by Ro *timentibus.*

9   As noted by Bartlett, *Metrical Division,* 29, the translator has ignored the mutual exchange of *mild-heortnesse* (mercy) and *soð* (truth) implied in Ro *sibi* and *se.*

11   Taking *fremsum god* as a rendering of Ro *benignitatem,* I read *god*

as a substantival plural adjective, rather than a noun denoting the deity; hence, "acts of kindness."

Psalm 85

1   *and* (Ro *quoniam*) here has a quasi-causal force, "seeing that"; see DOE B.5.a.

Psalm 86

4   *þa hehstan* (the most exalted one): the translator evidently rendered Ro *Altissimus* as if it were *altissimam* (referring to "the mother of Sion").

5   *frum-sprecend folces* (foretellers to the people): to explain the *hapax legomenon frum-sprecend* (Ro *principium*), Tinkler, *Vocabulary and Syntax,* 37, draws attention to Cassiodorus, *Expositio,* 792, 145–47, *Ipsi sunt enim principes Moyses et prophetae . . . quorum erat testimonium narraturus.*

Psalm 87

2   *gange min in-gebed* (let my secret prayer enter), Ro *intret oratio mea:* Tinkler, *Vocabulary and Syntax,* 25, discusses various emendations, but see DOE under *gangan* III.B.1.f.

7   *þu me ofer-hige on ealle gelæddest: ealle* could be either an adverb modifying *gelæddest* or an adjective qualifying *ofer-hige;* the latter (you brought down on me all your pride) would accord with the variant reading *omnes elationes meas,* where Ro has *elationes meas.*

11   *Cwist þu . . . manna ænig:* this verse, numbered verse 12 in Krapp's edition, has been relocated before the verse *Ne on ðeostrum . . . on eardige* (numbered v. 11 in Krapp's edition) to make the two conform to the sequence of content in Ro verses 11–12. The copyist may have been confused by the parallel Ro, which has three consecutive verses beginning with *Numquid.*

13   The construction *Ic me to ðe . . . clypade* (I invoked you), with *me*

as reflexive object, is odd. Grein emends *me* to *nu,* but against this is the independent presence of the same verse in the *Junius* Office with *me;* see Jones, *Shorter Poems,* 300 (3.12), and Krapp, *Paris Psalter,* 217.

15 *hwæðere næs gescended* (but not confounded): evidently the translator's own optimistic reading of Ro *confusus.*

Psalm 88

12 *Wesan hea mihte handa þinre / ahafen ofer hæleðas* (let the lofty powers of your hand be exalted over men), Ro *firmetur manus tua.* I follow Donoghue, *Style in Old English Poetry,* 193–94, in moving *is,* located by previous editors at the end of the second line, to the head of the third. The addition *ofer hæleðas* may owe something to Cassiodorus, *Expositio,* 807, 218, *firmetur in superbos.*

18 *halige ele* (with consecrated oil): *ele,* supplied by Grein, agrees with the context and Ro *oleo.*

22 *heane on mihtum* (that one exalted in power): in response to Donoghue's query, *Style in Old English Poetry,* 194, I take *heane* as accusative singular masculine, with *hine* as its pronominal antecedent, both referring to King David.

31 *Ne ic him . . . ac him:* despite Ro *eo,* both occurrences of *him* seem to be contextually plural.

31–32 Of these two verses, the first renders verse 34 of Ro, the second verse 36, so it appears that a translation of verse 35 is lacking, possibly the result of scribal haplography of *neque profanabo* (v. 35) with *neque nocebo* of the previous verse (34).

39 *onmettest:* an otherwise unattested verb, which Tinkler, *Vocabulary and Syntax,* 26, reads as *onmetan,* "to paint."

Psalm 89

10 *Wæran anlicast ure winter geonge-wifran . . . on nette* (Ro *anni nostri sicut aranea meditabuntur*): this comparison between the spider and the human life-span seems to be unique. Bartlett, *Metrical Division,* 30, argues that the translator misread Ro *aranea* (spi-

derweb) as "spider," but the issue is complicated by the fact that *aranea* could be read as plural of *araneum* (spiderweb) or as feminine singular, "a female spider." The latter interpretation might have been reinforced by the fact that the word "spider" was feminine in Old English and that in Medieval Latin *aranea* (singular) denoted a spider.

hundred (a hundred): it is unclear why Ro *septuaginta* (seventy) is rendered this way; perhaps under the influence of *Cassiodorus, Expositio,* 825, 201–4, who explained that the number seventy here was arbitrary and not in accord with reality, since some people could live into their nineties.

13   *Hwa ðæs soð ne cann sæcgean . . . standeð* (Who cannot say something of truth about how the terror of your anger endures?): since the negative particle in the manuscript reading, *ne cann,* goes against the sense of Ro *quis novit,* previous editors have suggested various emendations of *soð* and *ne.* However, if we accept that the translator has turned the Latin into a rhetorical question, no emendation is needed.

15   *Gehweorf . . . eað-bede:* this verse also occurs in the *Junius* Office; see Jones, *Shorter Poems,* 320 (5.11), but with *eað-bene* (pliant) for *eað-bede* (open to entreaty); and Krapp, *Paris Psalter,* 218.

18   This verse also occurs in the *Junius* Office, see Jones, *Shorter Poems,* 314–16 (4.6), and Krapp, *Paris Psalter,* 218.

Psalm 90

4   The suprascript entry, *scuan* (shadow, shelter) above *sceade* (protection) seems to be intended to supply a semantic equivalent rather than an explanatory gloss.

6   *on midne dæg mære deoful* (the notorious noonday devil), Ro *daemonio meridiano:* assuming that *mære* is not just an alliterative filler, it may refer to the demon of *acedia* (spiritual sloth), a familiar topic in monastic circles, based on John Cassian's *Institutiones* 10.2. See Introduction, xvii.

8   Taking *ðæs eagan* (with your gaze) as an instrumental genitive; see Mitchell, *Syntax,* §1393.

16   Another fragmentary witness to the Metrical Psalms, beginning
      at this verse and extending to Psalm 95.2, was discovered by
      M. R. James in the Old English gloss of the Eadwine Psalter
      (Cambridge, Trinity College, MS R. 17.1); edited by Baker,
      "A Little-Known Variant Text of the Old English Metrical
      Psalms," *Speculum* 59 (1984): 263–81.

Psalm 91

2   *his soðe sæcge* (to announce his truths): judging by Ro *ad adnun-*
      tiandum . . . veritatem tuam, soðe should be treated as a noun
      rather than an adverb, though its inflection is odd. Grein has
      emended to *his soð a sæcge* but in "Zur Textkritik," 426, further
      emended *a sæcge* to *asæcge*.

3   *lufades*t (you have shown your love): Bartlett, *Metrical Division,*
      30, suggests that Ro *delectasti* (you delighted) was confused
      with *dilexisti.*

12   Taking *Setta*ð (plant) as an imperative rather than third plural
      indicative, though Ro *plantati* might suggest the latter.

Psalm 93

1   *þu miht . . . ana gefreogan* (you alone has the power to . . . free): as
      suggested by Tinkler, *Vocabulary and Syntax,* 29, the translator
      treated Ro *libere* (freely) as if it were *liberare,* "to free."

6   For the meaning of *stundum* (savagely), see B-T headword *stund*
      "adverbial use of cases (2a)."

9   Despite the potential ambiguity of the *se ðe* construction in
      adjectival clauses, "whoever" or "he who," the present context
      clearly implies that God alone is intended; see Mitchell, *Syn-*
      tax, §2208.

Psalm 94

4   The first clause of this verse, *forðon ne . . . æt þearfe,* translates
      verse 3b of Ro, *quoniam non repellet Dominus plebem suam;* the
      second clause, *He þas heah-beorgas healdeð swylce,* verse 4b of Ro,

altitudines montium ipse conspicit, which leaves verse 4a of Ro, *quia in manu eius sunt omnes fines terrae,* unaccounted for. That a rendering was originally present is suggested by the presence of *swylce* (likewise) in verse 4b, which, as it now stands, is somewhat awkward in relation to the immediately preceding text but would fit well with a statement of God's territorial dominion such as that contained in verse 4a of Ro.

11   *ic . . . aðe benemde, gif hi on mine reste ricene eodon:* as pointed out by Mitchell, *Syntax,* §3415, the versifier's translation is botched because he did not grasp the Hebrew idiom latent in Ro *iuravi . . . si introibunt in requiem meam,* which should have been expressed by Old English *þæt* (instead of *gif*), followed by a negative form of the verb *eodon.* Properly reconstructed, the final two clauses of the sentence would translate, "what in my anger I had affirmed by oath, that they would not quickly enter into my rest."

Psalm 95

9   *from treowe becwom tirfæst rice Drihten ure* (from a tree has issued a famous ruler, our Lord): it is not clear whether this is merely a literal rendering of Ro *Dominus regnavit a ligno,* or suggestive of an interpretation whereby *treowe* might refer to Christ's Cross.

Psalm 96

1   As a result of two missing folios between 113 and 114, virtually all of the remaining text of Psalm 96 (Ro vv. 2–12) and the opening part of Psalm 97 (Ro vv. 1–7) is lacking.

Psalm 97

8   From Ro *flumina* (v. 8), one can reasonably supply "The rivers" as subject of this verse.

Psalm 98

5   Judging by the marked punctuation of a semicolon after *weorþiað* in the third line of this verse, it appears that Krapp read *he* of the next line as referring to God, but the subject is actually *scabellum* (OE *sceamul*, "a stool," masculine), as indicated by the neuter inflection of its qualifying adjective Ro *sanctum*.

Psalm 99

2   *we his syndon* (we belong to him), Ro *non ipsi nos:* as pointed out by Bartlett, *Metrical Division,* 30, the translator overlooked *non* and took *ipsi* as a dative of the preceding *ipse,* when in fact it is plural.

4   *niðum swæs* (gracious to humankind), taking *niðum* as *niððum,* a common scribal error, as in *Beowulf* 2215; see also *niða bearna,* Psalm 58.5. The final clause of the corresponding Ro, *et usque in saeculum saeculi veritas eius,* was not translated, perhaps because it would have detracted from the main theme of God's benevolent power over humankind.

Psalm 100

7   The translator omits a rendering of Ro *non direxit in conspectu oculorum meorum,* the final clause of the verse.

Psalm 101

1   This verse occurs also in the *Junius* Office; see Jones, *Shorter Poems,* 312 (3.47), 320 (5.12), and Krapp, *Paris Psalter,* 219.

3   *mearh-cofan* (bones, literally, "marrow chambers"); see Tinkler, *Vocabulary and Syntax,* 42–43.

     Following Tinkler, *Vocabulary and Syntax,* 23, I take MS *forspyrcende* as a copyist's error for *forswyrcende,* present participle of *forsweorcan* (to grow dark), here referring to bones blackened by heat.

11   *heah-sæl* (an opportune time): I follow Tinkler, *Vocabulary and Syntax,* 51–52, in reading the second element as denoting "time" rather than "happiness," as in the corresponding Ro *tempus (miserendi).*

16   *Ða . . . þæt he folc gesceop:* as pointed out by Bartlett, *Metrical Division,* 30, the translator mistakenly read Ro *(scribantur) haec* as referring to the noun clause beginning with *þæt,* when in fact it refers to God's benevolence in the previous verses.

21   *He him andwyrdeð . . . fæste standeð. Ic þe . . . sylfa wylt* (He will respond . . . permanently endures. I will relate . . . yourself agree): Judging by the punctuation of Krapp's text, a colon after *standeð* followed by quotations marks bounding *"Ic þe . . . sylfa wylt,"* the subject and speaker of all of this verse (except the final line) is God; so too in DOE under *andwyrdan* 1b. The problem with this reading is that while the first part of the verse does seem to envisage the deity, as suggested by the reference to his manifest strength, which endures permanently, the direct speech that follows implies a speaker who, by contrast, must endure miseries and a short lifespan, in other words, certainly not God. These are evidently the words of the psalmist, and they connect seamlessly with the final line of the present verse and the rest of the psalm.

     þæt þu me ne meaht . . . sona gecigean (so that you may not in the middle of my days summon me at once): as suggested by Donoghue, *Style in Old English Poetry,* 194, the negative particle *ne* (suggested by Ro *ne revoces me in dimidio dierum meorum*) was probably lost between *me* and *meaht* through haplography. I follow B. Mitchell, "Some Problems of Mood and Tense in Old English," *Neuphilologische Mitteilungen* 49 (1965): 52, who reads *þæt* as introducing a purpose clause.

Psalm 102

1   *Bletsa, mine sawle . . . Drihten* (Lord, joyfully bless my soul): here, and elsewhere, the translator inverts the subject-object relationship of Ro *benedic anima mea Dominum,* so that the speaker

becomes the recipient of the blessing. The purpose seems to be to impart a precatory tone to the psalms, thereby making them prayers of supplication rather than statements of worship. See further P. P. O'Neill, "Strategies of Translation in the Old English Versions (Prose and Metrical) of the Psalms in the Paris Psalter (Paris, Bibliothèque nationale de France, Fonds latin, 8824)," *Bulletin of the Institute of Oriental and Occidental Studies, Kansai University* 48 (Osaka, 2015):150–51.

1–5   These verses occur also in the *Junius* Office; see Jones, *Shorter Poems,* 308–10 (3.34–38), and Krapp, *Paris Psalter,* 219.

6   *poliað* (with punctum delens under *ð*) is read by Krapp as *polian,* "suffer" (presumably subjunctive). However, since Ro *faciens . . . iudicium omnibus iniuriam patientibus* points to an indicative, *poliað* is adopted in the present text. See further Mitchell, *Syntax,* §§2400 and 2402.

    Treaflice (painfully?): otherwise unattested, and with no recognized etymology, is emended by Tinkler, *Vocabulary and Syntax,* 28, to *tearflice,* but the latter is no less obscure.

12   *fæðme bewindeð* (encompasses this earth in its expanse) is explained by DOE (headword *bewindan*) as "loosely rendering *distare* 'to be distant, parted,'" but this meaning is otherwise unattested and hardly consonant with the semantics of Ro *distat.*

    betweonan þam (by the measure between them): *sc.* east and west.

15   With the construction *hine gærs-bedd sceal wunian wide-fyrh* (a grave must then enclose him for all time), compare the Old English poem *Soul and Body,* 43, *syððan ic ðe on worulde wunian sceolde* (after I was made to dwell within you in this world); Jones, *Shorter Poems,* 194–95.

19   *mægyn and mihta* (those Virtues and Powers): taking his cue from the explicit reference to angels (Ro *angeli*) immediately before, the translator took Ro *potentes virtutes* (a well-attested variant of *virtute* in Ro manuscripts) to refer to two of the angelic orders, hence *mægyn* and *mihta* denoting respectively the fifth and sixth ranks of that hierarchy.

Psalm 103

3   *hyde gelice* (like a skin): the translator read Ro *sicut pellem* in its primary sense, where the commentators usually take it in the derivative sense of "tent, pavilion."

16   *mid heora spedum* (with their substance), following the explanation of *spedum* offered by Meritt, *Fact and Lore,* 206–7. Tinkler, *Vocabulary and Syntax,* 45–46, suggests the influence of Cassiodorus, *Expositio,* 933, 390–95.

17   *uphebbean* (Ro *fulicae*): the conventional definition of *uphebbean* as a type of waterfowl that lifts up (OE *uphebbe*) its tail seems facile; see further Tinkler, *Vocabulary and Syntax,* 28.

  erinaces (coneys): presumably borrowed directly from Ro, some texts of which have the reading *erinacis;* see DOE.

24   *scrinde,* otherwise unattested, is problematic; B-T *scrind* defines it as "swiftness (?)" and BTS, 698, suggests emending to *scynde,* relating the latter to *scyndan* (to hasten), while Tinkler, *Vocabulary and Syntax,* 27, argues that *scrinde* is a scribal error for *scride/ scriðe* (swift).

25   *Dracan . . . þysne* (this dragon): a reference to Leviathan (see Job 40:20–41:25).

Psalm 104

9   For the references to Abraham and Isaac, see Genesis 15–17 and 28:13–15, respectively.

15–16   See Genesis 37:37 and 41:40.

16   *hine þam leodum . . . sette* (he established him as ruler over all the people), Ro *princeps populorum et dimisit eum:* As noted by Bartlett, *Metrical Division,* 30, *princeps* is wrongly linked in apposition to *eum* as object of *dimisit,* which is mistranslated by *sette* (he established), against the correct rendering, "the ruler set him free."

22   See Exodus 4:27.

31   *frumcynnes heora frean* (the lords of their highest lineage), Ro *pri-*

mitias omnis laboris eorum: as noted by Bartlett, *Metrical Division,* 30, the translator misread *primitias,* "firstfruits," as "lords."

33   This verse contrasts the jubilation of the Egyptians army as they gain on their opponents with the terror of the Israelites in flight when they realize that they are blocked by the Red Sea; see Exodus 14:10.

35   *ganetas* (gannets): Tinkler, *Vocabulary and Syntax,* 83–84, suggests that this rendering of Ro *coturnix* (a quail) may owe something to Numbers 11:31, which mentions that the quail came from the direction of the sea *(arreptas trans mare coturnices).*

     heofon-hlafe halige, literally, "holy bread from heaven," following Ro *pane caeli,* otherwise known as manna.

36   *na him . . . gengdan æfter* (they did not in the least wet their feet . . . later on), Ro *et abierunt in sicco flumina:* This mention of the miraculously dry feet of the Israelites after crossing the river Jordan seems to have been supplied by the translator from Joshua 3:14–17.

Psalm 105

1   *Ic andette* (I acknowledge; Ro *confitemini*): from here on this switch from first plural to singular is consistently made by the translator (see Psalms 106.1, 110.1, 117.1 and 28, and 135.1), and, since it normally occurs in the opening verse of the relevant psalms, may have served to set a personal, rather than communal, tone for the prayer.

8   *hi bysmredan* (they provoked), Ro *inritaverunt:* presumably in the first instance by neglecting to thank God for conducting them safely across the Red Sea and, later, by forgetting about this favor altogether.

     þa hi . . . randas bæron (when they . . . carried their shields into the broad waters of the Red Sea): the reference to carrying the shields has no basis in Ro, but see Old English *Exodus* 332b–333, *Randas bæron / sæwicingas ofer sealtne mersc* (the sea vikings carried their shields across the salty swamp).

17   *on þæne wyrsan had* (for the more depraved form): presum-

ably "more depraved" by comparison with conventional idols carved in human likeness.

21   *hi . . . wolde . . . todrifan* (intending . . . to disperse them): Bartlett, *Metrical Division,* 30–31, noting that *todrifan* does not match Ro *ut prosterneret,* suggests the influence of Ro *ut deiceret* in the following verse. See also Numbers 32:13.

23   *on hryre gefremedan* (they worked toward ruin for themselves): "for themselves" is supplied in the present translation to indicate that the Israelites were bent on their own destruction, as indicated by Ro *in eis ruina.*

24   Bartlett, *Metrical Division,* 37, argued that the translator substituted for the Ro text (which cryptically relates that Phinehas pacified God and thereby prevented further divine punishment of the Jewish people) a portrayal of Phinehas's role in "turning Israel from idolatory," which derives from Numbers 25. While the general notion of Phinehas's zeal may derive from that source, the two deeds attributed to him in the present verse, preventing the unlawful eating of food dedicated to false gods and shattering the idol, are actually associated with Moses (Exodus 32:20 and 34:14). The likely explanation for the translator's artifice in transferring the deeds of the latter to the former is that he deemed the horrific deed in Numbers 25 where Phinehas showed his zeal to be highly objectionable.

25   See Numbers 20:13.

35   *hi :* taken here as referring to the Israelites.

Psalm 106

2   The subject of *secge* (despite Ro *dicant*) is presumably the speaker of the previous verse, where first plural of Ro *confitemini* was modified in translation to first singular *ic andette* (I acknowledge), as in Psalm 105.1.

10   The meaning of *ægype* in *hi dydan drihtnes spræce æghwæs ægype* is unclear; my translation, "they treated the Lord's words as altogether worthless," is guided by Ro *quia exacerbaverunt eloquium Domini;* see DOE under *ægype.*

17   *by . . . drencyde wæran* (Ro *adpropiaverunt*): the translation "they
were drawn near" is tentative; DOE under *drencan* 5 merely
begs the question, while Tinkler's suggestion, 29, that "the
translator saw in *adpropiaverunt* the word *propinare,* 'to give one
to drink,'" does not suit the context very well and ignores the
fact that the translator elsewhere translates *adpropiaverunt* correctly.

25   *apindað* (they become puffed up): as suggested by B-T under
apindan, the translator misunderstood Ro *tabescere* (to pine
away) as *tumescere* (to swell); other examples occur at Psalms
111.9, 118.158, and 138.18.

28   *þa þe brimu wepað* (because the sea's surges abate), taking *þa þe*
as causal (see Mitchell, *Syntax,* §2580); for *wepað* (Ro *silverunt*),
see B-T under *wepan.*

41   *nemneð* (will invoke) is retained, rather than emended to *hemneð,*
as in Krapp, *Paris Psalter,* 220–21, a ghost word with the proposed meaning, "he will stop up." As argued by Meritt, *Fact and
Lore,* 28, it seems likely that the translator misread Ro *oppilavit*
as *appelavit;* see also Tinkler, *Vocabulary and Syntax,* 24.

Psalm 107

2   *on psalterio* (Ro *psalterium*): evidently a hybrid of Old English *on*
and dative singular of Latin *psalterium.*

6   *on Metibor* (in Metibor): see note to Psalm 59.5. In the present
verse, *bu* (both) refers to the two tents purportedly located in
Metibor and Sycimam and has nothing to do with "dwellings,"
the meaning assigned to *bu* by Kock, "Interpretations and
Emendations," 271.

7   *Effrem his agen broður* (Ephraim, his own brother); this additional
information about Ephraim (from Genesis 48:1) was first noted
by Bartlett, *Metrical Division,* 37.

8   *syndan me Moabitingas magas* (the Moabites are my kinsmen), Ro
Moab olla spei mei: the translator treated Ro *Moab* as epony-
mous ancestor of a people and in accord with that interpretation evidently rendered *olla* (a jar) by *magas* (kinsmen). Tinkler,

Vocabulary and Syntax, 42, points to Cassiodorus, *Expositio,* 989, 146, *Moab . . . significat ex patre,* but fails to record the rest of the comment, *quod est sine patre,* which undermines his suggestion.

Psalm 108

11   *reðe-mann* (Ro *fenerator*): I follow Grein in reading *reðe-mann* as a compound denoting "a userer"; alternatively, as argued by Tinkler, *Vocabulary and Syntax,* 45, it could be read as the collocation *reðe mann* (a cruel man), though given the presence of the descriptive adjective, *rice,* immediately before *reðe,* that seems less likely. Bartlett, *Metrical Division,* 31, correctly points out that Old English *gedæle* (will deal out) is not an accurate translation of Ro *scrutetur,* but compare Cassiodorus, *Expositio,* 996–97, 167–69, *fenerator eius, a iudice percepta fiducia, ingreditur domum obnoxii sui et omnia quaecumque habere potest diripit.*

15   *and hine adilgie . . . ealne* (and may he expel him perpetually): pointing to *hine,* which evidently lacks an antecedent, Grein argued that a line was missing after *swylce* of the previous line; however, although *hine* is somewhat abruptly introduced as a new persona, it has a counterpart, *he,* in the next four verses. While *ealne* would appear to qualify *hine,* it makes better contextual sense as a variant spelling of adverb *ealneh/ealneg* (perpetually).

18   In emending *ydwe* to *yðde* (ravaged) and reading *wan* as preterite singular of *winnan* (to fight, struggle), I follow the suggestion of BTS under *iþan.* Krapp's emendation of *ydwe* to *ywde* (appeared, manifested itself), that is, "seemed" (*Paris Psalter,* 221), is problematic, since the verb *iewan* is normally transitive, and in any case this reading hardly conveys the forceful import of Ro *intravit.*

28   *him si abrogden, swa of brec-hrægle hiora sylfra sceamu* (may their very own genitals be exposed on them, as if they had removed their trousers): this odd rendering of Ro *operiantur sicut deploide confusionem suam* (let them be covered in their shame as with a doublet) may be partly based on a misreading of *operiantur* as

aperiantur (let them be revealed) and of Ro *diploide* (a cloak) as Old English *brec-hrægle,* as first suggested by Bartlett, *Metrical Division,* 31; see DOE *abregdan* A.8.

Psalm 109

6   A folio missing between 132 and 133 presumably contained the translation of Psalm 109: 1–6ᵃ according to Ro numbering; that provided for the surviving Old English verses is conjectural. The acephalous opening, *hefige gefylleð* (he will carry out severely), is probably a translation of Ro *implebit (ruinas),* "he will fill ruins" (v. 6ᵃ).

Psalm 110

7   *þe hine wyllað well wyrcean and healdan* (those willing to observe and practice it well): *hine* (it) refers back to *godes egesan* rather than *snytru* (which is feminine) and thus seems to reflect Ga *(facientibus) eum* (with *timor* as its antecedent), rather than Ro *(facientibus) eam* (with *sapientia* as its antecedent). Ga *eum* is commonly found in English Ro psalters, including the parallel Latin of the Paris Psalter.

Psalm 113

2   *hæfdon ealdurdom ofer Israhelas* (they had dominion over the Israelites), Ro *Israel regnavit in ea:* Bartlett correctly points out that contrary to the Ro, Israel in the Old English version is portrayed as the one ruled rather than the ruler. However, this observation does not go far enough: the change is not a mistranslation but a deliberate recasting with interpretative significance. The translator has read the simple juxtaposition of Judah and Israel as a reference to the perpetual feuding between the two after (OE *syþþan*) they settled the Promised Land, and he wished to emphasize the ultimate victory of Judah, as he had done with an addition at Psalm 67.25. From a

Christian perspective, the concern with Judah's superiority was altogether appropriate, since Christ was said to have been descended from that house through David.

4   Attempts to link *restan* to its lemma Ro *exultaverunt* have not been very successful (see Krapp, *Paris Psalter,* 222), in part because the clause in which it is contained, *rammum þa restan gelice,* is an expansion of Ro *ut arietes.* Meritt, *Fact and Lore,* 179–80, argues that *restan* is plural preterite of the weak verb *restan* (to rest); hence, "they then rested like rams"; compare verse 6, below, *bliðe, gebærdon swa rammas* (joyful, behaving like rams).

6   The translator has removed the interrogative cast of Ro *quare exultastis,* making the verse purely declarative, as in Ga, which omits Ro *quare.*

18   The translator has modified the singular subject of Ro *domus Israhel speravit* to plural, *Israhela hus . . . helpe gehogedan* (the houses of Israel looked for help), no doubt having in mind the twelve tribes of Israel.

Psalm 114

3   I follow Grein's emendation of *Þar* to *Sar* (Sorrow), since the latter matches Ro *Dolores;* and the error is readily explained by the rubricator's insertion of the wrong initial.

swylde: perhaps dative/genitive singular of the otherwise unattested *swyld,* meaning "pang"; see B-T, and Tinkler, *Vocabulary and Syntax,* 27–28. Grein's emendation to *swylce* (also) seems plausible but does not suit the context, since it implies at least a loose connection with the immediately previous clause— which is not the case here.

ætfealh (clung): this emendation of *ætfeah* first suggested by Grein; see Psalm 118.31, and DOE under *ætfeolan.*

Psalm 115

1   In Ro (and Ga) Psalters the verses of this psalm are numbered in continuation of Psalm 114 (which ends with v. 9); and so the

Latin text of the present psalm begins with verse 10, which is marked suprascript in the modern English translation. On the other hand, in both the Old English text and its translation the normal protocol is maintained of beginning the numbering system anew with each psalm, so that the first verse is numbered "1," which for this psalm corresponds to verse 10 of the Ro. Note also that because verse 14 of the Ga (on which the numbering system of Latin Psalters is based) does not have a corresponding verse in the Ro, there is no 14 in Ro, which consequently jumps from 13 to 15.

1   *Ic þæt gelyfde* (I believed that), Ro *Credidi: þæt* seems to refer back to the message of the preceding psalm, that God always delivered him in time of need, thus linking the two psalms.

Psalm 117

5   *brædu,* with the present meaning of "a spacious place," is also used in the Old English glossed Psalters to translate Ro *in latitudine(m);* see DOE 3.a.

10–12   In these verses, the theme of revenge on enemies voiced in the second stichos (Ro *ultus sum eos/vindicabor in eis*) is transformed into statements of divine protection.

18   *Me clænsude* (He chastised me): emended from *Se clænsude,* as proposed by DOE *clænsian* 4.a.ii.

    se þe him clæne wæs (who in himself was exempt from sin): *him* refers reflexively to God. Evidently prompted by the wordplay of Ro *castigans castigavit,* the translator produced his own form with *clæne* and *clænsian.*

21   *teofrade,* usually taken to mean "he appointed," offers a reasonably close translation of Ro *factus est;* however, I follow the explanation of this *hapax legomenon* by Tinkler, *Vocabulary and Syntax,* 61, as "he decorated (with painting)."

22   This verse is cited in the Old English *Menologium,* ll. 60–62, where it is attributed to *se witega* (the prophet, presumably, King David); see Jones, *Shorter Poems,* 178–79 and 409, and J.

Toswell, *The Anglo-Saxon Psalter,* Medieval Church Studies 10
(Turnhout, 2014), 310–19.

26   Although structurally imperfect, the verse provides an ade-
quate translation of the Latin. For various suggestions—none
of them satisfactory—on dividing it into metrical lines, see
Krapp, *Paris Psalter,* 223.

Psalm 118

2   Throughout Psalm 118, Ro *testimonia* (22×), a plural form, is consistently translated by the singular *gewitness,* which suggests
that the translator had in mind a more technical meaning for
the latter word in this context than the one offered by DOE
(*geferan,* I.A.1.a), where Psalm 118.59, *on gewitnesse geferan,* is
explained as "to walk in (God's) testimony," that is, "to live a
godly life." Significantly, at Psalm 118.88, Ro *ut custodiam testimonia oris tui* is translated by *ic gewitnesse wel gehealde muþes
þines, þe þu men lærdest* (I will properly observe the "witness"
from your mouth, which you have taught humankind), where
the adjective clause implies that *gewitness* denotes a body of
knowledge transmitted, rather than a mode of conduct explained; likewise Psalm 118.167, where Ro *testimonia tua* is translated by *soð . . . þinre gewitnesse, worda æghwylc* (the truths . . .
of your "witness," each of its words). Certainly, Cassiodorus
recognized *testimonia* as having a written basis; thus, commenting on the first occurrence of the word in Psalm 118 (v. 2), he
refers to those *qui scrutantur sacrarum testimonia litterarum* (who
minutely examine the evidence of the sacred writings; *Expositio,* 1060, 86–87). In his use of *gewitness* in Psalm 118, the
translator arguably intended to denote a body of knowledge
transmitted by God to humankind, either orally or in written
form. Accordingly, in Psalm 118 *gewitness* is translated "revelation."

8   Here and throughout Psalm 118, *soðfæst(ness)* (true/truth),
whether used independently *(soðfæstness),* or as adjective quali-

fier *(soðfæst)* of the nouns *word* (vv. 20, 23, 80, 93, 124, 135) and
weorc (68, 71, 83, 94, 112, 141), translates Ro *iustificationes tuae;*
this practice may owe something to Cassiodorus, *Expositio,*
1079, 862–66, who explains that *iustificationes* refers to both
God's precepts *(mandata Domini)* and his works *(opera ma-
nuum).*

15–16   It appears that a translation of verse 15 (as found in the Ro) is
lacking: other than the phrase *soðe getreowe,* the present verse's
contents agree with those of Ro verse 16. Correspondingly,
while the first clause of verse 16 accurately translates the parallel verse 16a of Ro, the second clause seems to match Ro verse
17b. One can only surmise that verse 15 was lost at some point
in the text's transmission and that a verse was added (the present verse 16) to make up the correct number of verses, by con-
flating verses 16a and 17b. The verbal similarity between the
first lines of verses 15 and 16 *(Swa ic on þine soðfæstnysse soðe getreowe* and *Ic on þinre soðfæstnysse symble meteode)* suggests that
the problem originated in scribal dittography. And from the
fact that the parallel Ro text in the Paris Psalter follows the
proper sequence, one might conclude that the problem was
not the fault of the copyist, but a product of his exemplar.

29   *on þinre æ* (in the exercise of your law) may depend on the variant
reading *in lege tua* (Ro *de lege tua*).

30   *gedweled* (led astray): an odd rendering of Ro *oblitus* (forgetful);
perhaps the translator misunderstood it as *obliquus* (devious).

35   *hy:* as plural would refer to *bebodum,* the closest referent, but,
taken as feminine singular, it could be related to *stige* (path) of
the first line; the latter option seems preferable, judging by Ro
ipsam, which refers back to *semita* (path), the lexical equivalent
of *stige,* but no certainty is possible.

38   *oðer swylce* (another such mandate): Meritt, *Fact and Lore,* 196,
plausibly argues that *oðer* has nothing to do with "word,
speech," as reported in the dictionaries, but that in collocation
with *swylce* (such) it "is primarily a line filler." One might add
that in the present context *oðer swylce* does carry significant

meaning, implying "another such (mandate)" as that ordained in verse 33.

þinre spræce (of your speech): I follow Grein in emending *þine* to *þinre,* treating it as a genitive, qualifying *sped.* The latter noun often occurs in collocation with *spræc* in the Metrical Psalms, not only to facilitate alliteration but probably also to convey the semantic force of Latin *eloquium;* see Tinkler, *Vocabulary and Syntax,* 74–75, and note on v. 67, below.

45   *getrymede* (I have confirmed): a puzzling translation of Ro *exqui-sivi* (I sought).

47   *ic . . . mote gemetegian* (may I be allowed to consider) matches the subjunctive of the variant reading *meditabar* (Ro *meditabor*) and parallels the subjunctive construction of verse 44, *ic . . . wunian mote* (may I be allowed to dwell).

48   *bryce* (passionately): DOE under *brȳce* labels the word here as "perhaps . . . a mere intensifier," but it actually translates Ro *vehementer.*

61   On this adverbial use of the noun *ungemet* to mean "immeasur-ably," see K. Brunner, *Altenglische Grammatik nach der Angelsäch-sischen Grammatik von Eduard Sievers neubearbeitet,* 3rd rev. ed. Tübingen (1965), §319. B-T reads a compound, *ungemetgeneahhie* (extremely).

62   This verse's expansive rendering of Ro *media nocte surgebam ad confitendum tibi,* with additions referring to the seasonal chal-lenges *(mæla gehwylce,* "in whatever season") and the hurrying *(hraðe gange,* "I will quickly proceed") in good time *(eall ætgæ-dere,* "at once") to a place of worship *(þær,* "to the place where"), recalls similar exhortations in monastic rules about diligently observing the nocturnal hours.

67   *þinre spræce . . . sped* (the eloquence of your speech), Ro *eloquium tuum:* given the frequency of this phrase in Psalm 118, the emendation of *þine* to *þinre* (genitive) seems justified.

69   The meaning of *atredde* (I will investigate) and *atreddest* (you in-vestigated) at Psalm 138.2 has been deduced from Ro *scrutabor* (and *investigasti*); see DOE under *atreddan.* Tinkler, *Vocabulary*

and Syntax, 59, implausibly relates *atredde* to the verb *tredan* and suggests the translation "I will enter." See note on verse 161, below.

75   *reðe*, perhaps for *hreðe* (= *hraþe*, "speedily").

81   *swancur on mode* (slack of purpose): referring to the psalmist's soul, this is interpreted by Tinkler, *Vocabulary and Syntax*, 46, to mean "supple," with no pejorative connotation. Yet the two verses following emphasize the psalmist's fragility, as does Cassiodorus, *Expositio*, 1092, 1391–93, *Quapropter deficit anima mea, significat, lassata est atque fatigata; quod per nimia solet desideria provenire*, which explains that the soul is enervated by the intensity of its desire for God.

83   *ic eom nu geworden werum anlicast, swa þu . . . cylle* (I am now become very like other mortals, as fragile as a slender leather bottle exposed to hoar frost); Cassiodorus, *Expositio*, 1093, 1439–40, also introduces the comparison with humans, *Nec aestimes indecorum vivos homines utribus comparatos*.

93   *þæs* (that prospect): the disaster imagined in the previous verse.

98   *mine feondas . . . ealle* (all my . . . enemies) parallels the addition of *omnes*, an attested variant to Ro *inimicos meos*.

104   *ic . . . feode* (I . . . should detest): the original reading *ofeode* (preterite of *ofgan*, "to demand") does not make sense in the context, whereas *feode* (suggested to me by Professor R. Fulk) agrees with Ro *odio habui* and is used again at verse 163 to translate the same Latin phrase.

111   *eowde*, normally denoting "a flock of sheep," is an odd translation of Ro *hereditatem*; see Tinkler, *Vocabulary and Syntax*, 59.

115   *þenden* (as long as): this temporal translation of Ro *et* agrees with Cassiodorus, *Expositio*, 1109, 2071–72, *dum calumnias . . . concipiunt, ad scrutanda mandata Domini idonei non possumus inveniri*.

119   *ofer-hylmend* is defined by B-T as "one who conceals," but Tinkler, *Vocabulary and Syntax*, 32, argues that the word "seems to be associated with 'failure to listen,'" a meaning that fits somewhat with Ro *praevaricantes* (transgressors).

130   *eallum eorð-buendum* (to all earth's inhabitants): an odd transla-

tion of Ro *parvulis,* but see Augustine, *Enarrationes,* 1758, 18,
Sint omnes parvuli, et reus fiat omnis mundus tibi.

139   *ealles forgeaton . . . me wa dydan:* these two lines form the second half of verse 138 in the manuscript (and previous editions),
but since they actually translate the second part of verse 139,
Ro *quia obliti sunt verba tua inimici mei,* they have been relocated
to their present position, where they also harmonize syntacti-
cally with the clauses before and after them.

143   With plural *nearonessa,* compare the variant *angustiae* (Ro *angus-
tia*) found in some Ro Psalters.

146   *Do me cuðlice halne, heah-cyning . . . þæt ic ðine bebodu bliðe gehealde:*
the translator has expanded Ro *Exaudi me Domine iustificatio-
nes tuas requiram* (Lord, hear me; I will seek your justifications)
into a personal and Christian appeal, a characteristic feature of
his method of translation. See O'Neill, "Strategies of Translation," 150–52.

151   *wes* (may . . . it remain): the imperative agrees with the variant
Ro reading *esto* (Ro *tu es*).

152   "and also" is supplied in my translation in recognition of the fact
that *ongeat gleawlice* (I clearly recognized) serves as *koinon* between the previous and the following clauses.

159   *ic sylf geseah* (I myself perceived): evidently based on the inferior
Ro reading *vidi* (Ro *vide*).

161   *ic . . . tredde* (I . . . investigated), first singular preterite of weak
verb *treddan;* see note on verse 69, above.

162   *swa se bið bliðe . . . mannum losað* (like the lucky person who stumbles on a hoard of military booty, in a place where it is lost
to all): this elaboration of Ro *sicut qui invenit spolia multa* offers a rather apt characterization of "the Staffordshire Hoard"
of Anglo-Saxon objects discovered in 2009, near the village of
Hammerwich, Staffordshire.

169   *þæt þu me generige niða gehwylces* (your protection from every kind
of evil) does not translate the corresponding Ro *intellectum* and,
moreover, has a close counterpart in the next verse, where it
accurately translates the corresponding Ro *eripe me.* It may well
be a dittography, arising from the preceding clause, Ro *secun-*

dum eloquium tuum (*æfter þinre spræce*), which is shared by both verses.

172   *eodan* (sprang from): it is not clear whether the subject is *þine soðfæstnesse* (your truths) of the preceding verse, or *þin bebodu* (your commands) of the next line; the former has been preferred in the present translation.

175   This verse occurs in the *Junius* Office; see Jones, *Shorter Poems,* 300 (3.9), and Krapp, *Paris Psalter,* 223.

176   *þæt dysige scep, þætte forweorðan wolde huru* (that foolish sheep, which even wanted to die): this more optimistic rendering of Ro *sicut ovis quae perierat* (like a sheep that was lost) seems to imply that the sheep was saved, probably by the good shepherd, as recounted in Luke 15: 4–7.

Psalm 119

5   *min bigengea . . . on feorweg:* overall, an odd translation of Ro *incolatus meus prolongatus est,* since *biggenga* normally translates Latin *incola* (an inhabitant) rather than Ro *incolatus* (residence, exile), while *on feorweg* (far away) indicates that, contrary to conventional interpretation, the translator has read Ro *prolongatus* as spatial rather than temporal distancing. Moreover, the *bigengea* who departed (OE *gewat*) from the speaker represents a new subject, for which the Ro text offers no support. The closest parallel is the corresponding Old Latin, which for Ro *prolongatus* reads *elongatus est a me.* On the problem of *bryce,* which (with long *y*) could mean "beneficial, productive," or (with short *y*), "fragile," or could even be an alliterative filler, see DOE.

Psalm 120

6   *minne geweorðe:* B-T *min* suggests the meaning "small" and translates, "nor [may] the moon withhold her light," the interpretation apparently adopted in Krapp's text, *min ne geweorðe;* but the *Oxford English Dictionary* at *min* (adjective[1]) rejects *min* and

argues for *minne,* with the proposed meaning "wicked, harmful." From the context of Ro *luna [non uret] per noctem,* as well as the evidence of commentary (for example, Augustine, *Enarrationes,* 1799, 3–4, *A scandalis in sole, a scandalis in luna, ab omni malo te custodiet*), it is evident that baleful effects of the moon are intended; see further Tinkler, *Vocabulary and Syntax,* 43.

Psalm 121

4   *cneorisse cende wæron cynn æfter cynne* (Tribes were propagated . . . generation after generation), Ro *ascenderunt tribus, tribus Domini:* Bartlett, *Metrical Division,* 31, suggests confusion of *ascenderunt* with *descenderunt,* the latter in the sense of "to descend by lineage."

5   *Dauides hus . . . siteþ* (house of David, that sits in the heavens), Ro *sedes super domum David:* as noted by Bartlett, *Metrical Division,* 31, the noun *sedes* was misread as a verb and *domum David* treated as vocative instead of accusative

7   This verse occurs in the *Junius* Office; see Jones, *Shorter Poems,* 312 (3.46), and Krapp, *Paris Psalter,* 223–24.

9   *þæt ic god æt him begitan mote* (that I obtain good things from it): judging by the first line of the Old English verse, *him* probably refers to Jerusalem, rather than to God; Ro *quaesiui bona tibi* does not shed any light.

Psalm 122

4   The first line of this verse occurs in the *Junius* Office, as noted by Jones, *Shorter Poems,* 310 (3.42), but not Krapp, *Paris Psalter.*

5   *and we manegum synd manna wordum ure sawle swiðe gefylled mid edwite* (and we, our souls, are utterly permeated with shame by the many comments of people), Ro *multum repleta est anima nostra obprobrium abundantibus:* the manuscript reading *sawl* is emended to plural *sawle,* which not only provides an appositional subject to *we* but also mends a metrically deficient halfline (suggested to me by Professor R. Fulk).

Psalm 123

6   *neod-spearuwa* (a sparrow in difficulty): although *neod* is thought to have been supplied primarily to meet the requirements of alliteration (see Meritt, *Fact and Lore,* 195), it also suits the context semantically, if read as a variant spelling of *nied* (necessity, difficulty).

Psalm 124

3   *firenfulra tan* (the apportioned land of sinners), Ro *virgam peccatorum:* while *virgam* by itself means no more than "a rod" (usually translated by *gyrd*), its use here in collocation with Ro *sortem* (a lot) suggests a context of distributing land by means of casting lots. Thus, *tan* here seems to mean "a share of land determined by lot," as suggested by B-T II.

Psalm 125

5   *Þa . . . sawað* (those who sow), Ro *mittentes semina sua:* Bartlett, *Metrical Division,* 31, suggests that the translator confused *mitto* (I send) with *meto* (I harvest).

Psalm 126

3   *For hwan ge . . . bearnum:* Bartlett, *Metrical Division,* 38, notes this as the only instance in which a direct statement in the Latin (Ro *in vanum est . . . surgere*) is rendered as a rhetorical interrogative in the Old English.

     Arisað nu ricene and hraðe sittað (Rise now at once and sit down quickly), Ro *surgite postquam sederitis:* as pointed out by Bartlett, *Metrical Division,* 31, *postquam* seems to have been incorrectly read as an adverb (afterward) rather than a conjunction (after).

4   *herde bearn* (familial children): following the suggestion of BTS *heord* III (family); Tinkler, *Vocabulary and Syntax,* 32, implausibly reads *herde* as past participle of *hyrian* (to hire), translating Ro *(filii) mercis.*

6   *on ðon* (in that): Ro *ex ipsis,* but the referent is unclear, possibly
       the divine inheritance (*yrfe*) of verse 4.

Psalm 127

2   *on wyn-burgum* (in pleasant towns): Tinkler, *Vocabulary and Syn-
       tax,* 47–48, reads this addition as referring to the heavenly city,
       citing in support the eschatological interpretation of Cassio-
       dorus, *Expositio,* 1178, 84–85, but his explanation fails to explain
       the use of the plural form, *wyn-burgum,* and clashes with the
       overall literal tenor of the psalm, which extols the earthly,
       rather than heavenly, rewards destined for the virtuous man.

Psalm 128

3   *fæcne geðancas* (treacherous plans): in order to explain this trans-
       lation of Ro *cervices* (necks), Tinkler, *Vocabulary and Syntax,* 38,
       refers to the conventional allegorical interpretation of *cervices*
       as *superbia,* but a simpler explanation is that the translator drew
       on the corresponding He *laqueos* (snares).

6   *þa his cwide weoldan on ofergeate . . . hæbben* (those who would
       have entirely consigned his saying to oblivion): contrary to the
       exegetical tradition, which reads Ro *qui praeteribant* as "those
       who passed by," the translator apparently relied on another
       meaning of *praeteribant,* "they failed to mention."
       Us gebletsige . . . Drihten (May the Lord boldly bless us): with the
       verbal change of tense and mood and the switch in the object
       from second to third person, compare Old Latin *benedicamus
       nos* (Ro *benediximus vos*), though the variation is just as likely to
       be the translator's own pious recasting.

Psalm 129

5   *sawl min . . . aræfnede* (My soul has constantly adverted to): this
       odd rendering of Ro *sustinuit anima mea* (my soul waited for)
       evidently has its origins in the interlinear Old English glosses
       on the psalms; see DOE under *aræfn(i)an* 1.g.i.

Psalm 131

2 *Swa ic æt frymðe geswor* (So in the beginning I swore): Grein proposed emending *ic* to *he,* presumably influenced by Ro *sicut iuravit,* but, as is evident from the verses that follow, the primary subject is first person (David), and in any case the reading *ic* is supported by the variant *iuravi* (for Ro *iuravit*), which is attested, for example, in the twelfth-century Eadwine Psalter from Canterbury. Consequently, I have treated the clause *he geheold . . . þone mæran* (he behaved well toward the illustrious God of Jacob) as the translator's parenthetical comment on David.

2–5 The underlying meaning is that the psalmist swore to God that he would take no rest until he had found a suitable dwelling for the Lord. Unfortunately, the translator mishandled the syntax (reproduced in the present translation), using *þeah þe* (although) to introduce the first *si* clause, when he should have used *þæt* (that), as he had correctly done at Psalm 88.32. As argued by Mitchell, *Syntax,* §3415, his mistake stems from failure "to render correctly the Latin idiom" of *iurare* followed by a dependent clause introduced by *si* to express a strong negative. To rectify the error, one would have to translate *þeah þe* (v. 3) and *gif* (v. 4) by "that," while making their corresponding verbs negative. The resulting translation would read: "I swore . . . that I should not enter into the protection of my house or into my tent (whenever I pleased) or quickly ascend to my bed; that I should not grant sleep to my eyes or offer slumber to my eyelids, nor should I rashly give repose to my temples, until I found an excellent place, the choicest, for the Lord, a precious tent, thoroughly acceptable to the God of Jacob."

6 *wudu-feldum* (in the fields of the forest) is explained by Tinkler, *Vocabulary and Syntax,* 21, as a loan translation of Ro *(in) campis silvae,* though it is just possible that the translator understood it as a place-name (the view of modern biblical scholars) and, accordingly, treated it as a proper noun, *Wudu-feld,* a type of onomastic compound common in Old English.

17 Although the manuscript reading *Ec* is an attested spelling of *eac* (also) and is kept by Krapp, I follow Grein in emending to *Ic,* since there is no support in Ro for coordinating the two verses.

Psalm 133

1–2 In support of conjoining these verses, compare Cassiodorus, *Expositio,* 1211, 50–51, *Ideo duos versus simul posuimus, quoniam sibi invicem mutua connexione iunguntur. . . .*

4 *Ge* is likely an error for *Þe* (Ro *benedicat te*), caused by the rubricator's occasional lapses when supplying the colored initial of a new verse; Krapp retains *Ge.*

Psalm 134

3 *he wyrðe is* (he is esteeemed): more likely *he* refers to God than to God's name, judging by context, and Ro *suavis* (Ga *suave*).

11 The translator has omitted the reference to the Amorites (Ro *Seon regem Amorreorum*) and left untranslated the final clause, Ro *et omnia regna Chanaan occidit.*

21 *Lefes hus:* at some point in transmission this collocation was misread as *lifes hus* (house of life) and was so read by previous editors. In fact, it translates Ro *domus Levi,* "house of Levi." The spelling *Lefes* in the present emendation is based on that of the corresponding Old English gloss in the Vespasian Psalter (folio 130^r).

Psalm 135

3 *þæt his mild-heortnes is mycel to worulde* (that his mercy is great forever): this refrain, Ro *quoniam in saeculum misericordia eius,* which is present in every verse of the present psalm, occurs in the Old English translation only here and in the final verse, suggesting that its omission in the intervening twenty-four verses was a deliberate economy.

4–5   *He wundur dyde . . . se heofon worhte, hæleða andgit* (By himself he performed splendid wonders, he who created heaven and human understanding), Ro *qui fecit mirabilia magna solus . . . qui fecit caelos in intellectu:* taking the two verses as a single unit of meaning, and treating *se* as a relative rather than independent pronoun.

6   I follow DOE *æfter* II.A.7 in taking *æfter wæter* as a literal rendering of Ro *super aquas,* though the use of *æfter* (rather than *ofer*) is puzzling and, as noted by Cassiodorus, *Expositio,* 1225, 121–33, the notion of "upon the waters" itself is problematic.

27   *Andetað nu ealle . . . Gode* (Let all acknowledge . . . God), Ro *confitemini Deo caeli:* with this odd rendering of *caeli* by *ealle,* compare Cassiodorus, *Expositio,* 1230, 309–10, *Vnde uidentur per significationem caeli omnia potuisse concludi.*

Psalm 136

7   *oð þæt hi heora eard geceosan* (until they select their dwelling place), Ro *quousque ad fundamenta in ea:* as noted by Bartlett, *Metrical Division,* 35, "The translation perverts the [hostile] thought of the original," mistranslating Ro *quousque ad* (even to) as "until."

8   Although not so indicated in Ro, *þu* (you) seems to refer to Jerusalem, which the translator apparently equated with Ro *filia Babylonis* (*hire earm dohter,* "her wretched daughter"). As a result, the second half of the verse, which was usually interpreted by the commentators as a curse directed against Babylon in retribution for its treatment of the Jews, is here recast as an expression of gratitude to Jerusalem for the good things that it has done for its citizens.

9   *se þe nimeð and eac seteð his agen bearn on þone æþelan stan* (he who takes and also places his own children on that eminent rock): again, the translator has not followed the conventional interpretation of Ro *adlidet parvulos suos* (or *tuos*) *ad petram* (he will dash his [or your] children against the rock) as an expression of the psalmist's desire to take revenge on Babylon and its male

children. Instead, he provides a benign interpretation in keeping with that of the previous verse. Tinkler's argument (*Vocabulary and Syntax,* 30) for retaining the manuscript reading, *seceð,* is implausibly complicated.

Psalm 137

6   *þin wuldur* (your glory): the addition here of *þin,* as in previous editions, has some support in Ro *gloria Domini.*

Psalm 138

9   *þystru . . . me on nihte neode onlihte þæt ic minum bleom bregde neah-hige* (darkness may . . . actively give me light at night, such that I may frequently change my appearance): the translator envisages another way for the desperate psalmist to hide from God. This rendering is clearly not based on Ro *nox inluminatio mea in deliciis meis* (night will be my light in my pleasures); instead it may have been influenced by the corresponding He, *nox quoque lux erit circa me* (night also will be a light enveloping me).

Psalm 139

1   This verse occurs in the *Junius* Office; see Jones, *Shorter Poems,* 306 (3.29), and Krapp, *Paris Psalter,* 224.

13   *scylan eard niman . . . her rihte lifigeað* (those who live uprightly with good sense on earth are destined to take up residence in your sight): a similar eschatological interpretation of Ro *habitabunt recti cum vultu tuo* is more explicitly given by Cassiodorus, *Expositio,* 1260, 216–17, *Visio infastidibilis atque perpetua illum semper videre.*

Psalm 140

2   This verse occurs in the *Junius* Office; see Jones, *Shorter Poems,* 330 (8.4), and Krapp, *Paris Psalter,* 225.

3 *þonne ic þe æfen-lac estum secge* (whenever I devoutly recite to you the evening service), Ro *sacrificium vespertinum:* here *secge* indicates that the offering *(lac)* was a prayer (rather than a sacrificial object), which, collocated with evening *(æfen),* may refer to the Hour of Vespers.

4 *ne læt man sprecan* (to prevent it from speaking evil): this addition was probably suggested by Ro *ut non declines . . . in verbum malum* of the next verse, but see also Cassiodorus, *Expositio,* 1263, 70–71, *Petit sanctissimus propheta ne quid tale dicat quod pervenire debeat ad reatum.*

 æþele dor ymb-standende, þæt on welerum wisdom healde (a well-made door circumventing it, to guard wisdom on my lips), Ro *ostium circumstantiae labiis meis:* I take *þæt* as relative pronoun with *dor* as antecedent. Alternatively, *þæt* could be read as introducing a final clause (so that the door will guard wisdom on my lips); compare Cassiodorus, *Expositio,* 1263, 73, *nec prava voluntas in fatua verba prosiliat.*

8 *noldan heora deman . . . ne mihton* (their judges did not want to listen . . . they were not able to): an odd translation of Ro *iudices eorum audient verba mea quoniam potuerunt,* since, as pointed out by Bartlett, *Metrical Division,* 35, it involves two new negatives and the shifting of *iudices eorum* from the first to the second half of the verse.

9 *syndon þas moras myclum asprotene* (these raised bogs are thrown up abundantly): I take *mor* in the sense of low-lying wetlands or raised bogs, characterized by constantly rising peat domes. Just as Cassiodorus (*Expositio,* 1266, 201–3) interpreted Ro *sicut crassitudo terrae eructuat super terram* as the product of volcanic activity, so the Old English translator drew on another type of terrestrial overflow familiar to him.

11 On the form *beswice* (deceive) as a plural, see Hogg and Fulk, *Grammar of Old English,* 6.24.

Psalm 142

9   This verse occurs in the Old English gloss to the Eadwine Psalter; see P. O'Neill, "Another Fragment of the Metrical Psalms in the Eadwine Psalter," *Notes and Queries* 35(4): 434–36.

10   *þu me god dydest* (you have done good things for me): with this addition, compare Cassiodorus, *Expositio*, 1279, 194–95, *a clemente Domino ideo postulare beneficium, eo quod ipse sit Dominus supplicantis.*

Psalm 143

14–19   The abrupt shift in tone from negative to positive that occurs at this point in the Latin source (Ro v. 12) greatly confused medieval commentators, since it seemed to laud the wicked who had been castigated in the previous two verses. The metrical translator apparently did not advert to the problem.

14   *Þara bearn swylce begað æþelum settum beamum samed anlice* (Their children also incline quite like noble, planted trees), Ro *quorum filii sicut novellae plantationis:* I retain the manuscript reading, *begað,* as third person plural present of *bigan* (to incline). Krapp, *Paris Psalter,* 225, argues that Ro *novellae plantationis* requires a noun such as *bogum* (branches), in place of *begað,* but this requirement is already met by *settum beamum* (planted trees).

18   *Ne hreosað hi to hrusan* (They do not fall to the ground), Ro *non est ruina maceriae:* although according to Bartlett, *Metrical Division,* 32, *maceriae* has no Old English equivalent, it probably influenced the metaphor developed from *ruina* by the translator.

    fernes (passage), Ro *transitus:* perhaps a euphemism for death; compare the comment in *Anonymi "Glosa psalmorum ex traditione seniorum,"* ed. H. Boese, 2 vols. (Freiburg im Bresgau, 1992–94) II, 239, 14, 3–4, *NEQUE TRANSITUS neque mortui qui transiebant . . .*

    on worðum (in the streets): The emendation of *wordum* to *worðum* is supported by Ro *(in) plateis.*

Psalm 144

12   *and . . . and:* tentatively treating these conjunctions as correlative, "both . . . and."

15   *þa ðe hreosað ær* (those who fell just now): adverb *ær* serves to mark this present tense verb as prior in relation to the preceding present tense verb, *Ahefeð,* with the implication that God moves immediately to pick up the one who has fallen.

Psalm 146

5   *Micel* (1st) (great): this emendation of *Rice* provides alliteration, agrees with Ro *magnus Dominus noster,* and can be explained as the error of the rubricator entering the wrong intial letter.

Psalm 147

1   The run-on numbering of Ro verses from the previous psalm (as in Psalms 114 to 115) represents Jerome's solution to the problem of whether Psalm 147 constituted a new psalm (thus the Septuagint) or a continuation of the previous psalm.

5   As suggested by Bartlett, *Metrical Division,* 32, the translator has incorrectly collocated Ro *nebulam,* which belongs in the second clause, with *lanam* of the first. He has also made Old English *snaw* the object of both clauses.

9   *eldran cynne* (toward people of an earlier time): discussed by Krapp, *Paris Psalter,* 225–26.

Psalm 149

2   *swiðust ealra* (most of all): it appears that its complementary half-line is missing, probably a translation of Ro *super regem suum.*

6   *heo þæs wislice wynnum brucað* (they will certainly relish that with joy): with this addition to Ro *exultationes Dei in faucibus eorum,* and the rendering of *exultationes* by *gemynd,* compare Cassio-

dorus, *Expositio,* 1324, 112–15, *exsultationes in eorum faucibus constitutas, significans, quoniam sive cogitatione, sive lingua laudare non desinunt, a quo aeterna dona percipient.*

Psalm 150

3   A translation of the second part of this verse, corresponding to Ro *laudate eum in psalterio et cithara,* and the remaining verses of the psalm (Ro vv. 4–6), are missing due to the loss of a folio between 175 and 176.

Bibliography

EDITIONS AND TRANSLATIONS

Adriaen, Marcus, ed. *Magni Aurelii Cassiodori Expositio Psalmorum*. Corpus Christianorum, Series Latina 97–98. Turnhout, 1958–1973.

Assmann, Bruno, ed. *Die Handschrift von Exeter, Metra des Boetius, Salomo und Saturn, Die Psalmen*. Bibliothek der angelsächsischen Poesie, herausgegeben von Richard Paul Wülker. Vol. 3. Leipzig, 1898. (The Paris Psalter, 332–476).

Bright, James W., and Robert L. Ramsay, eds. *Liber Psalmorum: The West-Saxon Psalms, Being the Prose Portion, or the "First Fifty," of the So-Called Paris Psalter*. Boston, 1907.

Colgrave, Bertram, ed. *The Paris Psalter (MS Bibiothèque Nationale Fonds Latin 8824)*. Early English Manuscripts in Facsimile 8. Copenhagen, 1958.

De Coninck, Lucas, ed. *Theodori Mopsuesteni Expositionis in Psalmos, Iuliano Aeclanensi Interprete in Latinum Versae Quae Supersunt*. Corpus Christianorum, Series Latina 88A. Turnhout, 1997.

Dekkers, Eligius, and Iohannes Fraipont, eds. *Sancti Aurelii Augustini Enarrationes in Psalmos*. Corpus Christianorum, Series Latina, 38–40. Turnhout, 1956–1958.

Edgar, Swift, with Angela M. Kinney, eds. *The Vulgate Bible, Volume III: The Poetical Books, Douay-Rheims Translation*. Dumbarton Oaks Medieval Library 8. Cambridge, Mass., 2011.

Grein, Christian W. M., ed. *Bibliothek der angelsächsischen Poesie*. Vol. 2. Göttingen, 1858. (The Paris Psalter, 147–276).

Krapp, George Phillip, ed. *The Paris Psalter and the Meters of Boethius*. Anglo-Saxon Poetic Records 5. New York, 1932.

O'Neill, Patrick P., ed. *King Alfred's Old English Prose Translation of the First Fifty Psalms.* Medieval Academy Books 104. Cambridge, Mass., 2001.

Pulsiano, Phillip, ed. "The Old English Introductions in the *Vitellius Psalter.*" *Studia Neophilologica* 63 (1991): 13–35.

Thorpe, Benjamin, ed. *Libri Psalmorum versio antiqua Latina: cum Paraphrasi Anglo-Saxonica, partim solute oratione, partim metrice composita. . . .* Oxford, 1835.

Wansbrough, Henry, ed. *The New Jerusalem Bible.* London, 1985.

Weber, Robert, ed. *Le Psautier romain et les autres anciens psautiers latins.* Collectanea Biblica Latina 10. Vatican City, 1953.

———, ed. *Biblia Sacra iuxta Vulgatam Versionem.* 2 vols. 2nd improved ed. Stuttgart, 1975.

Secondary Works

Bartlett, Helen. *The Metrical Division of the Paris Psalter.* Baltimore, 1896.

Bright, James W. "On the Text of the Prose Portion of the 'Paris Psalter.'" *Modern Language Notes* 24 (1909): 77–78.

Bright, James W., and Robert L. Ramsay. "Notes on the West-Saxon Psalms." *Modern Language Notes* 33 (1918): 471–74.

Clark Hall, J. R. *A Concise Anglo-Saxon Dictionary, Fourth Edition with a Supplement by Herbert D. Meritt.* Cambridge, 1960.

Donoghue, Daniel. *Style in Old English Poetry: The Test of the Auxiliary.* New Haven, 1987.

Grattan, J. H. G. "On the Text of the Prose Portion of the 'Paris Psalter.'" *Modern Language Review* 4 (1909): 185–89.

Grein, Christian W. M. "Zur Textkritik der angelsächsischen Dichter." *Germania* 10 (1865): 416–29.

Hogg, Richard. H, and R. D. Fulk. *A Grammar of Old English, Vol. 2.* Oxford, 2011.

Holthausen, Ferdinand. *Altenglisches etymologisches Wörterbuch, second improved edition with additional bibliography by H. C. Matthes.* Heidelberg, 1963.

Meritt, Herbert D. *Fact and Lore About Old English Words.* Language and Literature 13. Stanford, 1954.

Mitchell, Bruce. *Old English Syntax.* 2 vols. Oxford, 1985.

O'Neill, Patrick P. "The Old English Introductions to the Prose Psalms of the Paris Psalter: Sources, Structure, and Composition." *Studies in Philology* 78, no. 5 (1981): 20–38.

Sisam, Kenneth. "Notes on the West-Saxon Psalms." *Modern Language Notes* 33 (1918): 474–76.

Tinkler, John D. *Vocabulary and Syntax of the Old English Version in the Paris Psalter: A Critical Commentary.* Janua Linguarum, *Series Practica* 67. The Hague, 1971.

Toswell, M. J. *The Anglo-Saxon Psalter.* Medieval Church Studies 10. Turnhout, 2014.

Index

Roman numerals refer to the page numbers of the general introduction to this volume; two-part Arabic numbers to psalm and verse number; Arabic numbers preceded by "In." to the Prose Psalm Introductions; and Arabic numbers followed by "n" to the Notes to the Translations.